D1571131

INTERPERSONAL REJECTION

INTERPERSONAL REJECTION

Edited by Mark R. Leary

OXFORD
UNIVERSITY PRESS

2001

OXFORD
UNIVERSITY PRESS

Oxford   New York

Athens   Auckland   Bangkok   Bogotá   Buenos Aires   Calcutta
Cape Town   Chennai   Dar es Salaam   Delhi   Florence   Hong Kong   Istanbul
Karachi   Kuala Lumpur   Madrid   Melbourne   Mexico City   Mumbai   Nairobi
Paris   São Paulo   Shanghai   Singapore   Taipei   Tokyo   Toronto   Warsaw

and associated companies in
Berlin   Ibadan

Copyright © 2001 by Oxford University Press

Published by Oxford University Press, Inc.
198 Madison Avenue, New York, New York 10016

Library of Congress Cataloging-in-Publication Data
Interpersonal rejection / edited by Mark R. Leary,
        p.   cm.
    Includes bibliographical references and index.
    ISBN 0-19-513014-6
        1. Rejection (Psychology)   I. Leary, Mark R.
    BF575.R35 I58   2000
    158.2—dc21   00-025023

9 8 7 6 5 4 3 2 1

Printed in the United States of America
on acid-free paper

Preface

Imagine for a moment that an extraterrestrial psychologist visited Earth to study the social behavior of the human beings who live here. Before studying us directly, the alien researcher would undoubtedly read the existing literature on human behavior, looking for information about why human beings behave as they do. Reading the research literature, our visitor would quickly learn much about the motives that underlie and guide human behavior—motives involving, for example, control, power, self-esteem, autonomy, self-consistency, and so on. However, once the extraterrestrial set out to observe and study us directly, it would still be unprepared to understand what it saw.

Based on what it read in the literature, the visitor might be very surprised about certain aspects of people's social relationships, including the sheer amount of time that people spend relating to one another, seeking other people's attention, vying for their approval, and trying to be liked and accepted. It would observe that humans do not interact with an endless stream of different individuals but rather move in and out of interactions with people with whom they already have ongoing relationships. The alien would also see that we have many different kinds of relationships—with mates, offspring, other family members, close friends, casual friends, authority figures, subordinates, group members, co-workers, team members, and so on—but would observe that, in all of them, people typically behave in ways that maintain those relationships (even unsatisfying relationships). In fact, people would be observed doing things to avoid being rejected from groups and relationships, things sometimes not in the best interests of themselves or others. Furthermore, assuming that it could read our minds (as an alien undoubtedly could), our friend might see that Earthlings often worry about being rejected and suffer distress when other people reject them.

Returning to its home planet, the alien might wonder why human psychologists seemingly have not recognized that human beings have a pervasive need to be accepted and valued by other people and an equally pervasive aversion to being rejected by other members of their species. (For example, few textbooks in social psychology give any indication that people are concerned about being accepted.) To be sure, theorists have discussed the bonds that develop between parents and their offspring and the difficulties that parental rejection creates. Furthermore, researchers have studied the causes and consequences of peer rejection among children and rejection in romantic relationships. In addition, the approval motivation literature at least acknowledges that people seek positive reactions from others. But, these isolated pockets of work aside, we have seemed to miss the big picture: human beings have a strong and pervasive drive to be accepted in virtually all of their interpersonal relationships, and this motive underlies much of their behavior. Of course, being accepted is only one of our goals. Yet, whatever else they may be doing, people typically try to behave in ways that will not jeopardize their social acceptance and lead to rejection.

The impetus for this book came from my realization that psychologists and other behavioral researchers have collectively underestimated the importance of actual, potential, and imagined rejection in human behavior. My hope was that a volume on *Interpersonal Rejection* would pull together existing work on rejection from psychological specialties (specifically, social, developmental, and personality psychology) and would also stimulate further scholarly interest in the topic.

Chapter 1 sets the stage for the book by critically examining the concept of interpersonal rejection. Because the term "rejection" has an all-or-nothing quality that makes it difficult to measure and study, I conceptualize acceptance and rejection as points along a continuum of relational evaluation, or the degree to which another person regards his or her relationship with an individual as valuable, important, or close. All rejection-related phenomena involve low relational evaluation, and reactions to rejection can be viewed as responses to perceiving that other people do not adequately value their relationships with the individual.

In chapter 2, Kip Williams and Lisa Zadro examine social ostracism. Williams and his colleagues have pursued research on ostracism for several years, and this chapter provides an excellent, integrative review of what they have learned. Two points about the research described in this chapter are particularly notable: it relies on a wide array of research approaches to study ostracism in both laboratory and real-life settings, and it provides researchers with several fascinating paradigms for ethically ostracizing participants in experimental research.

Although all rejection is distressing, there is something particularly poignant about instances in which the rejected individual is in love with the person who rejected them. Chapter 3, by Roy Baumeister and Dawn Dhavale, broadly treats unrequited love and romantic rejection. Of particular interest in this chapter is Baumeister and Dale's discussion of how the perceptions and experiences of the rejected person differ from those of the rejector. These differences in perceptions likely occur in most instances of interpersonal rejection and have implications for resolution of rejection episodes.

Betrayal is typically thought of as a breach of trust (which it is), but Julie Fitness suggests that much of the distress of being betrayed arises from the feeling that one is not valued and accepted. In chapter 4, Fitness uses an interpersonal script approach to examine recent research on betrayal. Fitness's insight is that the reactions of people in betrayal episodes (and presumably rejection episodes more generally) reflect individuals' socially shared beliefs about betrayal and how people should respond to such events.

In chapter 5, Steven Asher, Amanda Rose, and Sonda Gabriel examine rejection among children. (Asher and his colleagues have been interested in peer rejection for many years; in fact, Asher was co-editor of one of the few volumes that have studied rejection.) In this chapter, Asher, Rose, and Gabriel report on an extensive study of peer rejection in elementary school and provide a comprehensive and detailed taxonomy of rejection behaviors that not only contributes to our understanding of childhood peer rejection but undoubtedly will facilitate future research in this area.

The four chapters in part 2 deal with the immediate and long-term consequences of being rejected. In chapter 6, Erika Koch, Nancy Hechenbleikner, and I point out that a great deal of human emotion centers around real, anticipated, perceived, and potential rejection. We then examine several emotions—sadness, loneliness, hurt feelings, jealousy, guilt, shame, embarrassment, and social anxiety—and show how each arises from rejection (or, more accurately, from perceived low relational evaluation). Finally, we speculate on how these rejection emotions differ in terms of their associated cognitive appraisals and action tendencies.

Starting with the premise that rejection threatens people's self-esteem, Kristin Sommer devotes chapter 7 to ego-defensive strategies people use in the face of real and potential rejection. Distinguishing between self-enhancement and self-protection defenses, Sommer describes common ways in which people manage rejection in their important relationships, including maladaptive responses. She also addresses the topic of rejection in the workplace, an arena that warrants research focus.

In chapter 8, Carol Miller and Cheryl Kaiser examine how people deal with being stigmatized. Stigmatization invariably involves rejection, but unlike cases in which people are rejected because of others' idiosyncratic preferences, stigmatization is rooted in widely accepted beliefs and values. As a result, stigmatized people face negative reactions from many individuals. Miller and Kaiser apply recent insights in attachment theory to the question of why some targets of stigmatization cope more effectively with others' reactions than other targets. They conclude that differences in stigmatized individuals' mental models of themselves and of other people underlie differences in how they react to being stigmatized.

To date, the greatest amount of research on the topic of rejection has involved the effects of peer rejection on children's well-being. In chapter 9, McDougall, Hymel, Vaillancourt, and Mercer review this literature, showing us what we have learned about the consequences of childhood peer rejection since the publication of Parker and Asher's influential review in the mid-1980s. The authors examine both intrapersonal, internalizing problems that arise from peer rejection (such as depression, loneliness, poor self-concept, and psychopathology) and interpersonal, externalizing problems (such as aggression, school misbehavior, delinquency, and criminality).

People obviously react differently to instances of rejection, and the chapters in part 3 focus specifically on these individual differences. In chapter 10, Levy, Ayduk, and Downey examine individual differences in rejection sensitivity. Since Downey and Feldman's publication of the Rejection Sensitivity Scale in 1996, rejection sensitivity has been widely studied, and this chapter reviews what we know about rejection-sensitive people. Sadly, one consistent finding from this research is that highly rejection-sensitive people often behave in ways that ultimately lead others to reject *them*.

Chapter 11, by Kristine Kelly, concludes the book with a look at individual differences in reactions to rejection. After discussing the nature of rejection events, Kelly discusses common emotional, cognitive, and behavioral reactions to rejection and personality characteristics that moderate these reactions. Among the characteristics that she examines are trait self-esteem, narcissism, attachment style, trait social anxiety, depression, perceived social support, and gender.

Working with this group of authors has been an exceptionally rewarding experience, and I thank them for the time, effort, and expertise they invested in this project. Collectively, we hope that this volume will not only rectify the long-standing neglect of rejection as an important human experience but also stimulate future interest in this topic.

Winston-Salem, NC   M.R.L.
September, 1999

Contents

Contributors

Dr. Steven R. Asher
Duke University
Department of Psychology: Social and
    Health Sciences
Duke University
Box 90085
Durham, NC 27708-0085
asher@duke.edu

Ozlem Ayduk
Department of Psychology
Columbia University
406 Schermerhorn Hall
New York, NY 10027
ozlem@psych.columbia.edu

Dr. Roy F. Baumeister
Department of Psychology
Case Western Reserve University
Cleveland, OH 44106
rfb2@po.cwru.edu

Dawn Dhavale
Department of Psychology
Case Western Reserve University
Cleveland, OH 44106

Dr. Geraldine Downey
Department of Psychology
Columbia University
New York, NY 10027
gdowney@psych.columbia.edu

Dr. Julie Fitness
Department of Psychology

Division of Linguistics and Psychology
Macquarie University
NSW 2109
Australia
jfitness@bunyip.bhs.mq.edu.au

Sondra W. Gabriel
Director, Office of School-University
    Research Relations
University of Illinois at Urbana-
    Champaign
Bureau of Educational Research
236C Education Building, MC 708
1310 S Sixth Street
Champaign, IL 61820
sgabriel@staff.uiuc.edu

Nancy R. Hechenbleikner
601 Colville Road
Charlotte, NC 28207

Shelley Hymel
University of British Columbia
Psychoeducational Research and
    Training Centre
Scarfe 1120
Vancouver BC
Canada V6T 1Z4
shelley.hymel@ubc.ca

Cheryl R. Kaiser, Graduate Teaching
    Fellow
Department of Psychology
Dewey Hall
University of Vermont at Burlington

Burlington, VT 95401
Cheryl.Kaiser@uvm.edu

Dr. Kristine M. Kelly
Department of Psychology
109 Waggoner Hall
Western Illinois University at Macomb
Macomb, IL 61455-1390
KM-Kelly2@wiu.edu

Erika J. Koch
Department of Psychology
University of Florida
Gainesville, FL 32611
koche@ufl.edu

Dr. Mark R. Leary
Department of Psychology
Wake Forest University
Winston-Salem, NC 27109
leary@wfu.edu

Sheri R. Levy
Department of Psychology
Columbia University
406 Schermerhorn Hall
New York, NY 10027
sheri@psych.columbia.edu

Patricia McDougall
Department of Psychology
St. Thomas More College
University of Saskatchewan
1437 College Drive
Saskatoon, Saskatchewan
Canada S7N 0W6
patti.mcdougall@usask.ca

Louise Mercer
Educational and Counseling Psychology
   and Special Education
Faculty of Education
2125 Main Mall—Scarfe Building

University of British Columbia
Vancouver, B.C.
Canada V6T 1Z4

Dr. Carol T. Miller
Department of Psychology
360 Dewey Hall
University of Vermont at Burlington
Burlington, VT 95401
Carol.Miller@uvm.edu

Amanda J. Rose
210 McAlester Hall
Department of Psychology
Columbia, MO 65211
Rosea@missouri.edu

Dr. Kristin Sommer
Department of Psychology
Baruch College
Box G-1126
17 Lexington Avenue
New York, NY 10010
Kristin_Sommer@baruch.cuny.edu

Tracy Vaillancourt
University of British Columbia
Vancouver BC
Canada V6T 1Z4

Dr. Kipling D. Williams, Senior Lecturer
School of Psychology
University of New South Wales
Sydney NSW 2052
Australia
Kip.williams@unsw.edu.au

Lisa Zadro
School of Psychology
University of New South Wales
Sydney NSW 2052
Australia
l.zadro@unsw.edu.au

PART 1

VARIETIES OF INTERPERSONAL
REJECTION

1

Toward a Conceptualization of Interpersonal Rejection

MARK R. LEARY

Human beings are an exceptionally social species with a strong need to belong and an even stronger aversion to being rejected. We not only spend most of our lives in proximity with other people—living, working, playing, talking, eating, sleeping, and sometimes just "hanging out" with them—but also typically want those individuals to accept us at some minimal level. We know that not everyone will necessarily like us, but we usually hope that they will at least not find us so deficient or aversive as social interactants that they reject us outright. And when rejection does occur—when lovers leave us, friends drift away, potential employers decline to hire us, coaches deem us unsuitable for the team, strangers snub us, and so on—the experience is typically quite distressing. As a result, most people occasionally worry about rejection and generally try to avoid being rejected.

The Need to Belong

Elsewhere, Roy Baumeister and I have discussed the fact that human beings have a strong "need to belong"—a "pervasive drive to form and maintain at least a minimum quantity of lasting, positive, and significant interpersonal relationships" (Baumeister & Leary, 1995, p. 497). Extensive evidence supports the idea that people greatly desire social attachments, think often about their relationships with other people (particularly relationships in the process of forming or disintegrating), and expend considerable effort to maintain and protect social bonds, even bonds that have become unnecessary or a source of pain or trouble (Baumeister & Leary, 1995).

The strong and pervasive human quest for social acceptance may be an adaptation that evolved because it promoted survival and reproduction among our human and prehuman ancestors (Ainsworth, 1989; Barash, 1977; Baumeister & Leary, 1995; Buss, 1991; Tooby & Cosmides, 1996). Early hu-

3

man beings who lived in groups and fostered supportive relationships were more likely to survive and reproduce than those who lived alone or on the periphery of community life, leading over time to a pervasive drive to form and maintain connections with other people.

Yet evolutionary analyses of human sociality have not widely acknowledged that social living is a two-way street. Not only must a person desire to socialize with and be accepted by other people, but the other individuals must be willing, at minimum, to tolerate having him or her around. Thus, an adaptive drive to seek social acceptance must be accompanied by mechanisms for enhancing the likelihood that one will, in fact, be accepted rather than rejected by at least some other people. To develop and maintain the relationships people desire, they must be sensitive to how others regard them and behave in ways that avoid rejection. Thus, human beings may possess specialized psychological systems that monitor and regulate their quest for social acceptance (Baumeister & Leary, 1995; Bowlby, 1969; Leary & Downs, 1995; Tooby & Cosmides, 1996). People may have a "sociometer" that monitors other people's reactions to them, triggers negative affect when threats to their social well-being are detected, and motivates behaviors to restore acceptance (Kirkpatrick & Ellis, in press; Leary & Baumeister, 2000; Leary, Tambor, Terdal, & Downs, 1995).

Everyday observation and behavioral research confirm that people are, in fact, acutely attuned to how others perceive and evaluate them. Not only are they highly sensitive to indications of disinterest, disapproval, and disassociation, but they strategically adjust their behavior when they believe that others are not perceiving them in desirable ways (Baumeister & Leary, 1995; Hogan, Jones, & Cheek, 1985; Leary, 1995; Schlenker, 1980). Furthermore, people often experience strong emotions when they feel particularly rejected or accepted by other people. Sadness, hurt feelings, anxiety, loneliness, jealousy, anger, and shame are one's common responses to thinking that other people are disapproving or rejecting, and pride, happiness, and joy are common reactions to being respected, liked, and accepted (Baumeister & Tice, 1990; Leary, 1990; Leary, Koch, & Hechenbleikner, chapter 6, this volume).

Acceptance and Rejection as Relational Evaluation

Existing theory and research relevant to the topic of interpersonal rejection has focused on specific manifestations of rejection, such as ostracism, stigmatization, betrayal, unrequited love, rejection sensitivity, peer rejection, parental neglect, and so on. Unfortunately, there has been relatively little cross-fertilization among these topics, possibly because we lack an overriding conceptualization of acceptance and rejection that would allow us to move easily back and forth among various rejection-related phenomena.

The problem has been compounded by the fact that most writers, myself included, tend to use the terms "acceptance," "rejection," and their synonyms as if they reflect a dichotomy, juxtaposing the experience of "rejection" (exclusion, ostracism, neglect, and so on) against the experience of "acceptance" (inclusion, attention, approval, love, etc.). However, treating acceptance-rejection as a dichotomy makes it very difficult to talk about *degrees* of acceptance and rejection. People obviously accept some individuals more fully and unconditionally than they accept others, and likewise they more strongly and actively reject certain other individuals. Yet acceptance, rejection, and most terms that refer to them seem absolute: an individual is either accepted or rejected, and it seems awkward to talk about a person being partially rejected or mostly ostracized, or to regard one person's love as more or less requited than another's.

Elsewhere, I attempted to describe shades of acceptance and rejection by proposing a seven-category index of inclusionary-status (Leary, 1990). This index, shown in table 1.1, reflects differences in the degree to which people actively and deliberately seek out or reject the individual. This scheme is based on behavioral expressions of acceptance and rejection, specifically the effort to which other people go to include or exclude the individual. At one extreme are instances in which people seek the individual's company—for example, by going out of their way to interact with him or her, or making a special effort to maintain a relationship. The other extreme is characterized by deliberate efforts to reject, ostracize, or abandon the individual. In between are instances in which people accept or reject the individual but do not go too far out of their way to do so. For example, the index characterizes rejection as "passive" when we simply ignore other people (but don't physically avoid or reject them), "active" when we avoid them (but tolerate their presence when necessary), or "maximal" when we actually eject the individual from the social encounter (as when an individual is required to leave a party or is banished from an organization). Similarly, acceptance may be

Table 1.1 The Inclusionary-Status Continuum

Status	Definition
Maximal inclusion	Others make an effort to seek out the individual
Active inclusion	Others welcome the individual (but do not seek out him or her)
Passive inclusion	Others allow the individual to be included
Ambivalence	Others do not care whether the individual is included or excluded
Passive exclusion	Others ignore the individual
Active exclusion	Others avoid the individual
Maximal exclusion	Others physically reject, ostracize, abandon, or banish the individual

Note. Based on Leary (1990). Used with permission.

"passive" (allowing the person to be present), "active" (welcoming the individual), or "maximal" (exerting effort to seek out the individual's company).

Relational Evaluation

Although the scheme in table 1.1 is useful as a way of characterizing the "strength" of accepting and rejecting behaviors, it does not adequately capture the psychological reactions that underlie acceptance and rejection. The reactions that we colloquially call acceptance and rejection appear to reflect differences in *relational evaluation*—the degree to which a person regards his or her relationship with another individual as valuable, important, or close. As we will see, conceptualizing acceptance-rejection in terms of relational evaluation provides a useful way to operationalize acceptance and rejection and helps to eliminate awkward dichotomization.

People obviously value their relationships with other individuals to varying degrees. What we normally call acceptance involves a state of relatively high relational evaluation in which a person regards his or her relationship with another individual as very valuable, important, or close. As a result, the person seeks out the other individual's company, treats that person nicely, provides emotional support and other social provisions, does things to maintain a relationship with the person, and so on, depending on how much he or she values a particular relationship. Thus, relational value accounts for the variations in behavioral inclusion listed in table 1.1.

In contrast, what we call rejection is a state of low relational evaluation in which a person does not regard his or her relationship with another individual as valuable, important, or close. In extreme cases, people may regard the relationship as worthless or even give it a negative value, in which case they exclude, ostracize, abandon, or banish the individual. In milder cases, people may value their relationship with an individual only minimally and thus invest little or nothing in sustaining the relationship.

Viewing acceptance and rejection as points on a continuum of relational evaluation provides a precise way to operationalize the degree to which people accept and reject one another as well as a unifying construct with which to integrate research on various rejection-related phenomena. The concept of relational evaluation underlies all rejection experiences and provides a common language for discussing a variety of rejection-related processes, including those in this volume. Ostracism, for example, obviously conveys low relational evaluation; people don't ignore and reject people whose relationships they value (Williams, 1997; Williams & Zudro, chapter 2, this volume). Similarly, by definition, unrequited love involves a situation of low relational evaluation (Baumeister & Dhavale, chapter 3, this volume; Baumeister, Wotman, & Stillwell, 1993). Likewise, betrayal is often experienced as rejection because it conveys that another person does not value his or her relationship with us as much as we had believed or else the betrayal would not have occurred (Fitness, chapter 4, this volume).

The behaviors that have been studied in the context of peer rejection in childhood also involve low relational evaluation. Notably, all thirty-two types of peer rejection identified by Asher, Rose, and Gabriel (chapter 5, this volume) involve low relational evaluation. For example, refusing to include other children, expressing dislike for them, ignoring what they say, taking objects away from them, giving them less valuable resources than one gives others, mocking them, and physically or verbally assaulting them all convey that the perpetrator does not value his or her relationship with the victim. Similarly, stigmatization involves a process of relational devaluation; people are devalued because they possess characteristics that others consensually regard as legitimate criteria for rejecting other people (Leary & Schreindorfer, 1998; Miller & Kaiser, chapter 8, this volume). Clearly, low relational evaluation lies at the heart of all rejection. This does not, in any way, suggest that we abandon other terms that refer to types or degrees of rejection (ostracism, stigmatization, exclusion, neglect, and so on). Rather, the concept of relational evaluation offers a common currency in which we may study these constructs.

Perceived Relational Evaluation and the Experience of Rejection

Of course, when people *feel* accepted or rejected, they are reacting not to the objective degree to which others value their relationship but rather to their perceptions of the degree to which they are valued. Thus, people's emotional and behavioral responses to acceptance and rejection are a function of *perceived relational evaluation*—one's perception of the degree to which another person regards his or her relationship with an individual to be valuable, important, or close. People feel accepted when perceived relational evaluation exceeds a minimum criterion but rejected when perceived relational evaluation falls below that criterion.

The strongest experience of rejection arises from events that connote relational *devaluation*. Often people perceive not only that another individual does not value their relationship as much as they desire but that their relational value in that individual's eyes has declined relative to some earlier time. Perceiving less acceptance, love, respect, or warmth than one perceived previously may make a person feel rejected even though he or she knows that the other individual does, in fact, accept him or her. Because the other person does not value the relationship as much as before, one experiences a deep feeling of rejection. This helps to explain why people are often most hurt by those with whom they are already close (Miller, 1997). The more an individual feels relationally valued, the further he or she has to fall in relational value. Thus, being treated in a polite but formal manner by a previous intimate is often quite unsettling because it connotes relational devaluation. Similarly, people usually feel a greater sense of rejection if a long-term romantic partner abandons them than if a new object of romantic interest declines their offer for a date, and being fired from a job is worse than not be-ing hired. To fall in relational evaluation is typically quite distressing.

The concept of perceived relational evaluation implies that people pos-sess standards for assessing the degree to which other people value relation-ships with them. These standards differ both among individuals (one person may require greater relational evaluation to feel accepted than another) and among relationships (low relational evaluation may be experienced as rejec-tion in one relationship but not in another). Because people's reactions to re-lational evaluation vary, in part, according to their desires and standards for being relationally valued, their reactions to events that connote acceptance and rejection differ.

People's reactions to events that show how much they are relationally val-ued by another person are affected by the relational evaluation they desire. Thus, two people may experience the same interpersonal event—for exam-ple, being teased, the "cold shoulder," or a forgotten birthday—and both may infer a low relational evaluation from how they were treated. Yet one person may have little or no reaction because he or she does not care about being re-lationally valued by the offending individual, whereas the other person may react strongly. Thus, any explanation of people's reactions to rejection must take into account the degree to which they desire others to value having re-lationships with them (Kelly, chapter 11, this volume; Sommer, chapter 7, this volume).

In addition, people interpret interpersonal events differently in terms of their relevance for relational evaluation. Some people read evidence of rela-tional evaluation into many behaviors, perceiving high relational evaluation in a polite smile or utter rejection in a brusque reply. People who are highly rejection-sensitive, for example, interpret even minor slights and insensitive behavior as evidence that others do not value a relationship with them (Downey & Feldman, 1996; Levy, Ayduk, & Downey, chapter 10, this vol-ume). Similarly, people who have low trait self-esteem, who are socially anx-ious, depressed, or narcissistic, or who have an insecure attachment style of-ten see more rejection in people's behavior than is warranted (Kelly, chapter 11, this volume; Nezlek, Kowalski, Leary, Blevins, & Holgate, 1997; Sommer, chapter 7, this volume).

Often, people *feel* rejected even though they know that those who have "rejected" them do, in fact, like and accept them. For example, a woman may feel rejected when her overtures are spurned by a man although she knows full well that he likes and accepts her. The experience of rejection arises not because he has rejected her in an absolute sense but rather because his dis-missive reaction demonstrates that he does not value his relationship with her as much as she would like. Perceiving low relational evaluation leads her to feel quite rejected even though she knows that he accepts her, albeit not as much as she desires. Conceptualizing such paradoxical instances in terms of relational evaluation explains why the woman feels rejected even when she is not: subjective feelings of rejection arise when people perceive that re-lational evaluation is lower than they desire.

Viewing feelings of rejection as a response to low relational evaluation also helps us understand instances in which people feel rejected even though the behaviors of the other person do not involve rejection per se. For exam-ple, people may feel rejected when others tease them even though the others have not actually rejected them (Kowalski, Howerton, & McKenzie, in press). Similarly, people are often hurt by perceived slights and inconsiderate be-havior that make them feel rejected even when the other person did not re-ject them per se (Leary, Springer, Negel, Ansell, & Evans, 1998). People often see an insufficient level of relational value in these events, reasoning that people who value their relationships wouldn't tease them or treat them in-considerately. As a result, they experience a sense of rejection when true re-jection has not occurred and, in many cases, they know that the other person accepts them at some level.

Incidentally, viewing subjective feelings of rejection as a function of the discrepancy between desired and perceived relational evaluation may ac-count for why people sometimes feel rejected even though the rejector de-nies that rejection has occurred (and may, in fact, be oblivious to the fact that the individual feels rejected). The rejector does not perceive that he or she has rejected the individual, although he or she may concede acting in a thoughtless, inconsiderate, or hurtful manner. The victim, however, has in-terpreted those behaviors as reflecting low relational evaluation.

In brief, all rejection episodes involve low relational evaluation and, of-ten, relational devaluation. The concept of relational evaluation may be used to operationalize one individual's feelings toward another (e.g., person X val-ues his or her relationship with Y a certain amount), and the concept of per-ceived relational evaluation may be used to operationalize the psychologi-cal appraisal that underlies the subjective experience of acceptance and rejection.

Emotional Responses to Low Relational Evaluation

The perception that other people do not value their relationships with us as much as we desire (i.e., low perceived relational evaluation) is virtually al-ways accompanied by emotional distress. Depending on the context and the nature of the existing relationship between the individuals, people who feel inadequately valued may feel sad, anxious, lonely, hurt, jealous, guilty, or ashamed (Baumeister & Tice, 1990; Leary, 1990; Leary et al., chapter 6, this volume). For example, the breakup of marital and other intimate relation-ships almost always induces negative affect (Price & McHenry, 1988; Spanier & Casto, 1979), as do failures to be accepted into organizations and hired for desired jobs. Even seemingly minor indications of low relational evalua-tion—such as being teased, ignored, or having one's opinions disregarded—

can be quite upsetting (Leary & Springer, in press; Leary et al., 1998; Williams, 1997).

Furthermore, ongoing or long-term patterns of low relational evaluation can set the stage for chronic dysphoria. People who lack close social relationships tend to be unhappier than those who have them (Myers, 1992). People who are rejected or otherwise regard their social relationships as deficient are chronically lonely (Russell, Cutrona, Rose, & Yurko, 1984), and data suggest that perceived acceptance or belonging is the culprit rather than amount of social contact per se (Wheeler, Reis, & Nezlek, 1983). Children who are frequently rejected by their peers tend to be lonely and depressed and often experience other emotional and behavioral problems (Asher, Parkhurst, Hymel, & Williams, 1990; McDougall, Hymel, Vaillancourt, & Mercer, chapter 9 this volume). Similarly, children who are neglected or abused by their parents experience emotional difficulties, partly because being treated in such ways conveys that parents do not accept the child or value their relationship with him or her (Putallaz & Heflin, 1990). Likewise, long-term patterns of ostracism among adults can be quite frustrating and lead to depression (Williams, 1997).

Rather than being just an aversive annoyance, the emotions that accompany rejection appear to serve important functions. They "warn" people about events that have undesirable implications for their social acceptance, and they serve as negative reinforcement for behaviors that help to maintain quality relationships with other people (Baumeister & Tice, 1990; Miller & Leary, 1992). The inherent aversiveness of these emotions motivates people to protect their relationships and the people they care about (Leary et al., chapter 6, this volume). If we did not feel badly when we were rejected (or even when rejection was possible), we might not take steps to repair breaches in important relationships.

Promoting, Maintaining, and Restoring Relational Evaluation

Human beings devote great effort to obtaining the attention, approval, and acceptance of other people. Conceptualizing acceptance-rejection in terms of relational evaluation helps us characterize precisely what people are trying to do when they seek acceptance and avoid rejection. Specifically, people are motivated to maintain, if not increase, the degree to which other people value them as relational partners, whether as friends, group members, romantic partners, or something else.

Put differently, the things that people do to be "accepted" by others involve behaviors that they think will increase their relational value—that is, lead others to value having relationships with them more highly. The ways in which people try to gain acceptance and avoid rejection typically involve efforts to make themselves more desirable as potential relational partners.

People want to be seen as possessing characteristics that other people value. Depending on the nature of the relationship at stake (e.g., friend, group member, romantic partner), efforts to be accepted typically involve showing oneself to be some combination of likeable, competent, attractive, and, often, trustworthy (as least in the context of the relationship itself) (Jones & Pittman, 1982; Leary, 1995). Furthermore, people want to be seen as possessing special attributes that make them unique and irreplaceable among the individuals by whom they want to be valued (Tooby & Cosmides, 1996).

People have several distinct kinds of relationships, each with somewhat different criteria for judging relational value. For example, to be regarded as a desirable friend, one must demonstrate that one is likeable and loyal. In contrast, coalition membership requires primarily abilities or resources that facilitate the goals of the group. Thus, one's friendships are rarely threatened by signs of incompetence, whereas one's membership in a task-oriented group might be. Conversely, as long as people have the requisite skills, we may tolerate and even seek out those we do not particularly like as members of a task-oriented group (at least to a point), but we don't usually maintain friendships or romantic partnerships with people we don't like. Likewise, one's physical appearance may not make much difference to potential friends, coalition members, and exchange partners, but it might be relevant to one's relational value in the eyes of a potential mate. Because the criteria for relational value differ across relationships, people may be accepted and rejected for different reasons in different kinds of relationships.

Problems arise when people try to increase their relational value in one kind of relationship according to criteria more appropriate in another kind of relationship. For example, people who stress their attractiveness or likeability rather than competence in a task-oriented group may be disappointed by their low relational value in the group, as will people who hope to endear themselves to lovers and family members through their work-related achievements.

People promote their relational value in many ways. Perhaps the most straightforward is self-presentations expressly intended to convey a particular impression. Through what they say about themselves, their appearance and manner of dress, the topics they discuss, the attitudes they express, their nonverbal expressions, and so on, people try to project images of themselves that will lead others to value them as relational partners (Leary, 1995; Schlenker, 1980). In addition, many seemingly instrumental behaviors—such as achieving in one's job, winning at sports, or earning a good salary—are often performed more for the benefits to one's relational value than for their own sake. People can also regulate their relational value through the social circles in which they move and the kinds of interpersonal interactions they pursue. People seek social environments in which their attributes will be valued and avoid environments in which their attributes are not valued.

When relational value is threatened—when one has behaved badly, made a fool of oneself, or detects that others are uninterested or rejecting—people usually try to restore their relational value by increasing their apparent likeability, competence, attractiveness, and general social desirability or by shunting attention away from negative qualities that will undermine their relational value further (Miller, 1996; Schlenker, 1980; Sommer, chapter 7, this volume). The arsenal of remedial tactics that people use after embarrassing and guilt-inducing events—apologies, excuses, justifications, and the like— help to restore relational value when they have shown themselves to be a less-than-ideal relational partner.

The Inevitability of Social Rejection

One irony of interpersonal life is that, although everybody desires to be accepted and dreads rejection, people nonetheless regularly reject one another in small and large ways. In cases in which other people pose obvious threats to our well-being and safety, rejection seems quite reasonable. (Excluding mass murderers, child molesters, and other threatening individuals from our social groups is easy to understand, for example.) But when other people pose no obvious harm, shouldn't we want to accept everyone and to be accepted by them? Does the fact that we regularly avoid, ostracize, and reject one another reflect something dark or dysfunctional about human nature? In my view, the answer to both questions is decidedly "no." On the contrary, interpersonal rejection is an essential feature of social life.

Limited Relational Niches

Nobody can accept everyone. A person has only so much time and energy to devote to social relationships. As a result, each individual must choose with whom to spend time and foster relationships. Stated differently, people have a limited number of relational niches, and they must decide the best way to fill them with individuals who will provide the best long-term benefits to them (Tooby & Cosmides, 1996). Each choice to spend time with one individual necessarily inhibits opportunity to spend time with someone else.

Furthermore, most relationships require a sufficient amount of time and energy. Relationships that do not receive sufficient time and attention (whatever that might be for a particular relationship) cannot be sustained. An individual who spreads himself or herself too thin by trying to maintain too many relationships would not be valued as a relational partner by anybody. Thus, someone who valued his or her relationships with everybody to the same degree would be caught among conflicting loyalties and likely be rejected by everyone.

The relational niches of many contemporary Americans are strained to capacity, if not overflowing. From the first appearance of *homo sapiens* over one million years ago through the early part of this century, people interacted primarily with individuals who lived within the distance of a short walk (or a short horse or carriage ride) and rarely moved far from where they were born. Today, on the other hand, we interact with people from around the world, with global interaction facilitated by jet travel, telephones, and, most recently, e-mail. In addition, most Americans move many times during their lives, and, in each location, they develop new relationships. As a result, people today are exposed to an ever-growing circle of relational partners with whom they may try to sustain contact. Relinquishing past relationships as one formed new ones would be appropriate, but people often try to hold on to previous relationships even at great distance and effort. According to Gergen (1991), this state of affairs has led to a "saturated self" in which excessive relationships, roles, and responsibilities overwhelm individuals. Not only do saturated relational niches create stress, but people whose relational niches are already packed to capacity are usually unresponsive to opportunities for additional social engagements.

Of course, the individuals who are not chosen as a part of one's limited relational niches are not necessarily "rejected" in the strict sense of the word; rather, they are simply not among the person's relational choices. Even so, as we have seen, the experience of rejection arises not from rejection per se but rather from perceived low relational evaluation. Thus, when an individual currently outside our primary set of relationships desires for us to value our relationship with him or her, he or she is likely to feel rejected even though we have not actively rejected him or her at all. Gergen's (1991) notion of the saturated self raises the possibility that, because many people's relational niches are filled to capacity, everyone has the sense that other people are not as accepting as they would like. The alienation and estrangement from others that people sometimes feel may result because most other people lack the time or the energy to develop and sustain new relationships. In modern social life, limitations on time, energy, and relational niches require that each one of us "reject" certain individuals who might want us to value them relationally.

Judicious Relational Evaluation

Given these limitations on the number of interactions and relationships people can reasonably sustain, we must make choices, presumably judicious ones, regarding whom to accept and whom to reject. Many of these decisions reflect idiosyncratic preferences based on our attitudes, interests, abilities, goals, interpersonal style, and previous social experiences. People seek those with whom they can share rewarding experiences and ignore, avoid, or reject those whose proclivities are markedly different. These choices generally do not necessarily reflect prejudice or malice but rather an egocentric attempt to minimize acrimony and conflict by narrowing one's field of interactants.

Although many relational choices reflect personal preferences, a broad look at people's patterns of rejection reveals obvious regularities. In particular, people appear disposed to place a particularly low (if not negative) relational value on four particular categories of individuals.

First, we generally do not value relationships with people who may physically harm us. (Often, the only value of such a relationship is that maintaining the relationship may avoid the harm that might occur if one tried to terminate it.) Thus, to protect our well-being, we avoid individuals who are potentially violent, as well as those who might infect us with disease.

Second, we do not value relationships with people who have little to offer us. Other people may provide us with a variety of outcomes, not only material and financial gains but also social provisions such as interesting conversations, advice, emotional support, affection, practical assistance, a social identity, and so on (Shaver & Buhrmester, 1983). People who have little that we want, treat us badly, exact a greater emotional toll than we are willing to pay, or are otherwise unrewarding partners tend not to be valued and, thus, are not included in our relational niches. Similarly, in group settings, we tend not to value those who cannot contribute to the accomplishment of mutual goals.

Third, we devalue, avoid, and ostracize people who take more than they give or exploit us in other ways. Research on equity theory has documented the importance of fairness in human relationships. Inequity causes anger and other negative emotions, lowers contentment with the relationship, and undermines relationships (Hatfield, Walster, & Traupmann, 1978).

Fourth, we tend to devalue our relationships with people who don't like and accept us. One of the best predictors of interpersonal attraction is the degree to which people think that others like them (Kenny & Nasby, 1980). Such a heuristic makes sense because we are unlikely to benefit from associating with people who do not value their relationships with us. People who value their relationships with us should foster and protect our well-being, so we have a stake in fostering and protecting them as individuals as well as our relationships with them. Interestingly, once they detect that we now value our relationship with them, they have an increased stake in us. (This spiraling process may cause strong relationships to emerge from initially weak starting conditions [Tooby & Cosmides, 1996]). Conversely, detecting that other people do not value their relationship with us provides a signal that we ought not to go out of our way to benefit them because doing so would be "wasted," for our goodwill is not reciprocated. In fact, people who do not value their relationships with us may be inclined to use, misuse, or abuse us for their selfish ends.

The vast majority of the people whom we do not relationally value (and often reject) in everyday life fall into one or more of the four categories just described—people whom we perceive as dangerous, having little to offer, as exploitative, or rejecting of us. Of course, people often have special reasons

to foster relationships with these kinds of individuals, but the general inclination is to ignore or avoid them.

The Special Case of Stigmatization

Although many choices about whom to accept and whom to reject are idiosyncratic preferences based on personal likes and dislikes, members of certain groups in every society are particularly likely to be rejected. People who
are psychologically impaired, physically disfigured, and mentally retarded
are widely devalued, for example, as are those known to have diseases such
as leprosy, HIV/AIDS, epilepsy, and cancer. Members of racial, ethnic, and
religious groups unlike one's own are also disproportionally excluded in virtually every society.

We often refer to members of such groups as "stigmatized," but the concept of stigma has been exceptionally difficult to define and operationalize
(Goffman, 1963; Jones et al., 1984). For example, stigma has been previously
defined through characteristics that discredit the individual and spoil his or
her identity (Goffman, 1963), lead others to judge the individual as illegiti-
mate for participation in an interaction (Elliott, Ziegler, Altman, & Scott,
1982), or convey a devalued social identity (Crocker, Major, & Steele, 1998).
However, stigmatization appears to involve not simply a discrediting, derogation, or devaluation of the stigmatized person's identity but rather a low
evaluation of one's relationship with the person. (Of course, relational evaluation is partly mediated by perceptions of the person's identity.) Stigmatization occurs "when a shared characteristic of a category of people becomes consensually regarded as a basis for disassociating from (that is,
avoiding, excluding, ostracizing, or otherwise minimizing interaction with)
individuals who are perceived to be members of that category" (Leary &
Schreindorfer, 1997, p. 15). That is, we speak of members of a group being
stigmatized only when other people implicitly or explicitly agree that relationships with members of that group ought not to be valued and pursued.

The fact that members of certain groups are consensually devalued as relational partners suggests that something other than idiosyncratic preferences are at work. Of course, many prejudices are socially transmitted, often
arising out of historical events that put the outcast group into conflict with
one's own. However, Kurzban and Leary (in press) suggested that some patterns of stigmatization may arise from adaptations that evolved because they
promoted inclusive fitness in the ancestral environment. Because relationships with certain categories of people would have reduced the chances of
survival and reproduction, evolution may have selected for individuals who
avoided those categories of people.

First, adaptations may minimize the likelihood of contracting communicable diseases by leading us to avoid individuals who show signs of ill
health. Many species are sensitive to indications that conspecifics are dis-

eased and tend to stay away from those who are (Clayton, 1990; Hamilton & Zuk, 1982; Møller, 1990; Pomiankoski, 1989). Likewise, human beings are distinctly repulsed by indications that others are unhealthy, such as open sores, a bloated appearance, disfigurement, and behavioral symptoms of pathogens, such as movement disturbances and scratching (Grammar & Thornhill, 1994; Low, 1990; Shackelford & Larsen, 1997). With an ability for abstract mental representation, human beings (unlike other animals) also respond to the mere knowledge that other people may be carrying communicable pathogens. Thus, the stigmatization of people with conditions such as epilepsy, psoriasis, leprosy, and AIDS may arise from this fundamental aversion to people who appear unwell. Of course, awareness, education, and intention can override natural inclination, but an evolutionary analysis may explain why the fear of people who are thought to be contaminated is so strong.

Second, human beings appear to possess adaptations for detecting "cheaters"—individuals who take benefits from others without paying the cost or reciprocating in some other way (Cosmides & Tooby, 1992). Thus, people avoid and ostracize, if not punish, those who are known to be bad risks for social exchange. These include not only individuals who intentionally deceive and cheat them (such as criminals and con artists) but also those who are unable to hold up their end of relationships because they lack the resources or psychological ability. Thus, people may devalue, stigmatize, and reject homeless people and those who are mentally ill because they are "bad risks" for social exchange.

Third, adaptations may help us to maintain the superiority of our own group. Group psychology is such that groups selectively include certain individuals as members while systematically excluding other individuals. The members then cooperate among themselves, while explicitly or implicitly competing with other groups (Tooby & Cosmides, 1988). Thus, people desire to belong to groups (Baumeister & Leary, 1995; Buss, 1990; Tajfel & Turner, 1986) and to exclude other individuals from joining their groups. In these selections, people make inferences about who is most likely to help versus hinder their own causes. One piece of information used in this regard involves personal similarity. All other things being equal, the more dissimilar others are from oneself, the less likely they are to be liked and accepted into one's group (Byrne & Nelson, 1965; Neimeyer & Mitchell, 1988). Anything may be used to judge similarity and compatibility, but appearance appears to play a key role. In the ancestral environment, a decidedly different skin color or physiogomy would have been a valid cue that an individual was not a member of one's own group. Of course, today, such cues are regularly used to stigmatize others even though they may bear no relationship to the individual's actual suitability for group membership.

Evolutionary hypotheses are necessarily speculative and difficult to evaluate. Yet, if we assume that the human tendency toward sociality and group living evolved because it conferred a reproductive advantage, then we must also entertain the possibility that human beings evolved adaptations that put brakes on that sociality. As we have seen, indiscriminate sociality, in which people value and accept everyone equally, is not in an individual's best interests. Thus, evolution may have endowed us with mechanisms that provide "hints" about other people's value as relational partners. Unfortunately, the criteria that benefited early hunter-gatherers on the savannahs of Africa do not always serve us well in modern, industrialized societies. Thus, we may stigmatize people with HIV or AIDS even though we know that they are not contagious, avoid homeless people instead of helping them, or discriminate against members of diverse racial and ethnic groups with whom mutually satisfying and beneficial relationships ought to be fostered. Of course, such reactions are not immutable, but history attests to the difficulty in getting people to relationally value those who are quite different from themselves.

Conclusions

Rejection is an inevitable feature of social life. As a result, each of us will play the roles of the rejector and the rejectee many times in our lives. Most of the time, rejection arises not out of hate or malice but rather from a simple failure to value one's relationship with another individual. Of course, rejection is sometimes more pernicious, involving stigmatization, prejudice, hatred, and other forms of exceptionally low relational evaluation. Whatever its source and behavioral manifestation, conceptualizing rejection in terms of relational evaluation provides a way of operationalizing the subjective reactions of both the rejector (low relational evaluation) and the the rejectee (low perceived relational evaluation, if not perceived relational devaluation).

People desire greatly that others value them as relational partners, and much of human unhappiness and strife stems from feeling insufficiently valued. People appear to need a certain amount of social acceptance; failing to obtain it predicts both emotional distress and maladaptive behavior (Baumeister & Leary, 1995). Although we have long known that rejected children suffer (Asher & Coie, 1990), we may have underestimated the importance of being accepted to the well-being of adults.

References

Ainsworth, M. D. S. (1989). Attachments beyond infancy. *American Psychologist, 44,* 709–716.

Asher, S. R., & Coie, J. D. (1990). *Peer rejection in childhood.* Cambridge: Cambridge University Press

Asher, S. R., Parkhurst, J. T., Hymel, S., & Williams, G. A. (1990). Peer rejection and loneliness in childhood. In S. R. Asher & J. D. Coie (Eds.), *Peer rejection in childhood* (pp. 253–273). Cambridge, Cambridge University Press.

Barash, D. P. (1977). *Sociobiology and behavior.* New York: Elsevier.

Baumeister, R. F., & Leary, M. R. (1995). The need to belong: Desire for interpersonal attachments as a fundamental human motivation. *Psychological Bulletin, 117,* 497–529.

Baumeister, R. F., & Tice, D. M. (1990). Anxiety and social exclusion. *Journal of Social and Clinical Psychology, 9,* 165–195.

Baumeister, R. F., Wotman, S. R., & Stillwell, A. M. (1993). Unrequited love: On heartbreak, anger, guilt, scriptlessness, and humiliation. *Journal of Personality and Social Psychology, 64,* 377–394.

Bowlby, J. (1969). *Attachment and loss: Vol. 1. Attachment.* New York: Basic Books.

Buss, D. M. (1990). The evolution of anxiety and social exclusion. *Journal of Social and Clinical Psychology, 9,* 196–210.

Buss, D. M. (1991). Evolutionary personality psychology. *Annual Review of Psychology, 42,* 459–491.

Byrne, D., & Nelson, D. (1965). Attraction as a linear function of proportion of positive reinforcements. *Journal of Personality and Social Psychology, 1,* 659–663.

Clayton, D. (1990). Mate choice in experimentally parasitized rock doves: Lousy males lose. *American Zoology, 30,* 251–262.

Cosmides, L., & Tooby, J. (1992). Cognitive adaptations for social exchange. In J. Barkow, L. Cosmides, & J. Tooby (Eds.), *The adapted mind* (pp. 163–228). New York: Oxford University Press.

Crocker, J., Major, B., & Steele, C. (1998). Social stigma. In D. T. Gilbert, S. T. Fiske, & G. Lindzey (Eds.), *The handbook of social psychology* (vol. 2, 4th ed., pp. 504–553). Boston: McGraw-Hill.

Downey, G., & Feldman, S. (1996). Implications of rejection sensitivity for intimate relationships. *Journal of Personality and Social Psychology, 70,* 1327–1343.

Elliott, G. C., Ziegler, H. L., Altman, B. M., & Scott, D. R. (1982). Understanding stigma: Dimensions of deviance and coping. *Deviant Behavior, 3,* 275–300.

Gergen, K. J. (1991). *The saturated self.* New York: Basic Books.

Goffman, E. (1963). *Stigma: Notes on the management of spoiled identity.* Englewood Cliffs, NJ: Prentice-Hall.

Grammar, K., & Thornhill, R. (1994). Human (Homo sapiens) facial attractiveness and sexual selection: The role of symmetry and averageness. *Journal of Comparative Psychology, 108,* 233–242.

Hamilton, W. D., & Zuk, M. (1982). Heritable true fitness and bright birds: A role for parasites? *Science, 218,* 384–387.

Hatfield, E., Walster, G. W., & Traupmann, J. (1978). Equity and premarital sex. *Journal of Personality and Social Psychology, 37,* 82–92.

Hogan, R., Jones, W. H., & Cheek, J. M. (1985). Socioanalytic theory: An alternative to armadillo psychology. In B. R. Schlenker (Ed.), *The self in social life* (pp. 175–198). New York: McGraw-Hill.

Jones, E. E., Farina, A., Hastorf, A. H., Markus, H., Miller, D. T., & Scott, R. A. (1984). *Stigma: The psychology of marked relationships.* New York: Freeman.

Jones, E. E., & Pittman, T. S. (1982). Toward a general theory of strategic self-presentation. In J. Suls (Ed.), *Psychological perspectives on the self* (vol. 1, pp. 231–262). Hillsdale, NJ: Lawrence Erlbaum.

Kenny, D. A., & Nasby, W. (1980). Splitting the reciprocity correlation. *Journal of Personality and Social Psychology, 38,* 249–256.

Kirkpatrick, L. A., & Ellis, B. J. (in press). Evolutionary perspectives on self-evaluation and self-esteem. In M. Clark & G. Fletcher (Eds.), *The Blackwell handbook of social psychology, Vol. 2: Interpersonal processes.* Oxford, UK: Blackwell.

Kowalski, R. M., Howerton, E., & McKenzie, M. (2001). Teasing in interpersonal interactions. In R. M. Kowalski (Ed.), *Behaving badly: Aversive behaviors in interpersonel relationships* (pg. 177–202.) Washington, DC: American Psychological Association.

Kurzban, R., & Leary, M. R. (in press). Evolutionary origins of stigmatization: The functions of social exclusion. *Psychological Bulletin.*

Leary, M. R. (1990). Responses to social exclusion: Social anxiety, jealousy, loneliness, depression, and low self-esteem. *Journal of Social and Clinical Psychology, 9,* 221–229.

Leary, M. R. (1995). *Self-presentation: Impression management and interpersonal behavior.* Boulder, CO: Westview Press.

Leary, M. R., & Baumeister, R. F. (2000). The nature and function of self-esteem: Sociometer theory. In M. Zanna (Ed.), *Advances in experimental social psychology* (vol. 32, pp. 1–62). San Diego: Academic Press.

Leary, M. R., & Downs, D. L. (1995). Interpersonal functions of the self-esteem motive: The self-esteem system as a sociometer. In M. Kernis (Ed.), *Efficacy, agency, and self-esteem* (pp. 123–144). New York: Plenum Press.

Leary, M. R., & Schreindorfer, L. S. (1998). The stigmatization of HIV and AIDS: Rubbing salt in the wound. In V. J. Derlega & A. P. Barbee (Eds.), *HIV and social interaction* (pp. 12–29). Thousand Oaks, CA: Sage.

Leary, M. R., & Springer, C. (2001). Hurt feelings: The neglected emotion. In R. M. Kowalski (Ed.), *Behaving badly: Aversive behaviors in interpersonal relationships* (pp. 151–175). Washington, DC: American Psychological Association.

Leary, M. R., Springer, C., Negel, L., Ansell, E., & Evans, K. (1998). The causes, phenomenology, and consequences of hurt feelings. *Journal of Personality and Social Psychology, 74,* 1225–1237.

Leary, M. R., Tambor, E. S., Terdal, S. K., & Downs, D. L. (1995). Self-esteem as an interpersonal monitor: The sociometer hypothesis. *Journal of Personality and Social Psychology, 68,* 518–530.

Low, B. (1990). Marriage systems and pathogen stress in human societies. *American Zoology, 30,* 325–339.

Miller, R. S. (1996). *Embarrassment: Poise and peril in everyday life.* New York: Guilford.

Miller, R. S. (1997). We always hurt the ones we love. In R. M. Kowalski (Ed.), *Aversive interpersonal behaviors* (pp. 11–29). New York: Plenum.

Miller, R. S., & Leary, M. R. (1992). Social sources and interactive functions of emotion: The case of embarrassment. In M. S. Clark (Ed.), *Emotion and social behavior* (pp. 202–221). Beverly Hills, CA: Sage.

Møller, A. P. (1990). Parasites and sexual selection: Current studies of the Hamilton and Zuk hypothesis. *Journal of Evolutionary Biology, 3,* 319–328.

Myers, D. (1992). *The pursuit of happiness.* New York: Morrow.

Neimeyer, R. A., & Mitchell, K. A. (1988). Similarity and attraction: A longitudinal study. *Journal of Social and Personal Relationships, 5,* 131–148.

Nezlek, J., Kowalski, R. M., Leary, M. R., Blevins, T., & Holgate, S. (1997). Personality moderators of reactions to interpersonal rejection. *Personality and Social Psychology Bulletin, 23,* 1235–1244.

Pomiankoski, A. (1989). Choosing parasite-free mates. *Nature, 338,* 115–116.

Price, S. J., & McHenry, P. C. (1988). *Divorce.* Beverly Hills, CA: Sage.

Putallaz, M., & Heflin, A. H. (1990). Parent-child interaction. In S. R. Asher & J. D. Coie, *Peer rejection in childhood* (pp. 189–216). Cambridge: Cambridge University Press.

Russell, D., Cutrona, C., Rose, J., & Yurko, K. (1984). Social and emotional loneliness: An examination of Weiss' typology of loneliness. *Journal of Personality and Social Psychology, 46,* 1313–1321.

Schlenker, B. R. (1980). *Impression management: The self-concept, social identity, and interpersonal relations.* Monterey, CA: Brooks/Cole.

Shackelford, T. K., & Larsen, R. J. (1997). Facial asymmetry as an indicator of psychological, emotional, and physiological distress. *Journal of Personality and Social Psychology, 72,* 456–466.

Shaver, P., & Buhrmester, D. (1983). Loneliness, sex-role orientation, and group life: A social needs perspective. In P. B. Paulus (Ed.), *Basic group processes* (pp. 259–288). New York: Springer-Verlag.

Spanier, G. G., & Casto, R. F. (1979). Adjustment to separation and divorce: A qualitative analysis. In G. Levinger & O. C. Moles (Eds.), *Divorce and separation: Context, causes, and consequences* (pp. 211–227). New York: Basic Books.

Tajfel, H., & Turner, J. C. (1986). The social identity theory of intergroup behavior. In S. Worchel & W. Austin (Eds.), *Psychology of intergroup relations* (2nd ed., pp. 7–24). Chicago: Nelson-Hall.

Tooby, J., & Cosmides, L. (1988). *The evolution of war and its cognitive foundations.* (Institute for Evolutionary Studies Technical Rep. No. 88–1). Palo Alto, CA: Institute for Evolutionary Studies.

Tooby, J., & Cosmides, L. (1996). Friendship and the banker's paradox: Other pathways to the evolution of adaptations for altruism. *Proceedings of the British Academy, 88,* 119–143.

Wheeler, L., Reis, H. T., & Nezlek, J. (1983). Loneliness, social interaction, and sex roles. *Journal of Personality and Social Psychology, 45,* 943–953.

Williams, K. D. (1997). Social ostracism. In R. M. Kowalski (Ed.), *Aversive interpersonal behaviors* (pp. 133–170). New York: Plenum.

2

Ostracism

On Being Ignored, Excluded, and Rejected

KIPLING D. WILLIAMS AND LISA ZADRO

> "My father has given me the silent treatment
> whenever he's been upset with me ever since
> I was 12 years old. Now I'm 40 years old and
> my father hasn't talked to me for the last 6
> months. Recently, he was in hospital and I was
> told he might die. I decided I had to go see
> him, even if he wasn't talking to me. I walked
> up to him and held his hand and said 'Oh
> Daddy, please don't leave me.' He looked at
> me, his eyes were welled-up with tears, then
> turned his head away from me. He still
> wouldn't talk to me . . . his death would be
> the final silence."
>
> *From structured interview with 40-year-old*
> *female, taken March 12, 1998*

Humans are essentially social entities whose day-to-day lives place them almost continuously in the presence of loved ones and countless strangers. The presence of others provides us with opportunities not only for positive interactions but also for risks of being ignored, excluded, and rejected. We sit for an entire bus ride without speaking to the person next to us; individuals standing beside us in the elevator do not acknowledge us; at home, our partner may refuse to answer our questions during an argument. These are examples of ostracism, the act of individuals or groups excluding or ignoring other groups or individuals (Williams, 1997). Ostracism has many manifestations, ranging from the complete removal of an individual or group from the community (e.g., solitary confinement, exile, banishment) to exceedingly subtle signals of inattention (e.g., the removal of eye contact, no verbal response to a greeting or request).

Despite the pervasiveness of ostracism, little psychological investigation has been conducted on its nature. In this chapter, we will examine this complex phenomenon using a multi-method approach to demonstrate the short- and long-term effects of ostracism on both those who use it and those who endure it.

The Pervasiveness of Ostracism

Although exclusion has probably existed in some form in all human cultures, the term "ostracism" comes from the Greek *ostrakismos,* a practice originating in Athens around 488–487 BC used to remove those with dictatorial ambitions from the democratic state (Zippelius, 1986). The term derived from the shards of pottery or *ostrakon* on which the voters ascribed the name of the person they wished to remove from the community (Bury, 1951). Intriguingly, when the practice of ostracism was introduced in Syracuse after 454 BC, voters wrote the name of the potential target of ostracism instead on olive leaves. Their vote to exile deviant citizens was thus called "petalism" (Abbott, 1911).

The pervasiveness of ostracism is such that it has transcended time and is evident in many species and most, if not all, civilizations (Gruter & Masters, 1986). Many forms of ostracism have been documented among primates, including ostracizing members because of illness or abnormal behavior, unsuccessful attempts to take leadership, and forced immigration as a result of insufficient resources (Goodall, 1986; Lancaster, 1986). Ostracism may be beneficial among animal groups because it reduces both the demand on scarce resources and the chance of inbreeding (Goodall, 1986). However, rejection from the group, and thus from the protection of other members, is often the first step toward starvation and death for the ostracized member (Goodall, 1986).

Diverse cultures ranging from tribal civilizations to the Amish all practice some form of ostracism, whether ignoring members as a form of discipline (e.g., the Amish practice of *meidung;* Gruter, 1986), or exiling deviant individuals with the aim of protecting the remaining members of the group (such as that practiced by the Pathan tribes located in the Northwestern Frontier Province of Pakistan and the Slavic tribes of Montenegro; Boehm, 1986; Mahdi, 1986). Within our own culture, socially sanctioned forms of ostracism exist in almost all institutions, including schools (e.g., time-outs, expulsion; Scholz, McFarland, & Haynes, 1988), the legal system (e.g., placing those guilty of a crime in prison; Lynn & Armstrong, 1996; Zippelius, 1986), military academies (Davis, 1991), and the workplace (Faulkner, 1998; Miceli & Near, 1992). Furthermore, almost all religions punish noncompliance with ecclesiastical law through some form of excommunication, removing the deviate member from not only the congregation but also any privileges that church membership accrues in the afterlife, such as forgiveness for a lifetime of sins and ascension to heaven (Zippelius, 1986).

It would seem that ostracism, in its many guises, has a place in our day to day lives from the cradle to the grave. Our experiences with ostracism start early in life. Children have been observed to use forms of ostracism during supervised play. Barner-Barry (1986) documents a case in which a preschool class systematically ostracized a bully (i.e., ignored and excluded him from games and conversation) without adult prompting. This case study suggested that children's effective use of ostracism may indicate that exclusion, as a means of controlling the behavior of others, is both innate and adaptive (Barner-Barry, 1986). Ostracism is also evident during adolescence, although research suggests that adolescent girls favor it more than boys (Cairns, Cairns, Neckerman, & Ferguson, 1989).

As we grow older, all individuals become both a victim (i.e., a target) and a perpetrator (i.e., a source) of some form of ostracism within almost all of their relationships, whether with loved ones, colleagues, or strangers. In our day-to-day lives, apparently innocuous episodes of ostracism in which we ignore and are ignored by strangers on the street or fellow passengers on elevators are interwoven with more emotionally gruelling episodes in which we choose to ignore or are ignored by those we love. In fact, 67% of a representative U.S. sample admitted using the silent treatment (deliberately not speaking to a person in their presence) on a loved one, and 75% indicated that they had been a target of the silent treatment by a loved one (Faulkner, Williams, Sherman, & Williams, 1997). The silent treatment has been noted as a behavioral symptom of deteriorating marriages (Gottman & Krokoff, 1992), more likely to be used by couples who are less similar and well-matched (Buss, Gomes, Higgins, & Lauterbach, 1987).

Old age brings no immunity to ostracism. As we grow older, we may be steadily excluded from all facets of our life. In the workforce, we may be encouraged (or coerced) into retiring from our jobs, and our families may reduce the number of times they visit or phone us as they pursue their own lives. Furthermore, entering a nursing home or other institution that cares for the elderly excludes us from interacting with the greater part of society. How do such instances of ostracism affect the elderly? In a survey of older adults, Madey and Williams (1999) found that elderly persons who reported experiencing higher levels of ostracism from their work, family, and society expressed lower levels of life satisfaction.

Finally, ostracism may occur even during death. Researchers have documented the conceptual difference between biological death and social death (Sudnow, 1967; Sweeting & Gilhooly, 1992). Whereas biological death refers to clinical death (i.e., brain functioning has ceased), social death refers to the point at which other people cease to socially interact with the dying person. Social death may be perpetuated by health care workers or by dying persons' loved ones. Sudnow (1967) recounts several indicators of social death evident in the behavior of hospital staff, including preparing terminally ill patients for the morgue before they were clinically dead (e.g., pushing their eyelids shut), talking about the patient in the third person while in the patient's presence, and socially ignoring patients they believed showed no hope of recovery. Sudnow cites two physicians who spoke at the bedside of a terminally ill patient about the patient's forthcoming autopsy! Family and friends are also likely to contribute to the social death of the dying person by decreasing the frequency or duration of their visits or not visiting at all. Social death allows family members and friends the opportunity to distance themselves from the dying to minimize the emotional turmoil of seeing a loved one in considerable pain. However, for the dying individual, social death represents ostracism, from not only loved ones but also the roles they once occupied in society.

Social and Psychological Consequences of Ostracism

The prevalence of ostracism throughout the centuries, cultures, and species has led to a variety of research perspectives exploring it. Anthropologists, sociologists, biologists, physiologists, ethologists, zoologists, and legal experts, among others, have all examined the phenomenon (Gruters & Masters, 1986). However, there has been little psychological investigation into the phenomenology, variations, causes, or consequences of ostracism. Until recently, only a handful of studies had explicitly examined the consequences of being ignored, excluded, or rejected, and most of them were "one off" studies that were generally atheoretical. In these studies, the conceptual and operational definitions of what we would call ostracism varied greatly without acknowledgment. This undoubtedly caused a proliferation of idiosyncratic effects.

Early studies examined physical isolation to delineate the psychological effects of exclusion. For instance, Schachter (1959) isolated five volunteers in a windowless room for as long as they could endure being separated from others and found considerable individual differences in the amount of time participants could tolerate the isolation. One participant requested to be removed after only two hours ("almost hammering down the door to get out," p. 9), whereas another participant remained isolated for eight days without suffering any notable adverse reactions. Similarly, Volkart (1983) examined case studies of prisoners in solitary confinement and reported that whereas some prisoners attempted to commit suicide during their confinement, others were relatively unconcerned about their isolation.

Subsequent studies have tended to study psychological rather than physical isolation. The underlying assumption in these studies is that individuals may feel isolated even in the presence of other people. These studies achieved psychological isolation when participants were rejected, excluded, or ignored by others in their presence. In general, researchers tended to manipulate these forms of ostracism using a triadic social interaction consisting of one participant (the target of ostracism) and two confederates (the sources of ostracism).

The studies varied in their conceptualizations of rejection, exclusion, or ignoring. Pepitone and Wilpizeski (1960) examined explicit and implicit forms of rejection. During a brief recess in the experimental session, two confederates in the explicit rejection condition carried on a conversation with one another but ignored the target. The confederates were instructed to "present an unfriendly demeanor" (p. 360) when glancing at the target. In the implicit rejection condition, the confederates did not speak to each other or to the target for the duration of the recess. Dittes (1959) examined the effects of rejection by presenting participants with bogus ratings ostensibly reported by members of their group about the participant's desirability as a group member. Participants were given ratings that signaled either acceptance or rejection as a member of the group. In a more recent study, Nezlek, Kowalski, Leary, Blevins, and Holgate (1997) examined rejection by informing participants that they had been chosen to work in a group (the inclusion condition) or alone (the rejection condition). Snoek (1962) varied the strength of rejection by explicitly telling targets either that they were not accepted into the group (strong rejection) or that the group did not mind whether they stayed or not (mild rejection). Geller, Goldstein, Silver, and Sternberg (1974) examined the act of being ignored, which they operationally defined as minimal attention to the target, brief responses to direct questions, and minimal eye contact. Mettee, Taylor, and Fisher (1971) manipulated the experience of being shunned in terms of physical avoidance and verbal abuse. Targets experienced two potential incidents of ostracism. Either the confederates moved away from targets to sit closer to the other confederate with whom they engaged in conversation, or one of the confederates openly derogated targets' stances on a recent media issue.

Some of these early studies provided evidence that being ignored or rejected had negative effects on targets' self-evaluations. Participants who were ignored rated themselves less favorably than those who were not ignored (Geller et al., 1974; Pepitone & Wilpizeski, 1960). When asked to rate trait words, more than half of the participants in the ignored condition described themselves as withdrawn, shy, and alone, whereas those who were included described themselves as relaxed, friendly, and comfortable. Moreover, participants who simply imagined that they were ignored in a conversation produced fewer positive self-relevant statements than those individuals who imagined that they were included in a conversation. They also tended to report that they would feel far more lonely, sad, frustrated, puzzled, rejected, and unworthy (Craighead, Kimball, & Rehak, 1979).

Other researchers have investigated how individual differences moderated responses to ostracism. Nezlek et al. (1997) examined personality moderators (depression and self-esteem) to rejection. They found that individuals who scored low on trait self-esteem and high in depression more accurately perceived rejection. Specifically, these individuals felt less accepted when they believed others rejected them in the group because of their personal characteristics than participants who were high in self-esteem and low in depression. Their ratings of acceptance were not affected when their exclusion was based on random selection. Nondepressed and high self-esteem individuals, however, felt accepted regardless of whether exclusion was based on personality characteristics or random selection. The authors concluded that depressed and low self-esteem individuals may be more sensitive to interpersonal cues that suggest rejection and tend to perceive interpersonal feedback more accurately.

Several studies have investigated how being rejected or ignored affected targets' thoughts and feelings about their sources. Pepitone and Wilpizeski (1960) found that participants who had been rejected rated the rejectors as less likeable. Similarly, Geller et al. (1974) reported that participants who had been ignored rated confederates less favorably than did those who were not ignored. They also found that, in an altruistic performance task, those who had been ignored rewarded confederates less than those who were not ignored. Dittes (1959) found that male participants who were rejected by the group were less attracted to the group, especially if they were low in trait self-esteem.

Many of the studies also examined whether ostracism affected one's desire to affiliate with the sources of ostracism. In some studies, targets preferred to avoid being with the sources of rejection in the future (Mettee et al., 1971; Pepitone & Wilpizeski, 1960), whereas in other studies targets highly desired to be with (or work with) those who had ostracized them under some conditions (Snoek, 1962). In particular, Snoek found that when targets were rejected for personal reasons (i.e., they were deemed unworthy of group membership), their desire to continue their membership in the group remained high.

Summary and Limitations of Early Research

Overall, the studies presented the view that ostracism is an aversive interpersonal experience, producing a socially aversive environment for targets that leads them to view themselves, and those who ostracize them, unfavorably. However, beyond demonstrating the aversive nature of ostracism, the conclusions arising from these studies were fairly limited and, as noted, sometimes contradictory.

In all of the research presented, ostracism was examined solely from the targets' perspective. None of the studies attempted to examine the psychological effects of ostracizing, even though Geller et al. (1974) observed that the confederates in their study experienced considerable discomfort when ostracizing targets, noting that "being an ignorer may be almost as uncomfortable as being ignored" (p. 556). None of the researchers adequately acknowledged the complexities of ostracism. Many of the studies employed forms of ostracism that may be phenomenologically different. Take, for example, the differences between being ignored during a conversation (Geller et al., 1974) and having another individual physically move away (Mettee et al., 1971). Being ignored in a conversation includes many indicators of ostracism: the target's attempts to contribute to the conversation are repeatedly ignored, eye contact with the target will be avoided or not maintained, and other nonverbal gestures (such as body orientation) will connote distance and dislike. In contrast to the multiple, minute instances of being ostracized during a conversation, physically moving away from a target consists of a single gesture of rejection. Are both instances of ostracism equivalent? The early studies did not address whether such different forms of ostracism prompted different responses in the target. Despite the plethora of definitions, applications, and interpretations of ostracism in the literature, investigations have not thoroughly explored the ways in which people may be rejected and ignored or the consequences of ostracism.

A Model of Ostracism

Williams (1997; Williams & Sommer, 1997) recently developed a model that attempted to unify the many conceptualizations of ostracism. Williams broadly defined ostracism as the act of being excluded or ignored. Based on this definition, one aspect of the model (shown in figure 2.1) presents ostracism in a taxonomic structure including possible antecedents of ostracism and potential moderators of its impact. The model suggests that four needs are specifically affected by ostracism and identifies several immediate, short, and long-term reactions to ostracism.

Taxonomic Dimensions

The model acknowledges the complexity of ostracism by classifying instances of ostracism along four dimensions: visibility, motive, quantity, and causal clarity. A recurrent theme in the four dimensions is the accompanying ambiguity that seems peculiarly paired with the phenomenon of ostracism. Unlike other forms of explicit rejection, such as verbal or physical aggression, ostracism is cloaked in relative mystery. Often, ostracism occurs without explanation. Sometimes, it is perceived when it is not intended, even though the target considers the possibility that it may not have been intended. Sometimes, it occurs in degree, such that the target of ostracism is still acknowledged but less so than usual. We believe that the ambiguity often inextricably tied to ostracism is one reason why it is so powerful.

Visibility. Three types of visibility include social, physical, and cyber ostracism. *Social ostracism* involves ostracism that occurs in the physical presence of the target (e.g., removal of eye contact, no talking, and not listening).

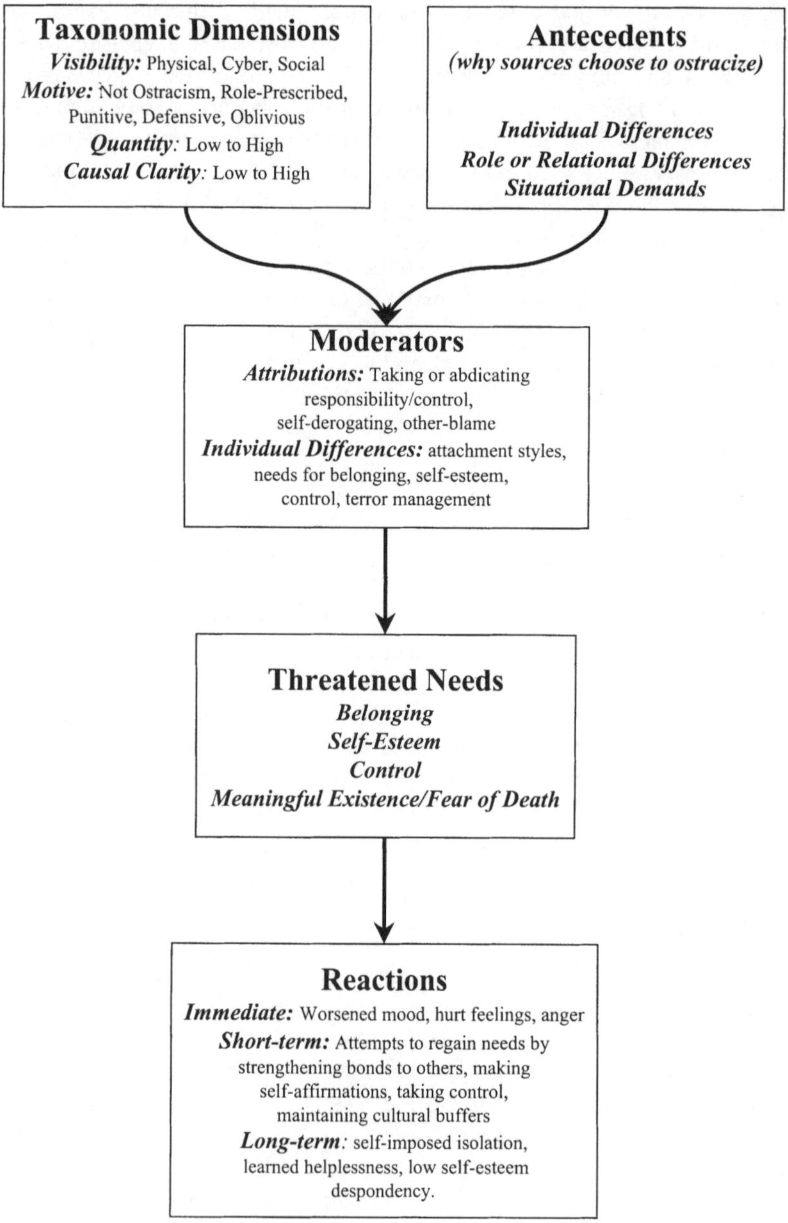

Figure 2.1 Williams's (1997) Model of Ostracism

Physical ostracism includes withdrawing from or leaving the situation (e.g., leaving a room during an argument, solitary confinement, and exile). *Cyber ostracism* encompasses all forms of being ignored or left out in interactions other than those that are face-to-face, such as not receiving mail (whether e-mail or posted letters), phone calls, or other forms of communication (e.g., memos).

Motives.   The model postulates five potential motives that ostracism may (or is perceived to) serve. Ostracism may be *punitive* in nature, that is, used as a form of punishment for perceived or actual wrongdoing on the part of the target. *Oblivious* ostracism occurs when the source does not deign to recognize the target's existence but is not designed as a punishment. *Defensive* ostracism is a protective response that occurs when we anticipate some form of negative interpersonal event, such as negative feedback or possibly being ostracized by others. *Role-prescribed* ostracism is a socially sanctioned form of ostracism, occurring when individuals are not expected to acknowledge the presence of others (e.g., ignoring those sharing a seat on public transport). *Not ostracism* occurs when behaviors indicative of ostracism (such as little eye contact, not speaking) are present, yet the act of ostracism is perceived to be purely unintentional. This form of ostracism fuels ambiguity because there is always the possibility that targets are not intentionally being ignored.

Quantity.   Ostracism varies in terms of the quantity of behaviors used to signal the ostracism, varying from low levels (e.g., answering only direct questions, making partial eye contact) to complete ostracism (e.g., offering no replies or conversation, removing oneself totally from the situation, avoiding all eye contact).

Causal clarity.   Ostracism may also vary in terms of the degree of *causal clarity.* In some situations, the cause of ostracism may be clear in that the source announces his or her intention to ostracize the target for a specific reason (e.g., situations when ostracism is imposed by law). Low causal clarity would occur when the reason for ostracism is unclear to the target or may stem from multiple motives (e.g., one determines that one's partner's silence could be because one is late getting home or has forgotten the partner's birthday).

Antecedents

Williams asserted three possible antecedents to ostracism. The first antecedent acknowledges individual differences in potential ostracizers (i.e., sources). Some people may be more inclined to use tactics of ostracism as opposed to violence or verbally expressing their emotions. Some sources may use ostracism to maintain control over the interaction or to prevent physical or verbal abuse. Certain types of ostracism may be preferred by some sources over other types. Ostracism may also be used when the individual is less adept at other forms of interpersonal conflict.

A second antecedent involves eliciting behaviors of the target. That is, some individuals may possess undesirable characteristics or behave in particular ways that cause others to ostracize them. These characteristics may include insensitivity to others, obnoxiousness, chronic complaining, loudness, or other undesirable traits.

Finally, social/situational forces may facilitate or inhibit the use of ostracism. For instance, an individual may choose to give his or her partner the silent treatment at a party, for it is a socially acceptable means of "fighting" with the partner in public and can be denied if one is confronted ("Oh no, I'm not angry with John, I'm just tired"). The "unobservable" and deniable nature of ostracism would also allow employees to use it quite easily in the workplace without fear of the recriminations that would accompany verbal abuse or violence.

Moderators.   The model proposes several moderators of ostracism. For example, a target's attributions for the ostracism should moderate its effects. Specifically, targets may view ostracism as the fault of others or as arising from the situation, thus attributing the blame externally. In other instances, individuals may believe that they caused the ostracism to occur (i.e., that it is their fault), thus attributing the blame to internal causes. Likewise, targets may make group-level attributions for being ostracized (e.g., "they don't like blacks"), which may be easier to cope with than individual-level attributions. Williams asserted that individual differences such as attachment style and the centrality of various needs may also moderate the effect of ostracism.

Threatened needs.   The essence of the model is that ostracism, in comparison to other aversive interpersonal behaviors, uniquely and quickly threatens four fundamental needs in targets: belonging, self-esteem, control, and meaningful existence. Extensive research and theory support the importance of each of these needs for human motivation and survival. Human beings need and seek to increase their sense of belonging (Baumeister & Leary, 1995), self-esteem (Steele, 1988; Tesser, 1988), control (e.g., Burger, 1992; Peterson & Seligman, 1984; Seligman, 1975), and meaningful existence (Greenberg, Pyszczynski, & Solomon, 1986; Greenberg, et al., 1990; Greenberg, et al., 1992). Although proponents for each need claim that theirs subsumes the others, the model assumes each need to be equally important to the individual. The four needs are not always mutually exclusive and, in fact, may overlap considerably.

First, ostracism is hypothesized to deprives targets of their sense of belonging. During ostracism, many signs of bondedness are removed. Ostracism is not simply disagreeing with targets or pointing out their shortcomings; it is an active denial of connection with the target. Ostracism also threatens targets' self-esteem because it is associated with punishment; it carries with it the implicit accusation that the target has done something wrong (of course, the feeling of threatened self-esteem may simply be an indicator of threatened belonging—see the sociometer hypothesis, by Leary, Tambor, Terdal, & Downs, 1995). Ostracism also threatens targets' perceived control over the interaction with the source(s) and simultaneously increases sources' sense of control. Exchanging verbal accusations or punches with sources, though unpleasant, can still provide targets with a sense of control or influence over the interaction. A sense of control is greatly diminished, however, when sources give no reactions to targets' queries or provocations. Finally, ostracism, perhaps more than any other form of aversive control, is a poignant metaphor for what life would be like if the target did not exist. Indeed, as discussed earlier, ostracism is often referred to as social death. Like other forms of mortality salience, ostracism should threaten people's sense of meaningful existence and remind them of the fragility of their lives. At this point, it is not clear whether meaningful existence should be affected in sources of ostracism.

Our discussion of threatened needs has focused on targets of ostracism. We are also interested in the impact of ostracism on the needs of those who are doing the ostracizing: the sources. Recently, we found some evidence to suggest that, at least in the short run, the same needs may indeed be fortified in sources. For instance, Williams, Shore, and Grahe (1998) and Sommer, Williams, Ciarocco, and Baumeister (in press) have found that sources report increased senses of control after ostracizing. In addition, some sources indicate initial enjoyment over heightened levels of self-esteem when they believe the tactic to be effective and beneficial. Whether ostracizing others increases a sense of control or self-esteem in the long term, however, is debatable.

Reactions.   The model identifies several reactions to ostracism in the immediate situation, short term, and long term. Immediate reactions to being ostracized likely include hurt feelings, bad mood, and physiological arousal. Because ostracism may threaten all four needs, the short-term effects of ostracism are predicted to drive individuals (behaviorally, emotionally, and cognitively) to regain these lost or threatened needs. For instance, threats to belonging can be remedied by establishing new bonds with others. Self-esteem may be regained by increasing one's self-importance or by remembering past achievements. Control may be re-established by taking a leadership role in a situation or exerting control over the lives of others. And threats to meaningful existence may be remedied by reasserting life goals and sense of purpose. However, in the long term, ostracism is hypothesized to lead to detrimental psychological and health-related consequences. Williams hypothesized that with repeated long-term exposure to ostracism, threatened needs will be internalized: a prolonged lack of belongingness may lead to feelings that one does not belong anywhere; the constant threat to self-esteem is likely to assist in the downward spiral of self-belief and affect resulting in chronic low self-esteem (Nezlek et al., 1997; Williams, 1997); prolonged loss of control over the environment and other people is likely to lead to learned helplessness (Seligman, 1975); and the sense of purpose, irreparably diminished, may then force people to question the purpose and the worth of their existence (Williams, 1997).

A Multi-Method Approach to Ostracism

With the model as a framework, it is evident that previous research on ostracism examined several types without acknowledging possible important distinctions. For instance, some studies used physical ostracism (isolating the target; Schachter, 1959; Volkart, 1983), others used social ostracism (e.g., not speaking to the target; Geller et al., 1974; Pepitone & Wilpizeski, 1960), and still others used a combination of both (e.g., not talking to the target, then moving away from them; Mettee et al., 1971). It is thus not surprising that this body of research has not led to uniform findings.

In contrast to these early studies, we have acknowledged the complexity of ostracism and have used a multi-method approach to examine it. There are several benefits in using a multi-method approach to examine ostracism. First, it is easy to be misled by results from a single paradigm. Often, empirical findings are idiosyncratic to a particular technique or measure and may not generalize to other seemingly similar situations. Second, certain aspects of ostracism cannot be investigated in the laboratory. Our laboratory studies focus on the short-term psychological effects of social ostracism. The experimental paradigms examining short-term ostracism are varied. They include conversation paradigms (the target is ignored during a conversation), a ball-tossing paradigm (the target is excluded from a spontaneous ball game), and Internet paradigms (the target experiences cyber ostracism in a cyber ball task and in the chat rooms). All of these experimental paradigms benefit from tight control and the certainty of cause-effect relationships. But, because of ethical constraints, we need to use other means to test the predictions of long-term effects. We have used role-play methods for looking at both short-term and long-term (week-long) effects. For especially long-term exposures to ostracism, we rely on self-report narrative accounts, structured interviews with both targets and sources, and event-contingent diaries. Although these approaches afford less control and are more open to alternative interpretations, they provide us with rich and vivid accounts of the phenomenology of ostracism.

We will now review our multi-method approach to the study of ostracism, beginning first with our experimental paradigms.

Experimental Paradigms

Conversation paradigms.   Several studies examined ostracism experimentally by having confederates ignore or exclude a participant during a conversation (e.g., Geller et al., 1974). A variation of this "conversation paradigm" was used by Ezrakhovich, Kerr, Cheung, Elliot, Jerrems, and Williams (1998) to determine whether targets are more affected when they are ostracized for something they clearly did wrong or for reasons that are unclear to them. In this study, female participants were either included or ostracized in a warm-up group decision task prior to performing a group task. The reason for the ostracism was either clear (participants were told that they were late to the experiment) or unclear (participants were not given any information as to why they were being ostracized).

Participants who were ostracized under less clarity worked harder than those who were ostracized under high clarity. Ezrakhovich et al. concluded that when the reason for ostracism was clear, targets were relieved of having to speculate about why they were being ostracized and were less likely to generate derogatory self-attributions. Working harder on the group task seemingly allowed participants to achieve group acceptance (belonging) and self-esteem.

Grahe and Williams (1998) also used a conversation paradigm to examine the effects of ostracism on sources as well as targets. Because asking individuals to ostracize someone is unlikely to mimic the psychological effects of real-world ostracism, we induced our participants into thinking they volunteered to ostracize another person. Thus, we hoped that they would cognitively justify their behavior to themselves. When three participants arrived for the experiment, they were first separated into three rooms. While they filled out informed consent forms and rank-ordered conversation topics that they were interested in discussing, two were approached by the experimenter, who asked them if they would volunteer to either include or exclude the third participant in the upcoming conversation. They were told that they could choose to do either, but that most participants chose to include the other person, and we really could use some excluders. This technique induced about 98% of our participants to comply, while giving them the illusion of volunteering. Once they received instructions on how to either include or exclude the third participant, all three participants were brought together to enter a conversation about a topic of mutual interest. (We made certain that the target participant's opinion on that topic did not deviate from the other two so that the ostracism could not be attributed to opinion difference.) We assessed not only the target's feelings and thoughts when ostracized versus being included but also the sources' feelings and thoughts. The results of this initial study replicated the aversive consequences for targets and also hinted at the possibility that sources derogated the ostracized targets (as in Lerner's [1980] finding of victim derogation as a consequence of beliefs in a just world). Further research, perhaps over a longer period of time, may allow us to examine the hypothesis that giving someone the silent treatment initiates a vicious cycle of face-saving and justification. In our structured interviews, which we discuss later, we have noted that sources frequently mentioned that once they begin the silent treatment, they had difficulty stopping. To stop would be an admission of wrongdoing, so they convinced themselves that their targets deserved the continued treatment.

Ball-tossing paradigm.   The conversation paradigm demonstrated that targets could feel excluded without being verbally derogated or physically abused simply by being precluded from social and verbal interaction. The ball-tossing paradigm examined a form of ostracism that dispenses with words altogether, excluding the target from an emergent group activity rather than a conversation. Two confederates either included or socially ostracized a participant during a 5-minute ball-tossing game. All participants were thrown the ball during the first minute, but those in the ostracized condition were not thrown the ball during the remaining 4 minutes. The experimenter then returned to conduct the subsequent part of the study.

Several studies have used the ball-tossing paradigm to examine how ostracism affects the primary needs elucidated in the model. Using this paradigm, Williams and Sommer (1997) examined the effect of ostracism on the need to belong. After the ball-tossing manipulation, participants were asked to generate as many uses for an object as possible within a set time limit. They performed this task in the same room either collectively (in which they were told that only the group effort would be recorded) or coactively (in which their own individual performances would be compared to that of the other group members) with the two confederates. Williams and Sommer hypothesised that ostracized targets would try to regain a sense of belonging by working comparatively harder on the collective task, thereby contributing to the group's success. Williams and Sommer found support for this hypothesis, but only for female participants. Whether they were ostracized or included prior to the task, men exhibited social loafing by being less productive when working collectively than when working coactively. Women, however, behaved quite differently depending on whether they had previously been ostracized or included. When included, they tended to work about as hard collectively as coactively, but when ostracized, they exhibited social compensation. That is, they were actually more productive when working collectively than when they worked coactively. There was also a distinct difference in the nonverbal behavior of men and women. Women demonstrated nonverbal engagement (i.e., leaning forward, smiling), whereas men disengaged faster and tended to employ face-saving techniques such as combing their hair, looking through their wallets, and manipulating objects. The researchers concluded that ostracism did lead to need threat for both men and women; however, there were gender differences in that ostracized women attempted to regain a sense of belonging, whereas men acted to regain self-esteem.

Lawson Williams and Williams (1998) used the ball-tossing paradigm to examine whether targets exhibited greater need for control when ostracized by two people who were friends with each other as opposed to two strangers. In one study, after the ball-tossing manipulation, male participants were asked take part in a mind-reading study. They were instructed to ask a newly arrived participant to turn his or her head from side to side until he or she could guess the design on the card that the new participant was holding. Social control was measured as the number of head turns that the participant requested of the new person. In a second study, female participants who had been ostracized by either two friends or two strangers in the ball-tossing paradigm filled out a questionnaire assessing their need for control. In both studies, only targets who had been ostracized by two friends exhibited greater need for control. We suggested that, in the presence of two people who were close friends with each other, a newcomer's subjective control over the situation is diminished from the onset of the interaction. Perhaps feeling less in control of the situation already because of feeling like the "fifth wheel" (or, in this case, the third wheel), the newcomer is at an immediate social disadvantage. He or she is not privy to the wealth of memories and experiences that the two friends may have shared and thus cannot partake of the private jokes, the shared reminiscences, or the mere familiarity that allows the two friends to remain at ease in each others' company. In the presence of two people who are friends, newcomers may compensate by trying to make a favorable impression as they face the undeniable knowledge that they cannot control the conversation when two friends talk about shared personal experiences.

Internet paradigms.   The conversation and ball-tossing paradigms examined social ostracism—the experience of being ostracized in the presence of others. As such, these paradigms reflected real-life situations such as when friends, colleagues, or loved ones ignore us. But ostracism need not occur only in face-to-face interactions. Cyber space has fast become a social medium to rival the tangible world in terms of the sheer possibility for interactions. Yet ironically, as phones, faxes, and computers promote the idea of bringing people closer together, these means of communication also allow many opportunities for ostracism. We wait for the promised fax; we keep checking for the invitation that is "in the mail;" we sit by our inboxes waiting for an e-mail from a close friend or are kept on call waiting to the tinny strains of "The Girl from Ipanema" as our partner answers another call. How does being ostracized in the cyber realm differ from being ostracized in real life?

Williams, Cheung, and Choi (in press) used a modified Web version of the ball-tossing paradigm in two experiments. In experiment 1, 1,486 participants from 62 countries accessed an on-line Internet experiment on mental visualization. They were led to believe that they were tossing a virtual flying disk with two other players (who were actually computer-generated). The extent to which participants were thrown the disk (and thus excluded from the game) was varied. Results showed that participants who were thrown the disk the least (and thus experienced the greatest amount of ostracism) quit the game sooner. These participants also found the experience to be highly aversive, experiencing the highest threat to the primary needs, and had the lowest mood when compared to participants who were ostracized less.

Experiment 2 involved 213 individuals in an investigation of behavioral consequences of cyber ostracism by ingroup, outgroup, and mixed-group members during a triadic Cyberball game. After the game, participants were told they would be put into a new group of six people. All participants were ostensibly randomly assigned to be the last person in a group of six (five computer-generated confederates) who were asked to make perceptual judgments. Ostracized individuals, especially those ostracized by ingroup or mixed group members, conformed the most to the incorrect unanimous majority judgments. This finding suggests not only that targets will try to regain their sense of belonging by conforming but also that *who* ostracizes targets has an important effect on the magnitude of the impact. Being ostracized by people with whom we share memberships is more painful than being ostracized by others outside our social groups.

Finally, ongoing research (Lam, 1998; Williams & Croker, 1998) on cyber ostracism in chatrooms is being conducted. Rintel and Pittam (1997) have observed that chatroom participants often report being ignored by others. In our research, we invited lone participants into a two-person computer chatroom and either included them or ignored them after an initial period of introductory conversation. We have found some interesting preliminary results. Targets of ostracism in this domain (computer-mediated communication, or CMC) seem to be more willing to acknowledge the ostracism, seeking clarification ("hey, are you ignoring me?") or voicing their objections to it (e.g., "hey, answer me!"), than those participants in our face-to-face paradigms. Although considered to be a "virtual reality," perhaps targets of cyber ostracism engage in a healthier repertoire of responses than those ostracized individuals in face-to-face reality.

Role-Play Paradigms

The train ride.   The ball-tossing and conversation paradigms followed the example of the early laboratory research into the nature of ostracism by exposing unsuspecting participants to brief periods of ostracism (Geller et al., 1974; Mettee et al., 1971; Pepitone & Wilpizeski, 1960). Because the duration of ostracism was only 5 minutes, we felt justified to impose this aversive experience on participants. With careful debriefing, our targets of ostracism seem to appreciate the necessity for deception. However, we have always been struck by how uncomfortable it is just to pilot-test the ostracism paradigms. Even though we know that we will not be getting the ball thrown to us, we still feel ostracized! This led us to try a role-play paradigm that might be just as powerful without having to deceive. It would also allow us to assess the effects of short-term social ostracism on both sources and targets.

We designed a role-play paradigm that manipulated ostracism during a 5-

minute simulated train ride (Zadro & Williams, 1998b). In this paradigm, participants were instructed to play the role of train commuters. Participants formed groups of three in which two participants were randomly assigned the role of source and the third was assigned the role of target. Participants were then seated in a configuration that we designed to look like the carriage of a train. It consisted of several rows of chairs, with three seats in each row, and train signage posted on the walls. Targets were seated in the middle seat between the two sources. All of the participants were given scenarios that detailed their role in the ostracism situation. Sources received a scenario that detailed how they were to ostracize the target (i.e., sources were instructed to speak only to the other source and not to speak to the target under any circumstance) and their motive for ostracizing the target (i.e., some groups were allocated punitive motive scenarios, whereas others received defensive or oblivious motive scenarios).

Data clearly show hat the train ride role-play paradigm obtains reliable psychological reports of the responses to social ostracism. General observation of participants while the train was in motion suggests that this paradigm is an exceedingly engaging means of examining social ostracism. As the train ride begins, all participants, both targets and sources, take on their roles with enthusiasm. Energy (and noise) levels are quite high, and there is often laughter and movement as participants lean forward or move closer to each other to start their conversation. However, as targets begin to perceive that their attempts to join the conversation are unsuccessful, they typically begin to grow quieter. Their comments become less frequent and their attempts to engage the sources nonverbally are curtailed to the point where (after about 2 minutes of ostracism) they remain seated with arms folded, staring off in the distance, and utterly silent as the noise and laughter continues around them. A few targets, when faced with ostracism, began to try harder to engage the sources' attention (e.g., imposing themselves prominently in the sources' line of vision, loudly answering questions that the sources directed to each other). However, by the third minute of ostracism, these targets too began to withdraw.

The train ride paradigm assisted us in investigating several aspects of the model, such as differences among punitive, defensive, and oblivious ostracism. First, in the punitive condition, sources were instructed to ostracize the target during the train ride "because the target failed to help an old lady after pushing her over, and you are angry with them." In the defensive condition, sources were asked to ignore the target because he or she appears dangerous ("quite frankly you are afraid of the target—you really don't want to start them talking"), whereas in the oblivious condition, sources were instructed to ignore the target simply because they are having an enjoyable time talking to each other ("it's as if though you don't even realize the target is there at all. The target doesn't even exist. In fact, it's almost as if there is no one sitting between you both"). We found that sources in both punitive and oblivious ostracism conditions showed no evidence of loss of belonging for ostracizing, whereas targets felt more left out when obliviously rather than punitively ostracized. Sources, however, evidenced lower self-esteem only after punitively ostracizing, whereas targets felt worse about themselves when they were obliviously ostracized.

Second, the paradigm permitted investigation of how participants regain threatened needs. Zadro and Williams demonstrated that after the train ride, targets of ostracism were more susceptible to the assumed similarity effect, whereby they overestimated the extent to which others agreed with their views, attitudes, and behaviors. Presumably, assuming similarity with others provided the target with a means of regaining a sense of belonging with others ("I think like them; they think like me") and validating their attitudes ("I am right because lots of others agree with me"), thus enhancing the target's self-esteem. Such complex and nonobvious findings suggest that the results attained from this role-play paradigm are beyond mere demand characteristics.

A week-long "real-life" simulation.   Whereas the train ride paradigm examined the short-term consequences of social ostracism, Williams, Bernieri, Faulkner, Gada-Jain, and Grahe (2000) used a form of role-play to examine the consequences of experiencing ostracism over an entire week. In this study, four colleagues ostracized one randomly selected member of the group per day. Thus, the study provided an opportunity to examine how ostracism affected both targets and sources of ostracism. Whenever ostracism was apparent to each participant (either as sources or as targets), he or she would make a diary entry of their thoughts, feelings, and behaviors. Examination of the diaries indicated that, although the participants were aware that ostracism would be taking place and that the reasons for the ostracism were intellectually motivated, they nevertheless recorded aversive feelings and attributional ambiguity for motives.

There were several interesting and surprising findings. Most notably, ostracism was cognitively effortful, particularly for the sources, but for targets as well. Often, when meetings had to occur, partial ostracism (e.g., reduced eye contact, fewer initiations to conversations, monosyllabic responses to questions) led interactants to be so concerned with ostracizing (or being ostracized) that they had difficulty recalling what was said in the meetings. On several occasions, targets expressed doubts as to the motives of the sources. Could they be ostracizing (or enjoying doing it) because of some preexisting attitude or conflict? Were they conspiring with others beyond the group of five to join in the ostracism? (The answer was no, but this paranoid perception was expressed by a few of the participants). Finally, some particularly strong behavioral reactions were unanticipated by any of the group. Some, as targets, tried to provoke the others into acknowledging them. One member placed a scarlet "O" on his forehead during a research practicum to get a reaction (which was not necessarily positive but was welcomed nonetheless). On another occasion, this same target honked his horn at one of the sources and felt victorious when that source threw up his hand to wave, before yanking it back down in disgust. Another target chose to ostracize the ostracizers. In fact, she was better at ignoring the others when she was a target than when she was a source (perhaps she was more motivated—defensively according to the model—to ostracize, when she was a target). Finally, several diary entries indicated that ostracizing a higher status person was enjoyable and that ostracizing a lower status person was easier.

Reactions of the participants underscored the power of ostracism. Despite foreknowledge about its occurrence and the reasons for it, there were numerous reports of aversive reactions, some so intense that many of the sources apologized to the targets on the following day. Although solely descriptive, the results of this simulation were interesting and provoked hypotheses for follow-up empirical research.

Qualitative Paradigms

Narratives.   We all know what it feels like to ostracize and to be ostracized. Thus, much can be learned about the nature of ostracism simply from systematically examining our experiences as targets and sources of ostracism.

Several studies have examined self-report narrative accounts of single incidents of ostracism. Williams, Shore, and Grahe (1998) used self-report narratives to investigate social ostracism, specifically the silent treatment. Participants were asked to list the specific behaviors they would experience when they gave the silent treatment to a friend, or when a friend gave them the silent treatment. Afterward, they were asked to report feelings that corresponded to each behavior they had listed. These were then coded by both independent raters and participants according to our model. We found evidence that, for targets, all four needs (belonging, control, self-esteem, and meaningful existence) were threatened by the silent treatment. Targets also felt a greater need to apologize for the incident. However, sources tended to feel need fortification, reporting a greater sense of control than targets when ostracizing.

Sommer et al. (in press) asked participants to write about two episodes of ostracism—one when they were a target, the other when they were a source—in order to examine whether trait self-esteem acted as a predictor of becoming either a target or a source of ostracism. Several findings emerged. Ostracism was most destructive when used as a preemptive defense against anticipated rejection. In contrast, ostracism was associated with positive relationship outcomes if used to control anger or to avoid an argument. Different forms of ostracism had different self-reported effects on the four needs. Analyses of participants' narratives indicated that oblivious ostracism tended to lead to greater threats to target's sense of belonging, self-esteem, and meaningful existence than punitive ostracism. When compared to punitive ostracism, oblivious ostracism also increased targets' tendencies to seek other relationships.

Sommer et al. also found that low self-esteem individuals were more likely to use the silent treatment in general, but they appeared to use it more as a manipulation tactic than as an indication of true disengagement. High self-esteem individuals were more likely than those with low self-esteem to use ostracism intentionally in order to terminate an undesired interpersonal relationship. Ironically, high self-esteem individuals were also more likely than those with low self-esteem to terminate their relationship with partners who ostracized them. For mixed self-esteem couples, the low self-esteem individuals are seemingly in a particularly poor position. They are more likely to use the silent treatment but only as a tactic. When they use it, their high self-esteem partners do not accept it and are inclined to leave (apparently because they are more likely to see themselves as having less difficulty meeting another person). To make matters worse, when the high self-esteem partner uses the silent treatment, he or she is ready to leave.

Self-report narrative accounts of ostracism have not been used solely to examine participants' actual experiences with ostracism. For instance, Samolis (1994) asked participants to imagine either being ignored or included in conversation at a party. Samolis found that participants who imagined being ignored generated fewer positive statements about themselves than those who imagined successfully conversing with others.

Structured interviews.   All of these paradigms (whether experimental, narrative, or role-play) examine a single, typically short-term episode of ostracism. For many individuals in the world beyond the laboratory, however, the reality of ostracism extends far beyond the 5-minute episode experienced by targets on the train ride or during the single working day of exclusion in the Williams et al. (2000) experiment. For many individuals, ostracism (particularly the silent treatment) by a loved one is a predictable consequence of any actual or perceived misdemeanor on their part. It is an interpersonal tactic that they are exposed to repeatedly throughout the duration of the relationship. For others, one single episode of ostracism may last for years so that regaining contact with a loved one is unlikely and the silence seems unending.

Ethical constraints make the lab the wrong place to examine the psychological consequences of long-term ostracism. Thus, the effects of prolonged exposure to ostracism have been explored in interviews conducted by Faulkner and Williams (1995) with long-term targets and sources of ostracism in the United States. These unstructured interviews have examined targets' responses to sustained episodes of ostracism, and why sources choose ostracism (particularly the silent treatment) rather than other forms of interpersonal conflict.

The interviews support the hypothesized long-term effects of ostracism on the four primary needs, with interviewees expressing thoughts, feelings, and behaviors indicating learned helplessness, low state self-esteem, and depression. Ostracism tended to evoke negative emotions such as anger, frustration, and despair. Many interviewees described their lives as being adversely affected by ostracism ("This has ruined my life—I have no chance for happiness now," Williams, 1997, p. 159). Several targets reported negative, self-destructive behaviors in response to being ostracized. For instance, one female interviewee developed an eating disorder after being ostracized by her mother for several years because she said she "saw it as the only way to maintain some control over my life" (Williams, 1997, p. 159). Some targets mentioned detrimental behaviors such as promiscuity as well as suicide attempts. Many also reported that ostracism had adversely affected their health.

Recently, we conducted a series of interviews on an Australian sample of long-term targets and sources of ostracism (Zadro & Williams, 1998a). Unlike Faulkner and Williams, who conducted their interviews using an unstructured interview protocol, we used a structured interview based on the stepwise "cognitive interview" designed for the purpose of interviewing children for eyewitness testimony (see Yuille, 1988). We selected the cognitive interview as a model for the ostracism interviews primarily because it included a free recall section that was uncontaminated by questions or conversation that may occur throughout the interview. Specific questions were tailored to address issues arising from the free recall section, so we could attain a progressively more detailed account of the interviewee's experiences. The structured interview contains three main "steps" or phases: establishing rapport, recalling the free narrative (the interviewee recalls the ostracism episode in his or her own words), and questioning (questions that examine specific aspects of experiences with ostracism and questions that pertain to aspects of the model of ostracism, such as perceived motive for ostracizing or being ostracized).

Although the structured interviews are still in progress, preliminary analyses indicate several emerging findings. For many of the interviewees (targets in particular), the interview is an extremely emotional experience. This is the first opportunity many targets have had to discuss often decades of experiencing multiple or prolonged episodes of the silent treatment. Many interviewees have expressed considerable surprise and relief when told that they are not alone in experiencing the silent treatment. One participant exclaimed, "I thought I was the only one. . . . I thought I had made up the term [the silent treatment]."

The personal experiences described by interviewees leave no doubt as to the devastating effects of prolonged ostracism on an individual. Take, for instance, the following letter sent to us by a young woman in her 20s:

> In high school, the other students thought me weird and never spoke to me. I tell you in all honesty that at one stage they refused to speak to me for 153 days, not one word at all doctor. That was a very low point for me in my life and on the 153rd day, I swallowed 29 Valium pills. My brother found me and called an ambulance. When I returned to school, the kids had heard the whole story and for a few days they were falling over themselves to be my friend. Sadly, it didn't last. They stopped talk-

ing to me again and I was devastated. I stopped talking myself then. I figured that it was useless to have a voice if no-one listened.

In all of the interviews conducted so far, targets have expressed sentiments indicating internalized need-threat including low self-worth ("I'm just no good at anything . . . failure, failure, failure"), a lack of belonging with others ("You didn't belong. You thought 'I'm a mistake, I shouldn't be here, I'm not wanted here.' That's what you felt."), very little control ("I felt helpless in so many areas of my life.") and a sense of purposeless ("It [the silent treatment] made me question 'what's it all for? Why am I still here?' whereas before I never questioned that. I knew why I was there and I knew what it was all for"). Furthermore, these sentiments often result in thoughts about, or attempts to commit, suicide ("I often think to myself' 'when is this going to end?' I've thought of suicide"). As a result of years of complete silence from loved ones, some targets have developed a sensitivity to silence such that even pauses in a phone conversation or the stillness that accompanies lying alone in bed at night is enough to induce severe anxiety. Jane, a woman in her fifties who received the silent treatment for 4 years by her stepfather, said: "I think one of the worst things in life would be to be deaf. I cannot bear silence. . . . I have to sleep with the radio on at night."

The effects of long-term ostracism are not merely psychological. During the free recall section of the interview, many targets have spontaneously asserted that they developed health problems in response to the silent treatment. These include stress-related ailments (e.g., migraines, heart palpitations, increased onset of asthma attacks), and those indicating suppressed immune functioning (e.g., recurring colds, bronchial problem, chronic fatigue syndrome, high blood pressure).

For many of the targets interviewed, the silent treatment often goes hand in hand with physical or verbal abuse. Yet many targets have stated that the silent treatment surpasses other weapons of conflict in sheer aversiveness. One female target received the silent treatment (which she referred to as "mental cruelty") from her third husband for 10 years. She said: "My second husband, who was an alcoholic, used to physically abuse me, but the bruises and scars healed very quickly and I believe that mental cruelty is far more damaging than a black eye."

The interviews conducted so far have also brought forward the notion of a familial tendency to use the silent treatment. One participant said that the silent treatment was used by four generations of men in her husband's family. One male source of ostracism wrote, "At the present moment, my sister aged 58 in the US won't talk to either my father or myself—for supposedly differing reasons. My father's sister has not spoken to him for over 30 years. My mother's brother once refused to talk to his wife for 6 months. My mother regularly refused to talk to me or my sister for days at a time. It seems like ostracism is a congenital condition in my family."

Although most interviews have been conducted with targets of ostracism, several sources of ostracism, both men and women, have also been interviewed. Some sources have said that that they are pleased with the effectiveness of ostracism ("I'm gonna use the silent treatment till the day I die"); however, others have emphasized the detrimental ramifications of using this tactic on loved ones. One particularly poignant example is the following experiences of a father who chose to give his son the silent treatment after a particularly heated argument:

> After two weeks, I woke up one morning with a blinding flash of insight: "What are you doing to your relationship with your son?" In that short period of time my son had already become intimidated by this treatment—he did exactly what his mother said at all times and whenever he spoke, it was in a quiet whisper. I am ashamed to say that I was sort of pleased with the effects of my ostracism but, as I say, one day I realized that it was making him weak and submissive and that it was eroding the future quality of our relationship.
> To terminate the ostracism, however, was an extremely difficult process. I could only begin with grudging monosyllabic responses to his indirect overtures. I was only able to expand on these responses with the passing of time and it is only now, about six weeks since the ostracism ceased that our relationship appears to be getting back to pre-row normality. . . . If it had lasted much longer, I might not have been able to stop and that not only would our relationship have been destroyed but also my son himself might have been permanently emotionally and physiologically disfigured. Further . . . it may have led to illness and perhaps, ultimately, to his premature death. . . . Ostracism can be like a whirlpool, or quicksand if you, the user, don't extract yourself from it as soon as possible, it is likely to become impossible to terminate regardless of the emergence of any subsequent will to do so.

In these interviews, all targets of ostracism agreed to be interviewed in the hope that they could learn of a remedy to stop the silent treatment. This research aims to determine methods to cope with or combat the silent treatment. On the basis of the interviews conducted by Faulkner and Williams and preliminary findings of these interviews, we suggest that the hope of a single cure to being ignored is unduly optimistic. Instead, hope may lie in identifying particular types of sources (i.e., those who will respond to confrontation, those who will be responsive to defensive ostracism) and developing strategies tailored to their method of ostracism.

Event-contingent records.   The structured interviews have provided an incredibly rich source of information about the nature of ostracism that could not possibly be obtained in the laboratory. However, for many of the interviewees (particularly those who have related ostracism episodes that happened many years ago), many of the perceived consequences of ostracism could conceivably be colored by retrospection.

Thus, to investigate the immediate effects of ostracism in day-to-day life, Williams, Wheeler, and Harvey (in press) developed the Sydney Ostracism

Record (SOR)—an event-contingent self-reporting method (also called a "diary format")—to study aspects of naturally occurring ostracism. In the last 15 years, event-contingent self-report methods have been successfully employed to test hypotheses about everyday social phenomena (see Reis & Wheeler, 1991, for a summary of this research). The SOR assesses everyday experiences with ostracism by having participants carry the SOR with them at all times for a set time period. When they encounter or perpetrate an ostracism episode, they record their experiences in the diary. Thus, the diary records the nature, frequency, and duration of ostracism and its effects on individuals when participants are either targets or sources of ostracism.

Preliminary research using the SOR has provided a rich description of everyday ostracism. Although research using this method is still in the initial stages, preliminary findings have indicated that the relationship between target and source may influence the impact of ostracism. In general, we have found that the closer the relationship between target and source, the greater the self-reported threat to the target's self esteem and sense of belonging, the greater the need to apologize and the higher the levels of self-reported anger. Targets reported that they felt the greatest threat to their sense of belonging and control when ostracized by a relationship partner, compared to being ostracized by a relative, friend, or stranger. When ostracized by a relative, targets expressed a greater threat to self-esteem and meaningful existence yet less threat to their sense of control. Being ostracized by an ordinary friend or stranger had very little effect on targets' needs. Apparently, it is not just being ostracized that is important; just as important is *who* is doing the ostracism. We take these preliminary results to suggest that the closer the relationship, the more threatening ostracism becomes. But why are people relatively less bothered when their family members ostracize them? We think that it may concern the fragility of the relationship. Blood is thicker than water, after all, and the possibility that one's mother, father, or sibling would disown the target of ostracism is remote compared to the possibility that one's relationship partner might leave.

Future research using the SOR may provide us with a detailed understanding of the long-term and cumulative effects of everyday ostracism: specifically, how ostracism adds to daily mental stress and information regarding the psychological impact of everyday ostracism as indicated by its effects on fundamental needs. This expanded understanding could lead to strategies aimed at helping people ameliorate the impact of ostracism.

Summary of Findings Related to the Model

The chapter has described a multi-method approach to studying ostracism. Our model of ostracism helps to distinguish among different types of ostracism and to predict the consequences of ostracism on the sources as well as on the targets. Here we review briefly what we have learned and conclude with what we need to explore further.

Antecedents

As yet, the experimental methods do not explain what factors instigate the use of ostracism. We can, however, look to our surveys, narratives, and structured interviews for plausible antecedents to ostracism. One likely antecedent is the behavior of targets. As the animal research suggested, members of groups or dyads are ostracized when they disrupt or do not abide by group norms. Our narratives and structured interviews suggest that sources often choose to ostracize in order to punish individuals who have violated implicit expectations and norms of the relationship. This is not to say that targets invariably deserve their fate. Often, sources' expectations are unfair or vague. Also, the punishment sometimes goes well beyond the crime in its severity and duration. Source characteristics are another possible antecedent. In our survey we found only negligible gender differences in the use of ostracism (i.e., the silent treatment); slightly more women than men admit to using it. We are currently studying the possible differences in the sorts of ostracism that men and women are likely to use. In our narratives we found that trait self-esteem may be negatively correlated with the tendency to use the silent treatment. Because of its widespread use, however, we should not regard the silent treatment as a tactic owned by individuals with low self-esteem. More research is needed to examine other possible individual difference variables that moderate ostracism. We are currently examining the possibility that attachment styles may be associated with the use of ostracism. Finally, the model also postulates that certain situational factors are associated with the use of ostracism. That is, because of its nonviolent nature and because some forms of ostracism (i.e., time out) are socially sanctioned, it may be used more often when concerns for impression management are high.

Taxonomic Dimensions

All four taxonomic dimensions have received some attention. Concerning the *visibility* dimension, we have investigated both social and cyber ostracism experimentally, and physical ostracism has been discussed in the structured interviews and narratives. Social ostracism appears to be aversive for targets and effortful for sources. Because there are no clear signals for when ostracism starts and when it will end, sources often find it difficult to cease ostracizing someone without admitting they were wrong and thus losing face. For targets, social ostracism is continuously salient. As a consequence, we suspect that social ostracism is most threatening to the four needs. By comparison, physical ostracism appears to offer a respite from conflict and allow a period of time for the target and the source to cool down. Physical ostracism is often accompanied by an implicit return to normalcy once the source and target are reunited. Cyber ostracism, in comparison, seems to provide the target the strength to summon the virtual courage to confront the source, either to clarify the ostracism (risking verification of being disliked or rejection) or to verbally attack the sources. Perhaps, while more immediately negative, reactions to cyber ostracism may shorten the duration of the ostracism and give the target more control than he or she has in social ostracism.

In our research, the *motive* for the ostracism is usually unstated. Participants are left to ruminate over the various possibilities. In the train ride studies, however, we manipulated motive. In the train ride, sources felt worse about using ostracism punitively, and targets felt worse about being ostracized obliviously. Similarly, the narrative research (Sommer et al., in press) indicated that individuals reacted most negatively to the silent treatment when the motive was coded as being oblivious (compared to punitive). This research also indicated that ostracism was most destructive to the relationship when used as a preemptive defense against anticipated rejection, whereas ostracism intended as a means to control anger or avoid an argument was associated with relatively positive relationship outcomes.

Only one study has examined *quantity* of ostracism. In experiment 1 of Williams, Cheung, and Choi (in press), the quantity of cyber ostracism was manipulated. Participants were either completely ostracized, in which they received no throws after the first round, or they were partially ostracized, in which they were included only half as often as they would have expected. Only in the complete ostracism condition did they report significant increases in aversive reactions. Although the manipulation check indicated that participants perceived partial ostracism, it was no more aversive than no ostracism or even over-inclusion. We suspect that this finding may be applicable only to this particular cyber ostracism experiment. In our structured interviews, we noted frequent reports of painful reactions to partial ostracism—the monosyllabic answers, the reduced eye contact, and the lack of initiations in conversations. Even a 40-year-old woman whose relationship with a man was primarily chatroom-based (another arena for cyber ostracism) reported negative feelings she experienced with the partial ostracism by her cyber partner. She said she knew he expressed his disappointment in her by saying "yep," "nope," and "k" (okay), instead of writing longer answers, and by his lack of initiating comments.

In the Ezrakhovich et al. (1998) study, we manipulated *causal clarity.* Here, we found that when the targets knew they were being ostracized by the co-participants for being late to the experiment, they were less likely to work hard for the group success than when there was no apparent reason for the ostracism. In the latter case, they expended more effort. This provides initial support for the notion that causally clear ostracism is not as threatening as when ambiguous.

Moderators

Individuals' membership status within the group who ostracizes or includes them may, in some cases, moderate the impact of ostracism. In experiment 2, Williams et al. (1998) found that individuals ostracized by outgroup or mixed-group members reported (correctly) receiving the Cyberball less often, but individuals who were ostracized by ingroup members reported receiving the Cyberball just as often as would be expected in a triad (near 33%). However, individuals ostracized by the ingroup members were the most likely to conform to another group on a perceptual judgment task. Lam (1998) also manipulated group membership status in a chatroom but found no differences in this variable's impact on ostracism.

Trait self-esteem was measured in experiment 1 of Williams et al. (in press) prior to the virtual flying disk game. Self-reported reactions to the disk game were more aversive for low self-esteem than for high self-esteem individuals, and this pattern held across all ostracism conditions. Yet other studies (e.g., Nezlek et al., 1997) have shown low self-esteem individuals to be more sensitive to rejection cues than high self-esteem individuals. Whether the reason for these different patterns of results are because of differences in method (Internet versus laboratory) or operational definitions (not throwing the disk to the individual versus explicit rejection of the individual) is not clear and warrants further research.

We are currently examining the potential moderating influence of attachment style on reactions to ostracism. Bowlby (1977) investigated attachment behavior by examining how infants forged emotional bonds with caregivers. Ainsworth (1989) created a paradigm, the strange situation, to examine attachment patterns based on responses to the child's separation from his or her parent. Three attachment patterns were recorded: secure, avoidant, and anxious/ambivalent (or resistant). These infant attachment patterns have been hypothesized to generalize to adult attachment patterns, including romantic attachments (Hazen & Shaver, 1987). Williams (1997) speculates that individuals who are securely attached should be less affected by ostracism because they are secure enough within themselves to withstand outside rejection. Anxious/ambivalent individuals should show the greatest negative affect because of their general anxiety and anticipation of rejection. Finally, avoidant persons may actually respond to ostracism by ostracizing others in return or in anticipation.

Need Threats and Reactions

As discussed, using a wide range of methods, we have found ample evidence that ostracism threatens self-esteem, control, and belonging. It is not surprising that, of the four needs, meaningful existence would be relatively difficult to influence within a short-term experiment. In the structured interviews, we see frequent mention of feelings of worthlessness and meaninglessness. We have also found some support for the notion that, for sources, control, and sometimes self-esteem, is fortified. We are interested in determining whether the temporary feeling of heightened control one gains by using ostracism persists over time or if, at some point, the compulsion to remain silent begins to control the ostracizer.

Short-Term Reactions

Individuals have attempted to regain control (or have expressed a desire for more control) when two others who were perceived to be friends ostracized them. Ostracized individuals have shown tendencies to work harder in groups, conform more to others, and assume a higher degree of similarity between their attitudes and the general public's—all effects that could increase their sense of belonging—than nonostracized individuals. So far, we have no evidence for attempts to increase self-esteem or meaningful existence (although the assumed similarity effect has been interpreted as a coping mechanism for mortality salience; see Pyszczynski et al., 1996).

Long-Term Reactions

In our structured interviews, we have observed ample support for the hypothesis that long-term exposure to ostracism leads to internalization and acceptance of a lowered sense of belonging, control, self-esteem, and meaningful existence. Our interviews with long-term targets of the silent treatment indicate that they frequently report severe bouts of depression, helplessness, alienation, and even attempts to commit suicide. Although extensive qualitative and quantitative analyses remain to be conducted, these ongoing interviews are replete with references to health problems and therapy.

Conclusion

We have presented a program of research attempting to discover the causes, consequences, and complexities of ostracism. We recognize that any one method enjoys certain advantages but also suffers certain restrictions and qualifications. Consequently, we have embarked on a multi-method approach, relying on laboratory and field experimentation, role-play, narratives, event-contingent diaries, Internet research, and structured interviews. Although research is still in progress, there is encouraging converging support for the hypotheses generated by the model of ostracism. In the next few years, we hope to shed more light on the powerful, yet relatively overlooked, phenomenon of ostracism. Currently, we are investigating the psychophysiological effects of ostracizing and being ostracized to further delineate the possible debilitating effects of ostracism on health. We are also examining a few, surprisingly neglected topics.

One such topic is the psychological impact of time-outs as used to discipline children at home and in schools. Our literature review suggests that time-out is carried out in several ways (e.g., time-out rooms, sitting in the presence of one's classmates with a bow tied around one's arm), yet there has been no systematic analysis of the effectiveness of these varying treatments. Given that this is a popular and socially sanctioned form of ostracism, it is especially important to determine whether some forms of time-out might have unanticipated side effects.

Another topic we hope to examine is the phenomenon of being disowned or disinherited. How do people feel after their parents say to them, "You are no longer my child, you are not a member of our family"? Only a few articles have been written on this potentially devastating form of ostracism, so we hope to conduct structured interviews with both targets and sources. This project may not only provide us with more information about long-term ostracism but also go beyond the effects of the silent treatment. Being disowned, perhaps more than any other form of ostracism, deprives individuals of their strongest, most permanent bonds and the roots to which their existence is tied.

Acknowledgments

This research was funded by two Australian Research Council Large Grants (A79800071 and A10007248) and two ARC Small grants awarded to the first author.

Correspondence concerning this chapter should be sent to Kipling Williams at the School of Psychology, University of New South Wales, Sydney 2052 Australia, or by electronic mail: kip.williams@unsw.edu.au.

References

Abbott, E. (1911). *A history of Greece—Part II.* (3rd ed.). London: Longmans, Green.

Ainsworth, M. D. S. (1989). Attachment beyond infancy. *American Psychologist, 44,* 709–716.

Barner-Barry, C. (1986). Rob: Children's tacit use of peer ostracism to control aggressive behavior. *Ethology and Sociobiology, 7,* 281–293.

Baumeister, R. F., & Leary, M. R. (1995). The need to belong: Desire for interpersonal attachments as a fundamental human motivation. *Psychological Bulletin, 117,* 497–529.

Boehm, C. (1986). Capital punishment in tribal Montenegro: Implications for law, biology, and theory of social control. *Ethology and Sociobiology, 7,* 305–320.

Bowlby, J. (1977). The making and breaking of affectional bonds. *British Journal of Psychiatry, 130,* 201–210.

Burger, J. M. (1992). *Desire for control: Personality, social, & clinical perspectives.* New York: Plenum.

Bury, J. B. (1951). *A history of Greece to the death of Alexander the Great.* (3rd ed.). London: Macmillan.

Buss, D. M., Gomes, M., Higgins, D. S., & Lauterbach, K. (1987). Tactics of manipulation. *Journal of Personality and Social Psychology, 52,* 1219–1229.

Cairns, R. B., Cairns, B. D., Neckerman, H. J., & Ferguson, L. L. (1989). Growth and aggression: I. Childhood to early adolescence. *Developmental Psychology, 25,* 320–330.

Craighead, W. E., Kimball, W. H., & Rehak, P. J. (1979). Mood changes, physiological responses, and self-statements during social rejection imagery. *Journal of Consulting and Clinical Psychology, 47,* 385–396.

Davis, B. O. (1991). *Benjamin O'Davis, Jr., American: An autobiography.* Washington, DC: Smithsonian Institution Press.

Dittes, J. E. (1959). Attractiveness of group as function of self-esteem and acceptance by group. *Journal of Abnormal and Social Psychology, 59,* 77–82.

Duck, S., Rutt, D. J., Hurst, M. H., & Strejc, H. (1991). Some evident truth about conversation in everyday relationships: All communications are not created equal. *Human Communication Research, 18,* 228–267.

Ezrakhovich, A., Kerr, A., Cheung, S., Elliot, K., Jerrems, A., & Williams, K. D. (1998, April). *Effects of norm violation and ostracism on working with the group.* Presented at the Society of Australasian Social Psychologists, Christchurch, NZ.

Faulkner, S. L. (1998). *After the whistle is blown: The aversive impact of ostracism.* Unpublished doctoral dissertation, University of Toledo.

Faulkner, S. L., & Williams, K. D. (May, 1995). *The causes and consequences of social ostracism: A qualitative analysis.* Paper presented at the Midwestern Psychological Association, Chicago, IL.

Faulkner, S., Williams, K., Sherman, B., & Williams, E. (1997, May). *The "silent treatment:" Its incidence and impact.* Presented at the 69th Annual Midwestern Psychological Association, Chicago.

Geller, D. M., Goodstein, L., Silver, M., & Sternberg, W. C. (1974). On being ignored: The effects of violation of implicit rules of social interaction. *Sociometry, 37,* 541–556.

Goodall, J. (1986). Social rejection, exclusion, and shunning among the Gombe chimpanzees. *Ethology and Sociobiology, 7,* 227–236.

Gottman, J. M., & Krokoff, L. J. (1992). Marital interaction and satisfaction: A longitudinal view. *Journal of Consulting and Clinical Psychology, 57,* 47–52.

Grahe, J., & Williams, K. D. (1998, April). *A conversation paradigm to study sources and targets.* Paper presented at the Midwestern Psychological Association, Chicago, IL.

Greenberg, J., Pyszczynski, T., & Solomon, S. (1986). The causes and consequences of the need for self-esteem: A terror management theory. In R. F. Baumeister (Ed.), *Public self and private self* (pp. 189–212). New York: Springer-Verlag.

Greenberg, J., Pyszczynski, T., Solomon, S., Rosenblatt, A., Veeder, M., Kirkland, S., & Lyon, D. (1990). Evidence for terror management theory II: The effects of mortality salience on reactions to those who threaten or bolster the cultural worldview. *Journal of Personality and Social Psychology, 58,* 308–318.

Greenberg, J., Solomon, S., Pyszczynski, T., Rosenblatt, A., Burling, J., Lyon,

D., Simon, L., & Pinel, E. (1992). Why do people need self-esteem? Converging evidence that self-esteem serves an anxiety-buffering function. *Journal of Personality and Social Psychology, 63,* 913–922.

Gruter, M. (1986). Ostracism on trial: The limits of individual rights. *Ethology and Sociobiology, 7,* 271–279.

Gruter, M., & Masters, R. D. (1986). Ostracism as a social and biological phenomenon: An introduction. *Ethology and Sociobiology, 7,* 149–158.

Hazan, C., & Shaver, P. (1987). Conceptualizing romantic love as an attachment process. *Journal of Personality and Social Psychology, 52,* 511–524.

Lam, A. (1998). *The effects of cyber ostracism and group membership on self-esteem: Does it matter who's ostracising me?* Unpublished honors thesis, University of New South Wales.

Lancaster, J. B. (1986). Primate social behavior and ostracism. *Ethology and Sociobiology, 7,* 215–225.

Lawson Williams, H., & Williams, K. D. (1998, April). *Effects of social ostracism on need for control.* Presented at the Society of Australasian Social Psychologists, Christchurch, NZ.

Leary, M. R., Tambor, E. S., Terdal, S. K., & Downs, D. L. (1995). Self-esteem as an interpersonal monitor: The sociometer hypothesis. *Journal of Personality and Social Psychology, 2,* 518–530.

Lerner, M. (1980). *The belief in a just world: A fundamental delusion.* New York: Plenum.

Lynn, P., & Armstrong, G. (1996). *From Pentonville to Pentridge: A history of prisons in Victoria.* Victoria: State Library of Victoria.

Madey, S. F., & Williams, K. D. (1999, March). *Ostracism and the elderly: Older adults' feelings of exclusion in relationships.* Paper presented at the Eastern Psychological Association, Boston, MA.

Mahdi, N. Q. (1986). Pukhtuwali: Ostracism and honour among the Pathan Hill tribes. *Ethology and Sociobiology, 7,* 295–304.

McGuire, M. T., & Raleigh, M. J. (1986). Behavioral and physiological correlates of ostracism. *Ethology and Sociobiology, 7,* 187–200.

Mettee, D. R., Taylor, S. E., & Fisher, S. (1971). The effect of being shunned upon the desire to affiliate. *Psychonomic Science, 23,* 429–431.

Miceli, M., & Near, J. (1992). *Blowing the whistle: The organizational and legal implications for companies and their employees.* New York: Lexington.

Nezlek, J. B., Kowalski, R. M., Leary, M. R., Blevins, T., & Holgate, S. (1997). Personality moderators of reactions to interpersonal rejection: Depression and trait self-esteem. *Personality and Social Psychology Bulletin, 23,* 1235–1244.

Pepitone, A., & Wilpizeski, C. (1960). Some consequences of experimental rejection. *Journal of Abnormal and Social Psychology, 60,* 359–364.

Peterson, C., & Seligman, M. E. (1994). Causal explanations as a risk factor for depression: Theory and evidence. *Psychological Review, 91,* 347–374.

Pyszczynski, T., Wicklund, R. A., Floresku, S., Koch, H., Gauch, G., Solomon, S., & Greenberg, J. (1996). Whistling in the dark: Exaggerated consensus estimates in response to incidental reminders of mortality. *Psychological Science, 6,* 332–336.

Reis, H. T., & Wheeler, L. (1991). Studying social interaction with the

Rochester Interaction Record. In M. P. Zanna (Ed.), *Advances in experimental social psychology* (vol. 24, pp. 270–312). New York: Academic Press.

Rintel, E. S., & Pittam, J. (1997). Strangers in a strange land: Interaction management on Internet Relay Chat. *Human Communication Research, 23,* 507–534.

Samolis, M. M. (1994). *The effects of ostracism and communication level on self and task-referents, feelings, and action.* Unpublished manuscript.

Schachter, S. (1959). *The psychology of affiliation.* Stanford, CA: Stanford University Press.

Scholz, D., McFarland, B., & Haynes, M. (1988). Time-out in schools. *Behavior Problems Bulletin, 2,* 12–16.

Seligman, M. E. P. (1975). *Helplessness: On depression, development, and death.* San Francisco: Freeman.

Snoek, J. D. (1962). Some effects of rejection upon attraction to a group. *Journal of Abnormal and Social Psychology, 64,* 175–182.

Sommer, K. L., Williams, K. D., Ciarocco, N. J., & Baumeister, R. F. (in press). Explorations into the intrapsychic and interpersonal consequences of social ostracism. *Basic and Applied Social Psychology.*

Steele, C. M. (1988). The psychology of self-affirmation: Sustaining the integrity of the self. In L. Berkowitz (Ed.), *Advances in experimental social psychology* (pp. 261–302). New York: Academic Press.

Sudnow, D. (1967). *Passing on: The social organization of dying.* Englewood Cliffs, NJ: Prentice Hall.

Sweeting, N., & Gilhooly, M. L. M. (1992). Doctor, am I dead? A review of social death in modern societies. *Omega, 24,* 254–269.

Tesser, A. (1988). Toward a self-evaluation maintenance model of social behavior. In L. Berkowitz (Ed.), *Advances in experimental social psychology* (vol. 21, pp. 181–227) San Diego: Academic Press.

Volkart, R. (1983). Eine literaturubersicht. *Revue Suisse De Psychologie Pure et Appliquee, 42,* 11–24.

Williams, K. D. (1997). Social ostracism: The causes and consequences of "the silent treatment." In R. Kowalski (Ed.), *Aversive interpersonal behaviors* (pp. 133–170) New York: Plenum.

Williams, K. D., Bernieri, F., Faulkner, S., Grahe, J., & Gada-Jain, N. (2000). The Scarlet Letter Study: Five days of social ostracism. *Journal of Personal and Interpersonal Loss, 5,* 19–63.

Williams K. D., Cheung, C. K. T., & Choi, W. (in press). CyberOstracism: Effects of being ignored over the Internet. *Journal of Personality and Social Psychology.*

Williams, K. D., & Croker, V. (1998, April). *Confronting the ostracizers: The role of anonymity and identifiability on the behavior of targets.* Presented at the Society of Australasian Social Psychology, Christchurch, NZ.

Williams, K. D., & Sommer, K. L. (1997). Social ostracism by one's coworkers: Does rejection lead to loafing or compensation? *Personality and Social Psychology Bulletin, 23,* 693–706.

Williams, K. D., Shore, W. J., & Grahe, J. E. (1998). The silent treatment: Perceptions of its behaviors and associated feelings. *Group Processes and Intergroup Relations, 1,* 117–141.

Williams, K. D., Wheeler, L., & Harvey, J. (in press). Inside the social mind of the ostracizer. In J. Forgas, K. Williams, & L. Wheeler (Eds.), *The social mind: Cognitive and motivational aspects of interpersonal behavior.* New York: Cambridge Press.

Yuille, J. (1988). The systematic assessment of children's testimony. *Canadian Psychology, 29,* 247–262.

Zadro, L., & Williams, K. D. (1998a). *Structured interviews with long-term sources and targets of the silent treatment.* Unpublished manuscript, University of New South Wales, Sydney, Australia.

Zadro, L., & Williams, K. D. (1998b, April). *Take the 'O' train: Oblivious versus punitive ostracism.* Presented at the Society of Australasian Social Psychologists, Christchurch, NZ.

Zippelius, R. (1986). Exclusion and shunning as legal and social sanctions. *Ethology and Sociobiology, 7,* 159–166.

3

Two Sides of Romantic Rejection

ROY F. BAUMEISTER AND DAWN DHAVALE

Rejection can be a painful and powerful experience in many contexts, but having one's love refused by the person one loves is perhaps the most painful of all. Recent Western culture has elevated romantic love to the status of a centrally important form of personal fulfillment, and popular culture, as well as serious intellectual work, continues to emphasize that the passionate love between man and woman is the most important route to blissful, fullfilled happiness. To fail at romantic love thus strikes at the core of one's sense of competent personhood.

Yet the poignant disappointment of unrequited love—that is, nonreciprical affection—is common. Surveys regarding unrequited love find that, by early adulthood, almost everyone has had such an experience, recalled with vivid, bittersweet detail even many years later. This is the dark side of our culture's relentless celebration of romantic love: many efforts to form a loving relationship with an appealing, carefully chosen partner end in grief.

The sadness, pain, and disappointment of the rejected lover are not difficult to understand. The greater mystery, in a sense, concerns the motives and inner processes of the person who does the rejecting. If both evolutionary selection and cultural conditioning shape people to seek loving attachments with others, why do so many people refuse offers of love?

This chapter will examine the two sides of unrequited love, comparing the experiences of the aspiring, would-be lover with those of the rejector. As we shall see, the rejector and the would-be lover have substantially different perspectives on these episodes of romantic rejection and sometimes have widely different views about what transpired.

Our main source for this work will be a series of studies carried out by the first author and several colleagues (Baumeister & Wotman, 1992; Baumeister, Wotman, & Stillwell, 1993). In these studies, people were asked to write open-ended descriptions (and in one case, respond to a structured questionnaire) about their own experiences in the roles of would-be lover and rejector. By comparing the two sets of accounts, we could delineate important differences in the two role perspectives.

The research samples of accounts of unrequited love did not permit direct comparisons of the views of the two interactants. In the first and largest study, for example, each person was asked to describe his or her most powerful experience in the rejector role as well as in the would-be lover role. We did not solicit complementary views from the other person involved in those events. We do have accounts by the same people in both roles, so any differences or biases are inherent in the roles themselves. In contrast, if we had obtained the rejector and would-be lover accounts from different people, the differences might simply mean that rejectors and would-be lovers are different kinds of people. In these data, however, the rejectors and would-be lovers are the same person.

Two issues of generality must also be acknowledged. First, the bulk of our findings pertain to love that has never been requited. In a few cases, however, people wrote about unrequited love that emerged from a relationship that had previously been characterized by mutual, reciprocal love. In theory, these might be vastly different contexts and experiences, but our impression was that in many respects they were quite similar. The anguish, the wondering about why the other doesn't return the love, and the rejector's awkward struggle to extricate the self from an unwanted entanglement are almost depressingly similar themes regardless of whether the love had ever been mutual.

The other issue concerns the broad context of human mating. We shall present unrequited love in the context of finding a long-term romantic partner. Still, some people experience unrequited love (as well as requited love) long before they are ready to settle down with a single long-term mate. On the other hand, most people who are in love want to have a lasting relationship, even if they do not necessarily envision marriage and family in the foreseeable future. Moreover, the human tendency to form romantic pair bonds may well be shaped by the evolutionary emphasis on mating and reproduction, so the natural impulse to find an attractive mate may shape the behavior even of those for whom marriage and reproduction are out of the question. To illustrate, evolutionary psychologists explain male jealousy and sexual possessiveness on the basis of paternity uncertainty (Buss & Schmitt, 1993). Men do not want their women to have sex with other men, for fear that the other man would impregnate their partner. Modern contraceptive technology has arguably rendered this concern obsolete, so in theory men should not mind their partner's infidelity as long as she uses a condom or takes the birth control pill. Yet men's emotions have not necessarily kept up with the pace of these technological developments.

Falling Upward

Let us begin with the basic question of why unrequited love should occur at all. If people were programmed (whether by nature or culture) to seek and accept love, rejection should be unnecessary. Clearly, however, rejection is commonplace. Why do so many people refuse so much love?

Obviously, people do not wish to enter love relationships with just anyone: they want a partner who has desirable qualities. People mate with others who are similar to themselves: in intelligence, cultural background, race, education, physical attractiveness, and other traits. This preference for similarity might seem to explain why people would reject romantic offers from some potential partners: the partner does not qualify.

The problem is exacerbated by opportunity costs. A person can marry only one person at a time, and in most circumstances one can sustain a serious romantic involvement with only one person at a time. Hence, to accept one person's love is implicitly to forego all others. Therefore one must be selective in finding a partner.

Still, this explanation is too facile. If the quest for similarity is so pervasive, why would the offer have been made in the first place? In other words, if two people are not well suited for each other, then one of them might well reject the other as a potential romantic partner. But why would the other have tried to mate with an unsuitable partner? This explanation works only if the two people disagree about how well suited they are to each other—in other words, if one person thinks the pair would make a good couple but the other person disagrees.

One way to resolve this paradox is to invoke the evaluative standards that people use to judge each other's (and their own) desirability as potential romantic partners. Many similar spousal traits, such as intelligence and physical attractiveness, are strongly evaluative. It is better to be intelligent and beautiful than stupid and ugly. On these dimensions, research suggests that attraction follows a pattern we labeled *falling upward* (Baumeister & Wotman, 1992): people desire mates who are higher but not lower than themselves. That is, they fall in love with people who rank above them.

These findings emerged from a research program that sought to find theoretically complex and sophisticated patterns of attraction. Walster, Aronson, Abrahams, and Rottman (1966) wanted to show that people were most attracted to potential partners who matched them on traits such as physical beauty or intelligence. They had to prove that people would reject others who were more attractive than themselves, so as to show maximum preference for the person most similar to oneself. This hypothesis failed to materialize in a series of studies. People were simply most attracted to the most desirable partners (Walster et al., 1966).

Thus, people are attracted to others whose total mate appeal equals or exceeds their own mate appeal. They are not generally attracted to people who have lower mate appeal, particularly in the quest for long-term mates. The major exception is that some men are willing to participate in short-term sexual liaisons with women who are relatively less desirable mates than the men are (Buss & Schmitt, 1993). Still, men seek these pairings explicitly as short-term adventures, so they do not count as part of the mate search. One may be attracted to a famous, glamorous superstar, but that person is not likely to return that attraction unless one has some claim to superstar appeal too.

Thus, people are attracted to people better than they are, but they generally marry people who are roughly equal to themselves (e.g., Jensen, 1977; Murstein & Christy, 1976). This discrepancy reveals one major source of unrequited love. If one falls upward, that is, if one falls in love with someone whose mate appeal is superior, that person is not likely to reciprocate one's love. Hence, that love will be unrequited, and if one has fallen far into love, one may experience major disappointment and heartbreak.

Unrequited love can thus be considered something of a "false start" on the way to mutual love. Consistent with this view, Hill, Blakemore, and Drumm (1997) found that as people got older, they reported more experiences of mutual love but not of unrequited love. When young, people routinely experienced unrequited love, but the frequency of these experiences tapered off. The implication is that young people often suffer through unrequited love, but as they grow older and develop a more accurate appreciation of their value in the mate market, they begin to have fewer unrequited and more mutual love experiences.

However, the picture is further complicated by several factors. First, people do not necessarily have accurate views of their own mate appeal. On the contrary, the norm is to overestimate oneself, at least at first. That is, the majority of North American citizens overestimate their intelligence, likeability, and other good qualities (see Taylor & Brown, 1988). Hence, one may be attracted to someone who looks like a perfect match, but this equity is based partly on one's inflated appraisal of his or her own desirability. An objective observer might be able to discern such disparity immediately. And, of course, the intended partner is also vulnerable to self-inflation. Even if an individual does find someone who is objectively a perfect match in terms of total mate appeal, that person may regard himself or herself as too good.

A further difficulty with finding a well-matched partner is that people do not necessarily judge themselves on the same criteria by which they judge others, so the calculation of total mate value might be susceptible to different results even if two people agreed about all specific appraisals. For example, a woman might regard a man's athletic prowess as irrelevant to his desirability, whereas he might see it as one of his most appealing features. Thus, even if they agreed precisely about his athletic skill, they might disagree about his desirability as a mate.

Gender differences also raise complications for the process of finding an equitable match. Women are generally more cautious about selecting mates than men (Buss & Schmitt, 1993) and are slower to fall in love (e.g., Kanin, Davidson, & Scheck, 1970). In unrequited love, men reported more frequent experiences of being the would-be lover, while women reported more frequent experiences of being the rejector (Baumeister et al., 1993). Hence, even if a couple were well matched, the man's love may often be unrequited by the woman for a time. Of course, this is a staple of movie and novel plots, in which the man's love for the woman is initially unreciprocated until he can persuade her to fall in love with him.

Another factor is that romantic attraction is susceptible to a broad range of subtle, poorly understood cues, which can also interfere with the mutuality of attraction. People may, for example, be attracted or repelled by someone who reminds them of a former lover or even a parent or sibling. Because such idiosyncratic influences are not likely mutual, they can spoil an otherwise equitable, appealing match between two potentially suitable partners.

Yet another factor that complicates the process of explaining unrequited love in terms of matching appeal is that some people may want to experience love even if it is unrequited. We have spoken thus far as if unrequited love is a false start in the search for mutual love, and we suspect that in most cases this is true. However, Aron, Aron, and Allen (1998) have emphasized that some people persist in loving someone who does not reciprocate that love, and these researchers found that such a "motivational paradox" (p. 787) can be explained in part by the appeal of the state of being in love. Love is an engrossing emotional state that yields moments of intense pleasure and provides meaning and purpose to many of life's activities. Moreover, love is celebrated throughout Western culture, from Christian theology to films and popular music lyrics, and being in love may enable people to feel they are participating in the greatest human adventure.

Gamble and Burden: Who Is Worse Off?

To appreciate the two sides of rejection in unrequited love, one must understand that the two roles operate in situations that differ radically in the range of possible outcomes. Differences in how people look back on these experiences can be understood in part by recognizing the differences in situation structure. Unrequited love is a situation of interdependence; Kelley and Thibaut's (1978) theory about interdependence offers a useful way to conceptualize how each person's outcomes depend on the other person's choices.

In the would-be lover's perception of the situation, an extremely wide range of outcomes is possible. If the would-be lover can persuade the other person to feel the same way (i.e., to fall in love too), the result could be a fulfilling, mutually satisfactory relationship that could well include the euphoric bliss of passionate love. At the other extreme, the beloved target could reject the aspiring lover in a cruel and humiliating fashion. One makes oneself vulnerable by loving, and this vulnerability entails risk. Indeed, the other person could ridicule the aspiring lover or publicly disclose personal information about the would-be lover, which could produce a distressful outcome. In between those extremes lies a wide range of partial, less severe outcomes, such as having a moderately satisfying relationship for a short time and then breaking up.

This broad range of possible outcomes contrasts sharply with what the rejector perceives. As long as the rejector is certain about not wanting to enter into a love affair with the would-be lover, the other person's love appears as mainly a problem to solve. At best, the other person might gracefully accept the rejection (or just lose interest) and go away. At worst, the person could continue to direct unwanted romantic advances and attentions toward the rejector, and these could shade into stalking or other harassing, intrusive behaviors. In fact, many stalkers are rejected would-be lovers, and in a surprising minority of cases stalkers eventually become the romantic partners of the people they have stalked (Nicastro, Cousins, & Spitzberg, 1999). Being pursued by an undesirable person could also be embarrassing for the rejector if others find out about it.

Comparing these two sets of possible outcomes reveals a stark difference. The would-be lover perceives outcomes ranging from agony to ecstasy, but the rejector perceives only those from bad to neutral. Thus, the situation offers little or nothing beneficial to the rejector. It is, in an important sense, a no-win situation, a problem to be solved or a burden to be borne. In contrast, to the would-be lover, the situation resembles a high-stakes gamble or adventure in which almost any outcome is possible.

The discrepancy in the perceived ranges of possible outcomes helps explain an otherwise puzzling, counterintuitive feature of the research findings. One initial hypothesis about unrequited love was that the would-be lovers (i.e., the rejected lovers) would tell sad, painful stories far more negative than those of the rejectors. In fact, however, the rejectors' stories were more uniformly and consistently negative in their affective tones. The would-be lovers did report suffering and heartbreak, but they also reported excitement, euphoria, and other positive feelings and looked back with a rich mixture of affection and regret. It was the rejectors who were more likely to express the wish that the whole thing had never happened. They had little or nothing good to say about the episode.

Thus, rejection is not a matter of one indifferent person calmly or merrily breaking the heart of the other person, who has a monopoly on suffering. On the contrary, the positive feelings (both at the time and in retrospect) seem to have been mainly those of the would-be lover. Stories about having one's heart broken have their happy moments. In contrast, stories about breaking someone else's heart seem almost entirely negative.

The reason, again, lies in the situation structure. The episode probably was an emotional roller-coaster for the would-be lover. The high points were generally quite high, and for a long time the person lived in the sweet illusion that the couple might fall in love and even live together happily ever after. The feelings toward the other person were positive, and unless the rejector was cruel or callous or exploitative, some of those positive feelings seem to remain.

In contrast, the rejector did not have an emotional roller-coaster, or at least not one that had any high points. There were relatively few positive feelings toward the person who offered love that the rejector did not want, and the entire episode may have been experienced as a difficult, unpleasant problem or burden. The rejector felt nothing good about it at the time, envisioned no happy future, and afterward recalled nothing positive.

We do not wish to overstate the case or undermine sympathy for the poor souls whose hearts are broken. In the questionnaire study (Baumeister et al., 1993), people were asked to rate the maximum severity of distress that they suffered at any point during the episode. The would-be lovers reported greater, more intense suffering than the rejectors. The pain of heartbreak is apparently greater than the guilt or distress over breaking someone else's heart.

But for many, the pain of having one's heart broken was substantially off-set by the many positive aspects of the experience. Love, attraction, hope, moments of euphoria when one believed that one was making progress, and similar experiences all helped to elevate the total experience for the would-be lover, even though the would-be lover's low points were generally lower than anything the rejector experienced.

Scriptlessness

Once one has decided to reject someone's offer of affection, how does one do it? As many people discover, the culture has not provided them with good, effective scripts for rejecting love. Unlike the would-be lovers, therefore, rejectors often struggle with a pervasive sense of scriptlessness. Many of the seemingly inconsistent and ineffective responses of rejectors may derive from ignorance of their role.

The discrepancy in available scripts can be appreciated by simply turning on the radio and listening to love songs for a day or so. One is likely to hear a fair number of songs about unrequited love, because they have long been a staple theme of lyricists. Yet it is quickly apparent that the two roles are not represented equally. Without having collected precise data, we would estimate that over 98% of the songs on unrequited love are based on the would-be lover's perspective. "I love you so much, why can't you love me too?" is the infinitely repeated theme of love songs—hardly any music is devoted to "please go away, I'm not interested in you."

Thus, the media offer plenty of advice about how to play the role of aspiring lover, but they offer very little guidance about how to administer rejection. For the would-be lover, at worst, there is the problem of how to switch from the hopeful-lover script to the heartbroken-and-rejected script, but both are well laid out. Would-be lovers know how they are supposed to think, feel, and act. Rejectors, in contrast, are often surprised at how little they understand how to play their roles. In their narratives, we repeatedly encountered comments such as "I didn't know what to do," "I wasn't sure how to handle the situation," and "nothing like this had happened to me before." On questionnaire ratings, would-be rejectors were much more likely than would-be lovers to say that they suffered from not knowing how to act.

Many of the problems that make unrequited love difficult for both parties can be traced to the lack of a script. Would-be lovers often suffer because the person they love seems inconsistent, confusing, and even fickle. They report that sometimes the person seemed friendly and warm but at other times aloof and cold. To the would-be lover, who is often painfully attentive to every detail and nuance of the love object's behavior, these deeply confusing shifts help make the experience into the emotional roller-coaster that we described. The inconsistent, inexplicable, and unpredictable behavior of the rejector was a common theme in would-be lovers' accounts.

This inconsistency can often be understood as arising from the scriptlessness, however. The rejector is not usually trying to confuse the would-be lover or deliberately setting out to send mixed messages and make life difficult. Rather, the rejectors don't know whether it's better to be consistently aloof and cold or, instead, to be friendly and warm while rejecting only the unwanted romantic advances. After they have already expressed their rejection, they might think it unnecessarily cruel to continue to be cold, so they may become friendly. Or they may simply oscillate between different patterns, simply because they do not know what is most appropriate and fair.

Persistence

A striking difference between rejectors' and would-be lovers' accounts of unrequited love concerns the persistence of the would-be lover after the initial rejection. To the rejectors, this persistence was a major theme and a significant source of vexation, aggravation, anger, and even sometimes fear. In their accounts, they forced themselves to make the rejection explicit, after which they thought the issue should end. To their surprise, however, the would-be lover often kept trying. The sense of being unable to escape from this person's unwanted attentions made some people feel frustrated and almost helpless. Although very little in our data approached the extreme of "stalking," in the sense in which people pursue and harass the individuals who have rejected them, stalking would not be much different from what some of our rejectors described.

In contrast, the excessive persistence was largely absent from the accounts and ratings furnished by the would-be lovers. In their stories, they kept trying until it was clear that the desired romance would never materialize, after which they became very sad and upset and began the slow process of recovery. They rarely or never spoke about bothering the person they loved once they accepted the fact that this person would never return the love.

This discrepancy is especially striking because it contraverts one of the standard patterns of autobiographical narratives: people's own actions tend to take center stage in their stories. It is quite unusual for A's actions to be featured more strongly in B's account than in A's own account. But the persistent pursuit of rejecting lovers is one instance of this unusual pattern.

A likely reason for the discrepancy is that the rejection is often far more explicit and final in the rejector's mind than in the pursuer's. We suspect that rejectors are often far less clear than they think in communicating the impossibility of romance. Some data supporting this hypothesis were provided by Folkes (1982), who showed that the reasons women express (to men) for rejecting dates are often not the real reasons. Women's real reasons for rejecting invitations involve factors that are internal (to the men), stable, and global, such as the fact that he is unattractive, unintelligent, or poor. The reasons they tell the men, however, tend to be external, unstable, and specific, such as being busy on that particular night or not wanting to see that particular movie.

One does not have to search far for explanations for this attributional misdirection. The woman often does not want to hurt the man unnecessarily or to provoke a scene, so making an excuse enables her to handle the immediate problem (of avoiding the particular date to which she has been invited). Unfortunately, these strategies succeed too well at minimizing the blow to the man's pride, so he asks again. If the woman says, "I can't go out with you next Saturday because my mother is coming over for dinner," he may well ask her again for the following week; indeed, to fail to do so would be foolish on his part. In contrast, if she said (more truthfully), "I don't want to go out with you because you are boring, and you smell bad, and you don't make enough money," he would not likely keep asking.

The scripts must also take some of the blame for the persistence problem. As we noted, countless books, movies, and songs have dealt with the theme of unrequited love, usually from the perspective of the aspiring lover. In many such stories, one person (more commonly the male) falls in love, is initially rejected, continues to try, and eventually wins the heart of the other person. We doubt that most modern Americans could possibly count how many movies they have seen in which persistent efforts are eventually rewarded by success in mutual love. In plain terms, the standard script for the aspiring lover calls for persistence despite initial rejection. Indeed, the happy endings of many such movies make it clear that both people end up blissfully in love, which means that the one who initially rejected the romance is very happy that the other persisted despite those rejections.

Those may be Hollywood fantasies, but they do constitute an important source of scripted knowledge that many people use in their own lives. Armed with several dozen such stories, the aspiring lover knows not to give up when the desired partner initially rejects the offers of romance. In our data, rejectors often expressed surprise and bewilderment at how the would-be lover could continue trying to initiate a romance after the rejector had said no.

They should not be surprised: thousands of movies have shown that initial rejection is a standard but temporary roadblock on the way to mutual, loving happiness.

Guilt

We turn now to two of the central themes of the respective roles. This section covers the dominant emotional and cognitive theme of the rejectors' accounts, which is guilt. (The next section will focus on the would-be lovers' central problem, self-esteem.) During and after the rejection, the rejector must often grapple with guilt.

The nature and roots of guilt have been a central theoretical problem for psychology for decades (e.g., Lewis, 1971), but recent research has offered new insights (see Tangney & Fischer, 1996). Guilt appears to be a strongly interpersonal emotion, for it is deeply rooted in close, communal relationships (see Baumeister, Stillwell, & Heatherton, 1994; Baumeister, Reis, & Delespaul, 1995). In short, people feel guilty about hurting people with whom they have relationships or bonds of mutual concern.

One might think that rejectors would feel little guilt, then, because they are hurting someone they do not care about. This interpretation is misleading, however, and in some cases downright wrong. Many cases of unrequited love involve pairs of friends, colleagues, or acquaintances, and the rejector often wants to maintain a good relationship with the person—just not a romantic relationship. To reject a friend's offer of romantic love while still remaining friends is a delicate matter indeed. And the pain one inflicts by rejecting the love will almost certainly cause guilt.

Because people usually have some relationship to the people who fall in love with them, there is some affective basis for feeling guilty about hurting that person. Rejecting a total stranger's offer of romantic love would likely be quite a bit easier (i.e., less likely to cause guilt) than rejecting the same offer from a close friend. Unfortunately, strangers do not often offer us love. People typically get to know each other to some degree before love emerges; in the process of getting to know each other, they form a relationship.

We believe that people are programmed by nature to form and maintain social attachments. Baumeister and Leary (1995) concluded that people have a basic need to belong, satisfied only in regular, pleasant interactions with a handful of other people, in the context of an ongoing bond characterized by mutual care and concern. Socially isolated people are rarely happy; people with strong social networks find happiness much easier to achieve (e.g., see Baumeister, 1991, on happiness).

If the need to belong is a basic and pervasive motivation, then one must assume that someone's offer of affection and intimacy is likely appealing at multiple levels. To reject that love, therefore, goes against the grain. To be sure, there are plenty of reasons why one might reject that love, including the constraint that one cannot have simultaneous romantic relationships with multiple partners. To accept one person's offer of love is implicitly to reject all others. Human nature may not automatically recognize those constraints, however, so people may feel badly about rejecting love even when the conscious, rational mind believes this particular person is not the right partner.

The issue of guilt was central in many rejectors' accounts, but it was largely absent from the would-be lovers' accounts. Not only were would-be lovers mostly immune from guilt—they seemed not even to recognize that the rejectors felt guilty. For the would-be lovers, the moral dimension and guilt were irrelevant.

For the rejectors, however, guilt was a central and ongoing problem. Many of them felt guilty even if at a conscious level their moral judgment insisted that they had done nothing wrong. And if they had done something wrong, the problem of guilt was often much deeper.

The main worry involved leading the other person on. Many rejectors seemed to agonize over the question of whether they had (even inadvertently) encouraged the would-be lover's interest. Some felt they might have done so, even fairly unwittingly, because initially they found the other's attentions flattering. Some rejectors' stories hinted at having regarded the episode as an opportunity for sexual pleasure, not realizing that a much greater emotional investment was at stake for the partner. In retrospect, they seemed to have taken advantage of the other person.

Rejectors took pains to establish their innocence, and these efforts at self-justification reflect the extent of their struggles with guilt. Many of them insisted that they had not led the other person on or provided any sort of encouragement. In some cases, these bordered on the absurd: one could read these stories and think that this unwitting individual seemed to have been minding his or her own business when abruptly someone else just fell in love with him or her out of the blue, the rejector doing nothing other than simply being such a marvelous person that others could not resist falling in love.

People are generally friendly with each other, and simple acts of friendliness can be interpreted as encouraging romantic interest (see Abbey, 1982). Another issue is scriptlessness: the rejector does not know how to act, and being pleasant, cheerful, and friendly is generally appropriate for many situations. Unfortunately, being pleasant, cheerful, and friendly to an aspiring lover may provide encouragement.

Although we have been rather hard on the rejectors in this subsection and expressed skepticism because they are not generally quite so innocent as they typically portray themselves, some sympathy is nonetheless in order. After all, the entire episode is generally aversive for them and offers relatively little in the way of pleasure or other positive outcomes. However, they often end up saddled with a load of guilt. Someone in love with one ought to be a good thing, but instead it provides short-term aggravation and inconvenience for a while, followed by long-lasting guilt. No wonder they often wish the whole thing had never happened!

How does one deal with guilt? In ongoing relationships, one can sometimes atone for a grievance, promise never to repeat it, or provide restitution in some other way. The rejector of love typically does not have these options, however. Escaping guilt then becomes a lasting problem.

Sadly, one strategy for reducing guilt used all over the world in different contexts is to disparage and devalue one's victim (see Baumeister, 1997; Baumeister, Stillwell, & Heatherton, 1995). From participants in laboratory studies (Lerner & Mathews, 1967; Katz, Glass, & Cohen, 1973) to mass murderers (Conquest, 1986; Lifton, 1986), people have been found to shift toward increasingly negative opinions of their victims. The strategy has a good rational basis. One feels guilty over harming someone important, someone one cares about, or someone with whom one has a close relationship. If one hurts someone, therefore, one can reduce the guilt by convincing oneself that the other person is not important, not worth caring about, or with whom no meaningful relationship is worth considering. Professional torturers, government killers, soldiers, and many others use such strategies to make inflicting harm emotionally easier.

In unrequited love, therefore, the rejector may be able to escape guilt by disparaging the would-be lover. This response may be all the more viable because of the pattern of "falling upward" that we mentioned earlier: in many cases, the rejector will regard himself or herself as being too good to be an appropriate partner for the would-be lover. Exaggerating the discrepancy may therefore be an especially appealing strategy for coping with the stress of having to reject someone.

There was certainly ample evidence of this strategy in our data. Many rejectors spoke in harsh, insulting terms about the people they rejected, describing them as losers, creeps, weird or deviant individuals, or otherwise unattractive partners. (To be sure, not all rejectors did this, and some spoke in carefully complimentary terms about the people they had rejected.) The would-be lovers' own accounts did not disparage either the self (such as by saying, "Looking back, she was really too good for me") or the rejector. Partner disparagement was confined to the rejectors' accounts, and it likely reflects a strategy for minimizing guilt.

Self-Esteem

If guilt was the main problem for rejectors, self-esteem was the main problem for would-be lovers—especially afterward. Having one's offer of love rejected is often a severe blow to one's ego. It can be acutely threatening if the rejector chose someone else instead of oneself, because the implicit message is that the other person has been judged more desirable than you. (Then again, self-esteem is not exactly protected if the person says he or she prefers to be alone rather than spend time with you! Yet somehow the rejection does not seem quite so personal if the love object rejects everybody, rather than liking others' company but rejecting one's own.)

The broader context for the self-esteem aspect of rejection is captured in sociometer theory (Leary & Baumeister, 2000; Leary, Tambor, Terdal, & Downs, 1995). In this view, self-esteem is largely an assessment of one's interpersonal appeal and hence of the likelihood that one will be able to form and maintain a good network of social relationships. Leary et al. (1995) provided ample evidence that self-esteem rises with social acceptance and falls with social rejection. To be rejected by a desired romantic partner, particularly if a person thought the two people would make a suitable pair, can be a cruel blow to one's appraisal of one's desirability. Not only is a particular relationship lost (which is bad enough), but one has the lingering suspicion that the future may hold similar rejections by others who will appraise one similarly.

Self-esteem was not entirely absent from the rejector's experience. Some rejectors noted that they were at least briefly flattered by the other person's interest. To be loved is to receive a message of validation and approval: someone else has chosen one as a person that he or she would like to spend time with and put at the center of his or her social world. Undoubtedly that is an esteem-boosting message.

In most cases, though, the rejector's feeling of boosted self-esteem was short-lived. Once the rejector began to regard the would-be lover as an unsuitable or undesirable partner, that person's approval meant little. Possibly the feeling of being flattered was simply overshadowed by the more negative feelings associated with having to reject someone and trying to avoid that person's unwanted attentions. Undoubtedly another aspect is that favorable evaluations by people who rank below ourselves are far less meaningful than favorable evaluations by peers or superiors. Once the rejector has decided that he or she is more attractive (in whatever way) than the would-be lover, the would-be lover's love carries little power to boost the self-esteem. Moreover, as we have seen, the rejector's efforts to escape from guilt often involve derogating the would-be lover, which makes that person's evaluation that much less meaningful.

If romantic rejection carries an implicit meaning to the rejector that he or she is more desirable than the would-be lover, that message is all the more salient (and hence painful) to the would-be lover. Having your heart broken is, among other things, a bitter blow to pride. Whatever the person might say about how one is a wonderful person in many respects and he or she values one's friendship and the lover will make a great partner for someone else, and so forth, one still feels that "I'm not good enough." In our data, rejected lovers wondered at length about what was wrong with them—what was it that made the person they loved decide that they were not a suitable partner.

Several factors contributed to the self-esteem problems. As we suggested, some degree of blow to self-esteem is implicit in the nature of romantic rejection. In some cases, though, this loss of self-esteem is exacerbated by the would-be lover's acceptance of indignities during the attempts to win the other person's heart. Aspiring lovers may beg, grovel, accept humiliating treatment, allow themselves to be exploited, and humble themselves in other ways. At the time, it seems foolish to let one's own pride get in the way of pursuing happiness and fulfillment through love. Afterward, though, people may particularly regret how they humbled themselves.

In particular, would-be lovers may humble themselves when they see the first signs of rejection but are themselves too involved emotionally to let go. Instead of quietly suffering or accepting the inevitable, they reveal their hurt feelings and ask the other person to make them feel better. They may pour out their feelings, cry, flatter the other, or simply beg for affection. These moments seem to haunt them later on: they wish they had held on to more of their dignity.

Recovering from heartbreak is therefore often a matter of rebuilding self-esteem. The rejection often carries an implicit message that one is not a desirable romantic partner, or at least not as desirable as one thought. Furthermore, one's own actions may aggravate the loss of self-esteem, insofar as one humbles oneself and sacrifice dignity on the altar of love. The heartbroken person is not fully recovered until he or she can return to the level of self-esteem he or she enjoyed before the incident.

And how is that done? Undoubtedly there are multiple ways to build and restore self-esteem. The favorite, though, is clear: find another relationship. We were surprised to see how many stories about heartbreak ended by mentioning that the person had now found someone else (and often supposedly better). Logically, these new relationships were irrelevant, because our research asked people to tell the story of the heartbreak, and the new boyfriend or girlfriend belongs to a different story. In the individual's mind, however, the new partner is part of the story about the heartbreak, because the new partner disproved the implication that the individual is not a desirable person. We suspect that this connection is important in the heartbroken person's own mind, because finding a good relationship with a new partner was an essential part of recovering from the self-esteem loss.

Conspiracy of Silence

As we noted, the communication between rejector and would-be lover often seemed to be damaged because such communication is hampered by a conspiracy of silence. The message of rejection is unpleasant for both parties, so neither one wants to say it. Hence, it probably does not get said as clearly or as often as it should.

The conspiracy of silence is an important theme, not just for unrequited love but indeed for this book's more general theme of rejection. Hardly anyone likes being rejected. And hardly anyone likes rejecting others, either. As we have seen, to reject someone often produces guilt (in the rejector) and low self-esteem in the person who is rejected. Both of these feelings are unpleasant, so both parties are motivated to avoid or at least minimize the explicit communication of rejection.

It is thus not surprising that would-be lovers report mixed messages and inconsistent behavior, even when rejectors often insist that they tried to be clear and consistent. Nor is it surprising that would-be lovers often persist in their courtship efforts past the point the rejector thinks reasonable. The communication likely did not come off very clearly. One person doesn't want to say it, and the other doesn't want to hear it.

Conclusion

Romantic rejection, like other forms of rejection, can be extremely distressing to the person who is rejected. People are motivated to avoid this form of rejection, and in many cases they seem to refuse to hear or believe the message of rejection. When rejection comes, it can be quite aversive emotionally can also carry a severe blow to self-esteem.

The work we have presented has also explored the psychology of the rejectors. Rejection appears to be quite aversive for them too. Many struggle with guilt feelings over having caused such pain to someone who loved them. Even if the guilt can be avoided, rejectors may suffer distress because of the excessive persistence and unwanted attentions of the person who is pursuing them.

Nor are these experiences rare. As we reported, nearly every adult seems to have had some experience of unrequited love, and many people have experienced it several times (in both roles). When researchers asked young adults to report on a recent experience, hardly anyone claimed not to have had such an experience.

When people widely engage in activity that periodically brings them suffering, it is fair to conclude that they are also getting something positive out of it. We have portrayed unrequited love as one seemingly inevitable consequence of assortative mating. The fact that people suffer so much during the quest for a good, satisfying romantic relationship is probably a strong indication that the quest is deeply important and that when the quest does succeed, the rewards of love compensate for one's suffering during the false starts and setbacks.

References

Abbey, A. (1982). Sex differences in attributions for friendly behavior: Do males misperceive females' friendliness? *Journal of Personality and Social Psychology, 42,* 830–888.

Aron, A., Aron, E. N., & Allen, J. (1998). Motivations for unreciprocated love. *Personality and Social Psychology Bulletin, 24,* 787–796.

Baumeister, R. F. (1991). *Meanings of life.* New York: Guilford Press.

Baumeister, R. F. (1997). *Evil: Inside human violence and cruelty.* New York: W. H. Freeman.

Baumeister, R. F., & Leary, M. R. (1995). The need to belong: Desire for interpersonal attachments as a fundamental human motivation. *Psychological Bulletin, 117,* 497–529.

Baumeister, R. F., Reis, H. T., & Delespaul, P. A. E. G. (1995). Subjective and experiential correlates of guilt in everyday life. *Personality and Social Psychology Bulletin, 21,* 1256–1268.

Baumeister, R. F., Stillwell, A. M., & Heatherton, T. F. (1994). Guilt: An interpersonal approach. *Psychological Bulletin, 115,* 243–267.

Baumeister, R. F., Stillwell, A. M., & Heatherton, T. F. (1995). Personal narratives about guilt: Role in action control and interpersonal relationships. *Basic and Applied Social Psychology, 17,* 173–198.

Baumeister, R. F., & Wotman, S. R. (1992). *Breaking hearts: The two sides of unrequited love.* New York: Guilford Press.

Baumeister, R. F., Wotman, S. R., & Stillwell, A. M. (1993). Unrequited love: On heartbreak, anger, guilt, scriptlessness, and humiliation. *Journal of Personality and Social Psychology, 64,* 377–394.

Buss, D. M., & Schmitt, D. P. (1993). Sexual strategies theory: An evolutionary perspective on human mating. *Psychological Review, 100,* 204–232.

Conquest, R. (1986). *The harvest of sorrow: Soviet collectivization and the terror-famine.* New York: Oxford University Press.

Folkes, V. S. (1982). Communicating the reasons for social rejection. *Journal of Experimental Social Psychology, 18,* 235–252.

Hill, C. A., Blakemore, J. E. O., & Drumm, P. (1997). Mutual and unrequited love in adolescence and young adulthood. *Personal Relationships, 4,* 15–23.

Jensen, A. (1977). Genetic and behavioral effects of nonrandom mating. In C. Noble, R. Osborne, & N. Weyl (Eds.), *Human variation: Biogenetics of age, race, and sex.* New York: Academic Press.

Kanin, E. J., Davidson, K. D., & Scheck, S. R. (1970). A research note on male-female differentials in the experience of heterosexual love. *Journal of Sex Research, 6,* 64–72.

Katz, I., Glass, D. C., & Cohen, S. (1973). Ambivalence, guilt, and the scapegoating of minority group victims. *Journal of Experimental Social Psychology, 9,* 423–436.

Kelley, H. H., & Thibaut, J. W. (1978). *Interpersonal relations: A theory of interdependence.* New York: Wiley.

Leary, M. R., & Baumeister, R. F. (2000). The nature and function of self-esteem: Sociometer theory. In M. Zanna (Ed.), *Advances in experimental social psychology* (vol. 32, pp. 1–62). San Diego, CA: Academic Press.

Leary, M. R., Tambor, E. S., Terdal, S. K., & Downs, D. L. (1995). Self-esteem as an interpersonal monitor: The sociometer hypothesis. *Journal of Personality and Social Psychology, 68,* 518–530.

Lerner, M. J., & Matthews, G. (1967). Reactions to suffering of others under conditions of indirect responsibility. *Journal of Personality and Social Psychology, 5,* 319–325.

Lewis, H. B. (1971). *Shame and guilt in neurosis.* New York: International Universities Press.

Lifton, R. J. (1986). *The Nazi doctors: Medical killing and the psychology of genocide.* New York: Basic Books.

Murstein, B. I., & Christy, P. (1976). Physical attractiveness and marriage adjustment in middle-aged couples. *Journal of Personality and Social Psychology, 34,* 537–542.

Nicastro, A. M., Cousins, A. V., & Spitzberg, B. H. (1999, June). *The tactical face of stalking.* Presented to the International Network on Personal Relationships and International Society for the Study of Personal Relationships (Joint Conference), Louisville, KY.

Tangney, J. P., & Fischer, K. W. (1995). *Self-conscious emotions: The psychology of shame, guilt, embarrassment, and pride.* New York: Guilford Press.

Taylor, S. E., & Brown, J. D. (1988). Illusion and well-being: A social psychological perspective on mental health. *Psychological Bulletin, 103,* 193–210.

Walster, E., Aronson, V., Abrahams, D., & Rottman, L. (1966). Importance of physical attractiveness in dating behavior. *Journal of Personality and Social Psychology, 4,* 508–516.

4

Betrayal, Rejection, Revenge, and Forgiveness

An Interpersonal Script Approach

JULIE FITNESS

Introduction

Throughout recorded human history, treachery and betrayal have been considered among the worst offenses people could commit against their kin. Dante, for example, relegated traitors to the lowest and coldest regions of Hell, to be forever frozen up to their necks in a lake of ice with blizzards storming all about them, as punishment for having acted so coldly toward others. Even today, the crime of treason merits the most severe penalties, including capital punishment. However, betrayals need not involve issues of national security to be regarded as serious. From sexual infidelity to disclosing a friend's secrets, betraying another person or group of people implies unspeakable disloyalty, a breach of trust, and a violation of what is good and proper. Moreover, all of us will suffer both minor and major betrayals throughout our lives, and most of us will, if only unwittingly, betray others (Jones & Burdette, 1994).

The Macquarie Dictionary (1991) lists a number of different, though closely related, meanings of the term "to betray," including to deliver up to an enemy, to be disloyal or unfaithful, to deceive or mislead, to reveal secrets, to seduce and desert, and to disappoint the hopes or expectations of another. Implicit in a number of these definitions is the rejecting or discounting of one person by another; however, the nature of the relationship between interpersonal betrayal and rejection has not been explicitly addressed in the social psychological literature. In fact, most scholars treat the two as distinct phenomena. For example, Jones and Burdette (1994) argued that rejection tends to occur early in the process of establishing a relationship, whereas betrayal occurs in an established relationship where partners are involved with and, to an extent, trust one another. According to their argument, rejection is painful, but the pain is for the loss of a potential relationship. Betrayal, however, is devastating because it disrupts an ongoing, meaningful relationship in which partners have invested material and emotional resources. Similarly, Jones, Couch, and Scott (1997) argued that rejection and betrayal are the two basic risks people take in close relationships, with betrayal being worse than rejection.

I will argue in this chapter, however, that this conceptualization of interpersonal rejection is too narrow and misses the essential meaning of what it is to betray, and to be betrayed, within an interpersonal relationship. Essentially, betrayal means that one party in a relationship acts in a way that favors his or her own interests at the expense of the other party's interests. In one sense, this behavior implies that the betrayer regards his or her needs as more important than the needs of the partner or the relationship. In a deeper sense, however, betrayal sends an ominous signal about how little the betrayer cares about, or values his or her relationship with, the betrayed partner. In particular, and as Gaylin (1984) noted, when those on whom we depend for love and support betray our trust, the feeling is like a stab at the heart that leaves us feeling unsafe, diminished, and alone. Psychologically, then, betrayal may be conceived as a profound form of interpersonal rejection with potentially serious consequences for the healthy functioning of the betrayed individual.

This chapter focuses on interpersonal betrayal and how relationship partners cope or do not cope with the rejection it implies. The first section reviews the theoretical and empirical work on the nature and causes of betrayal in different relational contexts, with a particular focus on perceived violations of relationship rules. The second section focuses on the cognitive, emotional, and behavioral concomitants of betrayal from the perspectives of both betraying and betrayed parties. The third section explores the aftermath of betrayal and presents relevant data from a recent study on forgiven and unforgiven marital offenses. The chapter concludes with a consideration of the long-term consequences of betrayal and suggestions for future research.

The Nature of Betrayal

As children grow to become adults, they learn from their caregivers and culture what relationships are all about; that is, they acquire theories, or knowledge structures, about relationships and how they work (Baldwin, 1992; Fletcher & Thomas, 1996; Knee, 1998). Although these lay theories of relational processes may have limited scientific validity, social cognitive research has amply demonstrated the power of such theories to influence laypeople's perceptions, judgments, and memories, both of relationships in general and of their own relationships in particular (e.g., see Fletcher & Fitness, 1996).

Relationship knowledge structures include beliefs about the importance of certain aspects of relationships such as passion and intimacy (Fletcher, Rosanowski, & Fitness, 1994), rules about proper conduct within relationships (Argyle & Henderson, 1985; Jones & Gallois, 1989), and expectations about how partners will (or ought) to behave toward one another (Kelley & Burgoon, 1991; Metts, 1994). When two partners play by the rules and meet each other's expectations, their relationship runs smoothly, and they experience relatively little emotion, positive or negative. However, when relationship partners behave in ways that violate each other's expectations, there is a "hiccup," or interruption, in the smooth running of the relationship (Berscheid, 1983); then the scene is set for an emotional interaction between the partners. In particular, the partner whose expectations have been violated must attend to the situation and decide what it means in relation to his or her needs, concerns, and goals (Fitness & Strongman, 1991; Lazarus, 1992).

Of course, not every interruption is unpleasant; some expectation violations may be highly positive and elicit emotions such as happiness and love (Kelley & Burgoon, 1991). For example, an individual who strongly believes that his mother must be kept happy at all costs but who also does not expect his relationship partner to behave well when his mother comes to stay may feel delighted when his partner violates his expectations with her exemplary behavior. On the other hand, an individual who strongly believes that sexual infidelity is wrong and who expects her partner will be faithful will likely be shocked and disappointed to discover his infidelity; because she had trusted him not to behave in such a fashion, she will also likely feel betrayed.

The key to betrayal, then, lies in people's theories, beliefs, and expectations about how relationships in general, and their own relationship in particular, should work, and also in people's trust that their partners will share, or at least respect, those beliefs and meet those expectations (Elangovan & Shapiro, 1998; Holmes, 1991). Indeed, trust is integral to betrayal because of its intimate connection with relational expectations. Boon (1994), for example, defined interpersonal trust as "the confident expectation that a partner is intrinsically motivated to take one's own best interests into account when acting, even when incentives might tempt him or her to do otherwise" (p. 88).

Clearly, trusting others exposes us to the risk of betrayal if they violate those confident expectations and take advantage of us. Moreover, if the relationship between two parties has been intimate then the implications of betrayal are especially painful: The person to whom we have disclosed and entrusted our deepest fears and vulnerabilities appears neither to care about our relationship nor to be committed to it. Little wonder, then, that such experiences of betrayal trigger feelings of rejection, abandonment, and aloneness.

Contexts of Betrayal: Who Betrays Whom?

Over the course of evolutionary history, humans have become finely attuned to the possibility of betrayal by others (Shackelford & Buss, 1996). Indeed, for social animals, knowing who to trust and how much to trust them is a critical survival mechanism. Shackelford and Buss (1996) have suggested that our "cheater-detector" mechanisms (Cosmides & Tooby, 1992) are some-what domain-specific and that human beings are attuned to detect different types of betrayal in different types of relationships (e.g., between spouses, friends, and coalition members). Typically, people tend to think of betrayal in the context of romantic relationships, and with good reason, for spouses and romantic partners are the most frequently cited sources of betrayal (e.g., Hansson, Jones, & Fletcher, 1990; Jones & Burdette, 1994). However, Shackel-ford and Buss (1996) have claimed that to understand betrayal, one must con-sider the relationship context within which it occurs because different rela-tionships involve different rules and expectations.

One line of research that supports this argument derives from the work of Clark and her colleagues (e.g., Clark & Mills, 1979; Clark & Waddell, 1985) on communal versus exchange relationships. In communal relationships, the expectations are that partners will care about one another's welfare and will support and help each other without expecting immediate reward. Typically, marital and familial relationships are characterized as communal in orienta-tion. However, in exchange relationships the expectations are that partners are not responsible for one another's welfare and that benefits obtained from either partner should be promptly reciprocated. Typically, relationships be-tween clients and service providers are characterized by exchange princi-ples. These differences in orientations and expectations set the scene for spe-cific types of relationship betrayal, such as might happen if a partner in a supposedly communal relationship demanded the kind of formal reciproca-tion of benefits normally associated with an exchange relationship (Shackel-ford & Buss, 1996). One recent example involved a man who, against his par-ents' wishes, married a woman of a different ethnicity and religion. On his wedding day he received an itemized bill from his embittered parents charg-ing him thousands of dollars for the "cost of his upbringing." The son felt be-trayed, not so much because his parents disapproved of his marriage but be-cause the itemized bill redefined a communal relationship as an exchange relationship. He was now expected to repay love with money.

Fiske (1992) made two additional distinctions among types of social rela-tionships. To what he called communal sharing relationships and equality matching relationships (ones based on exchange principles), he added au-thority ranking relationships, in which people are ordered according to sta-tus differences (such as those in the armed forces), and market pricing rela-tionships, in which people, like material resources, have a particular market value (e.g., as employees). Again, each type of relationship implies different rules, expectations, and forms of betrayal. For example, many older wives who have been "traded in" by their husbands for younger women perceive that a seemingly communal sharing relationship was actually a market pric-ing one in which they were a low-valued commodity. Similarly, part of the discomfort many people feel about prenuptual agreements derives from the belief that a communal relationship that should be based on love and trust is

being treated as an exchange, or market-pricing relationship. These violations of relational expectations have been termed "taboo trade-offs" by Fiske
and Tetlock (1997), who suggested that such violations are not just cognitively confusing, they also trigger negative emotional and behavioral reactions, including feelings of distress, anxiety, and punitive rage.

Betrayal, then, may occur in any kind of relationship context if one or the
other party violates salient relational expectations or "breaks the rules" in
some way. Close friends, for example, hold mutual expectations about one
another's behaviors, based on shared understandings of the rules of friendship (Wiseman & Duck, 1995). Such rules typically include respecting
privacy, volunteering help when needed, not criticizing one another in public, and sharing confidences but not disclosing them to others (Argyle &
Henderson, 1985). Violating any of these friendship rules may be appraised
as a betrayal and lead to the breakdown of the relationship (Fehr, 1996).
Indeed, Jones and Burdette (1994) found that women reported betrayal by
same-sex friends almost as frequently as betrayal by spouses.

The workplace is another potent context for interpersonal betrayal. Jones
and Burdette (1994) found that nearly 19% of men reported having been betrayed by a colleague at work; similarly, in a study of anger in the workplace,
Fitness (2000) found betrayal-related rule violations (e.g., lying and exploitation) were among the most frequently reported types of anger-eliciting
offences between coworkers. Betrayal may also occur in employer-employee
relationships. For example, employers may draw up a contract that specifies
the rights and responsibilities of both parties with respect to wages and working conditions. If either of the two parties violates a provision of the contract,
then technically speaking, a breach has occurred that may evoke anger in the
aggrieved party. However, not every kind of workplace-relevant rule is explicitly accounted for in an employment contract. Equally as important (and
perhaps more so) is the "psychological contract" comprising the beliefs employees hold about the reciprocal obligations between themselves and their
employers, including procedural and interactional fairness and the right to
be treated with respect. When employees are deceived or unjustly treated by
their employers, it is this perceived violation of the psychological contract
that elicits outrage and a sense of betrayal with potentially serious consequences, including industrial sabotage (Morrison & Robinson, 1997). Employers, too, may feel betrayed when deceived, cheated, and exploited by
trusted employees.

In summary, not every interpersonal rejection implies betrayal, but every
betrayal implies interpersonal rejection and/or a devaluation of the relationship between two parties. Moreover, and in line with Shackelford and
Buss's (1969) argument, relational context is clearly important with respect
to understanding the nature of betrayal. Even more important, however, is
knowledge of the socially-shared rules and expectations that are most salient
to any particular relational context.

The Process and Outcomes of Betrayal:
An Interpersonal Script Approach

Previously it was argued that people hold lay theories about the nature of re-lationships and how they work, as well as beliefs about what they can expect from their relationship partners. One important type of relational knowledge structure, called a script, includes beliefs and expectations about the ways in which relationship events typically unfold (Baldwin, 1992). For example, partners may have a "going out for a romantic dinner" script that involves expectations about how they will dress, where they will go, who will order what for dinner, how much wine they will drink, and what will happen once they have arrived home. Over time, relationship partners acquire a large number of relational scripts for the many routines of their lives together in-cluding domestic chores (who does what), conflicts (what they are typically about, who gives in first, who sulks, how the fight is resolved), and emotional interactions involving, say, jealousy, or anger (Fehr & Baldwin, 1996; Fitness & Fletcher, 1993).

The process and outcomes of interpersonal betrayal may also be regarded as a form of interpersonal script in that people hold socially shared beliefs about the kinds of behaviors that constitute acts of betrayal and expectations about the ongoing thoughts, feelings, and behaviors of both parties to the be-trayal. These beliefs and expectations play an important role in directing peo-ple's attention to particular kinds of relationship behaviors and in shaping their interpretations of those behaviors in relation to their needs and goals. The next section of this chapter examines some of the ways in which rela-tionship partners betray one another and explores the cognitive, emotional, and behavioral features of the interpersonal betrayal script from the per-spectives of the betrayed and betraying parties.

Acts of Betrayal

Theoretically, any kind of relational transgression may be appraised by rela-tionship partners as a betrayal, depending on the extent to which relational expectations and trust have been violated. However, the most commonly re-ported acts of explicit betrayal involve sexual and emotional infidelity, lies, and deception (Fitness & Mathews, 1998; Hansson et al., 1990; Jones & Burdette, 1994). Many regard sexual infidelity, in particular, as the epitome of marital betrayal, with good reason. Betzig (1989), for example, found sex-ual infidelity to be a significantly more common cause of marital dissolution than any other factor except sterility in 88 societies. Similarly, Pittman and Wagers (1995) observed that, in their clinical experience, more than 90% of divorces in established first marriages have involved sexual infidelity.

Clearly, the discovery that a spouse of romantic partner has been unfaith-ful strikes a devastating blow to an individual's sense of self-worth and needs for commitment and emotional security (Charney & Parnass, 1995; Weiss,

1975). However, an even more tormenting aspect to infidelity derives from the degree of deception that typically accompanies it. Indeed, many people regard deception in any relational context as the ultimate betrayal. Psychological research and popular literature alike attest to the multitude of ways in which relationship partners deceive one another, from simple nondisclosure, to half truths and white lies, to full-scale falsification and outright lies (De Paulo & Kashy, 1998; Metts, 1994; Peterson, 1996). As De Paulo and Kashy pointed out, people's reports of what they value most in their close relationships revolve around issues of authenticity and the ability to reveal their true selves to someone who can be counted on not to betray their trust. Lying is, by definition, inauthentic communication; thus, if my relationship partner lies to me, I may assume that he is promoting his own interests over mine and that he cares more about protecting himself than about caring for me or our relationship.

Despite the opinions of betrayed parties about partners' motives, however, liars frequently do not regard their deceptions as selfishly motivated. Metts (1989), for example, found the predominant motive for spouses' deception was actually to avoid hurting their partners or to help maintain their self-esteem. Similarly, in a study of relational deception, Barbee, Cunningham, Druen, and Yankeelov (1996) found 70% of participants admitted they had lied to their current partner at least once; however, 79% of these respondents also claimed their lies were motivated by a desire to protect their partners. An example might involve a husband who believes his wife would be upset to know he is dining with an ex-girlfriend, so he tells her he is working late to spare her the "unnecessary" pain of feeling betrayed. Ironically, however, this benevolent strategy may work against his interests if the deception is unmasked because research suggests that, compared to men, women view lies and deception as more profound relational transgressions (Levine, McCornack, & Avery, 1992). Thus, his wife may appraise her husband's lie as a more serious betrayal than his dinner.

Whether or not an act of betrayal involves lies, deception, or infidelity, one important aspect of the experience that intensifies its severity and painfulness is humiliation, or the perception that one has been shamed and treated with disrespect, especially in public (Gaylin, 1984; Metts, 1994). A number of studies have the examined the role of humiliation in exacerbating interpersonal conflict in different contexts. For example, Jones and Gallois (1989) found that not belittling or humiliating one's partner was one of the most important endorsed rules for handling marital conflict constructively. Similarly, Fitness and Fletcher (1993) found that being mocked or publicly shamed by one's spouse evoked strong feelings of hatred for him or her, and several researchers have noted the link between perceived humiliation and physical violence in marital and dating relationships (e.g., Dutton & Browning, 1988; Foo & Margolin, 1995; Lansky, 1987). In the workplace, too, Fitness (2000) found that public humiliation by superiors was associated with the most destructive long-term outcomes of an anger-eliciting incident, and Bies and Tripp (1996) claimed that workplace violations involving public ridicule may be virtually irreparable.

According to Miller's (1993) detailed exposition, humiliation involves the perception that one has been treated as contemptible or exposed as an inferior or ridiculous person. From an evolutionary perspective, our survival as social beings critically depends on the degree to which valued others accept and respect us, and people will go to extreme lengths to avoid looking weak or foolish—indeed, some will even die to protect their reputation (Miller, 1993). The horror of humiliation, then, derives not simply from its assault on a person's self-esteem, but also from the perceived loss of social status it evokes. So, for example, the humiliating discovery that one has been the "last to know" about a partner's infidelity, and the suspicion that one has been the subject of other people's gossip and pity, may trigger as much pain as the act of betrayal itself. Similarly, the humiliation of being discarded by one's partner for someone more physically attractive compounds the pain of betrayal and rejection (Shettel-Neuber, Bryson, & Young, 1978).

In summary, laypeople appear to have firm views about the kinds of acts that constitute betrayal in different relational contexts. Many such acts, however, involve a common, underlying theme: The power balance between two interdependent parties has been disrupted. In particular, when a betrayal has been accompanied by deceit or humiliation, the betrayer effectively assumes a "one-up" position to the betrayed, who has been duped or demeaned. Even without explicit humiliation, however, the betrayed party is disadvantaged relative to the betrayer, who has put his or her own interests first and discounted the needs and concerns of the betrayed party. The next important step in the interactional sequence, then, is for the betrayed partner to respond to the act of betrayal and to the shift of power it implies.

Discovering Betrayal

Discovering a betrayal may come "out of the blue" and constitute a deeply distressing shock. On the other hand, if relational trust is low, or the betrayer has been "on probation" because of a prior offense, a partner may actively search for evidence of deception, drawing on his or her implicit theories about the kinds of behaviors that suggest there may be "something going on." Once looked for, such evidence may not be hard to find, for research suggests people regard a wide range of partner behaviors as potential pointers to deception. For example, Shackelford and Buss (1997b) examined laypeople's beliefs about the kinds of cues that suggested a partner was being sexually or emotionally unfaithful and found a large number of supposedly diagnostic behaviors, including perceiving the partner was angry, critical, or apparently dissatisfied with the relationship; believing the partner was acting guilty, anxious, or emotionally disengaged; and an unaccountable increase *or* decrease in the partner's attentions or sexual interest. These findings suggest, in line with Berscheid's (1983) interruption theory, that a suspicious partner can interpret virtually any noticeable disruption to the normal day-to-day functioning of the relationship as an alarm signal.

Betrayal may also be revealed by way of a partner's confession. Confessing misdeeds has a long history in Western culture, and many Westerners believe that confession is good for one's bodily health and emotional well-being (Georges, 1995). According to Weiner, Graham, and Zmuidinas (1991), the function of confession derives from a naive, confession-forgiveness association; that is, offenders believe that "coming clean" will both ease their guilt and win them forgiveness from the person they have wronged ("a fault confessed is half-forgiven," p. 283.) Of course, this belief may be mistaken. Indeed, although confessing infidelity can provide great relief to the offender, it shifts a considerable burden of pain to the one who has been betrayed and frequently does not result in forgiveness (Lawson, 1988). Confession, then, like other forms of betrayal discovery, effectively sets the scene for the betrayed partner to make the next move in the interpersonal drama.

Reacting to Betrayal

According to Morrison and Robinson (1997), the initial discovery and experience of betrayal goes far beyond the mere cognitive awareness that a violation has occurred; rather, the feeling of violation is registered at a deep, visceral level. Other researchers have also noted that pain and hurt are among the first and most acute emotional reactions to the awareness that one has been betrayed (Leary, Springer, Negel, Ansell, & Evans, 1998; Vangelisti & Sprague, 1998). For example, Leary et al. (1998) found 20% of recalled "very hurtful" events reported by 168 students involved betrayal, with ratings of hurt positively associated with how rejected they felt. These findings support the central argument of this chapter that betrayal implies rejection and relational devaluation, or the realization that one's partner holds neither oneself nor the relationship in high regard (Leary et al., 1998).

Given the visceral impact of betrayal, it is interesting to speculate, in line with the evolutionary arguments proposed by Shackelford and Buss (1996), whether humans may affectively register betrayal before very much conscious cognitive work is undertaken at all, particularly when the revelation constitutes a severe interruption to the betrayed party's expectations of his or her partner. Under such circumstances people may register pain through an emotional calculus, rather than a so-called rational, cognitive one (see Planalp & Fitness, 1999). At some point, however, the powerful emotional impact of betrayal will motivate a considerable amount of conscious, cognitive effort to figure out its causes and implications, both for the betrayed partner and for the relationship. And, depending on how the betrayed partner interprets the situation, a variety of negative emotions other than hurt may then be experienced. For example, Fehr and Baldwin (1996) found students rated betrayal of trust as the most intensely anger-provoking type of relational transgression; anger that arises, no doubt, because betrayed individuals typically appraise the motives of their betrayers as malevolent, dispositional ("a mean streak"), and intentional (Hansson et al., 1990; Jones & Burdette, 1994). Such appraisals, along with perceptions of unjustness and moral "wrongness," reliably elicit anger in most relational contexts (Fehr & Baldwin, 1996; Fincham & Bradbury, 1992; Morrison & Robinson, 1997; Shaver, Schwartz, Kirson, & O'Connor, 1987).

Another emotion that may be experienced in response to betrayal is hatred—an emotion about which psychologists know little but that is considered by laypeople to be a powerful motivator of destructive and vengeful behaviors. As noted previously, Fitness and Fletcher (1993) found that humiliation and appraisals of relative powerlessness were important elicitors of hatred for an offending spouse; thus it might be expected that hatred would be experienced in response to deeply humiliating betrayals involving deceit, severe loss of social status, and appraisals of powerlessness. Moreover, betrayals that have involved sexual or emotional infidelity are likely to evoke the highly complex emotional syndrome known as jealousy, which includes fear of rejection, anger, and sadness (Sharpsteen, 1991). Of course, jealousy is not always destructive. Indeed, research has shown that laypeople tend to regard a partner's occasional, mild jealousy as a flattering signal of caring (Fitness & Fletcher, 1993). However, researchers have also noted the often serious concomitants and consequences of chronic or intense jealousy, including hostility, resentment, alienation, withdrawal, even murder (e.g., Daly & Wilson, 1988; van Sommers, 1988).

Specifying the kinds of emotions that one may experience in response to betrayal is not just an academic exercise because different emotions motivate different kinds of behaviors and therefore play a major role in the progress of the interpersonal betrayal script. Anger, for example, typically tend to motivate confrontation and engagement with the offending party, whereas hate tends to motivate avoidance or emotional withdrawal (Fitness & Fletcher, 1993; Frijda, Kuipers, & ter Schure, 1989). Jealousy, with its complex blends of emotions, may motivate behaviors from anxious clinging to depressed rumination and brooding, to angry confrontation or revenge (Sharpsteen, 1991; van Sommers, 1988). The emotional reactions of the betrayed party, then, are cues to how he or she has interpreted the betrayer's behavior and what the consequences might be. The next move is for the betrayer to react to those cues with his or her own interpretations, emotions, and behaviors.

Accounting for Betrayal

Once a betrayed individual has discovered and reacted to a partner's betrayal, the typical next step is for the betrayer to provide some kind of explanatory account of his or her behavior (Cody, Kersten, Braaten, & Dickson, 1992; Metts, 1994). As noted in the discussion of deception, betrayers may believe their intentions were good. They may argue they were doing their victims a favor, or at least, that their betrayals were unintended, excusable, and due to temporary, extenuating, or unstable causes (Baumeister, Stillwell, & Wotman, 1990; Hansson et al., 1990; Jones & Burdette, 1997; Leary et al., 1998). However, regardless of how benignly betrayers regard their own motives, the accounts they give of their actions must be carefully tailored if they are to achieve their relational goals. For example, whereas a fervent wish to repair the breach may call for a contrite account, a desire to end the relationship may call for a rather callous one. Making the issue more complex is the fact that relational goals may not always be compatible. For example, a betrayer may sincerely regret her behavior and desire her partner's forgiveness, but she may also want to defend herself to maintain self-esteem and save face. Or a betrayer may desire his partner's forgiveness but also want to end the relationship.

Studies from the communication literature suggest that accounts fall into one of four broad types, with each type serving to accomplish different relational goals (e.g., Cody et al., 1992). The first, most mitigating type of account involves conceding that an offense has been committed, along with a sincere expression of remorse, and perhaps an offer to make restitution. The second, not quite so mitigating type involves making excuses for the offense, such as extenuating circumstances (e.g., alcohol, stress, illness). The third, even more defensive type of account involves justifications; here the offender minimizes the wrongness or seriousness of the offence. Finally, the fourth, most aggravating type includes denials that the account-giver committed an offense or refusals to take any responsibility for it.

Naturally, the kind of account proffered by a betrayer has an important impact on the next stage of the betrayal script. For example, Gonzales, Haugen, and Manning (1994) found that victims judged aggravating accounts, involving justifications and refusals, more harshly than mitigating accounts. Similarly, in a study of hypothetical relationship transgressions, Hodgins, Liebeskind, and Schwartz (1996) found that offenders preferred to give more mitigating than aggravating accounts, expecting that victims would receive the former more favorably. However, they also found that the most blameworthy offenders told more lies and gave the shortest and most aggravating accounts. Perhaps these highly culpable offenders may have been more motivated to save face than to win forgiveness. Pittman and Wagers (1995) also remarked on the inventive excuses and justifications people give for having or continuing extramarital affairs, including one man who explained to his wife that "she was lucky to be married to him because she was such an ugly woman. She should feel proud to be married to a man who was able to get such a beautiful affairee" (p. 311). Needless to say, his wife was not mollified.

Without doubt, the most constructive account if the betrayer's goal is to repair the relationship is a concessionary one involving apologies and a sincere expression of remorse. A wealth of psychological literature attests to the power of the apology to ameliorate relational damage. For example, in a study of school-aged children, Darby and Schlenker (1982) found more profuse apologies resulted in less blame, greater forgiveness, less desire for punishment, greater liking, and a stronger belief that the offender was really sorry for his or her offense. Similarly, Ohbuchi, Kameda, and Agarie (1989) found apologies were helpful in softening partners' negative attitudes toward an offender and in reducing urges to aggressively retaliate.

Apologies, then, are powerful, but why? According to Tavuchis (1991), the original meaning of the term apology was to defend, justify, or excuse one's behavior. The modern meaning, however, is to admit one has no defense, justification, or excuse for behavior that has wronged another. Apologies, then, have been described as both paradoxical and powerful. No matter how sincere, an apology cannot undo what has been done, and yet somehow, it does (Tavuchis, 1991). Miller (1993) claimed that the magic of the apology derives from the submissive posture of the apologizer and its implications for restoring the face or esteem of the injured party. Essentially, the offender abases himself before the person he has wronged, unconditionally admits his offense, and, even if only briefly, invests the wronged person with a higher moral status than himself. The power of the apology to repair, then, derives from the gift of status that helps redress the power imbalance between the two parties.

Of course, apologizers may not actually feel sorry, but they must look sorry. As Miller (1993) pointed out, "if an apology does not look somewhat humiliating . . . it would be utterly ineffective in accomplishing the remedial work it is supposed to do. We have all given, witnessed, and received surly apologies that are intended and received as new affronts requiring more apology" (p. 163). Similarly, a truly contrite offender must take full responsibility for the offense; as Jacoby (1983) explained, there is a big difference between a friend or lover who simply says, "I'm sorry you're hurt," and one who says, "What I did was wrong; you have every right to be hurt and I'm sorry" (see also Cody et al., 1992).

Sincere apologies, then, imply that an offender is feeling guilt, one of the most essential emotions in the interpersonal betrayal script. Several researchers have demonstrated that people feel most guilty about offenses that threaten their relational bonds (e.g., Baumeister, Stillwell, & Heatherton, 1995; Jones, Kugler, & Adams, 1995), and Vangelisti and Sprague (1998) claimed that an offender's guilt sends a powerful signal to the hurt partner that the betrayer still cares and is committed to the relationship. However, another important facet of guilt in the context of interpersonal betrayal relates to its motivational aspect. Specifically, feelings of guilt theoretically derive from empathic distress over the suffering of the betrayed partner; the pain of guilt, then, motivates atonement and a desire to make the suffering partner feel better (Baumeister et al., 1995; Tangney, 1995). Indeed, the suffering of guilty offenders helps to compensate victims for their own suffering (referred to by O'Malley & Greenberg, 1983, as the "down payment" effect). For example, Baumeister et al. (1995) found that reproachers felt much better once they had successfully made offenders feel guilty, "as if some of the negative affect had been transferred out of one person and into another" (p. 266). Guilt, then, appears to more fairly apportion the suffering between script interactants.

Once a betrayed partner is feeling better because the betrayer is feeling guilty, it might be assumed that the emotional balance is more or less restored between the two parties and that the next act in the interpersonal drama will be the concluding one, involving the betrayed party's forgiving and forgetting the offense. However, forgiveness is not the only possible outcome of a betrayal event, regardless of an offender's remorse. For example, the betrayed partner may decide that an offense is simply unforgivable and terminate the relationship, or that an offense is unforgivable and warrants revenge. Or the partner may decide that long-term forgiveness is not impossible but that the betrayer has a great deal more suffering to do before the debt is paid. In the next section of the chapter I will discuss some of the betrayed partner's response options, beginning with the most potentially damaging for the long-term future of the relationship: revenge.

Coping with Betrayal: Revenge and Forgiveness

Revenge

A 27-year-old Perth woman who poured a pot of boiling liquid over her former partner's penis as he slept was jailed for seven years yesterday. She concocted and boiled the brew of floor cleaner, disinfectant, bleach, candle wax and honey because she was angry the man wanted to break up with her after four years together (*Sydney Morning Herald*, 24 Sept. 1998).

According to Frijda (1994), the ancient and universal desire to get even with those who have betrayed us is one of the most fundamental and potent of human passions. Despite the fundamental nature of the human urge to retaliate, however, revenge is generally regarded as an unhealthy signal of mental illness (Jacoby, 1983). Bagnall (1992) also noted how revenge has largely fallen out of our vocabulary, "as if modern humanity were embarrassed by its melodrama" (p. 37). Certainly, few admit to plotting revenge with Machiavellian relish, although some will freely admit to exacting revenge on their enemies; e.g., Australian politician Ros Kelly apparently claimed on television that she always exacted revenge on people who betrayed her, no matter how long it took (Bagnall, 1992).

Surprisingly, very little psychological research has focused on revenge, which Stuckless and Goranson (1992) defined as the infliction of harm in return for perceived wrong. In early times, people coped with injustice through revenge; indeed, for many peoples, including the ancient Greeks, revenge was equated with justice (Kim & Smith, 1993; Solomon, 1994). At various times in history it was even considered acceptable to take revenge against inanimate objects, such as trees, that were perceived to have harmed an individual (Cloke, 1993). Similarly, parents frequently "punish" inanimate objects on behalf of their hurt children (witness, for example, parents who console a toddler who has stumbled into a table by "smacking" the table and informing it of its "naughtiness").

What motivates betrayed individuals to take revenge on their betrayers? Clearly, one important motive is that revenge helps "even the score" between the two parties. In this sense, revenge and guilt are functionally similar in that both help to allocate the pain fairly—causing one's betrayer to suffer makes one feel better (Planalp & Hafen, 1998). Gabriel and Monaco (1994), for example, cited a case study in which an abandoned husband broke into his ex-wife's apartment and shredded all of her clothing. "This, he said, had made him feel 'much improved.'" However, he also "talked in some detail of his fervent wish and intention to do more than simply kill her. He wanted her to suffer the way in which he had suffered, i.e., feeling alone, frightened, and humiliated" (p. 173). Again, this case points to the strong links between humiliation, rejection, and revenge that have been noted by several researchers (e.g., Baumeister, 1997; Brown, 1968; Frijda, 1994; Kim & Smith, 1993; Vogel & Lazare, 1990). Given that humiliation inflicts such a deep and painful injury to a person's self-esteem and social status, taking revenge might well be regarded as a powerful means of restoring dignity and regaining some control over the situation.

In terms of actual revenge behaviors, there is no limit to human inventiveness, from everyday acts of vindictiveness (e.g., being unhelpful, gossiping), to torture, rape, or mass murder (Frijda, 1994). Jacoby (1983) claimed that people generally have some sympathy for the vengeful behaviors of rejected lovers; certainly, one famous case that recently inspired much public amusement, if not sympathy, concerned Lady Graham-Moon, an Englishwoman whose husband left her for a younger woman, who cut four inches off the sleeves of all her husband's suits, daubed his BMW with paint, and gave away his vintage wine collection to the local villagers (Bagnall, 1992). Usually, revenge is not so dramatic, though fantasies can be lurid. For example, in a study of students' experiences of desiring revenge, Frijda (1994) found "vivid thoughts of revenge . . . for erotic unfaithfulness, indiscretions, having been slighted, being cheated" (p. 264). Fortunately, students' fantasies tended to far outweigh vengeful actions; even so, a number of acts were reported, including the destruction of cherished possessions, public humiliation, and gossip.

The impulse to take revenge in response to a betrayal, then, is undoubtedly powerful and profoundly human, but actually taking revenge can cause problems, especially when the act of revenge itself constitutes a relational betrayal that encourages further revenge in a tit-for-tat cycle. Part of the problem derives from what Bies and Tripp (1996) refer to as the "different arithmetics" between victims and perpetrators. As discussed previously, betrayers and their victims interpret and respond to the same act of betrayal differently (see also Mikula, 1994). In particular, betrayers tend to minimize the harm they have caused, whereas the betrayed tend to maximize their own suffering (Baumeister, 1997). Thus, the betrayed party perceives that more pain and suffering is "owing" than the betrayer believes is fair and reasonable, and this perceptual mismatch leads to escalating cycles of revenge and counter-revenge (Kim & Smith, 1993).

Despite its unsavory reputation, revenge may play a constructive role in the relational context. Certainly, Frijda (1994) noted that the desire for revenge is not irrational, though its expression requires moderation. Solomon (1994), too, claimed that the dangers of vengeance are exaggerated and its importance for a "sense of self-esteem and integrity underestimated" (p. 308). Revenge can even motivate constructive behavior change ("I'll show them!") (Bies & Tripp, 1996). Clearly, people who have been rejected and deeply hurt feel a powerful impulse to reciprocate the pain; perhaps, then, society needs to find ways for helping people to deal constructively with this impulse. One innovative approach has been taken by an Australian florist shop called "Drop Dead Flowers," which organizes revenge packs for jilted and betrayed lovers including everything from a single dead rose to the "ultimate revenge pack": 13 dead roses and a box of melted chocolates packaged in black paper and a box. They claim divorcees are their main clientele and that many customers find it therapeutic to send a revenge pack because it means they can get on with their lives and not think about their betrayer any more.

Finally, Cloke (1993) claimed that if wished-for revenge is illegal or impossible to obtain, one can stay angry, which is bad for one's health, or one can deny one's anger and try to forget the betrayal, which is often impossible because of its painful nature. The third option is to forgive and, in so doing, to paradoxically achieve the highest form of revenge. In this respect, Cloke notes Oscar Wilde's (reputed) advice to "always forgive your enemies—nothing infuriates them so!" (p. 78).

Forgiveness

Until recently, the study of forgiveness was the almost exclusive preserve of philosophers, theologians, and clinicians; consequently there is very little material in the social psychological literature on laypeople's theories of how forgiveness works or what is forgivable or unforgivable in close relationships. Thus, there are many unanswered questions about the nature and process of forgiveness. For example, Tavuchis (1991) noted that sorrow and guilt are the energizing forces behind apology, but what motivates betrayed parties to forgive their betrayers? According to McCullough, Worthington, and Rachal (1997), empathic distress for a guilty party's suffering plays a crucial role in a victim's willingness to forgive; does this mean, however, that forgiveness can never occur if a betraying partner is unremorseful or, conversely, that forgiveness will always occur if the betrayer is patently sorry?

In a recent study of forgiven and unforgiven, self- and partner-caused marital offenses, I attempted a preliminary exploration of some of these issues (see also Fitness & Mathews, 1998). The study was based on the premise that laypeople hold implicit theories about how relational events unfold and that these event scripts may be accessed by having people recall episodes from their own relationship experiences. Based on the evidence discussed in this chapter, for example, one could argue that the prototypical interpersonal betrayal and forgiveness script works something like this: A relationship partner perceives that an offense has been committed; a rule has been broken or expectation violated. If the partner appraises the violation as caused by a close, trusted other who both intended to do it and is to blame for it, he or she will feel angry and betrayed and will call for an account from the offender. Now, the offender should concede an offense has been committed, accept responsibility for it, feel guilty, apologize, and make reparation; then the victim will perceive the offender is sorry, feel sorry for him or her, and forgive the offense. It might also be hypothesized, on the basis of folklore, that once the victim has forgiven the offense, it should also be forgotten; the relational slate is wiped clean.

But how might an unforgiven offense work? Given the previous discussion about the emotional consequences of betrayal, we would expect feelings of hurt and anger in both forgiven and unforgiven offense scripts. We would also expect offender guilt and apology to figure less prominently in unforgiven, as opposed to forgiven, offense scripts. However, a number of other potentially important emotions and behaviors may be more typical of unforgiven than forgiven offenses. For example, as previously noted, Fitness and Fletcher (1993) found marital hate accounts were characterized by themes of relative powerlessness, humiliation, and shame, all potent motivators of revenge. Anecdotally, several of their respondents also commented that if the researchers really wanted to know about hatred, they should have asked about unforgiven offenses committed by ex-partners, rather than current spouses. Taken together, these findings suggest that humiliation, shame, powerlessness, hatred, and revenge might be more distinctive of unforgiven rather than forgiven offense scripts.

It was also hypothesized in the current study that the role of shame in unforgiven offense scripts would not be restricted to the emotional reactions of the betrayal victim; rather, shame was also expected to figure prominently in offenders' feelings about their own betrayals, making forgiveness-seeking particularly difficult. As noted earlier, guilt is a generally functional emotion that derives in part from an offender's empathic distress in response to the pain he or she has caused. It is this distress that is held to motivate remorseful behaviors and attempts to restore the relationship. Shame, however, is a profoundly painful, self-focused emotion that typically motivates attempts to hide or escape from the situation, or alternatively, to retaliate against whoever has caused or even simply witnessed the shame in what Tangney (1995) called "externally-directed, humiliated fury" (p. 123). Clearly, if a betrayer's shame-induced withdrawal or defensive anger are misinterpreted by the betrayed party as signs of callous unrepentance then the delicate interactional negotiations involved in seeing and being granted forgiveness will run into problems.

In my study of the features of self- and partner-caused forgiven and unforgiven offenses, 90 long-term married (mean length of marriage = 21.3 years) and 70 divorced individuals recalled either a partner-caused or a self-caused marital offense; divorced participants described unforgiven offenses, and married participants described forgiven offenses. Respondents were asked to write an account of what had happened, what they had thought and felt at the time, how humiliating the offense had been, and how powerful they had felt relative to their partners. They also recalled their perceptions at the time of their partners' thoughts and feelings and answered a series of open-ended questions about their own and their partners' behaviors during and after the incident. Finally, respondents were asked either why they had forgiven or not forgiven their partner's offense, or why they thought they had or had not been forgiven by their partners.

Forgiven and Unforgiven Marital Offense Scripts

Offense Types

Overall, most of the offenses reported in this study could readily be classified as betrayals. Over half of the unforgiven, partner-caused offenses involved explicit betrayals such as lies, deception, and sexual infidelity, compared with 33% of forgiven partner-caused offenses, 17% of unforgiven, self-caused offenses, and 14% of forgiven, self-caused offenses. The bulk of remaining offenses such as "neglect, uncaring behavior," "public embarrassment," or "third party conflict" comprised implicit betrayals involving personal rejection or perceptions of relational devaluation. For example, a male respondent laconically describing a forgiven, self-caused offense explained that he had "fallen asleep during intercourse. Needless to say, partner was there at the time. She thought it meant I didn't love her." And a woman discussing a partner-caused, unforgiven offense explained how her partner had sided with his mother against her in a serious family conflict, an offense she clearly interpreted as a betrayal. As she said, "my husband should have put me first, not his mother. I should have been his priority."

Because betrayals appeared in forgiven as well as unforgiven accounts it was clearly not betrayal per se that made an offense unforgivable. In addition, and as predicted, respondents reported high levels of anger and hurt on behalf of the injured party, regardless of forgiveness condition. One important discriminating factor that did emerge between the two conditions, however, was offense repetition: Specifically, some 60% of unforgiven, partner-caused offenses had happened more than once, compared with only 30% of forgiven, partner-caused offenses and both forgiven and unforgiven self-caused offenses. Repeat offenses were typically regarded by respondents as a signal that the offender neither regretted his or her previous behavior, nor had any serious intention of behaving differently in the future, despite protestations to the contrary. As one woman explained, "I think the old Christian adage, turn the other cheek and just keep on forgiving, no matter how many times it happens, is for the birds who don't have the brains to figure out what's going on, not real human beings who have to move on with their lives."

Along with offense repetition, a second discriminating factor between forgiven and unforgiven scripts involved perceived humiliation and the emotions of shame and hatred. In particular, and as predicted, unforgiven offenses were significantly more likely to have involved humiliation than forgiven offenses; furthermore, unforgiven self-offenders reported feeling significantly more shame than forgiven self-offenders, and sadly, were significantly more likely than forgiven self-offenders to believe their partners hated them. Finally, and irrespective of forgiveness condition, feeling intense shame over a self-caused offense was positively associated with either withdrawing from or attacking the injured partner; feeling intense guilt, on the other hand, was positively associated with efforts to repair the damage to the relationship.

Overall, these data support the hypothesis that feeling shame in response to a self-caused offense, and subsequently withdrawing from or attacking an injured partner, may impede the flow of the prototypical forgiveness script and make it more difficult for the injured partner to forgive. However, the data also suggest that an initially hateful, unforgiving reaction from a rejected partner may heighten an offender's shame and so further reduce the possibility of constructively resolving the situation. Clearly, more fine-grained research is required to tease out the potentially disruptive and destructive roles of humiliation, hate, and shame in the process of interpersonal forgiveness, for both the betrayed and betraying parties.

Remorse and Forgiveness

Another important contrast between forgiven and unforgiven partner-caused offenses concerned the role of offender remorse. Over 50% of forgiven self-offenders claimed they were "truly sorry" (even if not entirely to blame) for the offense, compared with 31% of unforgiven self-offenders; similarly, nearly 50% of forgiven partners were believed to have been "truly sorry," compared with only 15% of unforgiven partners, even though unforgiven partners were more likely to have verbally apologized (40%) than forgiven partners (9%). Respondents' accounts made it clear that being "truly sorry" went far beyond verbal apologies. As several long-term married respondents observed, showing true remorse can take weeks, months, or even years, of "making up" for an offense and proving one's commitment to one's partner and the relationship. For example, in one moving account, an 81-year old man who had deceived his wife some 30 years previously described how it had taken some two years of patient and persistent effort following the betrayal to rebuild her trust in him, and to convince her that he truly wanted no other but her.

One reason that a betrayer might experience such difficulty in convincing a partner that he or she is truly sorry is that, along with feeling hurt and rejected, the partner appraises the offense to mean that the relationship is not important to the betrayer. To win forgiveness, then, a betrayer must reassure his or her partner that the offense was an inexplicable aberration reflecting only the betrayer's unworthiness, rather than any kind of partner or relational deficiency. In addition, a betrayer must convince his or her partner that their relationship is still of primary importance and that almost any sacrifice would be made to repair and restore it.

In the current study, repentant offenders used a number of strategies to demonstrate their contrition. For example, nearly half the respondents who had forgiven their partners referred explicitly to their remorseful partners' guilty, hang-dog expressions and dejected body language, including weeping. The majority of these respondents, however, along with the majority of forgiven self-offenders, claimed forgiveness was won through persistent, constructive efforts to repair the situation, e.g., by regularly demonstrating thoughtfulness or kindness, seeking counseling for drinking or gambling problems, resolutely ending extra-marital liaisons, and firmly admonishing troublesome third parties, including in-laws. In contrast, only a small proportion of unforgiven self- or partner-offenders were reported to have made such constructive efforts. They were more likely to have angrily retaliated, taken revenge (including physical abuse), or packed their bags and moved out—behaviors that may have been triggered in part by their feelings of shame but that also reinforced the impression that they cared neither for their partners nor for the relationship.

It should be noted, however, that even true contrition was not always a sufficiently good reason to forgive an offender. Of those respondents who claimed they could not forgive a clearly remorseful partner, 20% claimed the offense simply broke the rules and so fell outside the bounds of forgiveness, regardless of how sorry the offender was; 80%, however, cited betrayal severity and the complete breakdown of trust as the primary reason forgiveness was impossible. In particular, these respondents did not believe that spouses who really loved their partners would treat them as if they meant so little. For the most part, they appraised their partners' repentance as sincere; however, they did not believe they could ever be adequately compensated for the damage done. In line with these data, the majority of remorseful but unforgiven self-offenders believed it was the severity and painfulness of the betrayal, and the breakdown of relational trust, that had made forgiveness impossible.

There was more of a contrast, however, in respondents' reported reasons for forgiving an apparently unremorseful offender. Of these, 40% charitably accepted the extenuating circumstances involved in the offense (e.g., alcohol, stress); a further 30% reported, with some degree of resignation, that the passage of time had healed their wounds; 22% reported they had forgiven their partners simply because it was the right thing to do, either for the sake of the relationship or for their own personal well-being; and only 8% claimed they had forgiven their unremorseful partners because they loved them. Somewhat accurately, then, 40% of unremorseful self-offenders believed they had been forgiven because their partners had accepted their offense as more or less excusable. Less realistically, however, 60% believed they had been forgiven simply because their partners loved them. None believed that they had been forgiven because of the passage of time or because their partners believed it was their "duty" to forgive them. These findings suggest a number of different motives for forgiving betrayals that have little to do with offender remorse; however, it is interesting to speculate whether some unrepentant offenders may misinterpret the reasons for their partners' forbearance and even regard their apparent indulgence as license to repeat the offense.

Punishment and Forgiveness

As mentioned previously, one of the most important tasks for repentant offenders is to convince their partners that they would pay almost any price to repair and restore their relationships. One way for betrayed partners to assess the extent and sincerity of offenders' contrition and test their resolve to put things right is to inflict costs and seek compensation for the offense. Accordingly, respondents were asked if they had punished or been punished by their partners for the offense and to describe the kinds of punishments that were meted out.

Surprisingly, perhaps, over half the respondents reporting on forgiven, partner-caused offenses claimed they had punished their partners, compared with less than one third of respondents reporting on unforgiven, partner-caused offenses. However, the type and severity of punishments differed according to forgiveness condition. For example, nearly 75% of forgiven partners' punishments involved ongoing reminders of the offense; similarly, 100% of punished but forgiven self-offenders reported periodic reminders about what they had done. However, 70% of unforgiven partners' punishments and 58% of unforgiven self-offenders' punishments comprised acts of revenge including physical abuse, denunciation to family and friends, destruction of possessions, and abandonment. Both revenge and reminding were reportedly motivated by the betrayed party's need to communicate the depth of their hurt or to regain some power in the relationship—to feel "one-up" relative to the partner; however, reminders were also reportedly given to ensure the offender did not reoffend.

These findings have interesting implications for the delicate negotiations involved in the interpersonal betrayal and forgiveness script. For victims of betrayal, reminders appear to serve at least three purposes: fine-tuning the degree of mutual suffering, readjusting the balance of power, and behavioral deterrence. Clearly, as O'Malley and Greenberg (1983) theorized, expressing guilt goes some way toward making the betrayed party feel better, but guilt alone is not sufficient. Rather, as discussed previously, convincing partners in the aftermath of betrayal that they are, in fact, cherished, requires considerable effort and persistence on the part of remorseful offenders, especially if trust is to be fully restored.

This raises the interesting questions of how sorry is sorry enough, and when and how betrayed partners decide it is safe to fully trust again. Certainly, a number of forgiven respondents expressed some puzzlement, irritation, and sadness that they were still being reminded of something they had hoped was behind them. As one self-offender pointed out, "she said she had forgiven me, so she had no right to keep bringing it up and throwing it in my face." Pittman and Wagers (1995) also noted the extent to which punishments following infidelity may persist for years; indeed, they recommended a statute of limitations to such punishments, after which "all emotional rights should be restored" (p. 312).

One reason why betrayed spouses may refuse to forgive, despite the best efforts of their partners to behave well over an extended period of time, is that they believe letting their partners "off the hook" somehow diminishes the significance of the betrayal and exonerates their betrayers (Glass & Wright, 1997)—as if forgiving the offense served to legitimize it. Betrayed partners may also be reluctant to let go and lose the upper hand or moral advantage in the relationship. Indeed, refusing to forgive can be a very effective, if dysfunctional, way to exert relational power. At some point, however, remorseful offenders believe they have paid their dues and earned forgiveness, and their partners' reluctance to let go may be interpreted as a sign that they themselves do not truly care about the relationship, or about the offender. Indeed, ongoing punishment may itself constitute a relational betrayal that signals rejection to a confused partner. Given how little is known about the ways in which betrayed and betraying partners go about making these kinds of complex cognitive and emotional calculations over time, this is clearly a fascinating and fertile research area.

Summary

Overall, the findings of this study support the idea that laypeople hold elaborate theories about the nature of forgivable and unforgivable offenses in marriage. In particular, the results suggest that forgiven offenses tend to be once-only events, that sincere contrition is essential for forgiveness but that verbal apologies are not necessarily the best indicator of being "truly sorry," that forgiven offenders must work hard to regain their partners' trust and repair the damage, and that even then, offenders can expect to be periodically reminded about the offense. Unforgiven offenses, on the other hand, tend to involve humiliation, shame, hatred, and revenge; the offender is not perceived to be truly sorry, despite his or her verbal apologies, and there is a good chance that the same offense, or something similar, has happened before.

In line with previous research, the results of this study demonstrated the striking difference between perpetrators' and victim's perspectives. For example, although self-caused offenses involved exactly the same kinds of betrayal incidents as partner-caused offences, they were more likely to be justified as accidents, misunderstandings, or understandable reactions to prior partner provocation. In addition, many forgiven self-offenders were almost smug in their assumptions that ultimately they were understood, excused, loved, and forgiven by their partners. However, respondents recalling forgiven, partner-caused offenses emphasized the hard work that went into the forgiveness process; many claimed that even though the offense was officially forgiven, it was not forgotten. One might argue that self-offenders chose less serious offenses to remember and write about; however, types of offense and ratings of offense severity for self-offenses were the same as for partner-caused offenses, and as noted before, self-offenders acknowledged the degree of hurt and anger their partners had experienced in response to the offense.

The interesting point about these results is that respondents were randomly selected to report on a self- or partner-caused offense; thus, any one of them could have been asked to recall a marital betrayal from the opposite perspective, and presumably, they would have reported the entire sequence of events in line with the appropriate script. Thus, many long-term married couples may be privately nursing long-standing, partner-instigated hurts and rejections yet neither partner may realize that their own acts of betrayal are still remembered and still painful.

It should also be noted that the very few significant gender differences found in this study replicated other researchers' findings. As previously noted, Levine et al. (1992) found that women regard deception as a more profound relational transgression than men; similarly, Mikula (1994) found that women appraised relational offenses as more serious and unjustified than men did. He speculated that women have higher relational expectations and so feel more let down when their expectations are violated. Women in this study appraised forgiven partners' offenses as less fair and harder to forgive, and unforgiven partners' offenses as more serious than men did. However, although these findings suggest that, as one male respondent claimed, "women sure do find it hard to forgive and forget," it may be too simple to conclude that the results merely reflect women's more exacting standards. As Mikula (1994) pointed out, women generally have less power than men: they occupy lower status positions, earn less money, and have less economic power than men. Consequently, men's betrayals may really have more serious consequences for their partners than women's betrayals, and women's judgments may well derive from a complex combination of relational expectations, and social and economic realities.

The Long-Term Consequences of Betrayal

Predictably, the alleged long-term consequences of interpersonal betrayal depend on whether one asks the betrayed or the betrayer. For example, Hansson et al. (1990) found 26% of respondents reporting on their own betrayals claimed their behavior had actually improved the relationship, 41.5% reported no change or only temporary harm, and only 29% claimed their betrayal had damaged or ended the relationship. However, not one betrayal victim claimed the relationship had been improved by the partner's behavior; rather, 86% claimed it had damaged or destroyed it. Jones and Burdette (1994) obtained very similar findings.

The consequences of sexual infidelity may be particularly dramatic and long-lasting. Glass and Wright (1997) noted that the discovery of infidelity means the shattering of "long-held assumptions about the meaning of marriage, perceptions of the partner, and views of oneself" (p. 471), with the severity of reaction being associated with the strength of those assumptions. Similarly, Charney and Parnass (1995) found that 67% of betrayed husbands and 53% of betrayed wives suffered significant damage to their self-image and confidence, and 18% and 21%, respectively, suffered feelings of abandonment and attacks on their sense of belonging. Nevertheless, as demonstrated by the study of forgiven offenses reported in this chapter, many relationships survive infidelity and other forms of betrayal; so how do partners repair the damage and maintain the relationship?

According to Rusbult, Verette, Whitney, Slovik, and Lipkus (1991), one important factor involves accommodation—individuals' willingness to inhibit their destructive urges and to behave constructively in response to their partners' offenses. Rusbult et al. found a number of factors influenced people's willingness to accommodate, including the extent to which they felt invested in and committed to the relationship, and, reasonably enough, whether any promising alternatives were on the horizon. Other researchers, too, have found that the knowledge that one has access to desirable alternatives plays an important role in the decision to leave a relationship following partner betrayal. Shackelford and Buss (1997a), for example, found that women rated by observers as highly attractive were more likely to report they would seek a divorce if their husbands went on a date or had a one-night stand than women rated as less attractive; similar results were obtained for women judged to be more attractive than their husbands.

Partners who wish to repair or at least maintain their relationship in the aftermath of betrayal have a number of potential options available. Roloff and Cloven (1994) identified a number of relational maintenance strategies, including one called reformulation, whereby an offense is redefined so that it no longer violates a rule. Thus, a couple may decide that infidelity will be okay after all but that it must always involve safe sex or no emotional involvement. Another strategy is prevention, whereby partners agree to avoid conflict areas. Baumeister et al. (1990), for example, found that happily married spouses apparently do not tell each other up to 44% of their marital grievances, presumably in the belief that there is no point in "rocking the boat."

Roloff and Cloven (1994) also describe a strategy called minimization, whereby the offense is recast so that it no longer seems like a "big deal." As a respondent in the forgiveness study explained, "it was trivial; in the wider scheme of things, what did it matter?" Roloff and Cloven noted that this strategy may even encourage a victim to accept blame for the offense ("I made you do it!") to convince the partner that the relationship is worth maintaining. Wiseman and Duck (1995) have also pointed out that betrayed friends will often apologize first in an effort to repair the friendship.

A final strategy is relational justification, whereby partners focus on reasons for staying in the relationship. Bowman (1990) found that focusing on good memories, expressing positive feelings, and initiating shared experiences are common and functional strategies for coping with marital difficulties. Certainly, some of the comments made by forgiving partners in the study discussed previously reflected this theme. For example, one man claimed that "in a relationship, there is both pleasure and pain. If you concentrate on the pain, sooner or later the whole relationship will become painful, and you'll feel drained;" another respondent explained that "it's a matter of weighing up whether the result of non-forgiveness, i.e., unhappiness and the loss of that person in your life, is worth maintaining the rage for. If it isn't, you should let it go."

As a last resort, betrayed partners who have no viable alternatives may simply bide their time. As one recently divorced woman explained, "I just didn't love my husband anymore. . . . What he did killed my love for him. However, his betrayal made me realize I had to become more independent so that when the children got older I would have some options; so I just waited it out."

Conclusions

This chapter has examined the process and consequences of interpersonal betrayal and rejection from an interpersonal script perspective. Essentially, I argued that the drama of betrayal, rejection, revenge, and forgiveness is played out between relationship partners who hold beliefs and expectations about the rights and wrongs of relationship behavior, and about the consequences of breaking the rules. Clearly, our understanding of this fascinating area of human social behavior still has some way to go, particularly in relation to the various script components, such as the art of taking "just enough" revenge and the complex negotiations involved in winning forgiveness. Indeed, some of these components themselves constitute "mini-scripts" with important implications for the ongoing emotions and behaviors of the interacting parties. Much also remains to be learned about forgivable and unforgivable betrayals in different relational contexts, such as among family members and within different cultures. For example, in the forgiveness study described earlier, a Javanese respondent provided an intriguing account of why she had forgiven her husband's betrayal, suggesting that in this case, cultural prescriptives were far more relevant than either partner's feelings.

Researchers should also examine the ways in which individual differences moderate the process and outcomes of interpersonal betrayal. For example, using a self-report test called the Interpersonal Betrayal Scale, Jones and Burdette (1994) found divorced individuals were more likely to report betraying others than married individuals, and that high betrayers were less committed to their marriages, had more affairs, and told more lies than low betrayers. Presumably this propensity to betray is linked to people's beliefs that self-interest should usually take precedence over the interests of others. However, the tendency to betray may also be linked to people's beliefs about the inherent untrustworthiness of others. As Holmes (1991) noted, some individuals are chronically distrustful of relationship partners, possibly because they have experienced betrayal and rejection in past relationships.

This suggests an important role for attachment style in people's expectations of and responses to betrayal, given that insecurely attached individuals hold pessimistic beliefs about the likely trustworthiness and reliability of relationship partners (Shaver, Collins, & Clark, 1996). Rejection sensitivity, too, may mean individuals are always on the lookout for potential betrayal cues and interpret all kinds of partner behaviors as reliable signs of the rejection they dread (Downey & Feldman, 1996). High self-esteem has also been associated with destructive responses to relationship conflict (Rusbult, Morrow, & Johnson, 1987), apparently because people with high self-esteem believe they are valuable human beings who do not deserve to be badly treated. Ironically, however, too strong a sense of entitlement may make it difficult either to forgive a betrayal or to humble oneself sufficiently to acknowledge and be truly sorry for one.

In conclusion, there is clearly more to be learned about the nature and consequences of interpersonal betrayal. Hopefully this chapter will stimulate further exploration of its causes in different relational and cultural contexts, its psychological links with rejection, and its associations with the rich and endlessly fascinating relational phenomena of revenge and forgiveness.

Acknowledgment

The author acknowledges the support of a Large ARC grant A79601552 in the writing of this chapter.

References

Argyle, M., & Henderson, M. (1985). The rules of relationships. In S. Duck & D. Perlman (Eds.), *Understanding personal relationships: An interdisciplinary approach* (pp. 63–84). Beverly Hills: Sage.

Bagnall, D. (1992). Revenge: The urge to get even. *The Bulletin,* Aug. 4 issue (pp. 37–39). Sydney: APC.

Baldwin, M. W. (1992). Relational schemas and the processing of social information. *Psychological Bulletin, 112,* 461–484.

Barbee, A., Cunningham, M., Druen, P., & Yankeelov, P. (1996). Loss of passion, intimacy, and commitment: A conceptual framework for relationship researchers. *Journal of Personal and Interpersonal Loss, 1,* 93–108.

Baumeister, R. (1997). *Evil: Inside human violence and cruelty.* New York: W. H. Freeman.

Baumeister, R., Stillwell, A., & Heatherton, T. (1995). Interpersonal aspects of guilt: Evidence from narrative studies. In J. P. Tangney & K. W. Fischer (Eds.), *Self-conscious emotions: The psychology of shame, guilt, embarrassment, and pride* (pp. 255–273). New York: Guilford Press.

Baumeister, R., Stillwell, A., & Wotman, S. (1990). Victim and perpetrator accounts of interpersonal conflict: Autobiographical narratives about anger. *Journal of Personality and Social Psychology, 59,* 994–1005.

Berscheid, E. (1983). Emotion. In H. H. Kelley, E. Berscheid, A. Christensen, J. H. Harvey, T. L. Huston, G. Levinger, E. McClintock, L. A. Peplau, & D. R. Peterson (Eds.), *Close relationships* (pp. 110–168). New York: W. H. Freeman.

Betzig, L. (1989). Causes of conjugal dissolution: A cross cultural study. *Current Anthropology, 30,* 654–676.

Bies, R. J., & Tripp, T. M. (1996). Beyond distrust: "Getting even" and the need for revenge. In R. M. Kramer & T. R. Tyler (Eds.), *Trust in organizations: Frontiers in theory and research* (pp. 246–260). Thousand Oaks, CA: Sage.

Boon, S. (1994). Dispelling doubt and uncertainty: Trust in romantic relationships. In S. Duck (Ed.), *Dynamics of relationships: Understanding relationship processes, Vol. 4* (pp. 86–111). Thousand Oaks, CA: Sage.

Bowman, M. L. (1990). Coping efforts and marital satisfaction: Measuring marital coping and its correlates. *Journal of Marriage and the Family, 52,* 463–474.

Brown, B. R. (1968). The effects of need to maintain face on interpersonal bargaining. *Journal of Experimental Social Psychology, 4,* 107–122.

Charney, I., & Parnass, S. (1995). The impact of extramarital relationships on the continuation of marriages. *Journal of Sex and Marital Therapy, 21,* 100–115.

Clark, M. S., & Mills, J. (1979). Interpersonal attraction in exchange and communal relationships. *Journal of Personality and Social Psychology, 37,* 12–24.

Clark, M. S., & Waddell, B. (1985). Perceptions of exploitation in communal and exchange relationships. *Journal of Social and Personal Relationships, 2,* 403–418.

Cloke, K. (1993). Revenge, forgiveness, and the magic of mediation. *Mediation Quarterly, 11,* 67–78.

Cody, M. J., Kersten, L., Braaten, D. O., & Dickson, R. (1992). Coping with relational dissolutions: Attributions, account credibility, and plans for resolving conflict. In J. H. Harvey, T. Orbuch, & A. Weber (Eds.), *Attributions, accounts, and close relationships* (pp. 93–115). New York: Springer-Verlag.

Cosmides, L., & Tooby, J. (1992). Cognitive adaptations for social exchange. In J. Barkow, L. Cosmides, & J. Tooby (Eds.), *The adapted mind: Evolutionary psychology and the generation of culture* (pp. 163–228). New York: Oxford University Press.

Daly, M., & Wilson, M. (1988). *Homicide.* New York: Aldine de Gruyter.

Darby, B. W., & Schlenker, B. R. (1982). Children's reactions to apologies. *Journal of Personality and Social Psychology, 43,* 742–753.

DePaulo, B., & Kashy, D. (1998). Everyday lies in casual and close relationships. *Journal of Personality and Social Psychology, 74,* 63–79.

Downey, G., & Feldman, S. (1996). Implications of rejection sensitivity for intimate relationships. *Journal of Personality and Social Psychology, 70,* 1327–1343.

Dutton, D., & Browning, J. (1988). Concern for power, fear of intimacy, and aversive stimuli for wife abuse. In G. Hotaling, D. Finkelhor, J. Kirkpatrick, & M. Straus (Eds.), *Family abuse and its consequences: New directions in research* (pp. 163–175). Newbury Park, CA: Sage.

Elangovan, A. R., Shapiro, D. (1998). Betrayal of trust in organizations. *Academy of Management Review, 23,* 547–586.

Fehr, B. (1996). *Friendship processes.* Thousand Oaks, CA: Sage.

Fehr, B., & Baldwin, M. (1996). Prototype and script analyses of laypeople's knowledge of anger. In G. J. O. Fletcher & J. Fitness (Eds.), *Knowledge structures in close relationships: A social psychological approach* (pp. 219–245). Hillsdale, NJ: Lawrence Erlbaum.

Fincham, F. D., & Bradbury, T. (1992). Assessing attributions in marriage; The relationship attribution measure. *Journal of Personality and Social Psychology, 62,* 457–468.

Fiske, A. P. (1992). The four elementary forms of sociality: Framework for a unified theory of social relations. *Psychological Review, 99,* 689–723.

Fiske, A. P., & Tetlock, P. E. (1997). Taboo tradeoffs: Reactions to transactions that transgress spheres of justice. *Political Psychology, 18,* 255–297.

Fitness, J. (1996). Emotion knowledge structures in close relationships. In G. J. O. Fletcher & J. Fitness (Eds.), *Knowledge structures in close relationships: A social psychological approach* (pp. 195–217). Hillsdale, NJ: Lawrence Erlbaum.

Fitness, J. (2000). Anger in the workplace: An emotion script approach to anger episodes between workers and their superiors, co-workers, and subordinates. *Journal of Organizational Behavior, 21,* 147–162.

Fitness, J., & Fletcher, G. J. O. (1993). Love, hate, anger, and jealousy in close relationships: A prototype and cognitive appraisal analysis. *Journal of Personality and Social Psychology, 65,* 942–958.

Fitness, J., & Mathews, S. (1998). *Emotions, emotional intelligence, and forgiveness in marriage.* Paper presented at the 9th International Conference on Personal Relationships, Saratoga Springs, New York.

Fitness, J., & Strongman, K. T. (1991). Affect in close relationships. In G. J. O.

Fletcher & F. Fincham (Eds.), *Cognition in close relationships* (pp. 175–202). Hillsdale, NJ: Lawrence Erlbaum.

Fletcher, G. J. O., & Fitness, J. (Eds.). (1996). *Knowledge structures in close relationships: A social psychological approach.* Mahwah, NJ: Lawrence Erlbaum.

Fletcher, G. J. O., & Thomas, G. (1996). Close relationship lay theories: Their structure and function. In G. J. O. Fletcher and J. Fitness (Eds.), *Knowledge structures in close relationships: A social psychological approach* (pp. 195–217). Mahwah, NJ: Lawrence Erlbaum.

Fletcher, G. J. O., Rosanowski, J., Fitness, J. (1994). Automatic processing in intimate relationships: The role of close relationship beliefs. *Journal of Personality and Social Psychology, 67,* 888–897.

Foo, L., & Margolin, G. (1995). A multivariate investigation of dating aggression. *Journal of Family Violence, 10,* 351–377.

Frijda, N. (1994). The Lex Talionis: On vengeance. In S. H. van Goozen, N. E. van de Poll, & J. Sergeant (Eds.), *Emotions: Essays on emotion theory* (pp. 263–289). Hillsdale, NJ: Lawrence Erlbaum.

Frijda, N., Kuipers, P., & ter Schure, E. (1989). Relations among emotion, appraisal, and emotional action readiness. *Journal of Personality and Social Psychology, 57,* 212–228.

Gabriel, M., & Monaco, G. (1994). "Getting even": Clinical considerations of adaptive and maladaptive vengeance. *Clinical Social Work Journal, 22,* 165–178.

Gaylin, W. (1984). *The rage within: Anger in modern life.* New York: Simon and Schuster.

Georges, E. (1995). A cultural and historical perspective on confession. In J. W. Pennebaker (Ed.), *Emotion, disclosure, and health* (pp. 11–22). Washington, DC: American Psychological Association.

Glass, S., & Wright, T. (1997). Reconstructing marriages after the trauma of infidelity. In W. K. Halford & H. Markman (Eds.), *Clinical handbook of marriage and couple intervention* (pp. 471–503). New York: Wiley.

Gonzales, M. H., Haugen, J. A., & Manning, D. J. (1994). Victims as "narrative critics": Factors influencing rejoinders and evaluative responses to offenders' accounts. *Personality and Social Psychology Bulletin, 20,* 691–704.

Hansson, R., Jones, W., & Fletcher, W. (1990). Troubled relationships in later life: Implications for support. *Journal of Social and Personal Relationships, 7,* 451–463.

Hodgins, H. S., Liebeskind, E., & Schwartz, W. (1996). Getting out of hot water: Facework in social predicaments. *Journal of Personality and Social Psychology, 71,* 300–314.

Holmes, J. (1991). Trust and the appraisal process in close relationships. In W. Jones & D. Perlman (Eds.), *Advances in personal relationships, Vol. 2* (pp. 57–104). London: Jessica Kingsley.

Jacoby, S. (1983). *Wild justice: The evolution of revenge.* New York: Harper and Row.

Jones, E., & Gallois, C. (1989). Spouses' impressions of rules for communication in public and private marital conflicts. *Journal of Marriage and the Family, 51,* 957–967.

Jones, W., & Burdette, M. P. (1994). Betrayal. In A. L. Weber & J. H. Harvey

(Eds.), *Perspectives on close relationships* (pp. 243–262). Boston: Allyn & Bacon.

Jones, W. H.., Couch, L., & Scott, S. (1997). Trust and betrayal: The psychology of getting along and getting ahead. In R. Hogan, J. Johnson, & S. Briggs (Eds.), *Handbook of personality psychology* (pp. 465–482). New York: Academic Press.

Jones, W. H., Kugler, K., & Adams, P. (1995). You always hurt the one you love: Guilt and transgressions against relationship partners. In J. P. Tangney & K. W. Fischer (Eds.), *Self-conscious emotions: The psychology of shame, guilt, embarrassment, and pride* (pp. 301–321). New York: Guilford Press.

Kelley, D., & Burgoon, J. (1991). Understanding marital satisfaction and couple type as functions of relational expectations. *Human Communication Research, 18,* 40–69.

Kim, S., & Smith, R. (1993). Revenge and conflict escalation. *Negotiation Journal, 9,* 37–43.

Knee, C. R. (1998). Implicit theories of relationships: Assessment and prediction of romantic relationship initiation, coping, and longevity. *Journal of Personality and Social Psychology, 74,* 360–370.

Lansky, M. (1987). Shame and domestic violence. In D. Nathanson (Ed.), *The many faces of shame* (pp. 335–362). New York: Guilford Press.

Lawson, A. (1988). *Adultery.* New York: Basic Books.

Lazarus, R. (1992). *Emotion and adaptation.* New York: Oxford University Press.

Leary, M., Springer, C., Negel, L., Ansell, E., & Evans, K. (1998). The causes, phenomenology, and consequences of hurt feelings. *Journal of Personality and Social Psychology, 74,* 1225–1237.

Levine, T., McCornack, S., & Avery, B. P. (1992). Sex differences in emotional reactions to discovered deception. *Communication Quarterly, 40,* 289–296.

The Macquarie Dictionary (1991) (2nd ed.). Sydney: The Macquarie Library Pty. Ltd.

McCullough, M., Worthington, E., & Rachal, K. (1997). Interpersonal forgiving in close relationships. *Journal of Personality and Social Psychology, 73,* 321–336.

Metts, S. (1989). An exploratory investigation of deception in close relationships. *Journal of Social and Personal Relationships, 6,* 159–179.

Metts, S. (1994). Relational transgressions. In W. Cupach & B. Spitzberg (Eds.), *The dark side of interpersonal communication* (pp. 217–239). Hillsdale, NJ: Lawrence Erlbaum.

Mikula, G. (1994). Perspective-related differences in interpretations of injustice by victims and victimizers. In M. Lerner & G. Mikula (Eds.), *Entitlement and the affectional bond* (pp. 175–204). New York: Plenum Press.

Miller, W. I. (1993). *Humiliation.* Ithaca, New York: Cornell University Press.

Morrison, E. W., & Robinson, S. L. (1997). When employees feel betrayed: A model of how psychological contract violation develops. *Academy of Management Review, 22,* 226–256.

Ohbuchi, K., Kameda, M., & Agarie, N. (1989). Apology as aggression control: Its role in mediating appraisal of and response to harm. *Journal of Personality and Social Psychology, 56,* 219–227.

O'Malley, M., & Greenberg, J. (1983). Sex differences in restoring justice: The down payment effect. *Journal of Research in Personality, 17,* 174–185.

Peterson, C. (1996). Deception in intimate relationships. *International Journal of Psychology, 31,* 279–288.

Pittman, F. S., & Wagers, T. (1995). Crises of infidelity. In N. Jacobson & A. S. Gurman (Eds.), *Clinical handbook of couple therapy* (pp. 295–316). New York: Guilford Press.

Planalp, S., & Fitness, J. (1999). Thinking/feeling about social and personal relationships. *Journal of Social and Personal Relationships, 16,* 731–750.

Planalp, S., & Hafen, S. (1998). *Messages of shame and guilt.* Paper presented at the Western State Communication Association Convention, Denver, Colorado.

Roloff, M. E., & Cloven, D. H. (1994). When partners transgress: Maintaining violated relationships. In M. Roloff & D. Cloven (Eds.), *Communication and relational maintenance* (pp. 23–43). San Diego: Academic Press.

Rusbult, C. E., Morrow, G., & Johnson, D. J. (1987). Self-esteem and problem solving behavior in close relationships. *British Journal of Social Psychology, 26,* 293–303.

Rusbult, C. E., Verette, J., Whitney, G., Slovik, L., & Lipkus, I. (1991) Accommodation processes in close relationships: Theory and preliminary empirical evidence. *Journal of Personality and Social Psychology, 60,* 53–78.

Shackelford, T., & Buss, D. (1996). Betrayal in mateships, friendships, and coalitions. *Personality and Social Psychology Bulletin, 22,* 1151–1164.

Shackelford, T., & Buss, D. (1997a). Anticipation of marital dissolution as a consequence of spousal infidelity. *Journal of Personality and Social Psychology, 14,* 793–808.

Shackelford, T., & Buss, D. (1997b). Cues to infidelity. *Personality and Social Psychology Bulletin,* 1034–1045.

Sharpsteen, D. (1991). The organization of jealousy knowledge: Romantic jealousy as a blended emotion. In P. Salovey (Ed.), *The psychology of jealousy and envy* (pp. 31–51). New York: Guilford Press.

Shaver, P., Collins, N., & Clark, C. (1996). Attachment styles and internal working models of self and relationship partners. In G. J. O. Fletcher & J. Fitness (Eds.), *Knowledge structures in close relationships: A social psychological approach* (pp. 25–62). Mahwah, NJ: Lawrence Erlbaum.

Shaver, P., Schwartz, J., Kirson, D., & O'Connor, C. (1987). Emotion knowledge: Further exploration of a prototype approach. *Journal of Personality and Social Psychology, 52,* 1061–1086.

Shettel-Neuber, J., Bryson, J., & Young, C. (1978). Physical attractiveness of the "other person" and jealousy. *Personality and Social Psychology Bulletin, 4,* 612–615.

Solomon, R. C. (1994). Sympathy and vengeance: The role of emotions in justice. In S. H. van Goozen, N. E. van de Poll, & J. Sergeant (Eds.), *Emotion: Essays on emotion theory* (pp. 291–311). Hillsdale, NJ: Lawrence Erlbaum.

Stuckless, N., & Goranson, R. (1992). The Vengeance Scale: Development of a measure of attitudes toward revenge. *Journal of Social Behavior and Personality, 7,* 25–42.

Tangney, J. P. (1995). Shame and guilt in interpersonal relationship. In J. P. Tangney & K. W. Fischer (Eds.), *Self-conscious emotions: The psychology of shame, guilt, embarrassment, and pride* (pp. 114–142). New York: Guilford Press.

Tavuchis, N. (1991). *Mea culpa: A sociology of apology and reconciliation.* Stanford, CA: Stanford University Press.

Vangelisti, A., & Sprague, R. (1998). Guilt and hurt: Similarities, distinctions, and conversational strategies. In P. Anderson & L. Guerrero (Eds.), *Handbook of communication and emotion: Research, theory, application, and contexts* (pp. 123–154). New York: Academic Press.

Van Sommers, P. (1988). *Jealousy: What is it and who feels it?* London: Penguin Books.

Vogel, W., & Lazare, A. (1990). The unforgivable humiliation: A dilemma in couples' treatment. *Contemporary Family Therapy, 12,* 139–151.

Weiner, B., Graham, S., & Zmuidinas, P. (1991). Public confession and forgiveness. *Journal of Personality, 59,* 281–312.

Weiss, R. (1975). *Marital separation.* New York: Basic Books.

Wiseman, J. P., & Duck, S. (1995). Having and managing enemies: A very challenging relationship. In S. Duck and J. Wood (Eds.), *Confronting relationship challenges* (pp. 43–72). Thousand Oaks, CA: Sage.

5

Peer Rejection in
Everyday Life

STEVEN R. ASHER, AMANDA J. ROSE, AND
SONDA W. GABRIEL

The following conversation took place at an elementary school where we spent a year recording the everyday experiences of children as they interacted with their peers. Kate and Bill are in the lunch line when Kate points to a piece of meat that had fallen to the lunchroom floor from someone's tray and accuses Bill of "going to the bathroom in the wrong places." In the midst of this episode, Scott walks by and makes a rejecting comment, which Bill seems barely to notice in the context of the more challenging statements made by Kate.

Kate-Bill: Bill. Have you been going to the bathroom in the wrong places?

Bill-Kate: No. I wouldn't be talkin', girl.

Kate-Len, Bill: Bill's been going to the bathroom in the wrong places.

Bill-Len, Kate, Glen: She's tellin' me I've been goin' in the wrong place, to the bathroom.

Bill-Kate: That is not what you call it. You call it meat. That is meat on the floor. Somebody dropped it off their sandwich.

Kate-Bill: You ate it.

Bill-Kate: Nuh-uh, you did.

Kate-Bill: Nuh-uh, you ate it.

Bill-Kate: You did.

Kate-Bill: You did.

(A series of "You did" is exchanged.)

Bill-Kate: I'm tired of arguing with you. I'm tired of arguing with girls.

Kate-??: He went to the bathroom in the wrong place. (Kate is talking to an off-camera child who could not be identified from the videotaped recording.)

Bill-??, Kate: Nuh-uh.

Bill-Kate: You lie, that's a piece of meat.

Kate-Bill: No it ain't.

Bill-Kate: Yes it is.

Kate-Bill: It is not.

Bill-Kate: Fine.

Kate-Bill: Fine.

(A series of "Fine" is exchanged.)

Kate-Bill: You see, why do you keep goin' to the bathroom in the wrong places, Bill?

Bill-Kate: You're lyin'.

Scott-Bill: Hey, don't sit by me (Scott walks past Bill with his lunch tray).

Kate-Bill: No I'm not. Fine.

Bill-Kate: Fine.

Kate-Bill: Fine.

Bill-Kate: I'm not talkin' to you, so (Bill turns away).

Kate-Bill: I don't care, fine.

Bill-Kate: I said fine.

(Another series of "Fine" is exchanged.)

Kate-Bill: Fine. Shut up.

Bill: Aah (Bill bangs his head on the wall).

Kate-Bill: Fine.

This episode illustrates one of children's worst nightmares, a publicly humiliating interaction with peers that ends in complete frustration. Likely most people would remember this experience many years later. For Bill, unfortunately, this was only one of many highly negative peer experiences he had while we were at the school.

Introduction

The literature on interpersonal attraction within children's groups covers a 70-year period (Renshaw, 1981; Rubin, Bukowski, & Parker, 1998). Within this research literature, individual differences in children's integration into the fabric of their peer groups have been a central concern. This research consistently documents that, just as certain children are well liked or highly popular among their peers, other children are highly disliked by their peers. This latter group of children, referred to in the literature as sociometrically "rejected," can be identified by a combined use of positive and negative sociometric nominations in which children indicate the names of classmates or grade-mates they like most and the names of those they like least (e.g., Coie, Dodge, & Coppotelli, 1982; Newcomb & Bukowski, 1983). Peer-rejected children can also be identified by using rating-scale sociometric procedures in which children rate each of their classmates on a Likert scale in terms of criteria such as how much they like to play with or be in activities with each child (e.g., Ladd, 1981; Oden & Asher, 1977; Parker & Asher, 1993). Research reveals that children's sociometric status is fairly stable and that children who are highly popular or rejected are more likely than other children to maintain their sociometric status over time (Coie & Dodge, 1983; Newcomb & Bukowski, 1984; Parke et al., 1997).

Much of the research on sociometric rejection in childhood has focused on trying to delineate the behavioral characteristics that lead certain children to be rejected by their peers (see Asher & Coie, 1990, and Rubin et al., 1998, for reviews). This line of inquiry has been productive, leading to an understanding of the behavioral characteristics associated with peer acceptance versus rejection. These characteristics include prosocial behavior, aggression, disruptiveness, withdrawal, submissiveness, sense of humor, and academic and athletic competence. Research on the behavioral correlates of sociometric status has also led to the development of promising behavioral intervention strategies aimed at helping children who have serious peer relationship problems (for reviews, see Asher, Parker, & Walker, 1996; Coie & Koeppl, 1990).

Interestingly, despite its long history, relatively little of the behavioral research on peer rejection has focused on how peers actually treat rejected children. As a result, we need to know far more about how peer rejection as measured sociometrically is associated with overt behavioral rejection. Sociometric rejection is usually operationalized as a sociometric score substantially below the average for the group. One could argue that even though certain children receive relatively low ratings from peers on sociometric measures, their everyday experiences are not necessarily negative. More direct evidence is needed to make this inference. Especially helpful would be direct observations of the day-to-day experiences of children with their peers.

Our goal in this chapter is to lay the foundation for future research on behavioral manifestations of rejection by presenting an empirically derived taxonomy of the types of rejection that children experience in their everyday lives at school. We created the taxonomy by recording and content-analyzing children's conversations in the less formal and less closely supervised contexts of school, including the playground, the lunchroom, and physical education classes. We can envision the taxonomy used as the basis for a behavioral coding system of rejection (please contact the authors for a preliminary version of such a system). We also anticipate that the taxonomy could be used to develop self-report or peer assessment measures of rejection experiences, or to design studies in which children respond to contrived or hypothetical situations in which rejection occurs (see Erdley, Cain, Loomis, Dumas-Hines, & Dweck, 1997; Goetz & Dweck, 1980, for examples).

Our chapter is organized as follows. In the first major section, we briefly summarize prior studies that suggest that sociometric rejection is indeed often accompanied by overt rejection. These include studies of loneliness in childhood, observational studies of children's overt behavior toward one another, and studies that rely on peer assessment and self-report methods to learn about victimization and relational aggression. In the second major section, we describe our study of children's social lives at school and introduce a taxonomy of 32 different types of rejection. Each type of rejection is illustrated with a transcript from the conversations we recorded. Some of the 32 categories of rejection were anticipated based on prior research, whereas others were generated by watching the 200 hours of audio-video material we collected. We conclude the chapter with speculations about individual differences in how children respond to rejection and about the factors that might intensify or mitigate the effects of a particular rejection episode.

Prior Research on Rejection Experiences

Research on the connections between sociometric status and children's feelings of well-being suggest that rejected children are treated negatively by their peers. Peer rejection in childhood has been associated with such internalizing problems as depression (e.g., Cole & Carpentieri, 1990), low self-esteem (e.g., Patterson, Kupersmidt, & Griesler, 1990), social anxiety (e.g., Franke & Hymel, 1984), and loneliness. Of these problems, loneliness has received the greatest attention. Research shows that, at various age levels, children's feelings of loneliness are associated with their degree of acceptance by peers. Children rejected by their peers have been found to be more lonely than other children in early adolescence (Parkhurst & Asher, 1992), middle childhood (Asher, Hymel, & Renshaw, 1984; Asher & Wheeler, 1985; Boivin & Hymel, 1997; Crick & Ladd, 1993), and even as early as kindergarten and first grade (Cassidy & Asher, 1992).

These findings about the effects of rejection on children's feelings of well-being imply that children must be experiencing rejection in their everyday lives. They do not, however, tell us about the actual kinds of rejection children are experiencing. A relatively small number of observational studies, focused primarily on how rejected children behave toward others, also provide information about how peers treat rejected children. In an influential study, Gottman, Gonso, and Rasmussen (1975) compared third- and fourth-grade children at different levels of popularity on several dimensions pertaining to their social competence and their interactions with peers. One aspect of this study involved observing children's interactions in the classroom during lectures and small-group activities, in physical education class, and at recess. The more unpopular children received less positive reinforcement from their peers than did other children. For example, they were less likely to receive verbal approval or praise from their peers or to have their peers comply with their requests.

Several years later, a few additional studies also addressed rejected children's experiences with peers in natural settings. In one of these studies, fifth-grade children were observed in the classroom and on the playground (Dodge, Coie, & Brakke, 1982). Results indicated that children more frequently refused rejected children's prosocial approaches (e.g., asking another child to play) than those made by better-liked children. In another study (Putallaz & Wasserman, 1989), in which third- and fifth-grade children were observed on the playground, particular attention was paid to whether the children were successful in joining groups of peers. Compared to well-accepted children, rejected children were accepted less and ignored more when they were trying to enter a group of peers. Also, they were not able to sustain their interaction with a group over as long a period of time as were better-accepted children. Consistent with this finding, in another study (Ladd, 1983) in which third- through sixth-grade children were observed on the playground, rejected children spent less time in social interaction with peers than did better-accepted children. Perhaps rejected children's social interactions with peers were more limited because rejected children received negative treatment, such as being ignored or blatantly told to go away, that showed them they were not welcome.

Unpopular or rejected children's treatment by peers has also been examined in experimental settings (Coie, Dodge, Terry, & Wright, 1991; Putallaz, 1983; Putallaz & Gottman, 1981). In Putallaz and Gottman's research, children's sociometric status was related to how the children were treated when trying to join the ongoing interaction of a peer dyad. For example, in one study in which popular and unpopular children's attempts to enter a peer dyad were observed, popular children entered groups more quickly and with fewer entry bids than unpopular children. In contrast, unpopular children's entry bids were more frequently ignored than were those of popular children. In research by Coie et al., seven- to nine-year-old boys were observed in experimental play groups in a university laboratory. Each play group consisted of six boys from different schools who did not know each other prior to the play group experience. In this study, rejected boys were more likely than other children to be the targets of instrumental aggression, such as being pushed away by a child who wanted access to a toy or game.

The growing body of literature on peer victimization also suggests what rejected children's day-to-day experiences are like. Victimization is a type of peer maltreatment in which peers consistently target a particular child for aggression (see Kochenderfer & Ladd, 1996; Perry, Kusel, & Perry, 1988). Children who are rejected by their classmates are more likely than other children to be victimized, whether victimization is assessed using self-report (Ladd, Kochenderfer, & Coleman, 1997) or peer assessment methods (Perry et al., 1988). Examination of the items on self-report and peer assessment measures of victimization illustrates the types of behaviors that victimization entails. Some items focus on verbal victimization, such as the self-report item, "Does anyone in your class ever say mean things to you at school?" (Kochenderfer & Ladd, 1996). Some items focus on physical victimization, such as the peer assessment item asking children to nominate their classmates who "get beat up" (Perry et al., 1998). Additionally, some items are ambiguous in terms of the specific physical or verbal acts involved in the victimization, such as the self-report item, "How often have you been bullied at school?" (Olweus, 1991).

Research on "relational aggression" also suggests the types of experiences rejected children have with their peers. Relational aggression involves damaging (or attempting to damage) another person's relationships or someone's feelings of inclusion in the group (see Crick et al., 1999, for a review). Relational aggression has most frequently been studied using peer-report measures (e.g., Crick, 1995; Crick, Casas, & Mosher, 1997; Crick & Grotpeter, 1995), which assess how often children engage in behaviors such as keeping other children out of their group of friends, ignoring other children as a way of expressing anger, and telling other children that they will not be friends with them anymore unless they comply with a request. Children who are sociometrically rejected by their peers are more likely than other children to be frequent victims of relational aggression (Crick & Grotpeter, 1996).

A Taxonomy of Peer Rejection Experiences

The few relevant observational studies, the research on victimization, and the research on relational aggression help us to imagine daily life for children who are disliked by their peers. They receive less positive peer treatment than their better-liked classmates, and they are often the targets of physical and verbal victimization and relational aggression. Although we could use the studies described above to anticipate types of rejection (e.g., verbal aggression, physical aggression, ignoring), our expectation in conducting our observational study was that doing extensive observations over virtually an entire school year and using audio and video recording in less formal and less highly supervised school settings would reveal additional types of rejection that children encounter in their day-to-day lives. Indeed, by developing the taxonomy based on our observations, we discovered ways in which children reject one another beyond those described in earlier work.

In this section we describe our observations and the different types of rejection we identified. The children who participated in our observational research were from a public elementary school in a Midwestern community.

The school included kindergarten through sixth-grade children. The total school population was approximately 360 children and the average class size approximately 25 students. The 35 "focal" children we intensively observed were in third through sixth grade. This sample included 22 children in regular education classrooms and 13 children with mild mental retardation who were in special education classrooms for most of the school day and "mainstreamed" in regular education classrooms for classes such as art, music, library, and physical education. Half of the focal regular education students were sociometrically rejected, and half were average in sociometric status. We identified a rejected child in each of 11 different classrooms and then randomly picked an average sociometric status child from the same room of the same gender and race. The 13 children with mild mental retardation constituted the majority of the third- through sixth-grade children in the school with mental retardation.

To obtain a comprehensive picture of children's experiences, we observed each focal child in multiple school settings, including three separate occasions in the lunchroom and at recess and twice in physical education classes. Each observational session was 30–60 minutes long, resulting in approximately 6 hours of observational data for each child, for a total of more than 200 hours of observational data for the entire sample. Observing children in relatively unstructured school settings such as these presents several challenges (Asher & Gabriel, 1993; Pepler & Craig, 1995). If the observer is close enough to hear children's conversations, there is the risk of making children self-conscious about being observed; in any case it is not possible to write down everything that the child says or that others say to the child. Furthermore, children often talk quietly, even whisper, thereby making it very difficult to hear even at close range, especially in relatively noisy settings such as the lunchroom, playground, or gymnasium.

To meet these challenges, we used a wireless transmission system; children wore a small, lightweight lavaliere microphone and pocket transmitter while they were being observed. The microphone was clipped to the child's collar and the transmitter was contained in a small pouch on a belt fastened around the child's waist. The observer wore a backpack containing the necessary receiving equipment, including a battery pack and a specially adapted audio receiver. In lunch, recess, and physical education, we used a video camera to record children's behavior in sync with the audio recording of their speech. In classroom settings where videotaping would have been more intrusive, the observer recorded children's behavior "live," in sync with the audio recording of their speech.

Children wearing the microphone and transmitter were able to move about freely, since the devices weighed only seven ounces and no wires connected the child and the observer. The audiovisual technology we employed solved the problem of recording conversation and proved to be quite unobtrusive, for the observer could be as far as 300 feet away from the child wearing the microphone and transmitter. The observer wore a small "bug in the ear" earphone that carried sound from the receiving equipment, enabling the observer to hear the children's conversations. Despite their effectiveness, wireless transmission systems have been used infrequently in peer relations research. Such systems have been used in a few studies, including work on developmentally delayed boys' play (Guralnick & Groom, 1987), gender differences in peer conflicts (Sheldon, 1990), and aggressive behavior on the playground (Pepler & Craig, 1995).

Our observations began in October of the school year and ended in early June, and the observer was at the school every day from the opening to the closing bells. In conducting this research, an initial period of acclimation was necessary to habituate the children, their teachers, and other school staff to the observer and the recording technology. Thus, the observer spent 3 weeks at the school before beginning formal observations. This time was spent in pilot observations, learning the school layout and routines, meeting teachers and other school staff, and learning the names of all 287 third- through sixth-grade children at the school, as well as the names of all of the teachers and school staff (e.g., playground and lunchroom aides).

With our observational protocol, children were observed in the same setting no more than once per week, and at least one day elapsed between successive observational sessions with the same child. An observational schedule was constructed in advance, so that each of the children was observed two or more times in each of the settings over the course of the school year. Observations of a particular child were initiated, with the child's permission, when an activity such as lunch or recess began. These observations of a particular child ended when the activity concluded.

Following completion of the data collection, the children's conversations were transcribed verbatim from each of the videotaped observations, allowing us to attend to the details of children's conversations. The transcriber also noted important nonverbal behavior, such as behavior that was important for understanding the conversation (e.g., a child pointing to a classmate to signify whom he is talking about) or behavior that was itself a rejection (e.g., hitting). The transcription task required about 20 hours for each hour of tape, mainly because in the lunchroom, at recess, and in physical education class, several children often spoke at the same time and there was background noise as well. Approximately 150 children were in the lunchroom and recess settings at any one time, whereas about 25 children were present in physical education at one time. A densely layered audio-video recording of children's conversations resulted, which, while rich in detail, was also time-consuming to transcribe. The observer for the entire school year (Sonda W. Gabriel) was best able to accurately transcribe because she had heard the conversations as they took place. As a result, although multiple transcribers worked on this project, she produced or double-checked each transcript for accuracy.

We do not view our set of 32 categories as the full panoply of all types of rejection. Research with other samples, age levels, and cultures would likely reveal additional rejection types. Nonetheless, the rejection behaviors we observed were surprisingly varied. Some rejection behaviors were explicit and overt. Children could, for instance, loudly refuse to allow a child to sit at a particular lunch table, publicly insult the child, and convince other children not to let the child sit with them. Other rejection behaviors were more subtle, generally mild, and sometimes ambiguous. Rejection behaviors could also be public or private. For example, a child could insult a peer at recess with a crowd of children as an audience. Other rejection behaviors, however, were witnessed only by the researcher. Rejections also varied in terms of duration, some quick and done only once. For example, a child could walk past another child, punch the child in the back, say something mean, and then just keep walking. Other rejections lasted longer. In addition, rejection behaviors varied in their creativity. Some rejection behaviors were standard, such as hitting or calling names; others were less common. For instance, children relayed negative messages from other children or publicly reminisced about and repeated a form of rejection the child had previously endured. Finally, children displayed different numbers of rejection behaviors in a single episode. For example, verbal aggression and physical aggression often co-occurred.

In addition, rejections differed in severity. Several factors discussed above are related to the severity of the rejection. For example, rejections that were explicit and overt, public, and lengthy probably felt especially severe to the rejected child. We defined rejection broadly in terms of the severity of the rejection. Some behaviors that we describe (e.g., hitting) are clearly rejecting. Others (e.g., refusing to give a child a bite of a sandwich) are less severe and, therefore, more ambiguous. In recent work, Leary and colleagues (Leary, Springer, Negel, Ansell, & Evans, 1998; Leary et al., chapter 6, this volume) have introduced the construct of relational devaluation, which refers to an individual's perception that a relationship partner does not value the relationship to the same extent that he or she does. When a friend refuses to give a child a bite of a sandwich, for instance, the child might think that the friend would rather risk hurting the child's feelings than part with a small piece of the sandwich. Although the rejection types in our taxonomy range from rather mild to very severe, in each type it is reasonable to expect that the rejecter's behavior indicates to the rejected child that their relationship is not highly valued.

We have grouped our 32 rejection types into six major categories: Excluding and Terminating Interaction, Denial of Access, Aggression, Dominance, Moral Disapproval, and Involving a Third Party. The following six subsections describe each of the major categories as well as the specific rejection types in that category. We also present transcripts of conversation to illustrate the different types of rejection. In presenting conversation we have changed real names to pseudonyms designed to communicate accurate information about gender and, as much as possible, ethnicity. In our notation system, a hyphen distinguishes the speaker of an utterance from the listener(s).

Excluding and Terminating Interaction

The six rejection types in this category all involve excluding a child from the peer group or terminating interaction with a child. These behaviors are intended to make it clear to a child that he or she is not accepted by the other person or by the group.

Leaving.   The first rejection type in this category involves a child leaving another who presumably does not wish for the interaction to be terminated. In this example, Alice, Jessica, and Amy leave Janine after announcing that they are not going to play with her. This episode occurred at lunch time and seemed to be in retaliation for Janine becoming angry at these girls earlier during the lunch period. Janine had been talking about how "you need to have a daddy to make a baby" and repeatedly saying the word "sperm." The other girls had become angry at Janine for using that word, and Janine had then gotten angry in turn, saying that she was going to "bring a big bag of candy" to the school tomorrow and not give any to the girls.

> Alice-Jessica, Amy, Janine: All right now. Are we gonna play with Janine today?
>
> Amy-Alice, Jessica, Janine: No.
>
> Jessica-Alice, Amy, Janine: And maybe not tomorrow either.
>
> Amy-Alice, Jessica, Janine: We're not gonna play with her *ever.*
>
> (All the girls leave Janine; she sits for a while by herself.)

Refusal of offer.   This rejection involves a child refusing an offer made by another child, such as an offer to play, an offer of assistance, or an offer of resources. In the following example, Scott rejects Sandra's offer of candy. Scott was diagnosed as learning disabled and hyperactive, and he often interacted with children with mental retardation, including Sandra.

> Sandra-Scott: Scott. Scott. Scott! Here's a piece of candy. Here.
>
> Scott-Sandra: I don't care (Scott doesn't take the candy).

Sending away.   In this type of rejection, a child is told directly to leave a peer group or is nonverbally chased or directed away. In this episode, Carol sends Darlene, Vicky, and Chiquita away when they try to join a Red Rover game at recess. Darlene, Vicky, and Chiquita were all children with mild mental retardation who rarely attempted to join games with regular education children. They may have attempted it in this case because one of the teachers had organized the game and was one of the players.

> Carol-Darlene, Vicky, Chiquita: Get away from me, you too, get away. Get away!! (Carol screams this; other children turn to look).
>
> (Vicky, Darlene, and Chiquita back away and watch the other children play.)

Darlene-Vicky, Chiquita: No, we don't ever get to play.

The girls were eventually able to participate in the Red Rover game, after asking the teacher if they could play.

Expressing dislike or nonrelationship.   This form of rejection involves a child telling a peer directly that either the child does not like the peer or the child does not have a relationship with the peer. Examples are given to represent both the case of expressing dislike and the case of expressing nonrelationship. The first episode is an example of expressing dislike. In this example, Austin chooses a girl in the class to get the next turn in physical education class rather than choosing one of his male friends, Paul, Ronald, or Keith, each of whom had wanted Austin to choose him. In this example, Keith rejects Austin by expressing dislike.

Paul-Austin: And I picked you?

Ronald-Austin: Oh Aus-tin (Ronald lightly hits Austin's arm as he sits back down).

Keith-Austin: I don't like you.

(A 10-second pause follows.)

Keith-Austin: I don't like you anymore.

(A few minutes later, Keith deliberately kicks Austin in the leg.)

The next example involves a child expressing a nonrelationship. In this example, Belinda has become upset with her cousin, Anne, and retaliates by denying their relationship and claiming a (fictive) relationship with another child.

Belinda-Anne: You're not my cousin no more.

Anne-Belinda: Yes I am.

Belinda-Anne, Claudia: She's my cousin (referring to Claudia) and not you!

Ignoring.   This type of rejection occurs when one child intentionally ignores another child's comments or behaviors. In the following episode, Tommy has been playing basketball and Kathleen was watching and cheering for him. Tommy ignores Kathleen as he is leaving the court.

Kathleen-Tommy: All right, Tommy. Yeah. Gimme a five.

(Tommy walks by her without giving her five.)

Ignoring content.   In this rejection type, the rejecting child ignores the content of what the peer is saying, rather than completely ignoring the child. In the following example, Chiquita is in the doorway of the lunchroom as if she might leave. When Claudia approaches her and asks where she is going, Chiquita is preoccupied with where her friend, Belinda, is and does not answer.

Claudia-Chiquita: Where are you goin'?

Chiquita-Claudia: Where Belinda at?

Denial of Access

Children often depend on each other for access to various types of resources at school. For example, children depend on their peers for companionship and for shared access to resources, such as sports equipment. Children also rely on their peers for assistance, such as when they are having trouble with a class assignment or have lost the lunch they brought from home. Peers also can provide important information, such as whether the children are allowed to play on the jungle gym at recess or details about what a classmate missed due to an absence. A major form of rejection is to refuse access to these important resources. We identified eight types of rejection in this category.

Denial of access to self or self and others.   Children can deny a peer access to themselves and their playmates in many ways. For instance, they may refuse to let a peer join a kickball game or walk around with them on the playground, or attempt to prevent them from joining their team in physical education class. In the following example, Ellen is being denied access to a group of girls, part of a clique who called themselves the "Sugarbears" (our pseudonym for the name they called themselves). In this episode, Jodie will not let Ellen join the Sugarbears despite Ellen's repeated offers to become the club's pet. Jodie and Ellen were both disliked by many members of their class. Jodie is herself a marginal member of the Sugarbears and may feel threatened by Ellen's bid for inclusion.

Jodie-Joan, Gail, Ellen: Ellen is *not* in the club.

Jodie-Ellen: You aren't, aren't in the club.

(Ellen suggests to Melanie that she could be the club's dog.)

Jodie-Ellen, Melanie: No, we already have a dog.

Ellen-Jodie, Joan: I'll be the cat, I'll be the bunny.

Jodie-Ellen: No, we don't—

Joan-Jodie, Ellen: We don't need her.

Jodie-Ellen: Ellen you can't be our pet because we have just everything, there's every kind of pet.

Denial of access to other.   This rejection type involves denying a peer access to a third child. The following example involves Kate and Fran, who were best friends and who were both very possessive and jealous of the other, often accusing other girls of trying to "steal" their friend. Their friendship was also marked by many arguments and considerable strife. After their arguments, they would often go through periods of not speaking to one another before patching things up. In this episode, another girl in the class, Marcy, had thought that Fran wouldn't be able to play the games in physical education class that day because Fran was wearing a dress. When Marcy sees that Fran is playing, she tries to talk to Fran and is denied access to Fran by Kate.

Marcy-Fran: Oh, Fran, I thought you couldn't play.

Fran-Marcy: I didn't plan to do it.

Marcy-Fran: Fran.

(Kate overhears this conversation and comes over.)

Kate-Marcy, Fran: If she can or can't it's none of your business.

Denial of access to resources.   Children have access to physical resources that may be desired by their peers. This type of rejection involves refusing to grant a peer access to a desired object and often occurred at lunch when children asked others for samples of their lunches. In a previous episode, Ellen's disappointment at not being allowed in the Sugarbears was illustrated. In this example of *denial of access to resources,* Jodie refuses to share her Goldfish Crackers (a popular brand among children) with Ellen, using as a justification that Ellen is not a Sugerbear.

(Jodie had been passing out Goldfish Crackers to several of her classmates.)

Ellen-Jodie: I like Goldfish, can I have some too?

Jodie-Tracy (a child near Ellen): I'll give *you* a whole handful.

Jodie-Ellen: No.

Ellen-Jodie: Just one?

Jodie-Ellen: No.

Ellen-Jodie: You don't like me.

Jodie-Ellen: You're not in the Sugarbears.

Taking object or location away.   Children also reject their peers by taking resources away from children who already are in possession of them or by usurping children's locations, such as taking their lunch seat or their place on the swings. Two examples are given to illustrate, first, a rejection in which an object is taken away and, second, a rejection in which a location is taken away. In the first episode, Teresa is trying to take away the scooter that Jackee (her best friend) is playing on during physical education class. In a school with a small percentage of students of color, Teresa and Jackee were unusual in that they were cross-race best friends. They lived in the same trailer park, and that may have been the context for their initial friendship formation. Both girls also had similar, highly assertive, and even sometimes aggressive styles of interaction.

Teresa-Jackee: Jackee, get off (Jackee continues rolling around on the scooter).

Teresa-Jackee: Jackee, get your butt off.

(Teresa tries to pull Jackee off.)

Jackee-Teresa: You can't, you can't make me.

Teresa-Jackee: Get your butt off. Jackee, get off.

(Eventually, Jackee does get off the scooter.)

In the next example of this rejection type, Tawnika takes Tommy's location on the basketball court away from him. Tawnika was a tall and quite forceful girl who did not hesitate to use her size and personality to her advantage with both boys and girls, as in the following episode with Tommy.

Tawnika-Tommy: You have to move Tommy (Tawnika and some other girls, including Lynne, Maggie, and Nora are playing basketball on the court behind Tommy and his group).

Tommy-Tawnika: I *have* to be on this line.

Tawnika-Tommy: You're on our side, we're playin' a game.

(Tawnika moves closer to Tommy.)

Tommy-Tawnika: I'm on this line.

Tawnika-Tommy: No you're not, you're across that line.

(Tawnika shoves Tommy to make him move over the line.)

Assign less desirable resource or position.   The next type of rejection involves giving a peer an object of less value than that received by other children, such as giving a child the only broken cookie or assigning a child an unwanted position in a game or group. The first example illustrates assigning a less desirable resource, and the second illustrates assigning a less desirable position. In the following episode involving the distribution of resources, Vicky, Stephanie, Donna, and Babette are on the playground at recess. Stephanie has some gummy worms that she is sharing with the girls.

Vicky-Stephanie: God. God, they got bigger pieces than me (Stephanie is dividing the candy up among the girls).

Vicky-Stephanie: I only got little pieces.

The next episode illustrates assigning a less desirable position. Barry and Duane were playing ball at recess and taking turns pitching when Barry tells Duane he can no longer pitch.

Duane-Barry: Barry, it's my turn to pitch.

Barry-Duane: I'm sorry, Duane, you screwed up bad.

Duane-Barry: Ma-an!

Barry-Duane: You screw up too bad.

Duane-Barry: Just because I screw up doesn't mean I can't pitch (Barry pitches).

Denial of access to information.   This rejection type involves refusing to tell a child something he or she wants to know. In the following example, Bill refuses to answer Rose's question. Bill and Rose are both in the lunch line, waiting to get their lunch, when Bill first pretends to throw his new sunglasses on the floor and then accuses Rose of wanting to step on them.

Bill-Rose: Step on 'em, you'd be buyin' me another one, at the gas station.

Bill-Rose: Because I bought 'em at the gas station.

Rose-Bill: What gas station?

Bill-Rose: I ain't tellin'.

Denial of access to assistance.   This rejection type involves refusing to help a child who needs assistance. Children may encounter difficult tasks throughout the day, such as getting stuck on a math problem, having too many items to carry, or losing a homework assignment. In such cases they could benefit from help from a peer. In the following example of this rejection type, Belinda is denied access to assistance in opening her milk carton. Belinda and Vicky are both children with mild mental retardation. Belinda often asked other children for help and tattled on them to the teacher if they did not comply with her requests.

Belinda-Vicky: Please, Vicky, will you open this? (Vicky has already opened her own milk carton successfully).

Vicky-Belinda: Nope (Belinda pouts, then raises her hand to request help from one of the lunch ladies).

Refusal to comply.   In this type of rejection, the rejecter is denying the peer access to his or her cooperation. A refusal to comply with a request is a rejection when the request is reasonable, there is no clear basis for the child to refuse to comply, and the refusal is made in a hostile tone of voice. These rejections often seem more mild when they are read in a transcript than when they are seen on a videotape or in person, because the hostility of the tone of voice cannot be easily conveyed by a transcript. In the following example of *refusal to comply,* Vicky and Chiquita are playing on the tire swing, and Chiquita is standing in the middle of the swing.

Vicky-Chiquita: Siddown.

Chiquita-Vicky: I don't have to! (Chiquita leans toward Vicky when she says this and wiggles her shoulders to emphasize her words).

Aggression

Aggression is one of the few types of rejection that has received extensive attention in the peer relations literature. Studies of aggression have generally focused on physical aggression, verbal aggression, such as name-calling and insults, and, more recently, relational aggression (see Coie & Dodge, 1998, for a review). In our observations, aggression took diverse forms, including the types previously studied and a few that have not received much attention in past research. We identified nine distinct forms of rejection within the broader category of aggression.

Physical aggression.   The first rejection type involves a child physically attacking another child. Rough and tumble play accompanied by positive affect was not considered to be rejection. In the following example, Marjorie and some of the other Sugarbears are playing four-square together at recess. As in two previous examples, Ellen is rejected by this group of girls. In this example, Ellen is trying to join the game by inviting the other girls to hit her with the ball.

> Ellen-Marjorie: You guys've gotta hit my buttly (Ellen is calling her buttocks her "buttly").
>
> Marjorie-Ellen: We're not hitting your stupid buttly.
>
> Ellen-Marjorie: Hit my buttly.
>
> Marjorie-Ellen: We're not hitting it, Ellen. Now go and play with your own friends (Marjorie hits Ellen on the buttocks with her fist and then slaps her on the arm.)
>
> Ellen-Marjorie: You said you weren't hitting my buttly, you just did.
>
> Marjorie-Ellen: Do you want this in your face? If you don't shut up I am going to put it in (Marjorie draws the ball back suddenly as if preparing to throw it at Ellen's face.)

Flicking or throwing.   The next type of aggression involves flicking or throwing an object at a child (e.g., a paper, sweatshirt, food item), which, although annoying, is unlikely to actually do any physical damage. In this example, Scott and Bill have been arguing at the lunch table.

> Scott-Bill: Let's see, let's see you shut your mouth (Scott flicks crumbs across the table toward Bill).

Damaging possession of child.   This rejection type involves a child deliberately damaging a possession that belongs to a peer, for instance, breaking another child's pencil or scribbling on his homework. In the following example, Sam and Conrad, who are best friends, have been eating lunch together, along with several other boys from their class. Conrad has been repeatedly calling out, to one in particular, that he wants to trade his school lunch (pizza) with someone.

> Sam-Conrad: You're too late, it's ugh, ughh (Sam grabs Conrad's pizza and then wipes his hands on Conrad's jacket).
>
> Conrad-Sam: Fall out!

Sam-Conrad: Goobert!

Conrad-Sam: Whaah, whaah! (Conrad squawks in protest).

Sam-Conrad: Goobert! Goobert! (Sam wipes pizza on Conrad's jeans).

Half an hour later, as Sam and Conrad are going back in the school building after recess, Conrad points out to Sam the pizza stain on his jacket ("It's all over my new jacket").

Gestural aggression.   The next type of rejection involves any type of hostile gesture. This can include, for instance, shaking a fist at or giving a child "the finger." In the example below Josie, Ginny, Marcy, Fran, Connie, and Allison have been eating their lunch together and discussing their plans for the weekend, which include a sleep-over at one girl's house. Ginny (a marginalized member of this group) becomes confused about the plans, and Fran and Josie begin shouting at her, followed by gestural aggression from Marcy.

Fran-Ginny: Get it through your head, Ginny!

Josie-Ginny, Fran: Yeah, get it through your thick, greasy, poopy-head! (Josie giggles). (Marcy hears this remark, forms her hand into a gun shape, and pretends to "shoot" Ginny in the head and then recoil from the shot. Marcy then looks at Fran and Josie, seemingly for their approval, and smiles.)

Verbal aggression.   This rejection type consists of name calling and other verbal insults. This includes insulting the characteristics of another child, such as the child's appearance, behaviors, possessions, ideas, speech, or abilities. In the following episode, Tommy insults three different children in just a few minutes and is himself insulted by one of them in turn.

(Roy tries to tag Tommy and misses as Tommy walks by him in the lunchroom.)

Roy-Tommy: Hey.

Tommy-Roy: You can't tag a fly.

Roy-Tommy: You're crap. You can't.

Tommy-Roy: You couldn't either.

Ginny-Tommy: Tommy (Ginny is sitting on the bench next to Tommy's table).

Tommy-Ginny: You look like a rat, huh-huh.

Tommy-Bill: Bill, you know what you got in your brain? A load of bricks.

Insulting friends and kin.   This rejection type involves making negative comments about a child's friends or relatives rather than insulting the child directly. One example involves insulting friends, and another example involves insulting kin. In the first example, Viola insults Sam's choice of friends.

> Viola-Sam: Your friends. Who you call pal makes me sick, I don't know.
>
> (Viola shakes her head disapprovingly and returns to a game she is playing.)

In this example, several girls are arguing about who among them picks their noses. Vicky then insults Belinda's mother by claiming that she picks her nose.

> Vicky-Belinda: Nuh-uh you pick your nose and eat them, all the time, especially your mom, we saw her once.
>
> Belinda-Vicky: Oh baloney, my mom does not pick her nose!
>
> Vicky-Belinda: Yes she does, uuh—
>
> Belinda-Vicky: Shut up! I mean it!! (Belinda is very upset).

Mocking or taunting.   In this rejection type, children mock a peer's characteristics. This rejection type is quite different from *verbal aggression* in that the insults are delivered with sarcasm or in a humorous way intended to be amusing to other children who may be present to witness the rejection. For instance, some cases of *mocking or taunting* involve a child imitating another child's verbal or nonverbal behaviors. Children also used sarcasm to taunt another child, as is illustrated by the following example. Connie had been trying to keep Eric off the tire swing by using the rule that only a certain number of children were allowed on the tire swing at one time. Connie gets off the swing, Eric gets on, and Connie is then not allowed back on the swing for this reason. Eric sarcastically expresses sympathy for her.

> Eric-Connie: Poor little Connie. Got backfired by her ugly rule.
>
> Connie-Eric: Shut up Eric (Connie shoves Eric's leg).
>
> Eric-Connie: Poor little Connie.
>
> Connie-Eric: Shut up! (Connie shoves Eric again).
>
> Eric-Connie: Oh-oh I got shoved, oh-oh-oh-oh. Eat your heart out.

Reminiscing/Repeating.   Here children reject a child for something the child has done in the past, rather than for a current action. The defining feature of this category is that the focal child has not engaged in any action in the present that is eliciting the rejection. Rather, children bring up something from the past and explicitly discuss it, as they once again reject a child. The following episode involves a child, Andrew, who used to bring hard-boiled eggs to school for his lunch. Other children teased Andrew intensely about bringing boiled eggs to school, and in this episode, Ted does so once again, even though Andrew no longer brings eggs for his lunch.

Ted-Andrew: Did you bring an egg today?

Andrew-Ted: Why you—(Ted laughs).

Ted-Andrew: Did you bring an egg today?

Ted-Andrew: Andrew, did you bring an egg today?

Andrew-Ted: That does it.

Ted-Andrew: Yaah (Andrew runs after Ted).

Ted-Andrew: You brought an egg today.

Andrew-Ted: Why you—

Ted-Andrew: You brought an egg today.

Andrew-Ted: You—(some running/chasing among these two and other students).

Ted-Andrew: Did you bring an egg Andrew? (Ted yells this as he is running past Andrew).

Andrew-Ted: Uhh uhh.

Ted-Andrew: Didn't you, you brought an egg? (Andrew shakes his head no).

Ted-Andrew: Yuh-huh. Yuh-huh. You brought an egg. A big one. A big egg, an egg. An egg. An egg. An egg, an egg!

(Ted is backing up while he is yelling this as Andrew walks toward him. This episode goes on for several minutes longer and eventually includes three other children teasing Andrew about eating eggs.)

Aversive noises.   The last type of aggression involves children making obnoxious vocalizations (not words) directed toward another child. In this example, Bill is standing in the lunch line waiting to get his lunch. Bill passes the time by making obnoxious noises, annoying Freddy, the boy standing next to him.

Bill-Freddy: Woo-woo-woo-woo-eee, woo-ooo-ooo-ooo, wee-eee-eee (Bill makes noises and wiggles his hips).

Freddy-Bill: Bill, shut up.

Bill-Freddy: Woo-woo-woo-woo, woo-woo-woo-woo-eee. Woo-woo-woo-woo-eee. Uh-uh-uh, uh-uh-uh, oh-oh-uh-uh, oh-oh-oh-oh. Yea-eah, ohh yea-eah (Bill makes suggestive noises and pelvic thrusting).

Freddy-Craig, Don, Bill: Bill is a retard (Freddy says this to two other boys nearby in the lunch line, and also to Bill).

Bill-Freddy: My baby be dancin' the funky, ooh-ooh-ooh (Bill sings, and Freddy makes a fist and shows it to Bill).

(Bill continues making the noises and singing, and Freddy repeats "Bill's a retard" several times.)

Dominance

This category includes two types of rejection that involve children attempting to make a peer submit to their demands or agree with their opinions.

Ordering.   The first rejection type, *ordering,* involves either telling a child to do something or to stop doing something. Children often tell a peer to do something or not do something in a nonrejecting manner. However, it takes the form of a rejection when the children are speaking in hostile tones of voice and are clearly trying to dominate the situation and the peer. In the following example, Marcy and Kate are trying to pick up the same bean bag in physical education class, and Marcy orders Kate to stop trying to get the bean bag.

Marcy-Kate: Kate! Stop it, you fool.

Contradicting.   In this type of rejection a child tells a peer that something the peer said was incorrect. Again, context is important for this behavior to be rejecting. The child's tone of voice must be hostile or angry. In the following example, Zack and Barry disagree about how many fouls their baseball team gets.

Zack-Barry: You guys only get one out because you've got (unintelligible).
Barry-Zack: No, we get two.
Zack-Barry: Bull!

Moral Disapproval

This category contains three types and includes rejection behaviors that are intended to express to the rejected child that the child's behaviors are unacceptable, will cause someone harm, or will lead to a deserved negative outcome for the child.

Moral disapproval.   In this category one child tells another that the child's words or behaviors are morally unacceptable. In the example below, Kate and Eric have both been playing around the tire swing, and Kate criticizes Eric's use of foul language.

Kate-Eric: You've already said the A word (Eric said "ass").
Eric-Kate: So?
Kate-Eric: That's naughty.

Blaming.   In the second rejection type in this category, one child blames another for something negative that has happened or could happen, either to the blaming child, the blamed child, or a third party. In this example of *blaming,* Delores and Barry (who were brother and sister) had collided in the lunchroom, spilling Barry's lunch tray. Although it was not clear to the observer that one child was more at fault than the other, Franklin, a bystander, blamed Delores.

Franklin-Delores: Now look what you've done. Now look what you've done, you fool!

Predicting negative outcomes.   In the final rejection type in this category, the rejecting child predicts that a negative outcome will result from another child's actions or statements. The following example involves Eric and several girls. Eric often annoys and picks on these girls, and in this episode the girls predict that his behavior will lead to negative outcomes when he goes to junior high school.

Allison-Eric: I'll tell you somethin' Eric, here and right now, here and now.

Eric-Allison: Oo-oo-ooo.

Allison-Eric: There's nothin' I can warn you about junior high, because you're gonna get your butt kicked between the shoulder blades.

Eric-Allison: I don't care.

Allison-Eric: And maybe shoved in a locker.

Eric-Allison: I don't care.

Josie-Eric: A great big old—

Kate-Eric: Yeah but—

Josie-Eric: And then I'll kick you right in the balls and maybe they'll fall off.

Eric-Josie: Holy moley.

Kate-Eric: Uh Eric—

Eric-Josie: Hey-hey-hey-hey, it looks like you already had it. Arrk, arrk, hey aw hell, I won't smart off, I don't smart off to no big kids (Eric is referring to Josie's being overweight; Eric laughs).

Josie-Eric: You're gonna get—

Kate-Eric: You'll get your head busted in a locker, you'll get slammed, you'll get tripped, you'll get anything.

Involving a Third Party

The four rejection types in this category each involve bringing one or more people into the rejection episode other than the rejecter and the child being rejected.

Telling authority.   This type of rejection involves one child telling an adult about another child's perceived inappropriate behavior. In this example, several children are playing on the tire swing, and the boys are pushing the swing higher than the girls want it to be pushed. One of the boys is Janine's brother, Vincent. Before Janine gets off the swing, she asks Vincent to stop pushing, a request he ignores. The swing does slow down enough, however, for Janine to get off.

> Janine: I'm telling (Janine says this very quietly as she gets off the swing).
>
> Janine-Bob: Get Miss Smith (student teacher). They're not supposed to push it. They're pushin' it too high, and everybody's screaming (Bob ignores Janine's request).
>
> Janine: Ow ooh. I'm telling. They ain't supposed to do that.
>
> Janine-Meryl: Where's Missus S—Miss Smith? (Janine sees Miss Smith and runs over to her).
>
> Janine-Miss Smith: They're pushing that thing, and they're not supposed to. And they're scaring everybody. They're—
>
> Miss Smith-Janine: What's goin' on?
>
> Janine-Miss Smith: They're, they're pushing it and they're not supposed to.

Praising a rejecter.   In this rejection type, a child praises, congratulates, or otherwise supports a rejection made by another child to a third child. In this example, Tommy congratulates Roy on the name he called Bill.

> Roy-Bill: Billy-willy.
>
> Tommy-Roy: Yeah, good one (Tommy laughs and claps his hands).

Relaying negative messages.   In this rejection type, one child serves as the messenger of a negative statement from another child. In this example, Janine had been quarreling with two girls, Amy and Jessica, during lunch and recess. Alice comes over to Janine to deliver a negative message from Amy and Jessica.

> Alice-Janine: Now I'm supposed to tell you to please kiss off.
>
> Janine-Alice: Huh?
>
> Alice-Janine: They told me to say to kiss off.
>
> Janine-Alice: Well tell them, rub their face in doo-doo. Tell 'em that.

Third party rejection.   Here a child makes negative comments about a child that, although they are ostensibly directed to a third party, are said in the vicinity of the child being rejected and are clearly intended to be heard by the rejected child. In this episode, several children, including Vicky and Belinda, are playing on the tire swing when Vicky starts saying negative things about Belinda to other children that Belinda is intended to hear.

Vicky-LaVondra: I want that gross girl off here (referring to Belinda).

(Belinda gets off for a couple of minutes and then returns.)

Vicky-Alice: Oh God! Stinky's on here again (referring to Belinda).

LaVondra-Vicky: Oh God look!

Vicky-Belinda: Booger-nose.

Alice-Vicky: Which one?

Vicky-Alice: The one in the blue coat. The one that's beside you.

Alice-Vicky: Belinda?

Vicky-Alice: Yeah, she picks her nose and eats 'em, all the time.

LaVondra-Vicky: And when it's cold out, when it's real cold outside the uh the green snot come out her nose and she usually licks it. And I wouldn't be sittin' by her if I was you (Alice quickly moves away from Belinda and LaVondra laughs).

Summary of Rejection Categories and Types

In this section, we have described the ways in which children were observed to reject one another at school. Table 5.1 presents a list of the six major rejection categories and the specific rejection types we included in each major category. A brief definition of each rejection type is also given. In the next section, we discuss why being a victim of rejection might have a more intense impact on the subjective well-being of some children than of others.

Speculations about Overt Rejection and Children's Emotional Well-Being

Earlier in this chapter we briefly summarized evidence that rejected children suffer from higher levels of loneliness than do other children. Although the greater loneliness of rejected children is evident across many studies, there is considerable variability in loneliness even within the rejected group (see Asher, Parkhurst, Hymel, & Williams, 1990). This variability may be partially due to differences in the extent to which rejected children are actually the recipients of overt rejection. For example, rejected children who are aggressive in their behavioral style report less loneliness than children who are withdrawn or submissive (Boivin, Thomassin, & Alain, 1989; Parkhurst & Asher, 1992; Williams & Asher, 1987). Perhaps the aggressive subgroup of rejected children is actually less likely to be overtly rejected by peers. Children may hesitate to treat negatively a child who has a reputation for being aggressive. Also, children who are aggressive are more likely to have friends and be part of a network (see Cairns, Cairns, Neckerman, Gest, & Gariepy, 1988) and therefore have protectors (see Hodges, Malone, & Perry, 1997).

Table 5.1 Summary of the 6 Major Rejection Categories
and the 32 Rejection Types

Type	Definition
Excluding and Terminating Interaction Category	
Leaving	Leaving a child who presumably does not want the interaction to be terminated
Refusal of Offer	Refusing an offer made by another child (e.g., an offer to play)
Sending Away	Telling a child to leave or nonverbally chasing/directing the child away
Expressing Dislike or Non-Relationship	Telling a child that the child is not liked or does not have a relationship (e.g., a friendship) with the rejecter
Ignoring	Intentionally ignoring a child's comments or behaviors
Ignoring Content	Ignoring the content of what a child is saying (i.e., responding to a child's comments by saying something irrelevant to the child's comments)
Denial of Access Category	
Denial of Access to Self or Self and Others	Refusing a child access to oneself or to oneself and one's playmates
Denial of Access to Other	Refusing a child access to a third child
Denial of Access to Resources	Refusing a child access to physical resources (e.g., games, toys, snacks)
Taking Object or Location Away	Taking resources away from a child who is already in possession of them or usurping a child's physical location
Assign Less Desirable Resource or Position	Giving a peer an object of less value than that received by other children
Denial of Access to Information	Refusing to tell a child something he or she wants to know
Denial of Access to Assistance	Refusing to help a child who is in need of assistance
Refusal to Comply	Denying a child access to one's cooperation

(continued)

Table 5.1 Continued

Type	Definition
Aggression Category	
Physical Aggression	Physically attacking a child
Flicking or Throwing	Flicking or throwing an object at a child (e.g., a paper, food item)
Damaging Possession of Child	Deliberately damaging a possession that belongs to a child
Gestural Aggression	Making a hostile gesture to a child (e.g., shaking a fist or giving "the finger")
Verbal Aggression	Calling a child names or verbally insulting a child's characteristics (e.g, appearance, behaviors, belongings)
Insulting Friends or Kin	Making negative comments about a child's friends or relatives
Mocking or Taunting	Mocking a child's characteristics with the use of sarcasm or humor
Reminiscing/Repeating	Talking about and/or repeating previous rejections the child has suffered
Aversive Noises	Directing obnoxious vocalizations (not words) toward a child
Dominance Category	
Ordering	Telling a child in a hostile tone to do something (or stop doing something)
Contradicting	Telling a child in a hostile tone that something the child said was incorrect
Moral Disapproval Category	
Moral Disapproval	Telling a child that the child's words or behaviors are morally unacceptable
Blaming	Blaming another child for something negative that has happened, or could happen to the blaming child, the blamed child, or a third party
Predicting Negative Outcomes	Predicting that a negative outcome for a child will result from the child's actions or statements

(*continued*)

Table 5.1 Continued

Type	Definition
Involving a Third Party Category	
Telling Authority	Telling an adult about another child's perceived inappropriate behavior
Praising a Rejecter	Praising, congratulating, or supporting a rejection made to a child by a third party
Relaying Negative Message	Serving as a messenger of a negative statement about a child from a third party
Third Party Rejection	Making negative comments about a child to a third party in the vicinity of the child being rejected (i.e., so the comments can be overheard by the rejected child)

Variability in rejected children's loneliness also may be due to factors other than the degree to which children are overtly rejected. In this section, we offer hypotheses about additional sources of individual differences in children's emotional responses to peer rejection, hypotheses suggested to us by prior literature and by observing children's reactions to rejection episodes. Some children seemed to brush off being rejected and carried on with their day relatively undisturbed. For other children, though, being a victim of rejection appeared to be extremely upsetting. Why might rejection affect some children more severely? We speculate that at least eight factors influence children's tendency to suffer emotionally as a result of rejection. These are (1) how the child responds to an action that is ambiguous with regard to its rejecting intent, (2) the consistency with which rejecting behaviors occur, (3) the identity of the rejecter, (4) whether the child has social support, (5) the child's tendency to ruminate or brood about rejection, (6) whether the child attributes rejection to internal or external casues, (7) the child's beliefs regarding whether children can improve at how well they get along with others, and (8) whether the rejected child behaves in ways likely to mitigate or exacerbate the rejection experience. We offer these hypotheses in the hope that future research not only will focus on specific types of rejection experiences but also on the reasons why children react so differently to the rejection they encounter.

Consider, first, the issue of whether a child perceives ambiguous behaviors as rejecting. We found that children frequently engaged in behaviors that seemed ambiguous regarding whether a rejection was intended. For example, *ignoring* is a rejection only if a child hears a peer and purposefully does not respond. In a noisy lunchroom, however, whether the child actually hears the peer is not always clear. A second example involves *refusal of offer*. If a girl offered a peer half a sandwich, for instance, and the peer said, "I don't want half of your sandwich," one interpretation is that the peer does not want to eat a sandwich. Another interpretation, however, is that the peer does not want half of *her* sandwich. A third example of ambiguity is when children trade insults. Occasionally two children who were friends made comments such as, "You *wish* you could play basketball like me." This situation became more complicated when one child moved from good-natured and playful insults to comments that could be construed as ill-intentioned *verbal aggression*. Determining where joking around ends and rejection begins can be very difficult.

Research indicates individual differences in the interpretation of ambiguous provocation situations (Dodge, 1980; Dodge & Frame, 1982; Steinberg & Dodge, 1983); likely there are also individual differences among children in the interpretation of ambiguous rejection behaviors. Recent research shows that some children are rejection-sensitive (see Downey, Khouri, & Feldman, 1997; Downey, Lebolt, Rincon, & Freitas, 1998), meaning that they are more likely than other children to expect to be rejected by their peers. Rejection-sensitive children may be especially likely to interpret an ambiguous behavior as rejection. In contrast, some children may be rather insensitive to social cues (see, for example, Zakriski & Coie, 1996) and may therefore be particularly unlikely to interpret ambiguous behaviors as rejecting. Although this insensitivity could buffer these children from distress in the short term, insensitivity to social cues could lead to more problematic peer relationships for them over time.

A second factor that could affect the severity of the impact of rejection on children is the consistency with which rejection occurs. Research indicates that children who are repeatedly rejected over grade levels report higher levels of loneliness than children who are rejected only in one school year (Renshaw & Brown, 1993). Children who have difficulty handling particular social situations, such as finding a seat at the lunch table or getting on a team in physical education class, may also find that they are consistently rejected in these situations. These rejections may be particularly distressing for the children because they trigger painful feelings from previous rejections in the same context. In addition, the children may begin to feel distressed in anticipation of the social situation. A social tasks perspective on social competence (Dodge, McClaskey, & Feldman, 1985; McFall, 1982) suggests that for many individuals particular tasks are especially challenging.

Third, the identity of the rejecter could moderate the impact of rejection on children's emotional well-being. In our observations, we found that some children who were best friends were nevertheless capable of rejecting each other, sometimes quite cruelly. A number of the children at the school where we conducted our research had siblings or other relatives with whom they interacted regularly at school, and some times these children rejected one another. This observation is consistent with the findings that some children are relationally aggressive in their friendships (Grotpeter & Crick, 1996) and in their sibling relationships (O'Brien & Crick, in preparation). Rejections that come from trusted allies, such as close friends or family members, likely would be particularly hurtful, compared to those from children who have a more casual relationship with the child they reject. This speculation is consistent with Parker and Asher's (1993) finding that children whose best friendships were characterized by higher levels of conflict and betrayal were more lonely than children whose best friendships had lower levels of conflict and betrayal. It is also consistent with Leary's point in chapter 6 that declines in perceived acceptance by a relationship partner are acutely felt.

A fourth factor that may influence rejection behaviors' effects on children's well-being is whether children have social support. Friends serve many important functions in children's lives (see Asher & Parker, 1989; Bukowski, Newcomb, & Hartup, 1996; Furman & Robbins, 1985; Hartup & Sancilio, 1986; Sullivan, 1953), including providing assistance and validation in response to problems and difficulties. There are many ways in which a child could help a friend who has recently been a victim of peer rejection (see Rose & Asher, 1999b). For instance, a child could discuss the rejection experience with the friend, express sympathy, or reassure the friend that upsetting interactions sometimes happen to everyone. The child could also engage in an enjoyable activity with the friend to distract the friend from painful feelings. If the child were present when the friend was rejected, the child could stand up for the friend, perhaps decreasing the duration or the level of hostility of the rejection. Recent evidence indicates that lacking a friend contributes to loneliness independently from being poorly accepted (see Parker, Saxon, Asher, & Kovacs, 1999, for a review). One reason for this finding may be that children without friends are less likely to receive these forms of social support and, therefore, might suffer more than their befriended peers in response to rejection behaviors from peers.

A fifth factor that could affect the influence of rejecting behaviors on children's well-being is whether the children have a tendency to ruminate or brood about rejection experiences. Rejection occurred fairly frequently in our observations, and even a well-liked and socially competent child was unlikely to avoid entirely being a recipient of some form of rejection. Some children, after being rejected, may think about the rejection for days or weeks afterward. Rumination about upsetting events has been found to be linked to depression (e.g., Nolen-Hoeksema, Parker, & Larson, 1994); children who ruminate about painful experiences with peers might be more distressed than other children experiencing the same type of rejecting behavior.

A sixth factor affecting the impact of rejection behaviors involves the type of attributions that the child makes for the rejecter's behavior. Research on attributions and emotions in academic contexts indicates more negative emotional outcomes for individuals who attribute academic failure to internal causes, such as ability, than for those who attribute failure to external causes, such as the teacher writing an unfair test (e.g., Weiner, 1979; Weiner, Russell, & Lerman, 1979). Similarly, children who consistently attribute peers' rejection behaviors to internal causes (e.g., the rejection as a response to something that they did or said) would probably suffer more in response to rejection than children who attribute peers' rejection behaviors to external causes (e.g., the rejecter as a hateful child). Interestingly, in trying to comfort children who have been victims of rejection, some parents (and perhaps teachers) may tell children that the rejecting child is acting out of his or her own unhappiness or envy or that the rejecter has no manners and does not know how to get along well with others. For children who are generally well-liked and encounter rejection rarely, this type of comfort from adults may be relevant and helpful.

Two additional factors that could moderate how severely rejection influences children's emotional well-being are suggested by research on achievement motivation by Dweck and Erdley and their colleagues. Most research on achievement motivation has focused on children's beliefs and goals in response to academic failure situations (see Dweck & Leggett, 1988, for a review); however, the social domain has also received increasing attention (Benenson & Dweck, 1986; Erdley & Dweck, 1993; Erdley et al., 1997; Goetz & Dweck, 1980). These researchers hypothesize that some children are entity theorists (they think that children's abilities or personalities cannot be changed), whereas other children are incremental theorists (they think that children's abilities or personalities can improve) (e.g., Bempechat, London, & Dweck, 1991; Cain & Dweck, 1995). In one study in the social domain (Erdley & Dweck, 1993), entity theorists were more likely than incremental theorists to interpret another child's behavior as a behavioral trait that would be consistent over time. If entity theorists think about what happens to them as evidence of their own enduring traits, they may interpret a rejection from peers as evidence that they are, and always will be, unlikable. This belief could intensify the emotional consequences of a rejection experience.

Achievement motivation literature relates to rejection effects in another way. Children with entity versus incremental theories differ in their goal orientations (e.g., Bempechat et al., 1991; see Dweck & Leggett, 1988, for a review). Children who are entity theorists are more likely to have performance goals in achievement situations. They focus primarily on their performance outcome in achievement situations, since they interpret it as a direct indicator of their ability, which they presume cannot be easily changed. In contrast, children who are incremental theorists are more likely to have learning goals, and they focus on improving and on gaining new skills in achievement situations. Children with performance goals respond with helpless and ineffectual behavior to failure situations in social encounters with peers (Erdley et al., 1997), as well as in task-oriented situations (Elliott & Dweck, 1988; Smiley & Dweck, 1995), whereas children with learning goals try harder and maintain a positive attitude in response to failure. When children with performance goals encounter the types of rejection we documented, they may reduce their efforts and withdraw in response to failure. In contrast, children with learning goals may be more likely to think about what they could do differently to affect a better result. As a result, it seems plausible that these children would be less devastated by a social rejection experience.

A final factor that could moderate the influence of rejection on feelings of well-being is whether the children behave in ways likely to extend or exacerbate rejection or in ways likely to end or at least dampen the intensity or duration of the rejection. Children who feel inordinately angry or upset in response to rejecting behaviors may be likely to exacerbate the rejection episode. Consider, for example, a child who becomes very angry in response to a peer telling him to get off the basketball court because the peer was there first. This child might react intensely to the peer, perhaps by verbally or physically attacking him. Although in some cases this type of behavior might be intimidating enough to end the rejection, in other cases it could actually worsen matters if the peer responds similarly. Some children have been found to endorse revenge goals in conflict situations with classmates (Chung & Asher, 1995; Erdley & Asher, 1996; Lochman, Wayland, & White, 1993) and even with friends (Rose & Asher, 1999a). Children who seek revenge in response to relatively mild rejections will likely have increasingly problematic peer interactions.

Whereas some children might exacerbate rejection experiences due to an overly aggressive response, other children might exacerbate rejection because they are unwilling to stand up for themselves. Indeed, we observed children who responded to rejection with desperate attempts to gain the approval of the rejecting children. Recall the example of Ellen's offer to be any sort of a pet to the Sugarbears and her attempt to join their group by inviting them to hit her with a ball. Ellen wanted to be accepted so badly that, despite the other girls' repeated rejections, she kept trying to win their approval. By behaving desperately and not standing up for themselves, children like Ellen may inadvertently increase the amount and the intensity of rejection. They may actually encourage the children's rejecting behaviors with their continued pleas for acceptance and attention. Suffering this type of humiliation repeatedly may take more of a toll on children's well-being than if they were to accept that they were disliked or excluded by certain peers.

Other behavior patterns seemed more likely to mitigate rejection experiences. When rejections were mild or ambiguous or took place between friends, ignoring the rejection was sometimes effective. This example begins with Douglas telling Eric not to "just stand there" in their recess dodgeball game.

Douglas-Eric: Don't just stand there.

Eric-Douglas: Suck it, Douglas.

Douglas-Eric: Huh?

Eric-Douglas: I said suck it.

Douglas-Eric: Oh.

After clarifying that Eric said, "Suck it," Douglas said only, "Oh." The boys then continued to play without apparent animosity.

Children also could confront rejection effectively by responding with humor or a spirit of playfulness. In the following episode, Sam is trying to join a game of Red Rover. Sam amusingly pretends he cannot hear when the other children try to exclude him. Sam had an excellent sense of humor and frequently used it to his advantage when interacting with his peers.

Sherry-Sam, Clayton, Conrad, Howard, Viola: Now we've got *other* boys.

Clayton-Sam: Yeah, we don't need any more.

Howard-Sam: Sa-aa-am.

Conrad-Sam: You can't, you can't play Sam (Conrad is one of Sam's best friends).

Sam-Conrad: Huh?

Conrad-Sam: You can't play. Hey, you can't play man.

(Sam cups one ear, pretending he can't hear.)

Sam-Conrad: Who?

Conrad-Sam: You.

Sam-Conrad: I can't hear.

(Sam gets in line next to Conrad, despite Conrad's protests.)

Conrad-Sam: You can't play.

Clayton-Sam: You can't play, you can't play it's even already.

Conrad-Sam: You, you can't play because um—

Clayton-Sam: We've got five.

Sam-Conrad, Clayton: No, it isn't, four.

Conrad-Sam: No, because we already started.

(Sam steps out to count the other children in line.)

Sam-Conrad: Four and six, that isn't even.

(Sam steps back into line and successfully joins the game.)

This situation could have turned into a much longer, more intense rejection experience if Sam had responded angrily and aggressively or if he had whined and pleaded to be admitted. His tactics of pretending to be deaf to refusals and responding in a calm and reasoned manner, however, gained him access to the game. Children with a good sense of humor have been found to be particularly well-liked by their classmates (Sletta, Sobstad, &

Valas, 1995; Sletta, Valas, Skaalvik, & Sobstad, 1996). Perhaps one way in which their sense of humor helps is that they are able to turn potentially intense rejection experiences into positive, or even funny, interactions.

Conclusion

In this chapter we have proposed an empirically derived taxonomy of rejection experiences and have speculated about factors that could influence children's emotional responses to rejection. At this stage, research is needed on individual differences in the types of rejection children experience and on individual differences in children's reactions to rejection experiences. We need to know more about the extent to which sociometric rejection is actually accompanied by overt rejection, and we need to understand why some children respond to rejection with distress, yet others emerge from the experience with more adaptive views of others and of themselves. Research needs to test whether the factors proposed here moderate the relationship between being the victim of rejecting behaviors and becoming very lonely.

Research is also needed on the effects of intervention aimed at reducing peer rejection in school. Psychologists such as Olweus (1991, 1993) have led the way by creating programs to reduce bullying in schools. Some of the rejection episodes we have described would count as bullying. Many others, although they do not meet a definition of bullying, could be quite harmful, even devastating. In addition to intervening to reduce bullying, parallel efforts are needed to civilize life in school more generally. Educators who have called for creating more caring and emotionally responsive classrooms include Charney (1992), Noddings (1992), and Paley (1993). Schools have a responsibility to improve the emotional climate of schools and to reduce the level of peer rejection, even when it does not take the more extreme form that falls under the definition of bullying. Children should feel psychologically safe when they go to school, not just physically safe. Unfortunately, much of what happens at school, often out of the sight and earshot of adults, can undermine their feelings of safety.

Repeated peer rejection could contribute to a lifetime of the sort of wariness and rejection sensitivity that Downey and her colleagues have described. Most psychologists would view early familial experiences, especially abuse and neglect by parents, as being at the heart of later rejection sensitivities. However, for many people, peer experiences in childhood may give rise to later vigilance, wariness, and a tendency to lash out or retreat when problems arise in social relationships. Our hypothesis, then, is that educators who create more caring schools not only will contribute to concurrent feelings of well-being but will help children develop more healthy models of relationships that will enable them to respond more constructively to the inevitable bumps and bruises of social life they will later experience as adults.

Acknowledgments

The research reported in this chapter was supported by a grant from the W. T. Grant Foundation and by the National Institute of Child Health and Human Development Research Grant HD05951.

References

Asher, S. R., & Coie, J. D. (1990). *Peer rejection in childhood.* New York: Cambridge University Press.

Asher, S. R., & Gabriel, S. W. (1993). Using a wireless transmission system to observe conversation and social interaction on the playground. In C. H. Hart (Ed.), *Children on playgrounds* (pp. 184–209). Albany: State University of New York Press.

Asher, S. R., Hymel, S., & Renshaw, P. D. (1984). Loneliness in children. *Child Development, 55,* 1456–1464.

Asher, S. R., & Parker, J. G. (1989). The significance of peer relationship problems in childhood. In B. H. Schneider, G. Attili, J. Nadel, & R. P. Weissberg (Eds.), *Social competence in developmental perspective* (pp. 5–23). Dordrecht, The Netherlands: Kluwer Academic Publishing.

Asher, S. R., Parker, J. G., & Walker, D. L. (1996). Distinguishing friendship from acceptance: Implications for intervention and assessment. In W. M. Bukowski, A. F. Newcomb, & W. W. Hartup (Eds.), *The company they keep: Friendship in childhood and adolescence* (pp. 366–405). New York: Cambridge University Press.

Asher, S. R., Parkhurst, J. T., Hymel, S., & Williams, G. A. (1990). Peer rejection and loneliness in childhood. In S. R. Asher & J. D. Coie (Eds.), *Peer rejection in childhood* (pp. 253–273). New York: Cambridge University Press.

Asher, S. R., & Wheeler, V. A. (1985). Children's loneliness: A comparison of rejected and neglected peer status. *Journal of Consulting and Clinical Psychology, 53,* 500–505.

Bempechat, J., London, P., & Dweck, C. S. (1991). Children's conceptions of ability in major domains: An interview and experimental study. *Child Study Journal, 21,* 11–36.

Benenson, J. F., & Dweck, C. S. (1986). The development of trait explanations and self-evaluations in the academic and social domains. *Child Development, 57,* 1179–1187.

Boivin, M., & Hymel, S. (1997). Peer experiences and social self-perceptions: A sequential model. *Developmental Psychology, 33,* 135–145.

Boivin, M., Thomassin, L., & Alain, M. (1989). Peer rejection and self-perception among early elementary school children: Aggressive-rejectees vs. withdrawn-rejectees. In B. H. Schneider, G. Attili, J. Nadel, & R. P. Weissberg (Eds.), *Social competence in developmental perspective* (pp. 392–393). Boston: Kluwer Academic.

Bukowski, W. M., Newcomb, A. F., & Hartup, W. W. (1996). *The company they keep: Conceptual and methodological issues.* Cambridge, MA: Cambridge University Press.

Cain, K. M., & Dweck, C. S. (1995). The relation between motivational patterns and achievement cognitions through the elementary school years. *Merrill-Palmer Quarterly, 41,* 25–52.

Cairns, R. B., Cairns, B. D., Neckerman, H. J., Gest, S. D., & Gariepy, J. L. (1988). Social networks and aggressive behavior: Peer support or peer rejection? *Developmental Psychology, 24,* 815–823.

Cassidy, J., & Asher, S. R. (1992). Loneliness and peer relations in young children. *Child Development, 63,* 350–365.

Charney, R. S. (1992). *Teaching children to care : Management in the responsive classroom.* Greenfield, MA: Northeast Foundation for Children.

Chung, T., & Asher, S. R. (1995, July). *Children's goals are related to their strategies for responding to peer conflict.* Paper presented at the annual meeting of the American Psychological Society, New York.

Coie, J. D., & Dodge, K. A. (1983). Continuities and changes in children's social status: A five-year longitudinal study. *Merrill-Palmer Quarterly, 29,* 261–282.

Coie, J. D., & Dodge, K. A. (1998). Aggression and antisocial behavior. In W. Damon (Editor-in-Chief; N. Eisenberg, Ed.), *Handbook of child psychology: Vol. 3, Social, emotional, and personality development* (pp. 779–862). New York: Wiley.

Coie, J. D., Dodge, K. A., & Coppotelli, H. (1982). Dimensions and types of status: A cross-age perspective. *Developmental Psychology, 18,* 557–570.

Coie, J. D., Dodge, K. A., Terry, R., & Wright, V. (1991). The role of aggression in peer relations: An analysis of aggression episodes in boys' play groups. *Child Development, 62,* 812–826.

Coie, J. D., & Koeppl, G. K. (1990). Adapting intervention to the problems of aggressive and disruptive rejected children. In S. R. Asher & J. D. Coie (Eds.), *Peer rejection in childhood* (pp. 309–337). New York: Cambridge University Press.

Cole, D. A.. & Carpentieri, S. (1990). Social status and the comorbidity of child depression and conduct disorder. *Journal of Consulting and Clinical Psychology, 58,* 748–757.

Crick, N. R. (1995). Relational aggression: The role of intent attributions, feelings of distress, and provocation type. *Development and Psychopathology, 7,* 313–322.

Crick, N. R., Casas, J. F., & Mosher, M. (1997). Relational and overt aggression in preschool. *Developmental Psychology, 33,* 579–588.

Crick, N. R., & Grotpeter, J. K. (1995). Relational aggression, gender, and social-psychological adjustment. *Child Development, 66,* 710–722.

Crick, N. R., & Grotpeter, J. K. (1996). Children's treatment by peers: Victims of relational and overt aggression. *Development and Psychopathology, 8,* 367–380.

Crick, N. R., & Ladd, G. W. (1993). Children's perceptions of their peer experiences: Attributions, social anxiety, and social avoidance. *Developmental Psychology, 29,* 244–254.

Crick, N. R., Werner, N. E., Casas, J. F., O'Brien, K. M., Nelson, D. A., Grotpeter, J. K., & Markon, K. (1999). Childhood aggression and gender: A new look at an old problem. In D. Bernstein (Ed.), *Nebraska symposium on motivation* (Vol. 45, 75–141). Lincoln: University of Nebraska Press.

Dodge, K. A. (1980). Social cognition and children's aggressive behavior. *Child Development, 51,* 162–170.

Dodge, K. A., Coie, J. D., & Brakke, N. P. (1982). Behavior patterns of socially rejected and neglected preadolescents: The roles of social approach and aggression. *Journal of Abnormal Child Psychology, 10,* 389–410.

Dodge, K. A., & Frame, C. L. (1982). Social cognitive biases and deficits in aggressive boys. *Child Development, 53,* 620–635.

Dodge, K. A., McClaskey, C. L., & Feldman, E. (1985). Situational approach to the assessment of social competence in children. *Journal of Consulting and Clinical Psychology, 53,* 344–353.

Downey, G., Khouri, H., & Feldman, S. I. (1997). Early interpersonal trauma and later adjustment: The mediational role of rejection sensitivity. In D. Cicchetti & S. L. Toth (Eds.), *Rochester Symposium on Developmental Psychopathology: Vol. VIII. Developmental perspectives on trauma: Theory, research, and intervention* (pp. 85–114). Rochester, NY: University of Rochester Press.

Downey, G., Lebolt, A., Rincon, C., & Freitas, A. (1998). Rejection sensitivity and children's interpersonal difficulties. *Child Development, 69,* 1074–1091.

Dweck, C. S., & Leggett, E. L. (1988). A social cognitive approach to motivation and personality. *Psychological Review, 95,* 256–273.

Elliott, E. S., & Dweck, C. S. (1988). Goals: An approach to motivation and achievement. *Journal of Personality and Social Psychology, 54,* 5–12.

Erdley, C. A., & Asher, S. R. (1996). Children's social goals and self-efficacy perceptions as influences on their responses to ambiguous provocation. *Child Development, 67,* 1329–1344.

Erdley, C. A., & Dweck, C. S. (1993). Children's implicit personality theories as predictors of their social judgments. *Child Development, 64,* 863–878.

Erdley, C. A., Cain, K. M., Loomis, C. C., Dumas-Hines, F., & Dweck, C. S. (1997). Relations among children's social goals, implicit personality theories, and responses to social failure. *Developmental Psychology, 33,* 263–272.

Franke, S., & Hymel, S. (1984, May). *Social anxiety in children: The development of self-report measures.* Paper presented at the third biennial meeting of the University of Waterloo Conference on Child Development, Waterloo, Ontario, Canada.

Furman, W., & Robbins, P. (1985). What's the point? Issues in the selection of treatment objectives. In B. H. Schneider, K. H. Rubin, & J. E. Ledingham (Eds.), *Children's peer relations: Issues in assessment and intervention* (pp. 41–54). New York: Springer-Verlag.

Goetz, T. E., & Dweck, C. S. (1980). Learned helplessness in social situations. *Journal of Personality and Social Psychology, 39,* 246–255.

Gottman, J. M., Gonso, J., & Rasmussen, B. (1975). Social interaction, social competence, and friendship in children. *Child Development, 46,* 709–718.

Grotpeter, J. K., & Crick, N. R. (1996). Relational aggression, overt aggression, and friendship. *Child Development, 67,* 2328–2338.

Guralnick, M. J., & Groom, J. M. (1987). The peer relations of mildly delayed and nonhandicapped preschool children in mainstream playgroups. *Child Development, 58,* 1556–1572.

Hartup, W. W., & Sancilio, M. F. (1986). Children's friendships. In E. Schopler & G. B. Mesibov (Eds.), *Social behavior in autism* (pp. 61–80). New York: Plenum.

Hodges, E. V. E., Malone, M. J., & Perry, D. G. (1997). Individual risk and social risk as interacting determinants of victimization in the peer group. *Developmental Psychology, 33,* 1032–1039.

Kochenderfer, B. J., & Ladd, G. W. (1996). Peer victimization: Cause or consequence of school maladjustment? *Child Development, 67,* 1305–1317.

Ladd, G. W. (1981). Effectiveness of a social learning method for enhancing children's social interaction and peer acceptance. *Child Development, 52,* 171–178.

Ladd, G. W. (1983). Social networks of popular, average, and rejected children in social settings. *Merrill-Palmer Quarterly, 29,* 283–307.

Ladd, G. W., Kochenderfer, B. J., & Coleman, C. C. (1997). Classroom peer acceptance, friendship, and victimization: Distinct relational systems that contribute uniquely to children's school adjustment? *Child Development, 68,* 1181–1197.

Leary, M. R., Springer, C., Negal, L., Ansell, E., & Evans, K. (1998). The causes, phenomenology, and consequences of hurt feelings. *Journal of Personality and Social Psychology. 74.* 1225–1237.

Lochman, J. E., Wayland, K. K., & White, K. J. (1993). Social goals: Relationship to adolescent adjustment and to social problem solving. *Journal of Abnormal Child Psychology, 21,* 135–151.

McFall, R. (1982). A review and reformulation of the concept of social skills. *Behavioral Assessment, 4,* 1–33.

Newcomb, A. F., & Bukowski, W. M. (1983). Social impact and social preference as determinants of children's peer group status. *Developmental Psychology, 19,* 856–867.

Newcomb, A. F., & Bukowski, W. H. (1984). A longitudinal study of the utility of social preference and social impact sociometric classification schemes. *Child Development, 55,* 1434–1447.

Noddings, N. (1992). *The challenge to care in schools : An alternative approach to education.* New York: Teachers College Press.

Nolen-Hoeksema, S., Parker, L. E., & Larson, J. (1994). Ruminative coping with depressed mood following loss. *Journal of Personality and Social Psychology, 67,* 92–104.

O'Brien, H., & Crick, N. R. (in preparation). Relational aggression in sibling dyads.

Oden, S., & Asher, S. R. (1977). Coaching children in social skills for friendship making. *Child Development, 48,* 495–500.

Olweus, D. (1991). Bully/victim problems among schoolchildren: Basic facts and effects of a school-based intervention program. In D. Pepler & K. Rubin (Eds.), *The development and treatment of childhood aggression* (pp. 411–448). Hillsdale, NJ: Erlbaum.

Olweus, D. (1993). Bullies on the playground: The role of victimization. In C. H. Hart (Ed.), *Children on playgrounds* (pp. 85–128). Albany, NY: SUNY Press.

Paley, V. G. (1993). *You can't say you can't play*. Cambridge, MA: Harvard University Press.

Parke, R. D., O'Neil, R., Spitzer, S., Isley, S., Welsh, M., Wang, S., Lee, J., Strand, C., & Cupp, R. (1997). A longitudinal assessment of sociometric stability and the behavioral correlates of children's social acceptance. *Merrill-Palmer Quarterly, 43,* 635–662.

Parker, J. G., & Asher, S. R. (1993). Friends and friendship quality in middle childhood: Links with peer group acceptance and feelings of loneliness and social dissatisfaction. *Developmental Psychology, 29,* 611–621.

Parker, J. G., Saxon, J. L., Asher, S. R., & Kovacs, D. M. (1999). Dimensions of children's friendship adjustment: Implications for understanding loneliness. In K. J. Rotenberg & S. Hymel (Eds.), *Loneliness in childhood and adolescence* (pp. 201–221). New York: Cambridge University Press.

Parkhurst, J. T., & Asher, S. R. (1992). Peer rejection in middle school: Subgroup differences in behavior, loneliness, and interpersonal concerns. *Developmental Psychology, 28,* 231–241.

Patterson, C. J., Kupersmidt, J. B., & Griesler, P. C. (1990). Perceptions of self and of relationships with others as a function of sociometric status. *Child Development, 61,* 1335–1349.

Pepler, D. J., & Craig, W. M. (1995). A peek behind the fence: Naturalistic observations of aggressive children with remote audiovisual recording. *Developmental Psychology, 31,* 548–553.

Perry, D. G., Kusel, S. J., & Perry, L. C. (1988). Victims of peer aggression. *Developmental Psychology, 24,* 807–814.

Putallaz, M. (1983). Predicting children's sociometric status from their behavior. *Child Development, 54,* 1417–1426.

Putallaz, M., & Gottman, J. M. (1981). An interactional model of children's entry into peer groups. *Child Development, 52,* 986–994.

Putallaz, M., & Wasserman, A. (1989). Children's naturalistic entry behavior and sociometric status: A developmental perspective. *Developmental Psychology, 25,* 297–305.

Renshaw, P. D. (1981). The roots of current peer interaction research: a historical analysis of the 1930s. In S. R. Asher & J. M. Gottman (Eds.), *The development of children's friendships* (pp. 1–25). New York: Cambridge University Press.

Renshaw, P. D., & Brown, P. J. (1993). Loneliness in middle childhood: Concurrent and longitudinal predictors. *Child Development, 64,* 1271–1284.

Rose, A. J., & Asher, S. R. (1999a). Children's goals and strategies in response to conflicts within a friendship. *Developmental Psychology, 35,* 69–79.

Rose, A. J., & Asher, S. R. (1999b, April). *Seeking and giving social support within a friendship*. In A. H. N. Cillessen (Chair), *Social-cognitive processes in peer relationships: New concepts and methods*. Symposium conducted at the biennial meeting of the Society for Research in Child Development, Albuquerque, New Mexico.

Rubin, K. H., Bukowski, W., & Parker, J. G. (1998). Peer interactions, relationships, and groups. In W. Damon (Editor-in-Chief; N. Eisenberg, Ed.), *Handbook of child psychology: Vol. 3. Social, emotional, and personality development* (pp. 619–700). New York: Wiley.

Sheldon, A. (1990). Pickle fights: Gendered talk in preschool disputes. *Discourse Processes, 13,* 5−31.

Sletta, O., Sobstad, F., & Valas, H. (1995). Humour, peer acceptance and perceived social competence in preschool and school-aged children. *British Journal of Educational Psychology. 65,* 179−195.

Sletta, O., Valas, H., Skaalvik, E., & Sobstad, F., & (1996). Peer relations, loneliness, and self-perceptions in school-aged children. *British Journal of Educational Psychology, 66,* 431−445.

Smiley, P. A., & Dweck, C. S. (1994). Individual differences in achievement goals among young children. *Child Development, 65,* 1723−1743.

Steinberg, M. D., & Dodge, K. A. (1983). Attributional bias in aggressive adolescent boys and girls. *Journal of Social and Clinical Psychology, 1,* 312−321.

Sullivan, H. S. (1953). *The interpersonal theory of psychiatry.* New York: Norton.

Weiner, B. (1979). A theory of motivation for some classroom experiences. *Journal of Educational Psychology, 71,* 3−25.

Weiner, B., Russell, D., & Lerman, D. (1980). A cognition-emotion process in achievement-related contexts. *Journal of Personality and Social Psychology, 37,* 1211−1220.

Williams, G. A., & Asher, S. R. (1987, April). *Peer- and self-perceptions of peer rejected children: Issues in classification and subgrouping.* Paper presented at the biennial meeting of the Society for Research in Child Development, Baltimore.

Zakriski, A. L., & Coie, J. D. (1996). A comparison of aggressive-rejected and nonaggressive-rejected children's interpretations of self-directed and other-directed rejection. *Child Development, 67,* 1048−1070.

PART 2

DEALING WITH REJECTION
Immediate and Long-Term Reactions

6

Emotional Responses to Interpersonal Rejection

MARK R. LEARY, ERIKA J. KOCH, AND
NANCY R. HECHENBLEIKNER

Interpersonal rejection is inherently distressing. It is difficult to imagine anyone ever feeling good about being shunned, excluded, ostracized, or abandoned. Even when people are not rejected outright, they may become upset simply from feeling that others do not accept them as much as they would like. Just the possibility of being rejected may be quite troubling. Our focus in this chapter is on emotions caused by real, imagined, or anticipated interpersonal rejection. Some of these emotions—such as sadness and anxiety—may be experienced in nonsocial contexts as well as in interpersonal situations. Others—such as embarrassment, guilt, shame, hurt feelings, and loneliness—are purely social emotions that arise only in response to interpersonal events.

We begin this chapter with a brief primer on the adaptive significance of emotions and then discuss the interpersonal functions of rejection-related emotions. We then examine several emotions involved in the regulation of social acceptance and rejection. All of these emotions have been studied previously; however, we offer a new perspective: each of these emotions arises when people perceive that others do not sufficiently value relationships with them. As we examine evidence linking emotion to relational evaluation, we speculate about the cognitive appraisals and action tendencies that characterize each. Finally, we explain the implications of our analysis for enhancing understanding of social emotions.

The Adaptive Significance of Emotions

Since Darwin's (1872) insightful treatise, *The Expression of the Emotions in Man and Animals,* most theorists have regarded emotions as adaptations that provided an advantage to the survival and reproduction of our homonid ancestors (e.g., Frijda, 1986; Izard, 1977; Neese, 1990; Tomkins, 1962). In particular, emotions help organisms solve important problems in dealing with the physical and social environment. First, they signal events important to an organism's well-being, thereby causing it to focus on concerns that require immediate attention. Second, emotions motivate organisms to behave in adaptive ways. Because positive emotions typically signal conditions beneficial to the organism and negative emotions typically signal the opposite, a hedonically oriented animal will naturally tend to behave in beneficial ways. The mere prospect of experiencing pleasant or unpleasant emotions can thus steer behavior in particular directions. Once aroused, emotions involve a readiness to respond in a particular fashion (the emotion's "action tendency"). Smith and Kirby (2000) aptly described emotion as "a sophisticated well-being monitor and guidance system." Third, emotions usually involve not only subjective feelings but also expressive movements that communicate the organism's state to others. These emotional expressions often lead conspecifics to respond in desired ways, as when a wolf's threatening stare frightens intruders out of its territory, a particular smile induces one chimpanzee to groom another, or human crying leads other people to offer support.

Some emotions—such as fear, sadness, and anger—may arise in response to impersonal or interpersonal stimuli. We may fear an approaching tornado or we may fear being reprimanded by our boss, for example. However, other emotions are precipitated only by interpersonal events. Embarrassment, shame, hurt feelings, and loneliness are inherently social responses to real, anticipated, remembered, or imagined encounters with other people. However, people who are alone may experience these inherently social emotions, triggered by thoughts that have interpersonal relevance. In this chapter, we focus primarily on these inherently interpersonal emotions, although we also discuss the interpersonal determinants of emotions, such as anxiety, that may occur in both social and nonsocial contexts.

When events threaten our physical well-being, the function of the resulting emotion is usually easy to identify. For example, all psychology students learn that fear prepares animals to confront physical threats to their well-being. Fear is a response to events that require quick action, and its physiological concomitants prepare people to respond quickly (Marks & Neese, 1994). (We often hear that fear prepares people for "fight or flight," but this is not quite correct. For example, a pet owner may feel fear when she sees the family dog wandering across a busy highway, in which case neither fighting nor fleeing would serve much purpose.) In most cases, the link between an eliciting physical threat and the body's response is straightforward and its adaptive usefulness clear.

However, the function of interpersonal emotions may be more difficult to see. Precisely what is causing a person to feel anxious on a first date? Of what benefit is the feeling and action tendency associated with anxiety when one is performing on stage? When people's feelings are hurt, their hearts are broken, or they suffer other kinds of psychological pain at the hands of loved ones, what purpose do these highly aversive emotions serve? When one's stomach is tied in knots of jealous angst, what adaptation is involved? Surely there is some reason why people feel miserable in social situations such as these, but the function of social emotions is not always obvious. We hypothesize in this chapter that many, if not most, interpersonal emotions arise from events that signify whether people are accepted or rejected by other people (Leary, 1990). If this is true, emotions associated with rejection and acceptance must have served some important purpose in the evolutionary past that led to the promulgation of the genes of people who experienced them.

These emotions' adaptive significance can be seen when we consider the implications of interpersonal rejection in the ancestral environment where most of human evolution occurred. In many ways, the African savannah was a relatively hospitable environment for early human beings (and their prehuman ancestors), certainly more so than alternative habitats such as deserts, rainforests, tundras, and ice packs. Early human beings lived as nomadic hunter-gatherers, moving about seeking edible plants and animals. The primary dangers were predators, foreign bands of potentially hostile people, and starvation, particularly when one was too young, old, ill, or injured to find food on one's own.

Solitary individuals could not survive for long in such an environment. A lone human being is virtually defenseless against predators. A sick or injured solitary individual cannot easily acquire food and water for sustenance and is particularly vulnerable to attack. A pregnant woman would be particularly defenseless during the last stage of pregnancy and for a while after the birth if she and the child live by themselves. Unlike animals that protect their young in burrows or nests that are difficult to access, a female human who bears a child on the savannah cannot offer adequate natural protection. And children are less likely to survive to mate and reproduce if they are raised and protected by solitary mothers rather than by a clan. Thus, the prospect of long-term survival was not good for anyone who lived alone in the ancestral environment.

The Sociometer

The solution, of course, was for human beings to live in cooperative groups that provided protection, resources, and care for offspring. As a result of the distinct advantage of group living, natural selection favored prehuman and human beings who formed and maintained relationships with others. Because sociality and group living were favored in the human struggle to survive and reproduce, a drive to form and maintain lasting, positive, and significant interpersonal relationships evolved (Baumeister & Leary, 1995).

However, successfully living within the protective confines of a group meant not only that our ancestors were predisposed to form social bonds but also that the other members of the group were willing to accept (or, at minimum, tolerate) the individual as a member. Thus, people had to "behave themselves" and be perceived as the kind of people who made good group members and relational partners—friends, coalition members, trading partners, mates, or whatever. To remain in the good graces of other people, each person would have had to be attuned to cues that might indicate whether his or her positive standing in other people's eyes was in jeopardy. Because rejection had serious, sometimes fatal, consequences in the ancestral environment, people would have needed to avoid exclusion and ostracism at nearly all costs. Thus, human beings likely developed biopsychological mechanisms that led them to fear and avoid interpersonal rejection. They developed an aversion to cues that connote rejection and abandonment, as well as a system to apprise them of threats to belongingness.

This psychological system—characterized as a "sociometer" (Leary & Downs, 1995)—monitors the social environment for cues relevant to *relational evaluation,* or the degree to which other people regard their relationship with the individual as valuable, important, or close. Although one may speak loosely of the sociometer monitoring social "acceptance" and "rejection," such language may lead us to misconstrue acceptance and rejection as dichotomous. In fact, acceptance and rejection occupy the endpoints of a continuum of relational evaluation (see Leary, chapter 1, this volume). When the sociometer detects low or declining relational evaluation—when other people do not value their relationships with the individual at some minimum level—it produces emotional warning signals that attract the person's attention, alerting him or her to the possibility of a threat to social acceptance and, thus, well-being.

Explicit indications of rejection, such as when one's lover screams that "I never want to see you again!" or a member is expelled from a group, obviously trigger the sociometer. But, more commonly, cues signaling low relational evaluation involve subtle expressions of disinterest, disapproval, or dislike—for example, frowns, lack of eye contact, low responsiveness, distant body language, and avoidance. Furthermore, such cues do not need to convey rejection per se to trigger emotional reactions. Rather, the sociometer responds whenever relational evaluation falls below a minimum threshold of social acceptance. Thus, people may experience negative emotions even though they are being "accepted" if their acceptance falls below some critical point (Leary, chapter 1, this volume). Furthermore, changes in patterns of interaction over time can also cause an emotional response, such as when one realizes that a friend doesn't call as much as before or that one's lover hasn't said "I love you" in months. Feeling less valued, wanted, or appreciated than one once did can trigger the sociometer and its concomitant emotional responses. Even the mere possibility of relational devaluation causes negative emotions, as does the realization that one may have behaved inappropriately.

For many years, emotion theorists have been locked in a spirited debate regarding whether cognition is necessary for the experience of emotion. One camp, led by Zajonc (1980), argues that emotions can occur in the absence of cognition. The other side, championed by Lazarus (1984, 1991), insists that cognitive appraisals underlie all emotions. Part of the resolution of this question depends on how one defines "cognition." Clearly, emotions can occur in the absence of conscious, rational, and verbally mediated thoughts. However, if one assumes—as most theorists do—that appraisals can occur outside of focal awareness, then emotions likely do involve an appraisal of events that have implications for one's well-being. To unite these perspectives, Smith and Kirby (2000) proposed an appraisal model of emotion that includes both rapid, automatic, schematic appraisal processes and slow, deliberate, conscious appraisals. In the context of our model, the sociometer provides an automatic, ongoing, nonconscious appraisal of one's relational evaluation. However, once the sociometer detects cues that indicate low (or dropping) relational evaluation, focal attention is directed to the threat, and the appraisal becomes conscious and deliberate.

For sadness, loneliness, hurt feelings, jealousy, guilt, shame, embarrassment, and social anxiety, the critical appraisal appears to involve the perception of low relational evaluation or, often, a perceived *decline* in relational evaluation. Each of these emotions may be elicited by the perception that one or more other people do not value their relationship with the individual as much as desired or as much as they did previously.

Considerable evidence supports the notion that emotions respond primarily to *changes* in circumstances. For example, people feel most satisfied after recent improvements in life, but the good feelings decline after the new state persists for awhile (Hsee & Abelson, 1991), and romantic passion seems to result from increases in intimacy (and, thus, wanes when intimacy remains stable; Baumeister & Bratslavsky, 1999). Likewise, people who have experienced excessively good or bad fortune (such as winning large lotteries or being paralyzed in an accident) experience corresponding good and bad emotions for a time after the event but eventually are no more or less unhappy than they were before (Brickman, Coates, & Janoff-Bulman, 1978). In the same way, people appear to feel hurt, sad, lonely, and jealous primarily when events signal a deterioration in relational evaluation—that is, relational devaluation.

A central preoccupation of emotion theorists during the twentieth century has involved the optimal way to distinguish among varieties of emotion. Proponents of the discrete emotion perspective have suggested that only a few primary or fundamental emotions exist. Although theorists disagree regarding the number and identity of these basic emotions (as well as on the criteria by which emotions should be regarded as basic), certain emotions— such as happiness, sadness, fear, anger, shame, and disgust—appear on most lists. According to this view, all other emotional states emerge from combinations of these basic emotions.

Other theorists have insisted that emotions do not naturally fall into discrete categories and that it makes little sense to call some emotions more "basic" than others. Rather, supporters of dimensional perspectives insist that varieties of emotional experience can be characterized by a few underlying dimensions, such as valence (the pleasantness or unpleasantness of the experience) and arousal or activation (a dimension running from sluggishness at one pole to high arousal at the other; Larsen & Diener, 1992). A particular emotion occupies a position along these dimensions.

Proponents of both the discrete emotion and dimensional perspectives have amassed evidence to support their views, but the jury is still out. Our analysis in this chapter relies on a discrete approach to emotion, not necessarily because we believe the discrete emotion perspective is correct but because laypeople view emotions as falling into natural categories (Shaver, Schwartz, Kirson, & O'Connor, 1987). For our purposes, it is easier to talk about specific emotions and to specify the nature of the appraisals that underlie particular rejection-related emotional experiences. In the sections that follow, we examine eight emotions that stem from perceptions of low or decreasing relational evaluation: sadness, loneliness, hurt feelings, jealousy, guilt and shame (considered together), embarrassment, and social anxiety.

Sadness

Sadness has often been described as an emotional response to loss (e.g., Lazarus, 1991). In many, but not all instances, sadness is caused specifically by social losses that involve people's sense that others do not sufficiently value them as relational partners. For example, the dissolution of friendships and romantic relationships creates acute sadness (Tamako, 1983), and people become depressed after divorce and the breakup of other intimate relationships (Lorenz et al., 1997). When asked to write an account about a typical instance in which people feel "sad," 63% of Shaver et al.'s (1987) participants wrote about a loss of a relationship or separation from a loved one, and 28% wrote specifically about rejection. People are also saddened by rifts with family members, fallouts with good friends, and the realization that once close relationships have become distant. In these cases, an important aspect of the relationship is lost even though the relationship itself remains. Failure to be included—such as when one is denied membership in a group—leads to sadness (Atlas & Morier, 1994), and moving away from friends and family causes people to feel sad as well (Brown & Orthner, 1990). Children who perceive their relationships with their mothers and friends as less warm tend to be more depressed than those who feel closer to them (Stocker, 1994). People use the word "grief" to describe the intense sadness that results when the loss of a relationship seems permanent, whether the relationship ends because of death or breakup, or because the loved one has moved far away and will never be seen again.

As shown in these examples, sadness is not caused by rejection itself. Although rejection saddens people, the central cause appears to be low relational evaluation. Obviously, rejection inherently implies that the rejector does not value his or her relationship with the rejected individual, but other events that involve the deterioration or termination of relationships also lead people to feel less relationally valued than before. When people are bereaved or move away from good friends, for example, they do not feel rejected, yet relational evaluation has declined when those who once valued relationships with us are no longer available. Thus, we agree with Lofland's (1982) assessment that people experience grief as the result of "the rupturing of a relationship they define as significant" (pp. 221–222). We also find it informative that people are sometimes upset by the breakup of relationships even when they themselves terminated the relationship. This effect may occur because, although the person may have wanted the relationship to end, terminating a relationship typically leads the rejected party to value his or her relationship with the rejector less than he or she did before. So, although the breakup was desired, relational devaluation occurs nonetheless.

People are saddened even by temporary separations from loved ones. Homesickness, for example, is characterized primarily by feelings of sadness. In part, reactions to temporary separations may result simply from the expectation that one will not receive the desired positive outcomes while the loved one is absent. In addition, however, people may be dysphoric because they feel less relationally valued while the loved one is away than they did when he or she was present. From an evolutionary perspective, one's chances of survival plummet in the face of predators, starvation, or other disasters if the people who value us are not there, and people should thus be distressed even by temporary separations.

The action tendencies of sadness and depression, which typically involve inaction and withdrawal, have been a puzzle. Some theorists have suggested that the behavior of sad people may elicit nurturance and support from others (Coyne, 1967). Although this is sometimes true, sad withdrawal and lethargy often prolong the dysphoric state and impede the formation of new relationships (and, for that matter, engagement in alternative relationships that already exist). Furthermore, other people soon grow tired of those who are chronically unhappy, both because dysphoric moods are "contagious" (Segrin & Dillard, 1992) and because unhappy people tend to make excessive demands on others' time and patience (Katz & Joiner, in press). Evidence suggests that depressed individuals cause other people to distance themselves because they excessively seek reassurance and consolation (Joiner, 1996; Joiner & Metalsky, 1995). What function does sadness serve after relational devaluation has occurred?

We have three partial answers to this question. First, most research showing that negative moods lead others to withdraw from the sad individual has involved people who are chronically dysphoric, if not clinically depressed (see, however, Carver, Kus, & Scheier, 1994). Perhaps acute "normal" sadness elicits social support but prolonged depression does not. Furthermore, people's reactions are moderated by their relationship with the depressed person (King & Heller, 1984). For example, people are less tolerant of depressive behavior in strangers than in acquaintances (Segrin, 1993).

Second, depressed withdrawal may reflect a "time-out" strategy that allows the individual to reassess his or her situation or to wait for better times after receiving indications that the social environment is not sufficiently responsive (Kirkpatrick & Ellis, in press). Little is to be gained by pursuing social contacts when other people are not interested.

Third, the interpersonal function of sadness may lie not only in the reactions of others to the expression of sadness but in people's motivation to avoid dysphoric emotions. As we noted, emotions may motivate beneficial behaviors by serving as incentives and punishments. Thus, the mere possibility of debilitating sadness may prompt people to care for their loved ones and nurture their relationships with them. People's desire to avoid despondency may motivate them to protect the quality of their relationships, including behaving in ways that prompt other people to value their relationship with them. If this is true, the greatest interpersonal benefit of sadness is that it motivates behaviors that lead people to maintain relationships in which they are valued.

Loneliness

Feelings of loneliness emerge when people who value their relationships with us are not available for social interaction and support. In some instances, we have no one anywhere on whom we can count. At other times, we may know that certain other people do care about and value us, but they are not currently available. As in the case of sadness, the cause of loneliness appears to be low relational evaluation rather than rejection itself, although rejection can obviously make people feel lonely (Jones, 1990).

Research strongly suggests that loneliness is tied to factors that cause a sense of low relational evaluation. Loneliness is particularly common among people who have recently experienced bereavement, divorce, or the breakup of romantic relationships (Mitchell-Flynn & Hutchinson, 1993; Peplau & Perlman, 1982). Furthermore, lonely college students doubt their ability to develop satisfying relationships and believe that other people do not regard them as desirable friends and partners, even after their level of depression is statistically controlled, indicating that depression per se is not the culprit (Wilbert & Rupert, 1986). Children who are not accepted by their peers tend to be lonely (Cassidy & Asher, 1992), and peer rejection prospectively predicts feelings of loneliness (Boivin, Hymel, & Burkowski, 1995). Geographical relocation also causes loneliness by leading to the loss of relationships in which people feel relationally valued (Brown & Orthner, 1990; Rokach, 1998).

Are lonely people truly socially disadvantaged, or is the deficiency in their social relationships perceived rather than real? Research supports both points of view. Objective indicators of people's social networks—such as their number of close friends, the frequency with which they date, and the extent of their social activities—do predict loneliness (Jones, Carpenter, & Quintana, 1985). Compared to nonlonely people, lonely people appear to spend a higher percentage of their time with acquaintances than with family members and close friends (Jones, 1981), a pattern that may prolong episodes of loneliness because acquaintances are less likely to value their relationships than family members and friends. Furthermore, objective indices of a person's "social value" are linked to loneliness. For example, a study of elementary school children showed that lonely children were less physically fit and less physically active than their nonlonely peers (Page, Frey, Talbert, & Falk, 1992). Because physical skill is a socially valued attribute and a minimum level of physical prowess is necessary to participate in certain childhood activities, children with poor physical skills may have fewer opportunities to develop friendships and may be less valued as playmates, teammates, and friends.

Although loneliness is related to people's actual social experiences and personal attributes, their subjective judgments of their relationships account for variance in loneliness even after objective quality of social life is controlled. In fact, studies suggest that subjective perceptions of relationships may be more important than the objective quality of one's relationships (Jones et al., 1985; Wheeler, Reis, & Nezlek, 1983). Thus, although the objective nature of one's social contacts for relational evaluation can cause loneliness, people may experience low relational evaluation even when they seem to have many social contacts. Simply having a wide social network does not ensure that a person will perceive that he or she is an adequately valued member of that network.

Like depression, loneliness can undermine the quality of relationships. For example, studies show that lonely children are more likely to be stigmatized, rejected, and victimized by their peers than nonlonely children (Boivin et al., 1995; Rotenberg, Bartley, Toivonen, 1997). Over time, peer rejection increases loneliness, which then increases withdrawal and subsequent rejection in an insidious cycle (Boivin et al., 1995). Furthermore, lonely people often fear being rejected (Wilbert & Rupert, 1986), and that fear may deter them from seeking social contacts (Vorauer & Ratner, 1996).

Hurt Feelings

Of the emotions we discuss, the one that people colloquially call "hurt feelings" has received the least attention from psychologists. Even so, evidence strongly suggests that people's feelings are hurt by events that connote low relational evaluation—the perception that other people do not regard their relationship with the individual to be as valuable, important, or close as the individual desires (Leary & Springer, 2001). In a study of 168 hurtful episodes, Leary, Springer, Negel, Ansell, and Evans (1998) found that all but two of the episodes appeared to be caused by perceived relational devaluation and, furthermore, that ratings of participants' emotional pain correlated highly with the degree to which they felt rejected.

Criticism was the most common cause of hurt feelings, accounting for one-third of the hurtful incidents (Leary et al., 1998). Criticism appears to hurt people's feelings primarily when it implies relational devaluation. People seem to know this implicitly and, thus, qualify critical remarks when they do not want to hurt the other person's feelings ("You know I value our friendship, but . . ."). Instances of betrayal, which accounted for a fifth of the episodes, also indicate that the betrayer does not adequately value his or her relationship with the betrayed individual. Instances of active disassociation (explicit rejection) and passive disassociation (ignoring or avoiding the individual) also caused a high proportion of hurt feelings. In all these instances, people were hurt because they perceived that others did not value them as relational partners as much as they desired.

In another study, Hechenbleikner and Leary (1999) obtained an index of relational devaluation by asking participants how much they wanted to be valued and accepted by a particular individual, as well as how much they thought that individual valued and accepted them in a variety of hurtful episodes. Results showed that the magnitude of participants' hurt feelings was predicted by the difference between how much they wanted the other person to value them and how much they thought the person actually valued them—that is, by relational devaluation.

Although hurt appears to be a distinct emotional experience (Leary, Hechenbleikner, Strausser, Higgins, & Stiles, 1999), hurt feelings tend to occur in conjunction with other emotions, particularly sadness and anger, because situations that involve low relational evaluation often include features that naturally cause other kinds of emotions. For example, a rejection that hurts one's feelings might also cause one to feel sad if a relationship was damaged or angry if one perceived the rejection as unjustified.

Jealousy

Jealousy arises under a more circumscribed set of conditions than sadness, loneliness, and hurt feelings. People feel jealous when they believe that another person does not sufficiently value their relationship because of the presence or intrusion of a third party. Put differently, jealousy occurs when people perceive that another person values a relationship with them less because that person values his or her relationship with a third party more. People tend to think of jealousy primarily in the context of romantic and sexual relationships, but people may feel jealous whenever they believe that a third party has caused relational devaluation. For example, a child may be jealous of the attention that a parent devotes to a brother or sister, or an employee may feel jealous because the boss seems to prefer another employee.

Because jealousy arises from perceptions of relational devaluation, it is not surprising that people who are highly "rejection-sensitive" are more prone to jealousy than less rejection-sensitive people (Downey & Feldman, 1996; Pereti & Pudowski, 1997). Similarly, people who have an insecure or anxious attachment style are more jealous (Sharpsteen & Kirkpatrick, 1997), as are people who score high in interpersonal dependency (Pereti & Pudowski, 1997). Contrary to the popular notion that romantic jealousy reflects the jealous person's intense love for the target, excessive dependency and fear of rejection are sufficient to produce jealousy in relationships (Pereti & Pudowski, 1997).

Jealousy is a particularly complex emotion, usually accompanied by fear and sadness regarding the actual or potential loss of the relationship and anger toward the relational partner and the rival. The action tendency associated with jealousy appears to involve a motivation to restore the relationship by minimizing or eliminating the influence of the third party. Jealous people may try to attract attention to themselves, increase their desirability to the target, or diminish the influence of the third party by disparaging or threatening him or her.

Paradoxically, jealous people sometimes behave in ways that are anything but endearing to the target, including outbursts of anger, threats, and physical abuse. Such behaviors appear intended to intimidate the partner into disassociating from the rival, but, ironically, they may further undermine an already unstable relationship (Downey & Feldman, 1996). In extreme cases, jealousy may even provoke the murder of the rival, the partner, or (in the case of a well-known ex-football player) both. Extreme reactions such as these are baffling on the surface because they do not restore the threatened relationship and, in fact, sacrifice the well-being of the jealous murderer. The justifications of these jealous, jilted men (they are almost always men)—"If I can't have her, no one can"—are exceptionally puzzling. What is to be gained by injuring or killing one's former partner and, perhaps, her new lover?

Pinker (1997) has attributed responses such as these to the fact that human emotional reactions often resemble a "doomsday machine" (named for the device in the movie, *Dr. Strangelove*), designed to deter threats from opponents by initiating an inevitable retaliatory response that, once started, cannot be stopped. In the interpersonal realm, these doomsday-like deterrents send the message, "If you do X, I will be unable to stop myself from doing Y." Others will take more seriously a person's claims to respond to provocations, transgressions, and relationship threats if he or she appears to have no voluntary control over the response. Thus, to be effective, the doomsday messages of a jealous lover must be backed up by occasional instances of uncontrollable aggression. As Pinker notes, "For every killing of an estranged wife or girlfriend there must be thousands of threats made credible by signs that the man is crazy enough to carry them out regardless of the cost" (p. 489).

Guilt and Shame

Although they both involve violations of important moral and social standards, the psychological concomitants of guilt and shame differ somewhat.
The central distinction between them is that people feel guilty about engaging in a particular behavior, whereas they feel ashamed about the kind of person they are (Lewis, 1971; Tangney, 1995). A guilty person views his or her
bad behavior as an isolated transgression, whereas a shameful person views
his or her misdeed as a reflection of a flawed, objectionable, and often immoral self (see Tangney, 1995; Tangney & Salovey, 1999).

Beginning with Freud, most theorists trace shame and guilt to intrapsychic conflicts or to violations of one's personal standards (see Barrett, 1995,
for a review). However, more recently, social psychologists have suggested
that guilt and shame are inherently social emotions rather than reactions to
intrapsychic processes. Theorists of differing orientations (Morrison, 1983;
Thomas, 1995) have drawn a connection between guilt/shame and concerns
about social rejection. For example, Barrett (1995) traced shame (but not
guilt) to a concern about how others view one, and Retzinger (1995) suggested that, in shame, "self and other are alienated or are threatened to be
alienated" (p. 1106). Similarly, Baumeister, Stillwell, and Heatherton (1994)
presented an interpersonal analysis of guilt that focused on its relationship-
maintaining functions.

We believe guilt and shame are both reactions to events that have implications for relational evaluation. When people worry that something about
their behavior may lead other people to relationally devalue them, they feel
guilty. When they think that others' judgments of their character or personality may lead to relational devaluation, they experience shame, which is no-
toriously more aversive than guilt (Tangney, 1995). Being a wholly flawed
person is certainly worse than committing a single wrong deed.

The relatively little research on the interpersonal nature of guilt and
shame supports our hypothesis that these emotions arise from events that
have implications for relational evaluation. In a study of the everyday guilt
experiences of university students, Baumeister, Reis, and Delespaul (1995)
found that guilt was typically associated with distressing social events involving rejection, interpersonal conflict, and loneliness, events with the possibility to undermine relational evaluation.

Guilt and shame have sometimes been called "moral emotions," and, in
one sense, they are. However, the eliciting events typically violate *other people's* moral standards rather than one's own. (Mencken's quip that "con-
science is that little voice that tells us that someone may be watching" was
not far wrong.) In fact, other people have the power to make us feel ashamed
and guilty even when we do not think we did anything wrong!

The action tendencies of guilt and shame are different (Lazarus, 1991;
Tangney, Miller, Flicker, & Barlow, 1995; Tangney & Salovey, 1999). Guilty
people are motivated to repair the material and relational damage that their

behavior has caused. They apologize and atone, engage in remedial behaviors and restitution, ask forgiveness, and take other steps to affirm their social bonds with the people whom they have hurt (Baumeister et al., 1994). People who are ashamed, however, want to withdraw—to run away, hide. Because such reactions may appear extreme, many psychologists have interpreted them as undesirable if not dysfunctional (Lewis, 1971). However, these behaviors may be interpersonally advantageous for the shamed person. If others view one as an undesirable, flawed, immoral character, the best tactic may be to withdraw from further social interaction until one can make the personal changes necessary to become an acceptable interactant. Furthermore, if one's shameful behavior has made others angry and rejecting, a cooling-off period may help one to avoid punishment, retribution, and ostracism.

Embarrassment

Embarrassment, like guilt and shame, involves a concern for how one is perceived and evaluated by other people. However, embarrassment occurs as a result of violations of social rules rather than moral standards. Thus, embarrassment is a less intense emotion than guilt and shame, presumably because the infractions that elicit it are less weighty (Miller & Tangney, 1994).

The prevailing theory of embarrassment follows Goffman's (1955, 1959) insight that people become embarrassed when they cannot sustain desired images in other people's eyes (Leary & Kowalski, 1995; Miller, 1996; Schlenker, 1980). Self-presentational predicaments in which people believe that they have projected undesired impressions cause them to feel awkward, abashed, and anxious and lead them to repair the damage. A second theory, which also has empirical support, traces embarrassment to awkward social interactions. According to Silver, Sabini, and Parrott (1987), people become embarrassed when they are not able to participate in a social encounter in a poised manner. Both these perspectives, one stressing self-presentational predicaments and the other emphasizing awkward interactions, are parsimoniously subsumed by the idea that embarrassment is a reaction to real or imagined relational devaluation. If, through image or behavior, one appears to be a less-than-ideal social participant, one may worry that others will not value him or her as a relational partner.

Many observers have been puzzled because people are often more embarrassed than the objective situation seems to warrant. Goffman (1955) observed, for instance, that people give a "worst case reading" to embarrassing situations, assuming the worst about their plight. Not only do they often overestimate the potential damage to their social image, but they also seem not to realize that an embarrassing *faux pas* may actually be endearing under certain circumstances (Aronson, Willerman, & Floyd, 1966; Miller, 1996). Perhaps people are generally better off overestimating rather than underestimating the seriousness of events that pose a threat to their personal relationships. The mechanism that monitors threats to relational evaluation may be overly sensitive, thereby biased to detect "false positives" (Leary, Haupt, Strausser, & Chokel, 1998). The adaptive value of such a system is easy to see.

Social Anxiety

Social anxiety—feelings of nervousness and uneasiness in novel, uncertain, or other socially threatening situations (such as first dates, job interviews, public speeches, and casual conversations)—is an anticipatory response to the possibility of low relational evaluation. The self-presentation theory of social anxiety suggests that people feel socially anxious when they do not think that they will make the impressions they desire to make on other people (Leary & Kowalski, 1995; Schlenker & Leary, 1982). People who feel socially anxious are concerned simply about the *possibility* of making undesired impressions.

However, we can see that people worry about making undesired impressions primarily because they raise the specter of relational devaluation (Leary, in press). People know that other people accept or reject them based on how they are perceived. Being viewed as attractive, competent, likeable, and ethical, for example, will result in a more positive relational evaluation than being seen as unattractive, incompetent, despicable, or immoral. As a result, whenever people think that they cannot make the impressions they desire to make in a particular encounter, they feel socially anxious. To return to the evolutionary theme, social anxiety may have evolved as an "early warning system" that kept people from behaving in ways that would compromise their social images and, thus, their acceptance by group members (Leary, in press).

Emotion and Relational Devaluation

As we have seen, several interpersonal emotions reflect a response to concerns about relational evaluation. Whether measured as emotional states or as individual differences in the tendency to experience these emotions, sadness, loneliness, hurt feelings, jealousy, shame, guilt, embarrassment, and social anxiety are moderately correlated with one another (e.g., Leary et al., 1998; Leary et al., 1999; Segrin & Kinney, 1995). Since all of these emotions are responses to low (or declining) relational evaluation, interpersonal events that cause one emotion are likely to evoke one or more of the others as well.

Even so, the fact that these emotions are moderately correlated raises questions regarding how we ought to distinguish these emotions from one another. Are they really different emotions, or are they minor emotional variations on the same relational theme? Do they differ in some fundamental way that generalizes across cultures, or are the differences among them culture-specific? Theorists have wrestled for many years with the question of how to distinguish among various emotions and whether observed differences among emotions are culture-specific, and we will make no effort to resolve these issues here. Rather, we wish simply to speculate on how these emotions are differentially experienced and conceptualized by English-speaking people.

Salient Eliciting Features

Table 6.1 lists the salient eliciting features and dominant action tendencies for the eight emotions discussed in this chapter. Of the eight emotions, sadness and loneliness may be the broadest, most generic responses to low perceived relational evaluation. Loneliness occurs when people feel that an insufficient number of people value having relationships with them. When low relational evaluation has resulted from a loss of relationships in which they were previously relationally valued, people experience sadness as well. Because loneliness often arises when existing relationships weaken or end (through death, dissolution, or distance, for example), loneliness and sadness often occur together.

Hurt feelings occur when others indicate that they insufficiently value their relationship with the individual. Often, people's feelings are hurt within the context of ongoing relationships but also sometimes when their efforts to initiate interactions and relationships are ignored or rebuffed (Leary & Springer, 2001; Snapp & Leary, in press). When hurtful events involve relational devaluation and the loss of a real or desired relationship, hurt feelings are accompanied by sadness.

As we have seen, guilt, shame, and embarrassment are closely related, occurring when people think they have acted in undesirable ways that may lead to relational devaluation. Although the nature of the infractions that precede each emotion differs, the general concern is the same. Are these three reactions best regarded as a single emotion (and the distinctions are cultural and linguistic) or as three distinct emotions? Based on the similarities in the salient features and emotional action tendencies for guilt and embarrassment shown in Table 6.1, one could argue that guilt and embarrassment are essentially the same emotion but that they are distinct from shame.

Jealousy differs because of the specificity of the conditions that precipitate it. Jealousy is always experienced in a particular relationship, only when the presence or intrusion (which may be either real or imagined) of a third party compromises one's relational value in the eyes of a particular person.

Social anxiety, as an inherently anticipatory response, differs from the other emotions. In guilt, shame, and embarrassment, the misdeed has already occurred (although not necessarily the resulting relational devaluation, which may be impending); in jealousy, the threat of relational devaluation is either present or imminent; for hurt feelings, sadness, and loneliness, cues connoting relational devaluation have already been received. Only social

Table 6.1 Salient Features and Action Tendencies of Negative Social Emotions

Social Emotion	Salient Feature of Relational Devaluation	Emotional Action Tendency
Sadness	The individual has lost a relationship with a person who valued the relationship (e.g., through death, distance, or relationship termination)	Temporary withdrawal, followed by attention to alternative relationships
Loneliness	An insufficient number of people value their relationships with the individual	Seek additional relationships, if possible; if not, withdraw
Hurt feelings	Another person does not view his or her relationship with the individual to be as important, close, or valuable as the individual desires	Promote value of relationship if possible; if not, withdraw and seek alternative relationship
Jealousy	The presence or intrusion of a third party has led another person to devalue his or her relationship with the individual	Eliminate the presence or influence of the third party
Guilt	Morally undesirable behavior has led (or may lead) others to devalue their relationship with the individual	Remedial behaviors (e.g., apologize, make excuses, seek forgiveness, show oneself to be acceptable)
Shame	Morally undesirable personal characteristic has led (or may lead) others to devalue their relationship with the individual	Remedial behaviors (e.g., apologize, make excuses, seek forgiveness); temporarily withdraw
Embarrassment	Socially undesirable behavior has led (or may lead) others to devalue their relationship with the individual	Remedial behaviors (e.g., apologize. make excuses, seek forgiveness, show oneself to be acceptable)
Social anxiety	The individual fears that others may value their relationship less because of the impressions they may form of him or her	Self-presentational tactics to forestall relational devaluation

anxiety is cued by the mere possibility of behaving in ways that might lower one's relational value.

We do not claim that these are necessarily eight distinct emotions. In fact, one could say that they are variations of a single affective response to real, anticipated, or imagined relational devaluation. Data suggest that all negative social emotions share a common core of undifferentiated negative affect or distress (Leary et al., 1999). The emotions listed in Table 6.1 may be specific variations of this more general response, each with its own affective nuances, depending on the specific situation.

Action Tendencies

People seem to react to threats to relational evaluation in three primary ways. First, they may try to enhance their relational value to other people, behaving in ways that show them to be desirable relational partners. These efforts may be preemptive (as for social anxiety) or remedial (as for jealousy, embarrassment, or guilt). Second, they may seek alternative relationships in which they will be more highly valued. Third, they may simply withdraw from social interactions altogether for the time being; as we have seen, sadness, loneliness, and shame often involve inactivity and withdrawal. Withdrawal may be most common when people perceive that they can do little to re-establish interpersonal connections.

Aspects of all three reactions may occur with any of the emotions, but certain reactions predominate with each one. As can be seen in Table 6.1, sadness, loneliness, and shame tend to be accompanied by social withdrawal; hurt feelings by efforts to repair the relationship or to seek alternative relationships; jealousy by concerted efforts to eliminate the rival's influence; guilt and embarrassment by remedial actions; and social anxiety by protective self-presentations that ward off negative impressions.

One behavior that sometimes accompanies rejection emotions deserves special attention—suicide. People who kill, or try to kill, themselves virtually always experience one of the emotions described in this chapter at the time. Indeed, it is difficult to imagine someone taking his or her own life who did not feel depressed, lonely, hurt, jealous, guilty, or ashamed. (People don't appear to commit suicide from embarrassment or social anxiety.) We tend to think of suicidal people as deeply depressed—as they often are—but the underlying factor is often the feeling that no one cares about them or, in our terms, a feeling of profound relational devaluation. Indeed, many writers have suggested that suicidal people usually have deficient interpersonal relationships. In an extensive study of over 30,000 hospitalized suicidal patients, Osgood and Brant (1990) found that residents whom the staff rated as possibly suicidal felt rejection, abandonment, and loss of love. Many patients either had no close family members, or the family they had never visited them. Similarly, another study showed that most cases of suicide among patients in a psychiatric hospital were tied to events that estranged the individual from loved ones (Conroy & Smith, 1983). The link between low rela-tional evaluation and suicide calls for future attention.

Conclusions

Human beings typically become deeply distressed when they think that other people do not adequately value relationships with them. As aversive (if not downright painful) as these feelings sometimes are, they nonetheless serve an important function, motivating people to protect their interpersonal rela-tionships, alerting them to threats to those relationships, and prompting them to take action when relational problems arise. The emotions that were the focus of this chapter—sadness, loneliness, hurt feelings, jealousy, guilt, shame, embarrassment, and social anxiety—arise when people perceive that others do not adequately value relationships with them. Those perceptions may be accurate or inaccurate, and they may involve ongoing interactions or events merely remembered, expected, or imagined. But, in any case, low per-ceived relational evaluation, if not relational devaluation, is involved.

We have myopically focused in this chapter on negative emotions, but positive emotions also arise from interpersonal events. Many of individuals' most positive emotions result from exceptionally high relational evaluation. People experience intense happiness, if not joy, when they feel admired, ap-preciated, or deeply loved. Furthermore, overt evidence of high relational evaluation—such as being accepted into desired groups, forming friend-ships, and developing other kinds of social bonds—evokes pleasurable feel-ings. Even much of the emotional pleasure of sexual encounters may arise from a momentary sense of acceptance. Clearly, more attention should be de-voted to interpersonal acceptance and to the positive emotions that arise from high relational evaluation.

References

Aronson, E., Willerman, B., & Floyd, J. (1966). The effect of a pratfall on in-creasing interpersonal attractiveness. *Psychonomic Science, 4,* 227–228.

Atlas, G., & Morier, D. (1994). The sorority rush process: Self-selection, ac-ceptance criteria, and the effect of rejection. *Journal of College Student Development, 35,* 346–353.

Barrett, K. C. (1995). A functionalist approach to shame and guilt. In J. P. Tangney & K. W. Fischer (Eds.), *Self-conscious emotions: The psychology of shame, guilt, embarrassment, and pride* (pp. 25–63). New York: Guilford Press.

Baumeister, R. F., & Bratslavsky, E. (1999). Passion, intimacy, and time: Passionate love as a function of change in intimacy. *Personality and Social Psychology Review, 3,* 49–67.

Baumeister, R. F., & Leary, M. R. (1995). The need to belong: Desire for inter-personal attachments as a fundamental human motivation. *Psychological Bulletin, 117,* 497–529.

Baumeister, R. F., Reis, H. T., & Delespaul, P. A. E. G. (1995). Subjective and experiential correlates of guilt in everyday life. *Personality and Social Psychology Bulletin, 21,* 1256–1268.

Baumeister, R. F., Stillwell, A. M., & Heatherton, T. F. (1994). Guilt: An interpersonal approach. *Psychological Bulletin, 115,* 243–267.

Boivin, M., Hymel, S., & Bukowski, W. M. (1995). The roles of social withdrawal, peer rejection, and victimization by peers in predicting loneliness and depressed mood in childhood. *Development and Psychopathology, 7,* 765–785.

Brickman, P., Coates, D., & Janoff-Bulman, R. (1978). Lottery winners and accident victims: Is happiness relative? *Journal of Personality and Social Psychology, 36,* 917–927.

Brown, A. C., & Orthner, D. K. (1990). Relocation and personal well-being among early adolescents. *Journal of Early Adolescence, 10,* 366–381.

Carver, C. S., Kus, L. A., & Scheier, M. F. (1994). Effects of good versus bad mood and optimistic versus pessimistic outlook on social acceptance versus rejection. *Journal of Social and Clinical Psychology, 13,* 138–151.

Cassidy, J., & Asher, S. R. (1992). Loneliness and peer relations in young children. *Child Development, 63,* 350–365.

Conroy, R. W., & Smith, K. (1983). Family loss and hospital suicide. *Suicide and Life- Threatening Behavior, 13,* 179–194.

Coyne, J. C. (1967). Depression and the response of others. *Journal of Abnormal Psychology, 85,* 186–193.

Darwin, C. (1872). *The expression of the emotions in man and animals.* London: Murray.

Downey, G., & Feldman, S. (1996). Implication of rejection sensitivity for intimate relationships. *Journal of Personality and Social Psychology, 70,* 1327–1343.

Frijda, N. H. (1986). *The emotions.* New York: Cambridge University Press.

Goffman, E. (1955). On facework. *Psychiatry, 18,* 213–231.

Goffman, E. (1959). *The presentation of self in everyday life.* New York: Doubleday.

Hechenbleikner, N. R., & Leary, M. R. (1999, March). *Hurt feelings and relational devaluation.* Paper presented at the meeting of the Southeastern Psychological Association, Savannah, GA.

Hsee, C. K., & Abelson, R. P. (1991). The velocity relation: Satisfaction as function of the first derivative of outcome over time. *Journal of Personality and Social Psychology, 60,* 341–347.

Izard, C. (1977). *Human emotions.* New York: Plenum Press.

Joiner, T. E. (1996). Depression and rejection: On strangers and friends, symptom specificity, length of relationship, and gender. *Communication Research, 23,* 451–471.

Joiner, T. E., & Metalsky, G. I. (1995). A prospective test of an integrative interpersonal theory of depression: A naturalistic study of college roommates. *Journal of Personality and Social Psychology, 69,* 778–788.

Jones, W. H. (1981). Loneliness and social contact. *Journal of Social Psychology, 113,* 295–296.

Jones, W. H. (1990). Loneliness and social exclusion. *Journal of Social and Clinical Psychology, 9,* 214–220.

Jones, W. H., Carpenter, B. N., & Quintana, D. (1985). Personality and interpersonal predictors of loneliness in two cultures. *Journal of Personality
and Social Psychology, 48,* 1503- 1511.

Katz, J., & Joiner, T. E., Jr. (in press). The aversive interpersonal context of depression: Emerging perspectives on depressotypic behavior. In R. M. Kowalski (Ed.), *Aversive behaviors and relational transgressions: The under-
belly of social interaction.* Washington, DC: American Psychological
Association.

King, D. A., & Heller, K. (1984). Depression and the response of others: A re-
evaluation. *Journal of Abnormal Psychology, 93,* 477–480.

Kirkpatrick, L. A., & Ellis, B. J. (in press). Evolutionary perspectives on self-
evaluation and self-esteem. In M. Clark & G. Fletcher (Eds.), *The Blackwell
handbook of social psychology, Vol. 2: Interpersonal processes.* Oxford,
UK: Blackwell Publishers.

Larsen, R. J., & Diener, E. (1992). Promises and problems with the circumplex
model of emotion. In M. S. Clark (Ed.), *Emotion* (pp. 25–59). Newbury
Park, CA: Sage.

Lazarus, R. S. (1984). On the primacy of cognition. *American Psychologist,
39,* 124–129.

Lazarus, R. S. (1991). *Emotion and adaptation.* New York: Oxford University
Press.

Leary, M. R. (1990). Responses to social exclusion: Social anxiety, jealousy,
loneliness, depression, and low self-esteem. *Journal of Social and Clinical
Psychology, 9,* 221–229.

Leary, M. R. (in press). Social anxiety as an early warning system: A refine-
ment and extension of the self-presentational theory of social anxiety. In
S. G. Hofman & P. M. DiBartolo (Eds.), *Social phobia and social anxiety:
An integration.* New York: Allyn & Bacon.

Leary, M. R., & Downs, D. L. (1995). Interpersonal functions of the self-esteem
motive: The self-esteem system as a sociometer. In M. Kernis (Ed.),
Efficacy, agency, and self-esteem (pp. 123–144). New York: Plenum Press.

Leary, M. R., Haupt, A., Strausser, K., & Chokel, J. (1998). Calibrating the sociometer: The relationship between interpersonal appraisals and state
self-esteem. *Journal of Personality and Social Psychology, 74,* 1290–1299.

Leary, M. R., Hechenbleikner, N. R., Strausser, K. S., Higgins, K., & Stiles, K.
(1999). *The emotional nature of hurt feelings.* Manuscript under review.

Leary, M. R., & Kowalski, R. M. (1995). *Social anxiety.* New York: Guilford.

Leary, M. R., & Springer, C. (2001). Hurt feelings: The neglected emotion. In
R. M. Kowalski (Ed.), *Behaving badly: Aversive behaviors in interpersonal
relationships* (pp. 151–175). Washington, DC: American Psychological
Association.

Leary, M. R., Springer, C., Negel, L., Ansell, E., & Evans, K. (1998). The causes,
phenomenology, and consequences of hurt feelings. *Journal of Personality
and Social Psychology, 74,* 1225–1237.

Lewis, H. B. (1971). *Shame and guilt in neurosis.* New York: International
Universities Press.

Lofland, L. H. (1982). Loss and the human connection: An exploration into
the nature of the social bond. In W. Ickes & E. S. Knowles (Eds.), *Personality, roles, and social behavior* (pp. 219–242). New York: Springer-Verlag.

Lorenz, F. O., Simons, R. L., Conger, R. D., Elder, G. H., Johnson, C., & Chao, W. (1997). Married and recently divorced mothers and stressful events and distress: Tracing change across time. *Journal of Marriage and the Family, 59,* 219–232.

Marks, I. M., & Neese, R. M. (1994). Fear and fitness: An evolutionary analysis of anxiety disorders. *Ethology and Sociology, 15,* 247–261.

Miller, R. S. (1996). *Embarrassment: Poise and peril in everyday life.* New York: Guilford Press.

Miller, R. S., & Tangney, J. P. (1994). Differentiating embarrassment and shame. *Journal of Social and Clinical Psychology, 13,* 273–287.

Mitchell-Flynn, C., & Hutchinson, R. (1993). A longitudinal study of the problems and concerns of urban divorced men. *Journal of Divorce and Remarriage, 19,* 161–182.

Morrison, A. P. (1983). Shame, ideal self, and narcissism. *Contemporary Psychoanalysis, 19,* 295–318.

Neese, R. M. (1989). Evolutionary explanations of emotions. *Human Nature, 1,* 261–289.

Osgood, N. J., & Brant, B. A. (1990). Suicidal behavior in long-term care facilities. *Suicide and Life-Threatening Behavior, 20,* 113–122.

Page, R. M., Frey, J., Talbert, R., & Falk, C. (1992). Children's feelings of loneliness and social dissatisfaction: Relationship to measures of physical fitness and activity. *Journal of Teaching in Physical Education, 11,* 211–219.

Peplau, L. A., & Perlman, D. (Eds.). (1982). *Loneliness: A sourcebook of current theory, research, and therapy.* New York: Wiley.

Pereti, P. O., & Pudowski, B. C. (1997). Influence of jealousy on male and female college daters. *Social Behavior and Personality, 25,* 155–160.

Pinker, S. (1997). *How the mind works.* New York: Norton.

Retzinger, S. M. (1995). Identifying shame and anger in discourse. *American Behavioral Scientist, 38,* 1104–1113.

Rokach, A. (1998). The relation of cultural background to the causes of loneliness. *Journal of Social and Clinical Psychology, 17,* 75–88.

Rotenberg, K. J., Bartley, J. L., & Toivonen, D. M. (1997). Children's stigmatization of chronic loneliness in peers. *Journal of Social Behavior and Personality, 12,* 577–584.

Schlenker, B. R. (1980). *Impression management: The self-concept, social identity, and interpersonal relations.* Monterey, CA: Brooks/Cole.

Schlenker, B. R., & Leary, M. R. (1982). Social anxiety and self-presentation: A conceptualization and model. *Psychological Bulletin, 92,* 641–669.

Segrin, C. (1993). Interpersonal reactions to dysphoria: The role of relationship with partner and perceptions in rejection. *Journal of Social and Personal Relationships, 10,* 83–97.

Segrin, C., & Dillard, J. P. (1992). The interactional theory of depression: A meta-analysis of the research literature. *Journal of Social and Clinical Psychology, 11,* 43–70.

Segrin, C., & Kinney, T. (1995). Social skills deficits among the socially anxious: Rejection from others and loneliness. *Motivation and Emotion, 19,* 1–24.

Sharpsteen, D. J., & Kirkpatrick, L. A. (1997). Romantic jealousy and adult romantic attachment. *Journal of Personality and Social Psychology, 72,* 627–640.

Shaver, P., Schwartz, J., Kirson, D., & O'Connor, C. (1987). Emotion knowledge: Further exploration of a prototype approach. *Journal of Personality and Social Psychology, 52,* 1061–1086.

Silver, M., Sabini, J., & Parrott, W. G. (1987). Embarrassment: A dramaturgic account. *Journal for the Theory of Social Behavior, 17,* 47–61.

Smith, C. A., & Kirby, L. D. (2000). Appraisal and memory: Toward a process model of emotion elicitation. In J. P. Forgas (Ed.), *Feeling and thinking: The role of affect in social cognition* (pp. 83–106). Cambridge: Cambridge University Press.

Snapp, C. M., & Leary, M. R. (in press). Hurt feelings among new acquaintances: Moderating effects of interpersonal familiarity. *Journal of Personal and Social Relationships.*

Stocker, C. M. (1994). Children's perceptions of relationships with siblings, friends, and mothers: Compensatory processes and links with adjustment. *Journal of Child Psychology and Psychiatry and Allied Disciplines, 35,* 1447–1459.

Tamako, B. (1983). Mourning the dissolution of the dream. *Social Work, 28,* 391–392.

Tangney, J. P. (1995). Shame and guilt in interpersonal relationships. In J. P. Tangney & K. W. Fischer (Eds.), *Self-conscious emotions: The psychology of shame, guilt, embarrassment, and pride* (pp. 114–139). New York: Guilford Press.

Tangney, J. P., Miller, R. S., Flicker, L., & Barlow, D. H. (1996). Are shame, guilt, and embarrassment distinct emotions? *Journal of Personality and Social Psychology, 70,* 1256–1264.

Tangney, J. P., & Salovey, P. (1999). Problematic social emotions: Shame, guilt, jealousy, and envy. In R. M. Kowalski & M. R. Leary (Eds.), *The social psychology of emotional and behavioral problems: Interfaces of social and clinical psychology* (pp. 167–195). Washington, DC: American Psychological Association.

Thomas, H. F. (1995). Experiencing a shame response as a precursor to violence. *Bulletin of the American Academy of Psychiatry and the Law, 23,* 587–593.

Tomkins, S. (1962). *Affect, imagery, consciousness* (Vol. 1). New York: Springer.

Tooby, J., & Cosmides, L. (1990). The past explains the present: Emotional adaptations and the structure of the ancestral environment. *Ethology and Sociobiology, 11,* 375–424.

Vorauer, J. D., & Ratner, R. K. (1996). Who's going to make the first move? Pluralistic ignorance as an impediment to relationship formation. *Journal of Social and Personal Relationships, 13,* 483–506.

Wheeler, L., Reis, H., & Nezlek, J. (1983). Loneliness, social interaction, and sex roles. *Journal of Personality and Social Psychology, 45,* 943–953.

Wilbert, J. R., & Rupert, P. A. (1986). Dysfunctional attitudes, loneliness, and depression in college students. *Cognitive Therapy and Research, 10,* 71–77.

Zajonc, R. B. (1980). Feeling and thinking: Preferences need no inferences. *American Psychologist, 35,* 151–175.

7

Coping with Rejection

Ego-Defensive Strategies, Self-Esteem, and Interpersonal Relationships

KRISTIN SOMMER

There probably exists no greater threat to a person's self-esteem than to be the target of interpersonal rejection. Rejection signifies the loss of a potentially meaningful relationship, and termination of the bond alone may be devastating. But the implications of rejection go far beyond the broken relationship. Rejection may be interpreted as a sign that one lacks (or no longer possesses) the personal qualities that make one a desirable relationship partner. A person who is ignored by coworkers, excluded from a group, or jilted by a lover may infer that he or she is incompetent, unattractive, or unskilled in social graces. Thus, rejection not only severs a potentially important relational attachment but also poses a strong threat to one's overall sense of worth.

How do people cope? How do people preserve esteem in the face of information suggesting that they are not accepted, wanted, or desired by others? In this chapter, I review the cognitive and behavioral defenses that people employ in anticipation of, or response to, interpersonal rejection. I emphasize two major classes of ego-defenses—self-enhancement and self-protection—and discuss the relationship of these defenses to chronic self-esteem. I also present new research demonstrating how coping responses involving persistence and performance are so well ingrained that they arise quickly and implicitly in response to subtle rejection cues. Finally, I conclude with a discussion of how the ego-defensive strategies of people low in self-esteem may be maladaptive in both the interpersonal and performance spheres.

Two Classes of Ego-Defense

The strategies that people employ to preserve self-esteem in the face of ego-threatening information may be categorized into two major classes: self-enhancement defenses and self-protection defenses. Loosely defined, self-enhancement defenses include any cognitive or behavioral strategy intended to focus attention on one's positive qualities or characteristics. Enhancement strategies include focusing on one's positive traits, working hard to excel on difficult tasks, and, in response to interpersonal rejection, affirming one's desirability to others and reinforcing one's interpersonal relationships. Self-enhancement defenses preserve or create a highly positive attitude about the self, which includes the belief that one is good, competent, and attractive to others.

Self-protection defenses involve attempts to divert attention from one's perceived negative qualities or characteristics. Self-protection may be achieved by withdrawing from potentially humiliating social situations, avoiding tasks on which one might fail, and distancing oneself both cognitively and behaviorally from others perceived to be critical or faultfinding. Self-protection defenses do not reflect a direct attempt to enhance the self in response to unflattering or ego-threatening feedback. Rather, their role is to shield the self from events that threaten to lower esteem. These may include social or performance situations that might expose one's weaknesses, flaws, deficiencies, or other negative attributes.

Both self-enhancement and self-protection defenses are executed in response to threatening information about the self. Yet they operate differently. Self-enhancement defenses boost self-esteem in the face of information that threatens to lower it, whereas self-protection defenses prevent future (or additional) loss of esteem. Note that self-protection defenses do not necessarily prevent the internalization of negative feedback. Rather, their function is to interrupt negative feedback or curtail exposure to esteem-threatening events in the first place.

Self-enhancement and self-protection defenses are typically studied as responses to failure feedback on performance-based tasks (Brown & Gallagher, 1992; Tice, 1991; Wood, Giordano-Beech, Taylor, Michela, & Gaus, 1994). However, these two classes of defense can also be used as a framework for understanding how people cope with real or imagined interpersonal rejection.

Self-Esteem and Ego-Defense: Maximizing Gains versus Cutting Losses

Several studies have revealed that the defenses that people employ in response to ego-threatening feedback are closely related to their chronic feelings of worth. Specifically, self-enhancement defenses characterize primarily people high in self-esteem, whereas self-protection defenses are more frequent among people low in self-esteem (Baumeister, Tice, & Hutton, 1989; Blaine & Crocker, 1993; Wood et al., 1994). Along these lines, Arkin (1981) distinguished between acquisitive and protective strategies within the context of self-presentation. He noted that people with high self-worth seek to gain approval, whereas those with low self-worth attempt to avoid disapproval. Subsequent research findings have supported this view. In the face of failure, people with high self-esteem strive to be the best, to stand out, and to prove their superiority; people with low self-esteem try hard to avoid being the worst, to deflect attention from their faults, and to prevent total failure (Baumeister & Tice, 1985; Tice, 1991).

Similar effects may emerge in response to rejection threat. High self-esteem individuals may attempt to refute the negative implications of rejection by enhancing their own and others' opinions of them. Low self-esteem individuals, in contrast, may attempt to avoid situations that threaten to expose their perceived deficiencies or weaknesses.

To understand why individuals choose different ego-defensive strategies, one must consider the nature of trait self-esteem. First, self-esteem is based largely on the degree to which one feels included or accepted by others (Cooley, 1902; Leary, 1990; Leary, Tambor, Terdal & Downs, 1995; Mead, 1934). For example, in their sociometer theory of self-esteem, Leary and his colleagues (1995) argued that self-esteem functions as a gauge of one's perceived social acceptance. The authors showed that perceptions of inclusion are significantly higher among people with high compared to low self-esteem and that both false feedback and mental imagery techniques that create feelings of exclusion decrease state (temporary) self-esteem. Other studies have yielded similar support for the role of perceived social inclusion in self-esteem (Harter, 1987; Leary, Haupt, Strausser, & Chokel, 1998; Murray & Holmes, 1997; Sommer, Williams, Ciarocco, & Baumeister, in press). Hence, the higher one's self-esteem, the greater the perception that others will generally find one to be worthy of inclusion.

Second, self-esteem is related strongly to perceived competence (Harter, 1993; Harter & Marold, 1991). For example, consistent with their self-flattering (and perhaps inflated) assumptions regarding others' liking for them, people high in self-esteem are especially confident about their abilities. They are more willing than their low self-esteem counterparts to take risks (Baumeister, Heatherton, & Tice, 1993) and persist in the face of failure (McFarlin & Blascovich, 1981; Shrauger & Sorman, 1977), presumably because they expect to succeed. Further, unlike their low self-esteem counterparts, people with high self-esteem do not view failure as resulting in imminent rejection (Baldwin & Sinclair, 1996). On the contrary, their confidence in others' liking for them provides a buffer against less than perfect performance. Low self-esteem individuals, in contrast, have relatively lower confidence in their abilities. They do not necessarily hate themselves; rather, they have fragile and unclear self-concepts that subsume both positive and negative traits (Campbell, 1990; Campbell, & Lavallee, 1993). In addition, people low in self-esteem view acceptance and rejection as largely contingent on success and failure, respectively (Baldwin & Sinclair, 1996). For them, the prospect of failure is especially frightening.

Differential levels of perceived belongingness and competence result in different interpretations of and responses to interpersonal rejection. Put simply, rejection will likely come as a shock to people high in self-esteem. Being rejected is clearly inconsistent with their presumed attractiveness to others and their perceptions of themselves as competent and capable people. Therefore, rejection will be interpreted as a sign that others have failed to see or appreciate them for who they really are.

Conversely, rejection will be less of a surprise to people low in self-esteem. These individuals already question the degree to which they are accepted by others and are unsure about their strengths and weaknesses. Their tenuous self-views, in turn, may cause them to accept rather than refute feedback that casts them in a negative light. Among people low in self-esteem, rejection may simply confirm fears of being incompetent, inferior, or generally undesirable to others.

To defend against rejection, then, people high in self-esteem will attempt to magnify their desirable qualities, whereas people low in self-esteem will try to redirect attention away from their undesirable qualities. Indeed, evidence suggests that people with low self-esteem resist self-enhancement, even in the presence of positive, flattering feedback (Swann, Griffin, Predmore, & Gaines, 1987). They may avoid thinking of themselves in highly positive terms to avoid setting themselves up for a fall. Fearing that an enhanced self-image will be undermined by future failures, they tend to view themselves more neutrally (Swann et al., 1987).

Note that there appears to be a temporal difference between enhancement and protection defenses. As Blaine and Crocker (1993) noted, the self-protection defenses that characterize people low in self-esteem are largely anticipatory in nature. Unlike those with high self-esteem, people with low self-esteem do not possess a large number of highly positive self-conceptions to buffer the impact of ego-threatening feedback. Thus, they attempt to preserve or sustain what esteem they do have by avoiding situations that threaten to cast the self in a negative light. In principle, self-protection defenses may be employed following threat as well. For example, after learning that they are unliked or unwanted, low self-esteem individuals may shy away from challenging tasks or withdraw from social situations to prevent any additional loss of self-esteem. However, because people with low self-worth cannot easily affirm their positive qualities following rejection and thus cannot completely avert a loss in esteem, their self-protective defenses are usually preemptive.

In contrast, enhancement defenses are typically employed in response to threatening feedback. People high in self-esteem do not anticipate losing esteem, because they feel confident in their abilities and in others' positive impressions of them. Thus, these individuals seek opportunities to bolster the self when confronted with information that questions the veracity of their positive self-beliefs. Under some circumstances, high self-esteem individuals may self-enhance before negative feedback, for example, when the threat of rejection is particularly high. Yet, in the absence of salient cues that fore-

warn one of the possibility of rejection or exclusion, most self-assured people will find themselves engaging in self-enhancement strategies after the rejection has occurred.

Ego-Defense and Self-Evaluation

The magnitude and direction of change in the self-concept following rejection provide a strong indication of the degree to which people can counteract a loss of self-esteem. As noted, the self-protection defenses that characterize people low in self-esteem do little to ameliorate loss of esteem once
rejection has occurred. However, the self-enhancement defenses that typify
people high in self-esteem may buffer any loss of esteem. Thus, one has
achieved successful enhancement when threatening social feedback regarding one's inclusionary status fails to result in downward appraisals of the self.

An early study by Shrauger and Lund (1975) demonstrated that high and
low self-esteem individuals differed in the extent to which they internalized
negative social evaluations. Female participants received either favorable or
unfavorable feedback about their personalities from a novice clinician. They
then completed measures assessing their opinions about the evaluator. The
results indicated that high self-esteem participants perceived that the clinician knew them much better in the favorable than the unfavorable conditions, whereas low self-esteem participants reported no differences between
feedback conditions. Similar results were obtained for ratings of the clinician's objectivity, competence, and lack of emotional bias; high but not low
self-esteem participants discredited the source following the unflattering but
not flattering feedback. The findings suggested that people with high self-esteem tend to fend off unflattering feedback by derogating its source.

More direct evidence for the role of self-esteem in coping with interpersonal rejection was provided by Nezlek, Kowalski, Leary, Blevins, and
Holgate (1997). These researchers led half the participants to believe that
other group members had chosen to exclude them from a group task, whereas
the remaining half were told that the group had chosen to include them. All
participants then completed measures of perceived acceptance and self-
esteem feelings (i.e., state self-esteem). Analyses indicated that, when participants were excluded from the group, their perceptions of acceptance and
self-esteem feelings decreased with decreasing levels of trait self-esteem.
When participants were included, perceived acceptance and self-esteem
were not related to changes in trait self-esteem. These findings showed that
chronically high levels of self-esteem buffered the negative impact of rejection. Nezlek et al. found a similar pattern of results for depression; rejection
exerted a stronger negative impact on depressed than nondepressed individuals. Though manipulation checks confirmed that high self-esteem and
nondepressed participants were well aware of their exclusionary status, they
appeared relatively impervious to its evaluative connotations. Nezlek et al.

did not assess enhancement defenses directly, yet one could speculate that these participants counteracted a loss of esteem by drawing from a large reservoir of positive, self-flattering cognitions.

One could draw a parallel between these findings and the defense mechanism of denial (Shrauger, 1975). This defense, in its original, psychoanalytic form, reflects a complete erasure of threatening information from memory (Freud, 1936). However, studies have revealed no evidence that high and low self-esteem people are differentially aware of having been rejected (e.g., Nezlek et al., 1997). A modified definition of denial involves one's refusal to acknowledge the threatening *implications* of an event, not the event per se (Baumeister, Dale, & Sommer, 1998). The defense mechanism of denial may be viewed as a by-product of a broader motivation to affirm one's highly positive opinions of oneself following threat.

The ability to maintain highly positive views of the self in the face of rejection provides indirect evidence of self-enhancement. The self-concepts of people with high self-esteem resist downward adjustment in response to negative evaluations from others. Discrediting the source of negative evaluation helps high self-esteem people to counteract the impact of the evaluation and thereby maintain their highly positive self-perceptions.

Ego-Defensive Strategies in Close Relationships

Close relationships provide an important context for the study of rejection. The human quest for belongingness is typically satisfied by developing and maintaining a small number of intimate relationships (Baumeister & Leary, 1995). When emotional ties with close relationship partners are severed, threats to belongingness are more serious than those associated with the loss of relatively insignificant relationships. Further, it stands to reason that the opportunity for esteem loss will be especially high within close relationships, because it is here that the rejector has the most intimate knowledge of one's strengths and weaknesses. People generally disclose more to intimates than to strangers (Chaiken & Derlega, 1974; Gilbert, & Whiteneck, 1976); thus, people may assume that close relationship partners are particularly qualified to evaluate them. Rejection by intimates may deal a stronger blow to one's ego than rejection by nonintimates, whose evaluations may be more easily discredited or ignored.

This section provides an overview of the cognitive and behavioral strategies that people use to cope with real or anticipated rejection in close relationships. The discussion is couched in terms of whether these strategies enhance or protect the self. The ego-defensive tactics employed in response to real or imagined rejection are apparent in individuals' perceptions of, and behaviors toward, their rejecting partners. This includes the decision to forgive or hold grudges against partners who have transgressed.

Perceptions of Partner

Recall that self-protection defenses arise to avoid or minimize a future loss of self-esteem. Within the context of interpersonal rejection, self-protection may entail pre-emptively thwarting connections with others who are perceived as critical or faultfinding. People often distance themselves cognitively from a potentially rejecting relationship partner by devaluing the partner. Seeing the partner in less positive terms effectively reduces the perceived significance of the relationship and softens the blow of rejection if the partner threatens to terminate the relationship.

Probably the strongest evidence for partner devaluation in anticipation of rejection comes from a series of experiments by Murray and her colleagues (Murray, Holmes, MacDonald, & Ellsworth, 1998). Participants did or did not engage in a task that threatened feelings of worth (e.g., feelings of being inconsiderate or intellectually inept). They then completed measures assessing how positively they evaluated their partners and how confident they were in their partners' liking for them (reflected appraisals). The results indicated that, compared to nonthreatened individuals, low self-esteem individuals whose egos were threatened became less convinced of their partners' positive regard and lowered their evaluations of their partners. Low self-esteem people also reported a lower need for the relationship following threat. This was in stark contrast to high self-esteem people, who responded to ego-threat by inflating their evaluations of their partners as well as their perceptions of their partners' regard. Further, threat did not reduce their reported need for the relationship.

Low self-esteem individuals demonstrated clear evidence of self-protection. When events caused them to focus on their weaknesses or deficiencies, they became insecure about their partners' continued regard. Mediational analyses showed that these negative-reflected appraisals resulted in derogation of the partner and lower reported need for the relationship. The authors used the term "disruptive disidentification" to describe the distancing behaviors of people with low self-esteem. Low self-esteem individuals who were threatened feared that they would be rejected by their partners; thus, they defended against possible rejection by devaluing their partners. As Murray et al. (1998) noted, "it seems that self-doubt and associated fears of rejection put lows on the interpersonal offense, leading them to reject their partners before their partners have the opportunity to reject them" (p. 1476).

In contrast, high self-esteem individuals defended against threat by affirming their partners' continued positive regard and inflating ratings of their partners' virtues. Recall that enhancement defenses reflect an attempt to augment one's positive qualities in the face of information that threatens to damage self-esteem. The results from the Murray et al. (1998) study suggest that one method of refuting the unflattering feedback is to reinforce perceptions of the partner's commitment to the relationship. People high in self-esteem already assume high levels of interpersonal acceptance (Leary et al., 1995), and in times of threat they appear to use their close relationships as a resource for affirming the self.

Earlier I suggested that derogating the source of negative feedback functions to enhances the self, whereas this analysis treats partner derogation as a form of self-protection. Partner devaluation may serve both motives, albeit under different circumstances. Derogation serves enhancement when it elevates or maintains one's relative superiority. Thus, people with high self-esteem may devalue rejecting others to discredit them and thereby maintain self-perceptions of being worthy, liked, or respected. In contrast, derogation serves self-protection when it guards the self against future threat. Low self-esteem people may disparage others when they fear that their own deficiencies will eventually cause them to be rejected. In self-protection, derogation does not provide a means of boosting the self but rather reflects an effort to distance the self from potentially rejecting others.

Behaviors Toward a Partner

Self-enhancement or self-protection in response to interpersonal rejection is also evident in people's behaviors toward rejecting relationship partners. Consistent with their relatively low confidence in their own and others' impressions of them, individuals low in self-esteem may react to the threat of rejection by withdrawing and avoiding contact with the rejecting partner. Conversely, consistent with their highly positive self-conceptions, high self-esteem individuals may defend against rejection by attempting to prove their desirability to others.

In a recent study, my colleagues and I examined social ostracism, also known as the "silent treatment" (Sommer et al., in press). Respondents reported on 100-point scales how often they were subjected to the silent treatment and how often they used the silent treatment on others. They also wrote stories about incidents in which they gave and received the silent treatment. Consistent with sociometer theory, we found that trait self-esteem correlated negatively with perceptions of being silenced by others ($r = -.33$). On a more interesting (and seemingly ironic) note, we also discovered that self-esteem correlated negatively with the self-reported tendency to use the silent treatment on others ($r = -.45$). Thus, low self-esteem people were more likely than their high self-esteem counterparts to be both recipients and users of the silent treatment. Content analyses of the autobiographical narratives yielded evidence of a particular type of (motive for) ostracism used among people low in self-esteem—defensive ostracism. Defensive ostracism involves ignoring another person in a preemptive attempt to buffer the impact of anticipated rejection or esteem threat (Williams, 1997; Williams & Sommer, 1997). Defensive ostracizers reported using (or were described by the target as using) silence to avoid feeling bad, blameworthy, or inferior. Defensive ostracizers sometimes also reported that talking or arguing was futile because they always ended up "looking like the bad guy." Our findings were consistent with those of Murray et al. (1998), showing that people low in self-esteem may reject a potentially critical or rejecting partner as a means of protecting the self.

In contrast, we found that people who were high in self-esteem were more likely than those low in self-esteem to self-affirm, seek out external relationships, and terminate their relationships after receiving the silent treatment for ambiguous reasons (Ciarocco, Sommer, & Williams, 1998). Unclear ostracism (ostracism without a specific known cause) proved to be especially threatening; it resulted in more hurt and greater threats to self-esteem and belongingness than ostracism that had a specific known cause. In response to causally unclear ostracism, high self-esteem individuals exhibited a clear pattern of self-enhancement. They reported being hurt by the experience but then promptly left their partners. They often mentioned that they were better than their rejectors and that their true friends appreciated them. Those ostracized by a romantic partner emphasized the dedication and loyalty of their current romantic partners. High self-esteem targets were also more likely than low self-esteem targets to report seeking others' company following the ostracism. Apparently, people high in self-esteem felt confident in securing others' positive attention and could leave their rejecting partners and move on to other relationships.

Rusbult and her colleagues (Rusbult, Morrow, & Johnson, 1987) found similar support for the role of self-esteem in response to conflict. These researchers found that low self-esteem individuals were more likely than high self-esteem individuals to exhibit neglect, defined as ignoring the partner, criticizing the partner, and generally letting the relationship fall apart. In contrast, self-esteem correlated positively with the tendency to exit the relationship. Rusbult (1993) explained that high self-esteem individuals likely perceive greater options for securing alternative romantic relationships than do low self-esteem people. Thus, the former are more likely to leave the relationship when things are going badly. Rusbult et al. did not measure perceived partner rejection per se, but the findings are consistent with the notion that high self-esteem people will respond to the threat of relationship loss by terminating the relationship and finding new partners.

Note that both enhancement and protective defenses against rejection may result in relationship termination, albeit for different reasons. The neglect and defensive ostracism exhibited by people with low self-esteem could result in loss of the relationship. Indeed, low self-esteem individuals have less stable relationships than high self-esteem individuals (Hendrick, Hendrick, & Adler, 1988). Yet there is no indication that people low in self-esteem consciously try to ruin their relationships (Sommer et al., in press). Instead, they probably are trying to protect themselves against what they believe to be criticism or imminent rejection by the partner. People high in self-esteem, on the other hand, are more likely to actively sever connections when they feel that they are getting unwarranted negative attention from their partners.

Grudge Holding

A final manifestation of the desire for self-protection involves the tendency to hold a grudge. The inability or unwillingness to forgive an interpersonal transgression may provide low self-esteem individuals with a means of defending against future self-esteem loss. Forgiveness signifies that the relationship can revert back to its original state (Baumeister, Exline, & Sommer, 1998). Thus, a person contemplating forgiveness must consider whether forgiveness increases the chances of being hurt again. Consistent with their self-protective, defensive styles, people low in self-esteem may be particularly likely to withhold forgiveness in fear that their partners will betray or wrong them in the future. Research has revealed some support for this contention. Haley and Strickland (1986) found that depressed women were more likely than nondepressed women to respond to interpersonal betrayal on a prisoner's dilemma task with self-criticism and retaliation against the betraying partner. Other studies have shown that individuals who are depressed or low in self-esteem score lower on standardized measures of forgiveness than nondepressed or high self-esteem people (Al-Mabuk, Enright, & Cardis, 1995; Hebl & Enright, 1993; Mauger, Perry, Freeman, Grove, McBride, & McKinney, 1992; Subkoviak, Enright, Wu, & Gassin, 1995). For people who already question their desirability to others, then, forgiveness may pose a particularly difficult obstacle. Grudge holding may provide low self-esteem and depressed individuals with a buffer against esteem loss in case they are disrespected, neglected, or otherwise wronged in the future.

Summary

High self-esteem individuals exhibit self-enhancement defenses in response to real rejection, whereas low self-esteem individuals employ self-protection defenses in anticipation of rejection. People high in self-esteem cope with rejection by deliberately severing their relationships, self-affirming, and establishing relationships with others. They try to enhance themselves both cognitively and behaviorally in response to the implication that they are unworthy or undesirable. People low in self-esteem adopt a self-protective style of coping. For them, any event that draws attention to their negative traits activates fears of rejection. Low self-esteem individuals who perceive or anticipate rejection will devalue, ignore, avoid, hold a grudge against, and generally distance themselves from the rejector.

Implicit Rejection and Ego-Defensive Strategies

I now describe two studies that examined the effects of implicit rejection on ego-defensive strategies. These studies were based on the notion that coping responses to rejection can become so strongly ingrained that they may begin to emerge preconsciously (Sommer & Baumeister, 1997). By exposing some participants to simple rejection cues (primes), we hoped to activate a predictable set of ego-defensive strategies consistent with those found in response to more explicit forms of threat.

Prior research has demonstrated the automaticity of processes such as stereotyping (e.g., Banaji, 1996; Blair & Banaji, 1996; Bargh, Chen, & Burrows, 1996; Chen, & Bargh, 1997; Devine, 1989), impression formation (e.g., Gilbert, Pelham, & Krull, 1988; Srull & Wyer, 1979, 1980), and evaluation (Bargh, Chaiken, Raymond, & Hymes, 1996; Fazio, Sanbonmatsu, Powell, & Kardes, 1986). In a review of the literature, Bargh (1997) argued that goals or motivations, like percepts, are mental representations that may be elicited preconsciously (automatically) in response to a stimulus event. When people repeatedly choose certain goals or motivations in response to particular stimuli, then eventually these goals may begin to emerge without conscious intent. According to Bargh, preconscious processes require only the "proximal registration of the stimulus event to occur" (p. 6). The entire stimulus-response sequence is then carried out automatically without any conscious decision on the part of the perceiver.

Preconscious processes are typically tested with priming techniques. Participants are presented with subtle visual or auditory cues intended to activate mental representations of particular concepts (e.g., stereotypes). They are then assessed on some dependent measure theoretically related to the stimulus event (e.g., stereotypical behaviors). Automaticity occurs when participants exhibit a predictable pattern of emotions, cognitions, or behaviors in response to the primes and when participants have no awareness or recollection of the primes.

We tested the impact of implicit rejection on two facets of motivation: persistence and performance on a difficult task. Consistent with prior research, we predicted that implicit rejection would activate enhancement strategies among people with high self-esteem. Evidence for self-enhancement defenses would be indicated by high levels of persistence and performance on a difficult or challenging task (Trope, 1986). In contrast, we expected that the same manipulation would trigger protection or guardedness among people low in self-esteem. Self-protection defenses would be marked by low levels of persistence and performance. In our view, low motivation following a rejection threat may indicate concerns about failure and/or a desperate need to deflect attention from one's (perceived) substandard abilities.

A number of studies have demonstrated that ego threats (e.g., failure feedback) increase task motivation among high but not low self-esteem individuals. People high in self-esteem will take more risks (Baumeister et al., 1993), make more optimistic predictions about their future performance (McFarlin & Blascovich, 1981), and actually perform slightly better (Brockner, 1979) following a failure than a success. Under conditions in which persistence is counterproductive (i.e., impairs rather than enhances performance), high self-esteem may result in self-regulatory failure and decreased performance (Baumeister et al., 1993; McFarlin, Baumeister, & Blascovich, 1984). People low in self-esteem do not exhibit these self-enhancement strategies. In fact, they set their expectations for their performance low (McFarlin & Blascovich, 1981; Spencer, Josephs, & Steele, 1993) and tend to perform worse (Brockner, 1979; Shrauger & Rosenberg, 1970) following threat. Thus, like previous researchers, we expected that rejection priming would improve persistence and performance among high self-esteem individuals but worsen persistence and performance among low self-esteem individuals.

Participants completed a measure of trait self-esteem (Fleming & Courtney, 1984) during mass testing and were later classified as low or high in self-esteem using a median split. For the first study, participants completed one of three priming tasks. Priming was manipulated using the sentence unscramble task (Banaji, Hardin, & Rothman, 1993; Srull & Wyer, 1980), which required participants to form short phrases or sentences from a series of randomly ordered words. Half of the primes were neutral and constant across conditions. In the acceptance priming condition, the remaining primes were related to acceptance (e.g., "group the joined a"). In the rejection condition, the primes connoted rejection or exclusion (e.g., "from isolated on others"). Finally, a third condition included negatively valenced primes unrelated to rejection (e.g., "above crash hurt in"). All participants then completed a purported test of language abilities. They were presented with six anagrams, only three of which were actually solvable, and told to work on the anagrams as long as they desired. The primary dependent measure was the amount of time that participants persisted at the frustrating task before notifying the experimenter that they wanted to stop.

The results indicated striking differences in persistence between conditions. In the acceptance and negative priming conditions, low and high self-esteem individuals worked about equally hard trying to solve the unsolvable anagrams. In fact, those with low self-esteem persisted slightly (but nonsignificantly) longer. Yet, following the rejection threat, high self-esteem participants persisted significantly longer than low self-esteem participants. Put another way, persistence varied dramatically across priming conditions. Compared to the control primes, the rejection primes caused high self-esteem individuals to double their efforts, whereas they caused low self-esteem individuals to reduce their efforts by half.

The second study examined whether persistence differences translated into actual performance improvements or deficits. The procedure was essentially the same, but instead of measuring persistence on unsolvable anagrams, we recorded the number of solvable anagrams that people actually completed within 5 minutes. We found a significant interaction between self-esteem and performance. Following the acceptance primes, low self-esteem participants performed slightly better than high self-esteem participants. Yet the rejection primes boosted the performance of high self-esteem participants, whereas they impaired the performance of low self-esteem participants.

The first study showed that a defensive quest for self-enhancement drove high self-esteem individuals to continue working hard even though they were failing. The second study demonstrated that this defensive persistence paid off by way of improved performance on a difficult but solvable task. The findings parallel those of studies on close relationships by showing that people high in self-esteem cope with rejection by engaging in behaviors that accentuate their positive qualities and reinforce their highly positive self-views.

The pattern of findings was opposite for individuals low in self-esteem. The first study revealed a significant decline in persistence following implicit rejection, suggesting that these people were eager to quit working on the task. The second study showed that withdrawal translated into impaired performance. In the control condition, low self-esteem participants performed equally well as, if not a little better than, high self-esteem participants. But rejection threat threw things awry. Rejection caused people low in self-worth to avoid the task, possibly in efforts to deflect attention from their seeming incompetence. To these people, the challenging anagram task may have represented an opportunity to confirm their feared intellectual weaknesses. Thus, they abandoned the task to circumvent a potentially huge loss of self-esteem.

These studies demonstrate that rejection need only be primed to elicit ego-defensive behavior. Any event that cues individuals to the possibility of rejection may evoke compensatory enhancement or fearful withdrawal among high and low self-esteem individuals, respectively. Extensive debriefings indicated that participants were not able to decipher the true source of their motivation (or lack thereof). This suggests that goals for enhancement and protection may become automatic responses to rejection threat. Further, the entire stimulus-response sequence may occur without the perceiver's awareness that his or her behavior is being influenced.

Self-Esteem and Maladaptive Coping

The strategies that people low in self-esteem use to cope with rejection appear to be maladaptive, within both the relationship and performance spheres. In an apparent attempt to protect themselves from self-esteem loss, these individuals may cognitively and behaviorally distance themselves from their partners (Sommer et al., in press). People with low self-worth who are reminded of their past transgressions will even derogate their partners and diminish the perceived importance of the relationship (Murray et al., 1998). Low self-esteem and negative perceptions of the partner are, in turn, associated with lower relationship satisfaction, lower relationship stability, and lower likelihood of forgiveness following a transgression (Hendrick et al., 1988; Murray et al., 1998). Though more research on the topic is needed, the findings to date point to a self-fulfilling prophecy among low self-esteem individuals. To defend against rejection, people with low self-worth may actively thwart meaningful connections with their partners. The ensuing relationship termination further reinforces their already low perceptions of acceptance.

A more adaptive response to rejection threat would entail working hard to maintain the relationship, thereby reducing the likelihood of rejection. But low self-esteem individuals' own uncertainty about their desirability to others disrupts any hope of achieving and maintaining belongingness. From the perspective of someone with low self-esteem, then, the only effective way to guard against esteem loss when faced with the threat of rejection is to cognitively and behaviorally distance the self from the partner.

Other research has yielded similar evidence for the role of negative partner perceptions in overall relationship quality. Bradbury and Fincham (1992) examined relationship partners' attributions for conflict as well as their behaviors when attempting to resolve the conflict. Though the researchers did not assess trait self-esteem per se, they found that people who perceived hurtful or selfish intentions in their partners exhibited behaviors that were counterproductive to problem solving. Destructive behaviors included hostility and rejection of the partner. Similarly, Downey and Feldman (1996) found that people who were dispositionally high in rejection-sensitivity (i.e., those who anxiously expect and perceive rejection in the ambiguous behaviors of others) were more likely that those low in rejection-sensitivity to treat their partners with hostility and jealousy. Rejection-sensitivity, which correlates negatively with self-esteem, also predicted lower relationship satisfaction among both rejection-sensitive individuals and their partners. Taken together, these studies reinforce the conclusion that negative partner attributions contribute to the demise of the relationship.

Finally, maladaptive coping among people low in self-esteem is illustrated in the performance sphere as well. Rejection appears to instigate a pattern of underachievement wherein people with low self-worth withdraw, avoid challenging tasks, and underperform. There may be a self-fulfilling aspect to poor performance as well as relationship dissolution. That is, people low in self-esteem who begin to question their strengths in the face of threat will see their fears confirmed when they fail to live up to their own and others' standards.

The automatic nature of ego-defenses in response to rejection threat suggests that tactics intended to enhance or protect the self may be difficult to override. This is not especially problematic for people high in self-esteem, at least to the degree that their defenses eventually prove beneficial. Yet the automaticity of coping strategies may create a problem for people low in self-esteem. These individuals may, without knowledge or intent, engage in behaviors that eventually damage their relationships and undermine their success.

Are there circumstances under which the enhancement defenses employed by high self-esteem people are also maladaptive? Three lines of work have identified positive links between self-esteem, self-enhancement, and destructive behaviors. First, research by Rusbult et al. (1987) has shown that people high in self-esteem are more likely than those low in self-esteem to respond to relational conflict by actively leaving the relationship. Unfortunately, the studies that have explored this topic have failed to pinpoint the seriousness of relationship difficulties prior to the decision to leave. Thus, it is not clear whether among these participants leaving a bad relationship reflected a maladaptive tendency to destroy an intact relationship or a relatively healthy means of rebounding in response to a highly angry, hostile, or rejecting partner. Second, Baumeister, Smart, and Boden (1997) established a strong link between threatened egotism and violence, pinpointing high rather than low self-esteem as a cause of aggression. The self-esteem-violence link, however, appears to be specific to people who have either high, unstable self-esteem or an especially inflated sense of worth (i.e., narcissism). For example, Kernis, Grannemann, and Barclay (1989) found significant positive correlations between unstable (but not stable) high self-esteem and hostility. Other researchers (Raskin, Novacek, & Hogan, 1991; Rhodewalt & Morf, 1995) obtained similar correlations between narcissism and hostility. More recently, Bushman and Baumeister (1998) revealed that narcissism (defined by agreement with statements such as "The world would be a better place if I were in charge," "I am going to be a great person") predicted participants' decisions to administer aversive blasts of noise to a person who had ostensibly criticized them. However, self-esteem per se was not positively associated with aggressive responding. Finally, Baumeister and colleagues (Baumeister et al., 1993; McFarlin et al., 1984) showed that high self-esteem people's responses to ego threat prove detrimental to performance under conditions in which defensive persistence and overconfidence are counterproductive (i.e., impair rather than enhance one's ability to succeed).

Thus, some evidence suggests that enhancement defenses have a maladaptive side too. People whose self-esteem fluctuates may react to rejection threat with hostility and violence because their favorable self-views are at risk for downward adjustment. Also, narcissists are likely to lash out destructively when information suggests that they are unliked, disrespected, or otherwise held in low regard. Finally, people high in self-esteem may ultimately fail on tasks for which the contingencies between inflated confidence and performance are reversed.

A final issue to be considered involves the potential benefits of self-protection. Is self-protection adaptive in any way other than to make the person temporarily feel better? The existing literature suggests that few if any social benefits arise from self-protection. Withdrawing from social situations in anticipation of (or response to) rejection can only reduce one's chances of forming meaningful, rewarding relationships. However, as suggested above, self-protection may be beneficial under limited performance situations, such as when stronger efforts ultimately lead to worse outcomes. Baumeister et al. (1993) asked participants who had or had not been ego-threatened to complete a skill-based task on which they could set goals for their performance. The task was constructed such that setting high goals was linked to large monetary gains in the event of success but also large losses in the event of failure. In the absence of ego threat, high self-esteem individuals performed somewhat better than low self-esteem individuals. However, when people with high self-esteem were ego-threatened, they became overconfident, failed to reach their goals, and ultimately lost money. In other words, ego threat led to self-regulation failure among people with high self-esteem. People with low self-esteem demonstrated the opposite effect. When threatened, they set more modest goals for themselves, performed better, and increased their earnings. Thus, when the contingencies between confidence and large rewards were reversed, or when overoptimism became self-defeating, self-protective strategies proved to be relatively adaptive.

Implications for the Workplace

I have focused thus far on how self-esteem and rejection interact to affect personal relationships and performance within laboratory settings. However, coping responses to rejection may also appear in the form of changes in workplace behaviors. Specifically, the results from the priming studies suggest that lack of acceptance by one's employer or coworkers could disrupt performance among employees with low self-esteem. Rejection need not take the form of explicit devaluation of one's work. Rather, any information in the environment that threatens feelings of inclusion may exert a deleterious impact on the motivation and performance of a low self-esteem individual. To avoid failure and humiliation, people with low self-worth (who are otherwise competent and hard-working) may defensively withdraw from challenging tasks and exhibit a decline in performance.

In contrast, workplace rejection may pose a challenge to high self-esteem individuals, leading them to work even harder in efforts to prove themselves as smart, competent, and desirable people. Clearly, creating an unfriendly workplace as a means of improving employee productivity would not be advised. People with high self-esteem would probably just as well work elsewhere when confronted with chronic coworker or supervisor rejection, especially if the exact cause of rejection is unclear (Ciarocco et al., 1998). But when confronted with occasional perceptions of disrespect, exclusion, or ostracism within the workplace, people with high self-esteem will be much less likely than those with low self-esteem to respond with dejection and withdrawal. To the contrary, their need to prove their worth would likely result in defensive persistence and accelerated performance.

Summary and Conclusions

The defenses that people employ in the face of rejection may be broadly categorized into two classes: self-protection and self-enhancement. Self-protection strategies are typical of people low in self-esteem and usually emerge in anticipation of rejection. Strategies include derogating the partner, preemptively rejecting the partner, and withdrawing from tasks that threaten to reveal one's weaknesses. Self-enhancement tactics characterize people high in self-esteem and typically ensue in response to rejection. They include affirming the self, reinforcing existing relationships, and working hard to prove one's strengths. Both self-protection and self-enhancement defenses are employed in the service of self-esteem, although the evidence suggests that enhancement defenses more effectively counteract a loss of self-esteem following rejection.

People with high self-esteem are not immune to the detrimental effects of interpersonal rejection. The absence of downward changes in self-appraisals following rejection may lead some people to conclude erroneously that individuals who feel especially good about themselves do not care if they are disliked. Yet studies have revealed that high self-esteem individuals take great strides to defend against unwanted negative attention, such as by seeking interpersonal connections, reinforcing perceptions of partner commitment, and increasing efforts on difficult tasks. The need to belong is ubiquitous (Baumeister & Leary, 1995). The strategies that people employ to defend against threats to belongingness simply differ depending on their feelings of worth, which include their perceived abilities to garner acceptance. People who feel especially deserving of others' high regard and capable of winning that regard will work hard to refute the implications of being unwanted. Conversely, those who question their special desirability may try to dissociate from others to guard against future esteem loss.

Self-protective defenses against rejection are often maladaptive, within the context of both interpersonal functioning and individualistic performance. Low self-esteem individuals exhibit self-defeating responses to rejection by distancing themselves from close relationship partners instead of using those partners as a means of support and affirmation. They also withdraw from difficult tasks, which only incurs the failure they normally try to avoid. The enhancement defenses exhibited by people high in self-esteem are generally adaptive (though there are notable exceptions). Threats of rejection motivate high self-esteem individuals to bolster their confidence in both the relationship and performance domains.

Interpersonal rejection is a powerful social phenomenon that exerts an unparalleled negative impact on self-worth. People go to great lengths to avoid

feeling unwanted or undesirable, and they use several ego-defensive strategies to accomplish this goal. Real or anticipated rejection affects how both
high and low self-esteem individuals perceive and relate to their relationship
partners, and it determines their motivation on challenging tasks. Finally,
when enhancement and protection strategies are repeatedly chosen in response to interpersonal rejection, these defenses may begin to occur without
conscious intent.

Acknowledgments

Thanks go to Sherri Ondrus and Mark Leary for their helpful comments
on an earlier version of this chapter.

References

Al-Mabuk, R. H., Enright, R. D., & Cardis, P. A. (1995). Forgiveness education
with parentally love-deprived late adolescents. *Journal of Moral Education, 24,* 427–444.

Arkin, R. M. (1981). Self-presentation styles. In J. T. Tedeschi (Ed.),
Impression management theory and social psychological research
(pp. 311–333). San Diego, CA: Academic Press.

Baldwin, M. W., & Sinclair, L. (1996). Self-esteem and "if . . . then" contingencies of interpersonal acceptance. *Journal of Personality and Social
Psychology, 71,* 1130–1141.

Banaji, M. R. (1996). Automatic stereotyping. *Psychological Science, 7,*
136–141.

Banaji, M. R., Hardin, C., & Rothman, A. J. (1993). Implicit stereotyping in person judgment. *Journal of Personality and Social Psychology, 65,* 272–281.

Bargh, J. A. (1997). The automaticity of everyday life. In R. S. Wyer, Jr. (Ed.),
The automaticity of everyday life. *Advances in social cognition, Vol. 10*
(pp. 1–61). Mahway, NJ: Lawrence Erlbaum.

Bargh, J. A., Chaiken, S., Raymond, P., & Hymes, C. (1996). The automatic evaluation effect: Unconditionally automatic attitude activation with a pronunciation task. *Journal of Experimental Social Pyschology, 32,* 185–210.

Bargh, J. A., Chen, M., & Burrows, L. (1996). Automaticity of social behavior:
Direct effects of trait construct and stereotype activation on action. *Journal
of Personality and Social Psychology, 71,* 230–244.

Baumeister, R. F., Dale, K., & Sommer, K. L. (1998). Defense mechanisms in
modern personality and social psychology. *Journal of Personality, 66,*
1081–1124.

Baumeister, R. F., Exline, J. J., & Sommer, K. L. (1998). The victim role, grudge
theory, and two dimensions of forgiveness. In E. Worthington (Ed.),
*Dimensions of forgiveness: Psychological research and theological per-
spectives* (pp. 79–104). Radnor, PA: Templeton Press.

Baumeister, R. F., Heatherton, T. F., & Tice, D. M. (1993). When ego threats
lead to self-regulation failure: Negative consequences of high self-esteem.
Journal of Personality and Social Psychology, 64, 141–156.

Baumeister, R. F., & Leary, M. R. (1995). The need to belong: Desire for inter-
personal attachments as a fundamental human motivation. *Psychological
Bulletin, 117,* 497–529.
Baumeister, R. F., Smart, L., & Boden, J. M. (1996). Relation of threatened ego-
tism to violence and aggression: The dark side of high self-esteem.
Psychological Review, 103, 5–33.
Baumeister, R. F., Tice, D. M. (1985). Self-esteem and responses to success
and failure: Subsequent performance and intrinsic motivation. *Journal of
Personality, 53,* 450–467.
Baumeister, R. F., Tice, D. M., & Hutton, D. G. (1989). Self-presentational mo-
tivations and personality differences in self-esteem. *Journal of Personal-
ity, 57,* 547–579.
Blaine, B., & Crocker, J. (1993). Self-esteem and self-serving biases in reac-
tions to positive and negative events: An integrative review. In R. F.
Baumeister (Ed.), *Self-esteem: The puzzle of low self-regard* (pp. 55–85).
New York: Plenum.
Blair, I. W., & Banaji, M. R. (1996). Automatic and controlled processes in
stereotype priming. *Journal of Personality and Social Psychology, 70,*
1142–1163.
Bradbury, T. N., & Fincham, F. D. (1992). Attributions and behavior in marital
interactions. *Journal of Personality and Social Psychology, 63,* 613–628.
Brockner, J. (1979). The effects of self-esteem, success-failure, and self-consciousness on task performance. *Journal of Personality and Social Psychology, 37,* 1732–1741.
Brown, T. D., & Gallagher, F. M. (1992). Coming to terms with failure: Private
self-enhancement and public self-effacement. *Journal of Experimental
and Social Psychology, 28,* 3–22.
Bushman, B. J., & Baumeister, R. F. (1998). Threatened egotism, narcissism,
self-esteem, and direct and displaced aggression: Does self-love or self-
hate lead to violence? *Journal of Personality and Social Psychology, 75,*
219–229.
Campbell, J. D. (1990). Self-esteem and clarity of self-concept. *Journal of
Personality and Social Psychology, 59,* 538–549.
Campbell, J. D., & Lavallee, L. F. (1993). Who am I? The role of self-concept
confusion in understanding the behavior of people with low self-esteem.
In R. F. Baumeister (Ed.), *Self-esteem: The puzzle of low self-regard* (pp. 3–
20). New York: Plenum Press.
Chaiken, A. L., & Derlega, V. J. (1974). Variables affecting appropriateness
of self-disclosure. *Journal of Consulting and Clinical Psychology, 92,*
588–593.
Chen, M., & Bargh, J. A. (1997). Nonconscious behavioral confirmation processes: The self-fulfilling nature of automatically activated stereotypes.
Journal of Experimental Social Psychology, 33, 541–560.
Ciarocco, N. J., Sommer, K. L., & Williams, K. D. (May, 1998). *On being ignored and not knowing why: The detrimental effects of ambiguous silence.* Paper presented at the Midwestern Psychological Association conference, Chicago, IL.
Cooley, C. H. (1902). *Human nature and the social order.* New York:
Scribner's.

Devine, P. G. (1989). Stereotypes and prejudice: Their automatic and controlled components. *Journal of Personality and Social Psychology, 56,* 680–690.

Downey, G., & Feldman, S. I. (1996). Implications of rejection sensitivity for intimate relationships. *Journal of Personality and Social Psychology, 70,* 1237–1343.

Fazio, R. H., Sanbonmatsu, D. M., Powell, M. C., & Kardes, F. R. (1986). On the automatic activation of attitudes. *Journal of Personality and Social Psychology, 50,* 229–238.

Fleming, J. S., & Courtney, B. E. (1984). The dimensionality of self-esteem. II. Hierarchical facet model for revised measurement scales. *Journal of Personality and Social Psychology, 46,* 404–421.

Freud, A. (1936). *The ego and the mechanisms of defense.* New York: Hogarth Press.

Gilbert, D. T., Pelham, B. W., & Krull, D. S. (1988). On cognitive busyness: When person perceivers meet persons perceived. *Journal of Personality and Social Psychology, 54,* 733–739.

Gilbert, S. J., & Whiteneck, G. G. (1976). Toward a multidimensional approach to the study of self-disclosure. *Human Communication Research, 2,* 347–355.

Haley, W. E., & Strickland, B. R. (1986). Interpersonal betrayal and cooperation: Effects on self-evaluation in depression. *Journal of Personality and Social Psychology, 50,* 386–391.

Harter, S. (1987). The determinants and mediational role of global self-worth in children. In N. Eisenberg (Ed.), *Contemporary issues in developmental psychology* (pp. 219–242). New York: John Wiley.

Harter, S. (1993). Causes and consequences of low self-esteem in children and adolescents. In R. F. Baumeister (Ed.), *Self-esteem: The puzzle of low self-regard* (pp. 87–116). New York: Plenum Press.

Harter, S., & Marold, D. B. (1991). A model of the determinants and mediational role of self-worth: Implications for adolescent depression and suicidal ideation. In G. Goethals & J. Strauss (Eds.), *The self: An interdisciplinary approach.* New York: Springer-Verlag.

Hebl, J. H., & Enright, R. D. (1993). Forgiveness as a psychotherapeutic goal with elderly females. *Psychotherapy, 30,* 658–667.

Hendrick, S. S., Hendrick, C., & Adler, N. L. (1988). Romantic relationships: Love, satisfaction, and staying together. *Journal of Personality and Social Psychology, 54,* 980–988.

Kernis, M. H., Grannemann, B. D., & Barclay, L. C. (1989). Stability and level of self-esteem as predictors of anger arousal and hostility. *Journal of Personality and Social Psychology, 56,* 1013–1023.

Leary, M. R. (1990). Responses to social exclusion: Social anxiety, jealousy, loneliness, depression, and low self-esteem. *Journal of Social and Clinical Psychology, 9,* 221–229.

Leary, M. R., Haupt., A. L., Strausser, K. S., & Chokel, J. T. (1998). Calibrating the sociometer: The relationship between interpersonal appraisals and state self-esteem. *Journal of Personality and Social Psychology, 74,* 1290–1299.

Leary, M. R., Tambor, E. S., Terdal, S. K., & Downs, D. L. (1995). Self-esteem as an interpersonal monitor: The sociometer hypothesis. *Journal of Personality and Social Psychology, 68,* 518–530.

Mauger, P. A., Perry, J. E., Freeman, T., Grove, D. C., McBride, A. G., & McKinney, K. E. (1992). The measurement of forgiveness: Preliminary research. Special Issue: Grace and forgiveness. *Journal of Psychology and Christianity, 11,*170–180.

McFarlin, D. B., Baumeister, R. F., & Blascovich, J. (1984). On knowing when to quit: Task failure, self-esteem, advice, and nonproductive persistence. *Journal of Personality, 52,* 138–155.

McFarlin, D. B., & Blascovich, J. (1981). Effects of self-esteem and performance on future affective preferences and cognitive expectation. *Journal of Personality and Social Psychology, 40,* 521–531.

Mead, G. H. (1934). *Mind, self, and society.* Chicago: University of Chicago Press.

Murray, S. L., & Holmes, J. G. (1997). A leap of faith? Positive illlusions in romantic relationships. *Personality and Social Psychology Bulletin, 23,* 586–604.

Murray, S. L., Holmes, J. G., MacDonald, G., & Ellsworth, P.C. (1998). Through the looking glass darkly? When self-doubts turn into relationship insecurities. *Journal of Personality and Social Psychology, 75,* 1459–1480.

Nezlek, J. B., Kowalski, R. M., Leary, M. R., Blevins, T., & Holgate, S. (1997). Personality moderators of reactions to interpersonal rejection: Depression and trait self-esteem. *Personality and Social Psychology Bulletin, 23,* 1235–1244.

Raskin, R., Novacek, J., & Hogan, R. (1991). Narcissistic self-esteem management. *Journal of Personality and Social Psychology, 60,* 911–918.

Rhodewalt, F., & Morf, C. C. (1995). Self and interpersonal correlates of the Narcissistic Personality Inventory: A review and new findings. *Journal of Research in Personality, 29,* 1–23.

Rusbult, C. E. (1993). Understanding responses to dissatisfaction in close relationships: The exit-voice-loyalty-neglect model. In S. Worchel & J. A. Simpson (Eds.), *Conflict between people and groups: Causes, processes, and resolutions* (pp. 30–59). Chicago: Nelson-Hall.

Rusbult, C. E., Morrow, G. D., & Johnson, D. J. (1987). Self-esteem and problem solving behavior in close relationships. *British Journal of Social Psychology, 26,* 293–303.

Shrauger, J. S. (1975). Responses to evaluation as a function of initial self-perceptions. *Psychological Bulletin, 82,* 581–596.

Shrauger, J. S., & Lund, A. K. (1975). Self-evaluation and reactions to evaluations from others. *Journal of Personality, 43,* 94–108.

Shrauger, J. S., & Rosenberg, S. E. (1970). Self-esteem and the effects of success and failure feedback on performance. *Journal of Personality, 38,* 404–417.

Shrauger, J. S., & Sorman, P. B. (1977). Self-evaluations, initial success and failure, and improvement as determinants of persistence. *Journal of Consulting and Clinical Psychology, 45,* 784–795.

Sommer, K. L., & Baumeister, R. F. (1997, October). *Unleashing our worst fears: Rejection priming increases the ego-threatening implications of fail-ure.* Presented at the Society for Experimental Social Psychology confer-ence, Toronto, Canada.

Sommer, K. L., Williams, K. D., Ciarocco, N. J., & Baumeister, R. F. (in press). When silence speaks louder than words: The intrapsychic and interper-sonal consequences of social ostracism. *Basic and Applied Social Psy-chology.*

Spencer, S. J., Josephs, R. A., & Steele, C. M. (1993). Low self-esteem: The up-hill struggle for self-integrity. In R. F. Baumeister (Ed.), *Self-esteem: The puzzle of low self-regard* (pp. 21–36). New York: Plenum Press.

Srull, T. K., & Wyer, R. S., Jr. (1979). The role of category accessibility in the interpretation of information about persons: Some determinants and im-plications. *Journal of Personality and Social Psychology, 37,* 1660–1672.

Srull, T. K., & Wyer, R. S., Jr. (1980). Category accessibility and social per-ception: Some implications for the study of person memory and inter-personal judgment. *Journal of Personality and Social Psychology, 38,* 841–856.

Subkoviak, M. J, Enright, R. D., Wu, C., & Gassin, E. A. (1995). Measuring interpersonal forgiveness in late adolescence and middle adulthood. *Journal of Adolescence, 18,* 641–655.

Swann, W. B., Jr., Griffin, J., Predmore, S., & Gaines, B. (1987). The cognitive-affective crossfire: When self-consistency confronts self-enhancement. *Journal of Personality and Social Psychology, 52,* 881–889.

Tice, D. M. (1991). Esteem protection or enhancement? Self-handicapping motives and attributions differ by trait self-esteem. *Journal of Personality and Social Psychology,* 60, 711–725.

Trope, Y. (1986). Self-enhancement and self-assessment in achievement be-havior. In R. M. Sorrentino & E. T. Higgins (Eds.), *Handbook of motivation and cognition: Foundations of social behavior* (pp. 350–378). New York: Guilford Press.

Williams, K. D. (1997). Social ostracism. In R. Kowalski (Ed.), *Aversive in-terpersonal behaviors* (pp. 133–170). New York: Plenum Press.

Williams, K. D., & Sommer, K. L. (1997). Social ostracism by coworkers: Does rejection lead to loafing or compensation? *Personality and Social Psy-chology Bulletin, 23,* 693–706.

Wood, J. V., Giordano-Beech, M., Taylor, K. L., Michela, J. L., & Gaus, V. (1994). Strategies of social comparison among people with low self-esteem: Self-protection and self-enhancement. *Journal of Personality and Social Psychology,* 67, 713–731.

8

Implications of Mental Models of Self and Others for the Targets of Stigmatization

CAROL T. MILLER AND CHERYL R. KAISER

Rejection is so much a part of the experience of stigmatized people that it is difficult to imagine stigma without rejection. Because stigmatized groups have a devalued social identity, they face prejudiced attitudes, stereotyped expectations about their characteristics, and discriminatory behavior (Crocker, Major, & Steele, 1998). Although everyone experiences rejection at some point, stigmatized people belong to a group assumed to possess negative characteristics that justify avoidance, exclusion, and ostracism. Their social identity condemns them to chronic, pervasive, and sometimes extreme rejection and neglect.

Goffman (1963) suggested a classification of stigmas that is still useful today. He suggested that some people are stigmatized because of tribal stigmas; they belong to groups that differ from others in race or ethnicity. Many ethnic minority groups are targets of tribal stigmas. Other people are stigmatized because of their presumed character flaws (for example, substance abusers and homosexuals). Finally, some people are devalued because they are physically distinct from other people or, in Goffman's more colorful terms, suffer from "abominations of the body." People with heavy body weights, facial scars or birthmarks, and people with physical disabilities fall into this category.

In this chapter we use insights derived from attachment theory to highlight strategies that stigmatized people use to cope with potential rejection from stigmatizers. We propose that, to deal with prejudice, stigmatized people use a variety of strategies according to their models or expectations about others and about themselves. Depending on the relevant model, stigmatized people will approach or avoid stigma-tainted interactions with different degrees of uncertainty. Finally, we contend that stigmatized people develop

189

skills to navigate through situations in which their stigmatized status could precipitate rejection.

Stigma as Rejection

Rejection as an Indicator of Stigma

Rejection and stigma are so intimately related that researchers measure prejudiced attitudes toward stigmatized groups by asking people to indicate the ideal social distance between themselves and the stigmatized group (Bogardus, 1933; Dovidio & Gaertner, 1998; Triandis & Triandis, 1960). The argument that racist attitudes are on the decline in the United States frequently relies on studies showing that decreasing percentages of survey respondents indicate that they would reject African Americans in various situations. For example, since 1963 the percentage of people who say they would move if African Americans moved into their neighborhood has dropped from approximately 80% to 20% (Schuman, Steeh, Bobo, & Krysen, 1997). The percentage of Americans who believe that European Americans have a right to keep African Americans out of their neighborhoods has decreased from about 55% to about 10% (Schuman et al., 1997). A well-qualified African American candidate for the U. S. presidency would be acceptable to an overwhelming majority (90%) of people surveyed in 1994, whereas only a small minority of people found this acceptable in 1958 (Davis & Smith, 1994). Similarly, only a small minority supported racial integration of public schools in 1942, whereas this percentage increased to 90% in 1980 (Myers, 1999).

Changes such as these often are interpreted as evidence that rejection of some stigmatized people is declining. Although increasing acceptance of stigmatized people certainly is a hopeful sign, stigmatized people continue to report rejection and exclusion from social activities (Hurtado & Carter, 1997). For example, 53% of African American college students reported feeling excluded from social activities (Hurtado, Dey & Trevino, 1994). The more intimate and close a relationship or interaction is, the more likely that stigmatized people will not be fully accepted (Bogardus, 1933; Triandis & Triandis, 1960). In a study of the social acceptance of Middle Eastern and Western junior high school students attending integrated high schools in Israel, Schwarzwald and Hoffman (1993) found that almost all classmates (89%) were accepted in the most distant relationship included in this study (lend child a book or pen in class). As relationships became more intimate (for example, playing together at recess, doing homework after school, being best friends, and sharing intimate secrets), acceptance declined. This decline was especially precipitous for Middle Eastern children of low academic status, a stigmatized group in this setting. Thus, stigmatized people may be accepted in some types of relationships but not others.

Consequences of Rejection

The extensive research literature on rejection indicates that it is a formidable problem for the rejected person. Rejection by parents or caregivers has long-term effects on a child's social interactions with peers and on adult relationships (Downey, Khouri, & Feldman, 1997; Griffin & Bartholomew, 1994; Hazan & Shaver, 1987). Rejected children become extremely sensitive to rejection (Downey et al., 1997; Downey & Feldman, 1996); consequently, their ability to form romantic and other interpersonal attachments as adults may be impaired (Hazan & Shaver, 1987). Rejection is implicated in poor interpersonal functioning, including problems with hostility, aggression, depression, and jealousy (Boivin, Poulin, & Vitaro, 1994; Downey & Feldman, 1996; French & Waas, 1985; Waas & Graczyk, 1998; Wentzel & Asher, 1995). Children rejected by their peers exhibit problems with aggression, social skills, academics, hyperactivity, and loneliness (Coie, Dodge, & Kupersmidt, 1990; French & Waas, 1985; Parker & Asher, 1987; Waas & Graczyk, 1998; Wentzel & Asher, 1995; Zakriski, Jacobs, & Coie, 1997). Later on, they are more likely than more popular children to drop out of school, become delinquent, abuse alcohol and drugs, attempt suicide, and develop psychopathology (French & Waas, 1985; Kupersmidt & Patterson, 1991; Parker & Asher, 1987; Zakriski et al., 1997). In short, the implications of this research on rejection suggest that stigmatized people may not survive the onslaught of stigma-related rejection with their psychological functioning and interpersonal relationships intact.

However, recent theory and research indicate that stigmatized people may develop strategies to cope with rejection. In this chapter we describe some of these strategies, using theory and research on the consequences of rejection, especially its effects on psychological functioning and interpersonal relationships. This literature provides a framework for conceptualizing how stigmatized people may cope with rejection.

Mental Models of Self and Others

Attachment Theory

One influential theory about the consequences of rejection is attachment theory (Ainsworth, Blehar, Waters, & Wall, 1978; Bartholomew & Horowitz, 1991; Bowlby, 1969, 1973, 1980; Griffin & Bartholomew, 1994; Hazan & Shaver, 1987, 1994). Attachment theorists believe that early experiences with acceptance and rejection create relatively stable mental models about others and self. These mental models of others and self become the basis for the individual's style of relating to others.

According to Bartholomew and her colleagues (Bartholomew & Horowitz, 1991; Griffin & Bartholomew, 1994), four different interaction styles result from the combination of general expectancies about others (model of others) and general expectancies about self (model of self). Individuals with positive models of self and of others are secure in their relationships, confident about their acceptance, and able to approach others with relative ease. Individuals with positive models of others but with negative self-models have a preoccupied relationship style. They believe that others can provide acceptance but are uncertain about whether they deserve it. Consequently, they are often preoccupied with how others react to them. Negative models of others are associated with avoidance tendencies, which form a pattern of dismissive behavior for those with positive self-models. Such individuals may segregate themselves from others and deny the importance of relationships. In contrast, individuals who combine negative models of others with negative self-models tend to withdraw from interpersonal relationships in a fearful manner, to avoid the pain of rejection.

Stigma-Specific Mental Models

Research generally has confirmed the usefulness of conceptualizing attachment styles as a product of mental models of self and others (Bartholomew & Horowitz, 1991; Brennan & Shaver, 1995; Cozzarelli, Sumer, & Major, 1998; Griffin & Bartholomew, 1994). Many attachment theorists have assumed that people have general models of self and others that are similar across different relationships. However, there are theoretical and empirical questions about the stability of these constructs. People may have a variety of mental models or relationship schema (Baldwin, 1992; Baldwin, Keelan, Fehr, Enns, & Koh-Rangarajoo, 1996; Pierce, 1998) that may be evoked in different types of relationships (Baldwin, 1992; Berscheid & Reis, 1998). In other words, relationship styles may vary more across situations and relationships than they do across individuals (Pierce, 1998).

In coping with rejection, stigmatized people also may use a diversity of potential models of self and others. Specifically, stigmatized people have different relationships with other members of their group than they have with those who stigmatize them. Thus, an unchanging style based on a single model of others and self cannot account for their adaptations in diverse social interactions.

Stigma-specific models of others.   We propose that stigmatized people's coping responses to potential rejection by nonstigmatized others are shaped in large part by stigma-specific models of self and others. In any interaction nonstigmatized others are almost always potential stigmatizers (Crocker et al., 1998; Crocker, Voelkl, Testa, & Major, 1991). Even if the other person is not prejudiced toward the stigmatized group, the stigmatized person may still be uncertain whether this interaction or relationship is truly free of prejudice (Crocker & Major, 1989; Crocker et al., 1991; Major & Crocker, 1993; Ruggiero & Taylor, 1995, 1997). Thus, one important component of stigmatized indi-

viduals' models of others is their expectation about who may harbor prejudiced reactions toward them (Feldman Barrett & Swim, 1998). Stigma-specific models of others also include expectations about whether prejudice will
prevent others from meeting the stigmatized person's needs and whether others will reject the stigmatized person (Feldman Barrett & Swim, 1998).

In general, then, stigma-specific models of others are expectations about
the probability of success of social interactions with nonstigmatized people.
Stigmatized people with low expectations anticipate that social interactions
with potentially prejudiced people will not produce desired outcomes
whereas those with high expectations are confident that interactions will
produce desired outcomes. Some factors that can create positive expectancies include interactions with minimally prejudiced others, social norms that
discourage the expression of prejudice, equal status roles, and social support
from other stigmatized people. Thus, positive interaction expectancies do
not require that the other person be nonprejudiced. If the situation discour-
ages or prevents the expression of prejudice, the outcome of the interaction
can be quite positive for the stigmatized person.

Attachment theory proposes that positive models of others are associated
with approach tendencies and negative models of others are associated with
avoidance. These approach and avoidance tendencies occur because an individual's model of others includes expectations about how benevolent,
good, or accommodating others are. In contrast, a stigma-specific model of
others that promotes approach tendencies does not necessarily represent others as good, benevolent, or unprejudiced. Rather, it can be a model that includes positive outcome expectancies even though the other interactant
might be prejudiced. It also might include expectations that the other person
can be induced to provide resources. For example, if the other individual
controls resources that the stigmatized person needs, approach tendencies
may be strong despite potential rejection due to prejudice (Operario & Fiske,
1998).

Stigma-specific models of self.   Similarly, the model of self relevant to our the-
orizing is not a model of individual worth in general. Rather, it is a model
of how worthy, competent, or efficacious the stigmatized person *believes*
himself or herself to be in relationships with potential stigmatizers. As we
pointed out earlier, stigmatized people are rejected because of their social
identity. Although this might be expected to damage their self-worth, both
theory and research suggest that stigmatized people do not necessarily suffer from low self-regard (Crocker & Major, 1989). This suggests that stigmatized people can separate their general self-worth from their acceptance by
potential or actual stigmatizers. Thus, in our adaptation of attachment theory, our model of self is the stigmatized person's confidence about his or her
ability to garner the acceptance of nonstigmatized others.

Leary and Atherton (1986) discussed a similar concept that may be helpful in delineating the stigmatized person's model of self. *Self-presentational*

efficacy expectancy is a person's confidence in his or her ability to convey a desired impression. Devine and Vasquez (1998) suggested that self-presentational efficacy expectancy is an issue for nonstigmatized people when they interact with stigmatized people. Often nonstigmatized people are motivated to appear nonprejudiced or to express egalitarian values, but they lack confidence in their ability to convey this desired impression. Likewise, stigmatized people may be uncertain about whether they can present the images they desire to nonstigmatized people (Steele, 1997; Steele & Aronson, 1995). Stigmatized people who have high self-presentational efficacy expectancy may believe that they can present themselves in a way that will lead to acceptance from others. These people may have positive self-models that can promote confident approach strategies. In contrast, stigmatized people whose self-presentational efficacy expectancies are low may feel that that they cannot successfully negotiate social interactions with nonstigmatized people. Their negative self-models can cause them to fearfully withdraw from social interactions with nonstigmatized others or to approach interactions in a preoccupied, unconfident, or defensive manner. The approach style of stigmatized people who are low in self-presentational efficacy expectancies likely will be awkward and often result in negative outcomes.

Rejection and Relationship Skills

Another important modification we made in applying attachment theory to rejection of stigmatized people concerns the assumption that rejection creates deficiencies or deficits in the relationship styles of rejected individuals. Conventional attachment theory presumes that childhood rejection by significant others impairs an individual's ability to form secure relationships. Likewise, much of the research on peer rejection in childhood takes a skills deficit approach, documenting a number of ways in which unpopular children render themselves obnoxious to others. In some theories rejected children are the "architects of their own difficulties" (Ladd, 1985, p. 243, as cited in Hymel, Wagner, & Butler, 1990, p. 156).

However, we believe that stigmatized people do not necessarily suffer from skill deficits (although they can) like children rejected by parents, caregivers, or peers. Rather, we propose that stigmatized people often develop skills that enable them to avoid rejection and its aftermath. We call this the *skills repertoire model,* in contrast to most models of rejection, which adopt a *skills deficit model.*

In fact, stigmatized people may have a larger repertoire of relationship strategies than do nonstigmatized people because their stigma-specific models of self and others likely differ from their more general models of others. Consequently, they may use specialized strategies in close relationships with in-group members or in relationships with nonprejudiced people but other strategies in interactions with prejudiced people (Agerton & Moran, 1995; Cross & Strauss, 1998; Townsend, 1998). In other words, we suggest that stigmatized people vary their strategies depending on which model of others best describes the people with whom they are interacting.

For example, African Americans use Standard or Black English depending on the race and speech of their listeners (Agerton & Moran, 1995; Townsend, 1998). They may speak Black English to another African American, especially if that person speaks in Black English but switch to Standard English for a European American listener. Such code switching has been shown to occur in African Americans as young as four years old (Agerton & Moran, 1995). We believe code switching is a skill African Americans use to decrease the likelihood of rejection.

Summary

To summarize, stigma-specific models of self and others result in four different styles of relating to others in stigma-tainted social interactions. Stigmatized people may approach or avoid social interactions depending on whether their model of others is positive or negative. In addition, their model of self, or the belief that they can obtain acceptance, may determine how they approach or avoid interactions. Although we are not suggesting these styles as a typology, we believe they are a useful way to understand how stigmatized people interact with potential stigmatizers. Stigma-specific models of self and others may illuminate the variety of strategies that stigmatized people use to cope with prejudice and rejection.

Avoidance Coping Strategies

These diverse coping strategies may be either avoidance or approach-based responses. Avoidance strategies involve physical, social, and psychological withdrawal or disengagement from interactions that may involve stigma-based rejection. By avoiding or withdrawing from stigma-tainted interactions, the stigmatized individual need not confront rejection. Conversely, approach strategies involve attempts to engage in physical, social, and psychological interactions with potential stigmatizers. Approach strategies may prevent the stigmatized person from being rejected in the first place. The stigmatized person's models of self and others will determine whether the stigmatized individual approaches or avoids interactions with others who may stigmatize them and the type of approach or avoidance strategy.

Physical Avoidance

Much of the existing research on how stigmatized people cope with rejection examines avoidance-based strategies (Crocker et al., 1998; Crocker & Major, 1989). Avoidance may take the form of avoiding physical and social contact with potential stigmatizers. For example, women avoid situations in which they might encounter gender-based prejudice (Swim, Cohen, & Hyers, 1998). Women also avoid interacting with men who have reputations as sexual harassers or sexists (Adams, Kottke, & Padgitt, 1983; Junger, 1987).

Avoidance of nonstigmatized people often co-occurs with selective affiliation with members of the stigmatized group. Selective affiliation can range from seeking similar others to share stigma-related concerns to joining militant groups to fight oppressors. Research has indicated that selective affiliation and group identity are extremely important to the well-being of stigmatized people (Branscombe & Ellemers, 1998; Cunningham, 1997; Hurtado & Carter, 1997; Root, 1995). The need to feel accepted by a group, regardless of its status, is a basic human need (Baumeister & Leary, 1995; Branscombe & Ellemers, 1998). For example, in a study on racial identity among African Americans, one male participant who attended a mostly European American school described how he and a fellow African American classmate were able to feel connected to their African American community: "We went to the Apollo every Saturday. This was our chance to kind of take a break from the stresses of this environment. And I enjoyed it. I felt, when I got into the Apollo . . . the audiences were not integrated in those days. I could share with a lot of these folks the hominess, the security, the safety they felt. It was almost like church" (Cunningham, 1997, p. 386).

Psychological Avoidance

Stigmatized people can also cope with rejection by psychological avoidance. Psychological avoidance can take the form of avoiding comparisons with nonstigmatized people to protect the self-esteem of stigmatized people (Crocker & Major, 1989; Major, Sciacchitano, & Crocker, 1993; Major, Testa, & Blysma, 1991). By avoiding invidious comparisons, stigmatized people need not acknowledge that others have more social status and opportunities. Moreover, Miller (1982, 1984) suggested that same-group comparisons are especially relevant and informative. Comparisons with similarly disadvantaged others provides an accurate gauge of personal accomplishments by controlling for any disadvantages arising from group membership. Group identity also may be an important factor in same-group comparisons. Social identity as a member of a stigmatized group is a core feature of self-concept. Thus, comparison with members of the stigmatized person's group affirms an important component of his or her self-concept (Felicio & Miller, 1994; Miller, 1982, 1984).

Psychological avoidance also is exemplified in disengagement and disidentification with domains in which the stigmatized group fares poorly (Crocker et al., 1998; Major & Schmader, 1998; Steele, 1997). Disengagement occurs when the stigmatized person discounts or devalues the importance of feedback in a stereotyped domain. In disidentification, a long-term coping strategy, the person's identity and self-esteem are disconnected from the stereotyped domain (Crocker et al., 1998; Osborne, 1997). For example, Americans have pervasive negative stereotypes about African Americans and academic achievement. Steele and his colleagues (Steele, 1997; Steele & Aronson, 1995) proposed that, through chronic experiences with negative expectations about academic performance, African Americans learn to disengage their self-esteem from academic domains. African Americans depend less on academic performance for self-esteem than European Americans do (Major, Spencer, Schmader, Wolfe, & Crocker, 1998).

Stigmatized people also may devalue the importance of being accepted by potential stigmatizers (Crocker et al., 1998; Major & Schmader, 1998). Eventually, *cultural inversion* may occur, when stigmatized groups abandon the values of the dominant culture and adopt their own values (Ogbu, 1991). The attitudes of African American women toward body weight may provide an example. Even though they are likely heavier than the ideal in Western culture, they are less concerned about weight than their European American counterparts (Hebl & Heatherton, 1998). Moreover, self-esteem and heavy body weights are less highly related for African Americans than for European Americans (Miller & Downey, 1999). Apparently, African Americans have avoided identification with some aspects of the dominant culture.

Another form of avoidance takes the form of self-protective attributions in which negative interaction outcomes are attributed to prejudice (Crocker & Major, 1989; Crocker et al., 1991). Rejection may hurt less if the stigmatized person knows that it was motivated by prejudice and does not reflect his or her personal shortcomings. Attributions to prejudice can lead the stigmatized person to discount feedback from others (Crocker et al., 1991). By discounting the relevance of this feedback, the stigmatized person can mitigate the damage that performance-based rejection would otherwise cause (Crocker & Major, 1989; Crocker et al., 1998). Thus, attributions to prejudice can protect the stigmatized person's self-worth from the detrimental effects of rejection (Crocker & Major, 1989).

Model of Self in Avoidance Strategies

We have thus far discussed avoidance without regard to the model of self. Often it is difficult to determine whether avoidance is a fear-based withdrawal that results from negative models of self or a dismissive type predicated on a positive self-model. For example, selective affiliation may be either a dismissive or a fearful coping response to rejection. On one hand, selective affiliation may be motivated primarily by a negative self-model that makes the stigmatized individual anxious about acceptance by nonstigmatized others. Fear of rejection thus drives the individual into the company of similarly stigmatized individuals. On the other hand, stigmatized people with more positive models of their own efficacy and worthiness may withdraw from nonstigmatized others because they have ceased caring about others' acceptance. They affiliate with stigmatized others because they value these relationships more than those with nonstigmatized people.

Some research explicitly considers the stigmatized person's model of self in avoidance strategies. Pinel (1999) found that women who are high in stigma consciousness (the expectancy that they will be stereotyped) tend to avoid situations that might result in gender stereotyping. In this study, female undergraduates who had either high or low stigma consciousness were allowed to choose to compete in a traditionally masculine domain or a gender-neutral domain against male or female competitors. The results indicated that highly stigma-conscious women avoided competition in the masculine domain only when they expected to compete against men. Pinel suggested that these women avoided the masculine domain to avoid performing poorly. In this experiment, the women's negative model of self (i.e., fear of performing poorly in masculine domains) caused them to avoid the situation.

Similarly, playing the role of a "token" is a stressful situation for stigmatized people. When stigmatized people are the only representative of their group, increased attention and more extreme evaluations of their behavior can result (Taylor, Fiske, Etcoff, & Ruderman, 1978). Accounts of women married to foreigners who relocated to their husbands' country of origin illustrate the rejection that token individuals face. These women, who usually lack compatriots and feel their token status acutely, report that their solo status causes people to judge them harshly and make dispositional attributions for their behavior (Imamura, 1990). Similarly, Jackson, Thoits, and Taylor (1995) studied the stress highly successful African Americans experience in workplace settings. Compared to those in integrated settings, those with token status reported more multiple demands due to being African American and having to demonstrate more competence than their peers. It would not be surprising for stigmatized people to avoid stressful situations in which they are tokens. However, their reaction may depend on their model of self. Cohen and Swim (1995) showed that women who were given feedback that raised doubts about their ability to perform an experimental task were less willing to be the token woman in a group of men than were women who received feedback suggesting they were highly competent. People with positive self-models may have the confidence to face situations involving tokenism.

Summary

Avoidance strategies can involve avoidance of social interactions with nonstigmatized others or psychological withdrawal from interactions. Avoidance strategies should predominate when the stigmatized person's model of others is negative. The stigmatized person does not necessarily perceive that the other person is prejudiced (although sometimes this will be the case). Negative models of others also can arise when stigmatized people no longer value relationships with nonstigmatized people. Avoidance coping does not reflect an impairment of the stigmatized person's ability to relate to others. Rather, stigmatized people may use avoidance to cope with prejudice. Far from being a "cop-out," avoidance may be a rational and strategic response to reality. For example, if the other person is an unreformed bigot, the stigmatized person might be foolish to engage in any interaction. In summary, avoidance strategies constitute part of a repertoire of skills that a stigmatized person may use to deal with stigma-based rejection.

Approach Coping Strategies

Compensation

Although most research to date has focused on avoidance strategies, approach strategies may be equally important weapons in the stigmatized person's arsenal of skills to cope with rejection. Confident individuals, who have a positive model of self, may engage in compensatory behaviors, in which one adapts social interaction strategies to gain acceptance despite the existence of prejudice (Miller & Myers, 1998). Several studies in our laboratory have demonstrated that stigmatized people often engage in compensatory behaviors when they encounter potential prejudice. For example, heavyweight women reported that they behaved in a more socially skillful manner when they thought they were visible to their interaction partners than when they thought they were not visible. By adjusting their behavior, heavyweight women overcame their interaction partners' negative reactions to their appearance (Miller, Rothblum, Felicio, & Brand, 1995). As this study indicates, compensation can ameliorate stigmatized peoples' social interactions with nonstigmatized people.

Evidence of compensation also appeared in Kaiser and Miller's (1999) study, which examined how women cope with gender discrimination. Female undergraduates took an essay test that purportedly measured their future career success. We wanted to examine how the anticipation of prejudice would affect the manner in which the women completed the test. We told the participants that 100%, 50%, or none of the panel of male judges from which their judge would be selected discriminated against women. In addition, we manipulated the timing of this information. Some of the women learned of the potential for discrimination before completing the test, and others heard about the possibility of discrimination only after completing the test. We hypothesized that women who were aware that they might be discriminated against (because they learned about prejudice before completing the test) would compensate for the prejudice by behaving in a less stereotypically feminine fashion. After the experiment, judges who were blind to condition rated the women's test answers. The results indicated that the women who were forewarned that they would face prejudice compensated by producing essays judged to be less feminine than those produced by the women who did not anticipate facing prejudice. One interpretation of this finding is that the women who anticipated prejudiced reactions believed that they could overcome the barriers of prejudice if they acted in a less stereotypic fashion.

Similar compensatory effects have been shown among women in work settings. Women who occupy stereotypically masculine jobs assumed to demand agentic rather than communal characteristics often must overcome gender stereotypes to gain respect and avoid rejection (Eagly, Karau, & Makhijani, 1995). For example, female MBA candidates who role-played a telephone conversation with work associates from their managerial internships spoke in a more competent-sounding manner (as rated by naïve observers) to a former boss than to a former peer (Steckler & Rosenthal, 1985). In contrast, men spoke less competently to former bosses than to former peers. This appearance of women's greater competence in interactions with bosses can be interpreted as compensation.

Overcompensation

The studies described above reveal that stigmatized people sometimes alter their social interaction strategies when interacting with potential stigmatizers. Although compensatory behaviors can reduce the likelihood of being rejected (as shown in the study on heavyweight women), many things can go awry when people engage in compensation. In some situations, compensatory behaviors can negatively affect the social interactions of stigmatized people, particularly when they overcompensate. Overcompensation refers to the unskilled or inappropriate use of compensatory strategies (Miller & Myers, 1998; Miller & Rudiger, 1997). Stigmatized people who overcompensate may be perceived as too aggressive or inept.

Overcompensation can be associated with both negative and positive models of self. For people with a negative self-model, efforts to compensate may be marred by preoccupation or anxiety about acceptance. Compensation must be learned through trial and error, so overcompensation may occur when stigmatized people are learning and honing new social interaction strategies. Their anxiety and inexperience with these strategies may cause awkward social interactions and ultimately may lead to poor outcomes.

In contrast, overcompensation could occur when a stigmatized person with a positive self-model has high self-presentational efficacy expectations. The individual may be confident about acceptance by others but may misjudge the effects of his or her compensatory efforts on the other's response. This could easily occur when the other person is assumed to be prejudiced but actually is not. For example, when invited to take minutes at a meeting, a woman may assume that she was asked because she is the only woman present. If she makes a point of compensating for this perceived attempt to confine her to a stereotypical role, even though the request was not actually mo-

tivated by prejudice, her resistance may seem to be simply uncooperative behavior rather than a heroic effort to overcome prejudice. In this example, she
may be confident about her ability to present herself in a counter-stereotypic
fashion, but she may create hostility because she overreacted to a simple request.

Our study on gender prejudice demonstrated overcompensation (Kaiser
& Miller, 1999). Women who were forewarned about gender prejudice made
a less feminine impression. The women who compensated for prejudice
may have been trying to gain acceptance by disconfirming gender stereotypes, but they were not entirely successful. Although they did seem less
feminine, they were evaluated less favorably. Naïve undergraduate raters
formed more negative impressions of these women than of the women who
did not anticipate prejudice. This overcompensation effect may have been
the result of a positive or negative self-model. The judges did not know that
these women were threatened by sexism. Thus, their essays might have appeared inappropriate in the context in which they were judged. Alternatively, the women who faced certain or possible sexism may have done
their best to present an image of competence on the task, but the threat of
impending evaluation by a sexist judge created enough anxiety to interfere
with performance.

Development of Compensation

Stigmatized people sometimes cross the line from compensation to overcompensation because effective compensatory strategies may require relatively high social, cognitive, and behavioral skills. These skills may require
substantial experience; consequently, young children may have less well-
developed compensatory skills than older people do. For example, results of
a study by Dion and Stein (1978) suggest that physically unattractive children may show rudimentary attempts to compensate for their disadvantaged
status in social interactions. Unattractiveness is a highly stigmatized condition related to low sociometric status among school children (Hymel et al.,
1990). In this study, attractive and unattractive school children attempted to
convince another child to eat a cracker coated in a bitter-tasting substance.
Unattractive girls were among the most persistent in their efforts to persuade
another child to eat the cracker, but they also were not successful. Unattractive boys were the only ones who used the threat of physical force to
convince another child to consume the crackers. Although they accom-
plished their mission with boys, bullying, intimidating, and threatening
other children is not a harbinger of future social acceptance (Zakriski et al.,
1997). Attractive boys and girls both successfully motivated bitter-tasting
cracker consumption among other-sex children. This study suggests that unattractive children were at a disadvantage in this situation. Although it is not
possible to know the children's intentions, the strategies adopted by unattractive boys and girls may have been an effort to overcome their disadvan-

tage. The strategy adopted by the unattractive girls was potentially effective but did not succeed. The strategy adopted by the unattractive boys worked in the short run but over time may result in rejection.

Unattractive adults still show evidence of the consequences of their stigmatized status. They are less popular and lonelier than attractive people are. However, the overall psychological well-being, including self-esteem, of people who are unattractive in the eyes of others equals that of attractive people (Feingold, 1992). This suggests that unattractive people may develop ways to compensate for the effects of unattractiveness on their social relationships. In fact, although unattractive people have fewer relationships than attractive people do, the quality of their relationships may be roughly the same. For example, in a study in which college students recorded their daily social interactions in a diary, attractive and unattractive college women reported equally satisfying social relationships (Reis, Wheeler, Speigel, Kernis, Nezlek, & Perri, 1982). Despite evidence of pervasive prejudice toward unattractive people, unattractive women had social lives on a par in some respects with attractive women. One explanation for this paradox is that unattractive women also scored higher on measures of assertiveness than attractive women did. Reis et al. (1982) suggested that attractive women rely on their looks, whereas unattractive women assert themselves to gain acceptance. In short, this research suggests that both unattractive and attractive people can form successful social relationships; however, the route they take to that success may be different.

The most direct evidence of a developmental progression in compensation among stigmatized people derives from a study of peer acceptance among hearing-impaired children (Cappelli, Daniels, Durieux-Smith, McGrath, & Neuss, 1995). Although this study indicated that hearing-impaired children were more likely to be socially rejected than their nonhearing-impaired classmates, this difference decreased with age. Younger hearing-impaired children (grades one to three) experienced greater rejection than the older (grades four to six) hearing-impaired children. In addition, the older hearing-impaired children focused on social relationship goals and were more fearful of being rejected by their classmates than were the younger hearing-impaired children. Age was unrelated to relationship goals and fear of negative evaluations among hearing children. Perhaps hearing-impaired children learned how to avoid rejection by focusing their attention on their social skills and interpersonal relationship goals.

Summary

Relatively little is known about approach strategies. This is unfortunate because in many instances stigmatized people are highly motivated to approach interactions with nonstigmatized people (Kaiser & Miller, 1999; Miller et al., 1995; Steckler & Rosenthal, 1985; Townsend, 1998). In these situations, stigmatized people need strategies that enable efficacious interactions with nonstigmatized people who may be prejudiced against them. We believe that compensation is one strategy that stigmatized people use to obtain their goals, despite prejudice. Although compensation can produce beneficial outcomes, attempts to compensate can sometimes backfire. The successful use of compensation requires time and practice; unfortunately, stigmatized people have many opportunities to practice these skills in coping with rejection.

Skill Repertoires or Skill Deficits?

Apparent Skill Deficits

We already have mentioned the extensive research indicating that rejected people exhibit less socially skillful and less socially appropriate behavior than better-accepted people do. These data are correlational, so we do not know for certain whether the skill deficits cause the rejection or vice versa. Researchers interested in the problem of rejection among the general population have commonly assumed that skill deficits cause rejection. In research on stigma, researchers have tended to assume that rejection causes deficits in social skills (Adams, 1977; Miller & Turnbull, 1986; Skrypnek & Snyder, 1982; Snyder, 1984; Snyder, Tanke, & Berscheid, 1977; Word, Zanna, & Cooper, 1974). Prejudice often limits resources, such as access to education, income, and health care, which are important in the development of life skills (Duijkers, Drijver, Kromhout, & James, 1988; Jackson & Adams-Campbell, 1994; James, Hartnett, & Kalsbeek, 1983). For example, prejudice-based rejection may deny stigmatized people opportunities and experiences fundamental to the development of social skills. For all these reasons, stigma is often assumed to cause deficits in social skills.

In accordance with this premise, Goldman and Lewis (1977) found that physically unattractive people are less socially skilled than attractive people, just as stereotypes about them predict. In their study, college students conversed by telephone and rated each other after the conversation ended. Unattractive students (determined by independent ratings) were liked less and perceived as less socially skilled than attractive students. In a similar study, heavyweight women were liked less and perceived as less socially skilled by their partners in a telephone conversation and by judges who listened to recordings of what they said (Miller, Rothblum, Barbour, Brand, & Felicio, 1990).

These findings suggest that stigmatized people may have skill deficits that elicit rejection from others. We propose a skills repertoire model despite evidence that appears to document skill deficits because these behavioral deficits appeared only when stigmatized people thought that others were unaware of their stigmatizing condition. In both studies, the interaction was a telephone conversation in which the participants could not see each other and thus were unaware whether the other person was ugly or fat. In subsequent research, Miller et al. (1995) replicated the finding that heavyweight women made a poor impression when they conversed without being seen by the other person. However, when the women knew they were visible to the other person, they made impressions as positive as those created by nonheavyweight women. In fact, in the only other condition in which heavyweight women received relatively negative evaluations, the women thought they were not visible to their partners, but they actually were. In that condition, the other person's prejudice may have been unanticipated. Therefore, the women had not made the compensatory efforts they usually make when others may be prejudiced against them.

Resource Conservation

Why should stigmatized people who feel safe from prejudice because their stigmatized condition is unknown behave in a less positive manner than those who know another person is aware of their stigmatized status? Unrevealed stigmas may promote overly positive self-presentational efficacy expectations. If the other person cannot be affected by prejudice, then the stigmatized person need not act in a particularly efficacious manner. Thus, the stigmatized person may approach such situations with high confidence and low anxiety (i.e., positive model of self). Unfortunately, stigmatized people may become overconfident about such situations because ordinarily they *do* have to contend with prejudice. When things do not go well, they may (correctly) assume that the other's prejudice may be at fault. This could lead to misperceptions about how efficacious they would need to be if prejudice were not a part of the picture. As one extremely heavyweight participant in a study of coping with weight-related stigma said, "If I were not overweight, I wouldn't have to deal with negative reactions" (Myers & Rosen, 1999). People who attribute problems to their stigmatizing condition may underestimate how efficacious and effortful anybody has to be to relate well to others. Moreover, the tendency to compare and affiliate with similar (i.e., stigmatized) others prevents stigmatized people from observing the efforts and skills that nonstigmatized people must use to achieve their interaction goals.

This reasoning suggests that stigmatized people may underestimate the personal resources required in interactions uncontaminated by prejudice. However, it fails to explain why stigmatized people do not immediately discover their misperception about "safe" interactions and take remedial action. We believe "unsafe" interactions drain the energy, attention, and resources of stigmatized people. Constant vigilance to stigma-based rejection can be exhausting. As one multiply stigmatized person of our acquaintance described it, at the end of the day she is just tired of dealing with others' reactions to her stigmas. Thus, interactions in which stigmatized people think they are safe from prejudice are opportunities to conserve resources. Thus, they make more negative impressions on others when they think they are safe from the effects of prejudice.

We do not mean to say that stigmatized people are "super-humans" with vast arrays of skills to cope with prejudice. Coping responses partly depend on the resources available, and being stigmatized can indeed drain personal resources or prevent people from acquiring them. This increased strain can affect stigmatized people detrimentally. For example, John Henryism, or the belief that personal outcomes can be controlled through hard work, has been shown to predict high blood pressure among less educated African American men (Duijkers et al., 1988; James et al., 1983), suggesting that persistence in the face of strong adversity may cause health problems among people with few resources. These men may experience many stressors and difficulties as they attempt to control environmental outcomes. Stigmatized people likely will take advantage of the opportunity to engage in resource conservation when they feel safe from prejudice. Resource conservation may help them save their energy for situations in which it will be most beneficial.

Skills Come from Experience with Stigma

Despite these potentially negative outcomes, we propose that stigmatized people cope as best they can with the situations they confront and in the process learn something about how to cope effectively. The most dramatic demonstrations of this are in studies that examine stigmatized and nonstigmatized people's reactions to being stigmatized in the eyes of another. This research suggests that stigmatized people are better equipped to cope with prejudice than nonstigmatized people. Because nonstigmatized people have not had the opportunity to learn compensatory skills, we believe that they will experience greater difficulty when they are portrayed to another as stigmatized because of both their perceived inabilities to cope with prejudice (negative self-model) and their expectations that others will reject them (negative model of others).

In an experiment by Prail and Miller (1997), self-perceived attractive and less attractive women conversed with a male confederate by telephone. Prior to the conversation, each woman was shown a photograph of an attractive or a less attractive woman, and we asked if we could show a copy of the photograph to the man and tell him that it was her photograph. The women then were charged with telephoning the man and conversing with him for whatever they liked for as long as they liked. Before and after the conversation, the women rated themselves on how likable and socially skilled they would be/ were during the conversation. They also completed questions about what topics they intended to emphasize or did emphasize, how hard they intended to try, and how difficult they thought the conversation would be. The male confederates, who were blind to the woman's attractiveness and how she thought she had been depicted, rated their impressions of the women. Transcripts were made of the first 15 minutes of each conversation, and naïve undergraduate raters rated their impressions of the women based on this information.

The results of this study revealed evidence of both compensation and overcompensation among the unattractive women. However, these effects, though interesting, occurred on relatively few measures. The most consistent finding was that attractive women fared poorly when faced with the challenge of being portrayed as unattractive. When attractive women thought they were depicted as unattractive, they subsequently rated themselves as less likable and skilled than when they thought they were depicted as attractive. Attractive women in the unattractive depiction condition also rated the conversation to be more difficult—a difficulty they had not anticipated in the preconversation ratings. The judges also rated attractive women in the unattractive depiction condition more negatively on several dimensions, including social skill (two measures), likability, confidence, and physical attractiveness. To summarize, in this experiment only the attractive women showed consistent stigma confirmation effects because, we argue, they lack experience coping with stigma.

Conclusions

Being stigmatized is virtually synonymous with being rejected. The rejection a stigmatized individual experiences is a consequence of possessing a devalued social identity and is not warranted by the individual's behavior, personality, or abilities (or lack thereof). Stigmatized people respond to rejection in four main ways, depending on whether they have positive or negative models of others and of self. Negative models of others are associated with physical, social, and psychological avoidance. Stigmatized people with positive self-models avoid in a "dismissive" fashion, withdrawing from the mainstream into their own social and cultural realms. Those with less positive self-models may avoid nonstigmatized others in a more fearful manner with less motivation to approach members of their own group. In contrast, positive models of others promote approach strategies, many of which involve efforts to compensate for or overcome the effects of prejudice on social interaction. Depending on the stigmatized person's model of self, nonstigmatized people may be approached with confidence and relatively little anxiety, or with considerable preoccupation. Although rejection can circumvent the development of interaction skills, and although people often become rejected because they lack such skills, stigmatized people may develop special skills to cope with the rejection of being stigmatized.

References

Adams, G. R. (1977). Physical attractiveness research: Toward a developmental social psychology of beauty. *Human Development, 20,* 217–239.

Adams, J. W., Kottke, J. L., & Padgitt, J. S. (1983). Sexual harassment of university students. *Journal of College Student Personnel, 27,* 484–490.

Agerton, E. P., & Moran, M. J. (1995). Effects of race and dialect of examiner on language samples elicited from southern African American preschoolers. *Journal of Childhood Communication Disorders, 16,* 25–30.

Ainsworth, M., Blehar, M., Waters, E., & Wall, S. (1978). *Patterns of attachment: A psychological study of the strange situation.* Hillsdale, NJ: Lawrence Erlbaum.

Baldwin, M. W. (1992). Relational schemas and the processing of social information. *Psychological Bulletin, 112,* 461–484.

Baldwin, M. W., Keelan, J. P. R., Fehr, B., Enns, V., Koh-Rangarajoo, E. (1996). Social-cognitive conceptualizations of attachment working models: Availability and accessibility effects. *Journal of Personality and Social Psychology, 71,* 94–109.

Bartholomew, K., & Horowitz, L. M. (1991). Attachment styles among young adults: A test of a four-category model. *Journal of Personality and Social Psychology, 61,* 226–244.

Baumeister, R. F., & Leary, M. R. (1995). The need to belong: Desire for interpersonal attachments as a fundamental human motivation. *Psychological Bulletin, 117,* 497–529.

Berscheid, E., & Reis, H. T. (1998). Attraction and close relationships. In D. Gilbert, S. T. Fiske & G. Lindzey (Eds.), *Handbook of social psychology,* 4th ed. (vol. 2, pp. 193–281). Boston: McGraw Hill.

Bogardus, E. S. (1933). A social distance scale. *Sociology and Social Research, 17,* 265–271.

Boivin, M., Poulin, F., & Vitaro, F. (1994). Depressed mood and peer rejection in childhood. *Development and Psychopathology, 6,* 483–498.

Bowlby, J. (1969). *Attachment and loss, Vol. 1: Attachment.* New York: Basic Books.

Bowlby, J. (1973). *Attachment and loss, Vol. 2: Separation.* New York: Basic Books.

Bowlby, J. (1980). *Attachment and loss, Vol. 3: Loss, sadness, and depression.* New York: Basic Books.

Branscombe, N. R., & Ellemers, N. (1998). Coping with group-based discrimination: Individualistic versus group-level strategies. In J. K. Swim & C. Strangor (Eds.), *Prejudice: The target's perspective* (pp. 243–266). San Diego, CA: Academic Press.

Brennan, K. A., Shaver, P. R. (1995). Dimensions of adult attachment, affect regulation, and romantic relationship functioning. *Personality and Social Psychology Bulletin, 21,* 267–283.

Cappelli, M., Daniels, T., Durieux-Smith, A., McGrath, P. J., & Neuss, D. (1995). Social development of children with hearing impairments who are integrated into general education classrooms. *Volta Review, 97,* 197–208.

Cohen, L. L., & Swim, J. K. (1995). The differential impact of gender ratios on women and men: Tokenism, self-confidence, and expectations. *Personality And Social Psychology Bulletin, 21,* 876–884.

Coie, J. D., Dodge, K. A., & Kupersmidt, J. B. (1990). Peer group behavior and social status. In S. R. Asher & J. D. Coie (Eds.), *Peer rejection in childhood.*

Cambridge studies in social and emotional development (pp. 17–59). New York: Cambridge University Press.

Cozzarelli, C., Sumer, N., & Major, B. (1998). Mental models of attachment and coping with abortion. *Journal of Personality and Social Psychology, 74,* 453–467.

Crocker, J., & Major, B. (1989). Social stigma and self-esteem: The self-protective properties of stigma. *Psychological Review, 96,* 608–630.

Crocker, J., Major, B., & Steele, C. (1998). Social stigma. In D. Gilbert, S. T. Fiske, & G. Lindzey (Eds.), *Handbook of social psychology,* 4th ed. (vol. 2, pp. 504–553). Boston: McGraw Hill.

Crocker, J., Voelkl, K., Testa, M., & Major, B. (1991). Social stigma: The affective consequences of attributional ambiguity. *Journal of Personality and Social Psychology, 60,* 218–228.

Cross, W. E, & Strauss, L. (1998). The everyday functions of African American identity. In J. K. Swim & C. Strangor (Eds.), *Prejudice: The target's perspective* (pp. 267–279). San Diego, CA: Academic Press.

Cunningham, J. L. (1997). Colored existence: Racial identity formation in light-skin Blacks. *Smith College Studies in Social Work, 67,* 375–400.

Davis, J. A., & Smith, T. W. (1994). *General social survey, 1972–1994: Cumulative codebook.* Chicago: National Opinion Research Center.

Devine, P. G., & Vasquez, K. A. (1998). The rocky road to positive intergroup relations. In J. L. Eberhardt & S. T. Fiske (Eds.), *Confronting racism: The problem and the response* (pp. 234–262). Thousand Oaks, CA: Sage.

Dion, K. K., & Stein, S. (1978). Physical attractiveness and interpersonal influence. *Journal of Experimental Social Psychology, 14,* 97–108.

Dovidio, J. F., & Gaertner, S. L. (1998). On the nature of contemporary prejudice: The causes, consequences, and challenges of aversive racism. In J. L. Eberhardt & S. T. Fiske (Eds.), *Confronting racism: The problem and the response* (pp. 3–32). Thousand Oaks, CA: Sage.

Downey, G., & Feldman, S. I. (1996). Implications of rejection sensitivity for intimate relationships. *Journal of Personality and Social Psychology, 70,* 1327–1343.

Downey, G., Khouri, H., & Feldman, S. I. (1997). Early interpersonal trauma and later adjustment: The mediational role of rejection sensitivity. In D. Cicchetti & S. L. Toth (Eds.), *Developmental perspectives on trauma: Theory, research, and intervention. Rochester symposium on developmental psychology, Vol. 8* (pp. 85–114). Rochester, NY: University of Rochester Press.

Duijkers, T. J., Drijver, M., Kromhout, D., & James. S. A. (1988). "John Henryism" and blood pressure in a Dutch population. *Psychosomatic Medicine, 50,* 353–359.

Eagly, A. H., Karau, S. J., & Makhijani, M. G. (1995). Gender and the effectiveness of leaders: A meta-analysis. *Psychological Bulletin, 117,* 125–145.

Feingold, A. (1992). Good looking people are not what we think. *Psychological Bulletin, 111,* 304–341.

Feldman Barrett, L., & Swim, J. K. (1998). Appraisals of prejudice and discrimination. In J. K. Swim & C. Strangor (Eds.), *Prejudice: The target's perspective* (pp. 11–36). San Diego, CA: Academic Press.

Felicio, D. M., & Miller, C. T. (1994). Social comparison in medical school:

What students say about gender and similarity. *Basic and Applied Social Psychology, 15,* 277–296.

French, D. C., & Waas, G. A. (1985). Behavior problems of peer-neglected and peer-rejected elementary-age children: Parent and peer perspectives. *Child Development, 56,* 246–252.

Goffman, E. (1963). *Stigma: Notes on the management of spoiled identity.* Englewood Cliffs, NJ: Prentice-Hall.

Goldman, W., & Lewis, P. (1977). Beautiful is good: Evidence that the physically attractive are more socially skillful. *Journal of Experimental Social Psychology, 13,* 125–130.

Griffin, D., & Bartholomew, K. (1994). Models of self and other: Fundamental dimensions underlying measures of adult attachment. *Journal of Personality and Social Psychology, 67,* 430–435.

Hazan, C., & Shaver, P. (1987). Romantic love conceptualized as an attachment process. *Journal of Personality and Social Psychology, 52,* 511–524.

Hazan, C., & Shaver, P. R. (1994). Attachment as an organizational framework for research on close relationships. *Psychological Inquiry, 5,* 1–22.

Hebl, M. R., & Heatherton, T. F. (1998). The stigma of obesity in women: The difference is black and white. *Personality and Social Psychology Bulletin, 24,* 417–426.

Hurtado, S., & Carter, D. F. (1997). Effects of college transition and perceptions of the campus racial climate on Latino college students' sense of belonging. *Sociology of Education, 70,* 324–345.

Hurtado, S., Dey, E. L., & Trevino, J. G. (1994). *Exclusion or self-segregation? Integration across racial/ethnic groups on college campuses.* Paper presented at the American Educational Research Association annual meeting.

Hymel, S., Wagner, E., & Butler, L. J. (1990). Reputational bias: View from the peer group. In S. R. Asher & J. D. Coie (Eds.), *Peer rejection in childhood. Cambridge studies in social and emotional development* (pp. 156–186). New York: Cambridge University Press.

Imamura, A. E. (1990). Strangers in a strange land: Coping with marginality in international marriage. *Journal of Comparative Family Studies, 21,* 171–191.

Jackson, L. A., & Adams-Campbell, L. L. (1994). John Henryism and blood pressure in Black college students. *Journal of Behavioral Medicine, 17,* 69–79.

Jackson, P. B., Thoits, P. A., & Taylor, H. F. (1995). Composition of the workplace and psychological well-being: The effects of tokenism on America's Black elite. *Social Forces, 74,* 543–557.

James, S. A., Hartnett, S. A., & Kalsbeek, W. D. (1983). John Henryism and blood pressure differences among Black men. *Journal of Behavioral Medicine, 6,* 259–278.

Junger, M. (1987). Women's experiences of sexual harassment. *British Journal of Criminology, 27,* 358–383.

Kaiser, C. R., & Miller, C. T. (2000). *Reacting to impending discrimination: Compensation for prejudice and attributions to discrimination.* Manuscript submitted for publication.

Kupersmidt, J. B., & Patterson, C. J. (1991). Childhood peer rejection, aggression, withdrawal, and perceived competence as predictors of self-reported behavior problems in preadolescence. *Journal of Abnormal Child Psychology, 19,* 427–449.

Leary, M. R., & Atherton, S. C. (1986). Self-efficacy, social anxiety, and inhibition in interpersonal encounters. *Journal of Social and Clinical Psychology, 4,* 256–267.

Major, B., & Crocker, J. (1993). Social stigma: The affective consequences of attributional ambiguity. In D. M. Mackie & D. L. Hamilton (Eds.), *Affect, cognition, and stereotyping: Interactive processes in intergroup perception* (pp. 345–370). New York: Academic Press.

Major, B., & Schmader, T. (1998). Coping with stigma through psychological disengagement. In J. K. Swim & C. Strangor (Eds.), *Prejudice: The target's perspective* (pp. 191–218). San Diego, CA: Academic Press.

Major, B., Sciacchitano, A. M., & Crocker, J. (1993). In-group versus out-group comparisons and self-esteem. *Personality and Social Psychology Bulletin, 19,* 711–721.

Major, B., Spencer, S., Schmader, T., Wolfe, C., & Crocker, J. (1998). Coping with negative stereotypes about intellectual performance: The role of psychological disengagement. *Personality and Social Psychology Bulletin, 24,* 34–50.

Major, B., Testa, M., & Blysma, W. H. (1991). Responses to upward and downward social comparisons: The impact of esteem-relevance and perceived control. In J. Suls & T. A. Wils (Eds.), *Social comparisons: Contemporary theory and research* (pp. 237–260). Hillsdale, NJ: Lawrence Erlbaum.

Miller, C. T. (1982). The role of performance-related similarity in social comparison of abilities: A test of the related attributes hypothesis. *Journal of Experimental Social Psychology, 18,* 513–523.

Miller, C. T. (1984). Self-schemas, gender, and social comparison: A clarification of the related attributes hypothesis. *Journal of Personality and Social Psychology, 46,* 1222–1229.

Miller, C. T., & Downey, K. T. (1999). A meta-analysis of heavyweight and self-esteem. *Personality and Social Psychology Review, 3,* 68–84.

Miller, C. T., & Myers, A. (1998). Compensating for prejudice: How obese people (and others) control outcomes despite prejudice. In J. K. Swim & C. Strangor (Eds.), *Prejudice: The target's perspective* (pp. 191–218). San Diego, CA: Academic Press.

Miller, C. T., Rothblum, E. D., Barbour, L., Brand, P. A., & Felicio, D. M. (1990). Social interactions of obese and nonobese women. *Journal of Personality, 58,* 365–380.

Miller, C. T., Rothblum, E. D., Felicio, D., & Brand, P. (1995). Compensating for stigma: Obese and nonobese women's reactions to being visible. *Personality and Social Psychology Bulletin, 21,* 1093–1106.

Miller, C. T., & Rudiger, L. (1997, October). *Compensation for prejudice: How the stigmatized obtain desired outcomes despite prejudice.* Paper presented at the annual meeting of the Society of Experimental Social Psychology, Toronto, Ontario, Canada.

Miller, D. T., & Turnbull, W. (1986). Expectancies and interpersonal processes. *Annual Review of Psychology, 37,* 233–256.

Myers, A., & Rosen, J. C. (1999). Obesity stigmatization and coping: Relation to mental health symptoms, body image, and self-esteem. *International Journal of Obesity, 23,* 221–230.

Myers, D. G. (1999). *Social psychology.* 6th edition. Boston: McGraw Hill College.

Ogbu, J. U. (1991). Minority coping responses and school experience. *Journal of Psychohistory, 18,* 433–456.

Operario, D., & Fiske, S. T. (1998). Racism equals power plus prejudice: A social psychological equation for racial oppression. In J. L. Eberhardt, & S. T. Fiske (Eds.), *Confronting racism: The problem and the response* (pp. 33–53). Thousand Oaks, CA: Sage.

Osborne, J. W. (1997). Race and academic disidentification. *Journal of Educational Psychology, 89,* 728–735.

Parker, J. G., & Asher, S. R. (1987). Peer relations and later personal adjustment: Are low accepted children at risk? *Psychological Bulletin, 102,* 357–389.

Pierce, T. (1998). *Global and specific relational models in the experience of social interactions and significant life events.* Unpublished doctoral dissertation, McGill University, Montreal.

Pinel, E. C. (1999). Stigma consciousness: The psychological legacy of social stereotypes. *Journal of Personality and Social Psychology, 76,* 114–128.

Prail, D., & Miller, C. T. (1997). *Compensation and slacking off: Effects of physical attractiveness on women's reactions to being portrayed to another as beautiful or plain.* Unpublished manuscript. Burlington: University of Vermont.

Reis, H. T., Wheeler, L., Spiegel, N., Kernis, M. H., Nezlek, J., & Perri, M. (1982). Physical attractiveness and social interaction: II. Why does appearance affect social experience? *Journal of Personality and Social Psychology, 43,* 979–996.

Root, M. P. P. (1995). The multiracial contribution to the psychological browning of America. In N. Zack (Ed.), *American mixed race: The culture of microdiversity* (pp. 231–236). Lanham, MD: Rowan & Littlefield.

Ruggiero, K. M., & Taylor, D. M. (1995). Coping with discrimination: How disadvantaged group members perceive the discrimination that confronts them. *Journal of Personality and Social Psychology, 68*(5), 826–838.

Ruggiero, K. M., & Taylor, D. M. (1997). Why minority group members perceive or do not perceive the discrimination that confronts them: The role of self-esteem and perceived control. *Journal of Personality and Social Psychology, 72*(2), 373–389.

Schuman, H., Steeh, C., Bobo, L., & Krysen, M. (1997). *Racial attitudes in America: Trends and interpretations* (rev. ed.). Cambridge, MA: Harvard University Press.

Schwarzwald, J., & Hoffman, M. A. (1993). Academic success and ethnicity as determinants of social acceptance. *Journal of Cross Cultural Psychology, 24,* 71–80.

Skrypnek, B. J., & Snyder, M. (1982). On the self-perpetuating nature of stereotypes about men and women. *Journal of Experimental Social Psychology, 18,* 277–291.

Snyder, M. (1984). When belief creates reality. In L. Berkowitz (Ed.).

Advances in experimental social psychology, Vol. 18 (pp. 247–305). San Diego, CA: Academic Press.

Snyder, M., Tanke, E. D., & Berscheid, E. (1977). Social perception and social behavior: On the self-fulfilling nature of social stereotypes. *Journal of Personality and Social Psychology, 35,* 656–666.

Steckler, N. A., & Rosenthal, R. (1985). Sex differences in nonverbal and verbal communication with bosses, peers, and subordinates. *Journal of Applied Psychology, 70* (1), 157–163.

Steele, C. M. (1997). A threat in the air: How stereotypes shape intellectual identity and performance. *American Psychologist, 52*(6), 613–629.

Steele, C. M., & Aronson, J. (1995). Stereotype threat and intellectual performance of African Americans. *Journal of Personality and Social Psychology, 69,* 797–811.

Swim, J. K., Cohen, L. L., & Hyers, L. L. (1998). Experiencing everyday prejudice and discrimination. In J. K. Swim & C. Strangor (Eds.), *Prejudice: The target's perspective* (pp. 37–60). San Diego, CA: Academic Press.

Taylor, S. E., Fiske, S. T., Etcoff, N. L., & Ruderman, A. J. (1978). Categorical and contextual bases of person memory and stereotyping. *Journal of Personality and Social Psychology, 36,* 778–793.

Townsend, B. L. (1998). Social friendships and networks among African American children and youth. In L. H. Meyer, H. Park, M. Grenot-Scheyer, I. S. Schwartz, & B. Harry (Eds.), *Making friends: The influence of culture and development* (pp. 225–241). Baltimore: Paul H. Brookes.

Triandis, H. C., & Triandis, L. M. (1960). Race, social class, religion, and nationality as determinants of social distance. *Journal of Abnormal and Social Psychology. 61,* 110–118.

Waas, G. A., & Graczyk, P. A. (1998). Group interventions for the peer-rejected child. In K. C. Stroiber & T. R. Kratochwill (Eds.), *Handbook of group intervention for children and families* (pp. 141–158). Boston: Allyn & Bacon.

Wentzel, K. R., & Asher, S. R. (1995). The academic lives of neglected, rejected, popular, and controversial children. *Child Development, 66,* 754–763.

Word, C. O., Zanna, M. P., & Cooper, J. (1974). The nonverbal mediation of self-fulfilling prophecies in interracial interaction. *Journal of Experimental Social Psychology, 10,* 109–120.

Zakriski, A., Jacobs, M., & Coie, J. (1997). Coping with childhood peer rejection. In S. A. Wolchick & I. N. Sandler (Eds.), *Handbook of children's coping: Linking theory and intervention. Issues in clinical child psychology* (pp. 423–451). New York: Plenum Press.

9

The Consequences of Childhood Peer Rejection

PATRICIA MCDOUGALL, SHELLEY HYMEL,
TRACY VAILLANCOURT, AND LOUISE MERCER

The note being passed around the classroom read, "Everybody who hates Graham sign here." The page was filled with signatures. Graham was clearly rejected by his fourth grade classmates. What happens to children like Graham? What are the long-term outcomes associated with early rejection by one's peers? These questions are the focus of this chapter.

Graham's story typically evokes feelings of sympathy, sadness, and sometimes pity or disgust, as most of us view rejection by peers as an uncomfortable and undesirable experience for any child. Beyond the assumed discomfort associated with peer rejection, psychologists require empirical evidence regarding its long-term consequences for the developing child. In 1987, Parker and Asher published a seminal review paper on the consequences of peer rejection, asking whether children who are disliked, unpopular, or rejected by their peers are truly at risk for later maladjustment. Their article has been cited over 400 times in the past decade.

A primary motivation for the Parker and Asher (1987) review was to legitimize or justify the increased scholarly attention devoted to children's peer relations. The 1970s and 1980s ushered in a period of rapid growth in studies of children's peer relations. However, given the traditional, longstanding emphasis on parents as the primary agents of socialization, there appeared to be a need to demonstrate that how individuals get along with their peers *matters*. Indeed, as Parker and Asher argued, "If peers contribute substantially to the socialization of social competence, it follows that low-accepted children might become more vulnerable to later problems" (p. 358). The search for the consequences of peer rejection, then, began in part as a way of demonstrating that peer relations contributed critically to a child's overall development.

Over the past decade, the tide appears to have turned. Within both the academic and public arenas, the critical role of social relations with peers has been acclaimed more emphatically than ever before. Developmental theorists (e.g., Piaget, Sullivan, Maslow) had long ago pointed to the contributions of early peer relationships in children's lives, but psychologists, sociologists, and educators only recently came to appreciate the essential role of interpersonal relations, recognizing that the social need to belong is a fundamental human motivation (Baumeister & Leary, 1995). Furman and Robbins (1985) specifically argued that acceptance within a *peer* group, as opposed to friendship at a dyadic level, provides a sense of belongingness. In the popular literature, Goleman (1995) convincingly argued that emotional (social) intelligence is as important, if not more important, than academic intelligence for life success. And Harris (1995, 1998) has openly questioned psychology's traditional acceptance of the "Nurture Assumption," arguing that the influence of parents is *less* significant, and the role of peers *more* significant, than previously acknowledged. As the 1990s came to a close, it was no longer critical to ask whether peers affect child development. The question became: *how* do peers affect development?

In this chapter, we essentially begin where Parker and Asher left off in their 1987 review. We consider research over the past decade that has continued to address the consequences of early peer rejection, highlighting recent comprehensive reviews (e.g., Kupersmidt, Coie, & Dodge, 1990; Rubin, Bukowski, & Parker, 1998) and an impressive collection of studies from a special issue of *Development and Psychopathology*, edited by Cicchetti and Bukowski (1995). We begin with a review of the links between early peer rejection and four broad types of long-term outcomes: academic, general psychopathology, internalizing problems, and externalizing problems. After considering the consequences associated with early peer rejection, we discuss how and *why* rejection contributes to later adjustment. However, prior to reviewing this literature, we want to consider what is meant by the consequences of rejection, as the constructs of "rejection" and "consequence" raise issues for consideration.

Definitional Issues

What Is Rejection?

As we use the term, *rejection* refers to active dislike on the part of one's peers. This dislike may or may not be accompanied by varying degrees of victimization, exclusion, or intentional isolation from peer activities. Our focus is on rejection by one's primary social group rather than rejection by particular individuals, but we do not mean to suggest that rejection at the dyadic level is not important. Indeed, rejection by a friend, partner, or spouse may have serious implications for one's life, as reflected in the literatures on divorce, death, and friendship termination. Moreover, a growing body of research demonstrates that dyadic relationships may actually buffer the negative consequences of interpersonal rejection and victimization in groups (e.g., East & Rook, 1992; Hodges, Boivin, Vitaro, & Bukowski, 1999; Parker & Asher, 1993).[1] A review of these areas, however, is beyond the scope of this chapter (see Parker, Rubin, Price, & DeRosier, 1995; Parker, Saxon, Asher, & Kovacs, 1999).

Within the research on children's peer relations, the primary focus has been on rejection at the group level, as in the case of Graham. Several approaches have been used to identify rejected individuals, and debates continue over the advantages and disadvantages of various techniques (see Landau & Milich, 1990; Maassen, van der Linden, & Akkermans, 1997; Newcomb & Bukowski, 1983; Newcomb, Bukowski, & Pattee, 1993; Terry & Coie, 1991). Typically, however, rejection has been operationalized using either rating scale or nomination sociometric techniques to assess interpersonal attraction among members of a specified group.[2]

The peer *nomination* approach requires that children identify individuals within the group in terms of specified positive and/or negative criteria, such as liking and disliking (e.g., name three classmates you like a lot; name three classmates you don't like). Over the years, nominations have been used to compute both acceptance (sum of positive nominations) and rejection (sum of negative nominations) scores, social impact (acceptance + rejection), and social preference (acceptance − rejection) scores (see Maassen et al., 1997, for a review). These scores, in turn, have been used to create five distinct status groups (see Asher & Dodge, 1986; Coie, Dodge, & Coppotelli, 1982): popular, rejected, neglected, controversial, and average children. Critics say that nomination measures require individuals to make negative designations and do not provide information on how individuals feel about *all* group members (Williams & Gilmour, 1994).

In the peer *rating* technique, children are asked to rate each member of their peer group in terms of how much they like them or like to be with them. The average rating received provides a single index of peer acceptance/rejection, with lower ratings indicating greater rejection. For example, Graham was consistently rejected by classmates and received an average rating of 1.5 on a 5-point sociometric scale. One advantage of the rating scale approach is that scores are based on evaluations by all members of the group (Asher & Hymel, 1981). Rating-scale methods have good psychometric properties and provide continuous data applicable to a broader range of research designs (see Maassen et al., 1997; Parker et al., 1995). One criticism of rating scale measures is that, unlike the nomination approach, they do not permit distinctions between two poorly accepted subgroups: rejected and neglected children. However, with regard to peer rejection, children categorized as rejected using nomination measures are also those rated as highly disliked on rating scales (Hymel & Rubin, 1985; Rubin, Chen, & Hymel, 1993; Rubin, Hymel, LeMare, & Rowden, 1989), lending some confidence that the same "rejected" children are identified across measures.[3]

Childhood peer rejection appears to be a relatively stable phenomenon, with about 30%–45% of rejected children staying rejected over a 4-year period (Coie & Dodge, 1983). Rejected, popular, and average status categories tend to be more stable than neglected and controversial categories, but rejected status shows the greatest long-term stability of all categories (Rubin et al., 1998). Various indices of rejection/acceptance are also stable over time, with test-retest correlations of .55 and .65 for acceptance and rejection scores, respectively, over a 6-month interval (Asher & Dodge, 1986), for both nomination and rating measures. Over longer time periods, Roff, Sells, and Golden (1972) reported test-retest correlations of .42 for acceptance and .34 for rejection scores from grades 3 to 6, and Hymel, Rubin, Rowden, and LeMare (1990) reported correlations of .56 for peer ratings of acceptance/rejection from grades 2 to 5. Thus, for many children the experience of rejection is long-lasting. In terms of prevalence, Terry and Coie (1991) considered two large samples of elementary children and categorized about 62%–69% of children as average in social status, 13%–16% as rejected, and 12%–14% as popular in status across several different classification systems. In some systems, 5%–7% of children are classified as neglected and another 6%–15% are classified as controversial. Research also demonstrates that boys are more likely to be classified as rejected than girls (Coie et al., 1982).

Although sociometric evaluations have been widely used in research on children's peer relations, they still have limitations. First, most studies have evaluated peer acceptance and rejection only within the context of the school or classroom, a convenient context for assessing status within a salient peer group. With increasing age, however, children develop more extensive reference groups beyond the classroom (Brown, 1990; Kinney, 1993), so that classroom-based assessments are only a narrow window on the child's breadth of interpersonal experiences. Further, as children enter secondary school, the expanded size and fractionation of the peer reference group increases administration problems and raises the issue of "knowing" who your peers even are (Inderbizen, 1994). Even more difficult is the assessment of rejection in adulthood when there is no longer a common milieu, and participation in social groups varies across individuals. With these methodological challenges, it is not surprising that few studies of peer rejection have been conducted with adolescents and no comparable studies have been conducted with adults.

What Are "Consequences"?

The notion of "consequences" carries with it an implicit assumption of causality—that rejection leads to or causes particular outcomes. However, studies that truly lend themselves to causal interpretations of rejection experiences are rare. Facing this dilemma, Parker and Asher (1987) considered only longitudinal studies in their review, distinguishing between "follow-up" and "follow-back" studies. Follow-back studies, which compare adults who do or do not demonstrate a specific outcome on particular childhood social indicators (e.g., rejection), are suggestive but cannot be interpreted as reflecting predictive risk. The more traditional follow up study assesses the same individuals over time, examining whether childhood characteristics predict particular outcomes in later life. In this chapter, we consider both follow-back and follow-up studies, as well as intervention studies and concurrent and short-term longitudinal studies when they provide information relevant to our evaluation of the consequences of peer rejection.

Concurrent Correlates of Peer Rejection

Researchers have identified several personal characteristics consistently associated with peer rejection (see Asher & Coie, 1990; Rubin et al., 1998, for reviews). In a large-scale meta-analysis, Newcomb et al. (1993) found rejected children to be more aggressive, more withdrawn, less sociable, and less cognitively skilled than their more accepted peers, although it is not clear whether these are consequences or causes of rejection or both. For example, as our review will show, poor cognitive skills have most often been examined as a *consequence* rather than a *cause* of peer rejection, but at least one intervention study (Coie & Krehbiel, 1984) suggests that the reverse causal sequence is also plausible.

The two major behavioral correlates of peer rejection—aggression and withdrawal—have figured more prominently in recent research on the consequences of rejection yet were first proposed as *causes* of peer rejection. Specifically, Rubin, LeMare, and Lollis (1990) proposed two distinct behavioral pathways to peer rejection, one characterized by aggressive and inappropriate behavior and the other characterized by social withdrawal, shyness, and inhibition. However, once aggression and withdrawal became underlying causes of peer rejection, researchers began to question whether the long-term outcomes associated with rejection could instead be attributed to these behavioral tendencies. At the time of the 1987 review, Parker and Asher noted that most studies had considered behavioral tendencies *or* sociometric status but not both, and they called for consideration of the relative influence of status *and* behavior on long-term adjustment.

Over the last decade evidence has pointed to at least two distinct subgroups of rejected children: aggressive-rejected and withdrawn-rejected children (see Boivin, Hymel, & Bukowski, 1995, for a review). About 40% to 50% of rejected children are behaviorally aggressive, and about 10% to 20% are behaviorally withdrawn (Rubin et al., 1998). These subgroups are believed to be at risk for different types of negative outcomes: aggressive-rejected children at risk for externalizing difficulties (e.g., delinquency, acting out behavior), and withdrawn-rejected children at greater risk for internalizing difficulties (e.g., depression, loneliness, low self-esteem). An important consideration in this chapter, then, is whether the outcomes associated with peer rejection are more accurately viewed as consequences of the behaviors underlying one's poor social status rather than one's social status per se.

Accordingly, we consider both the isolated effects and joint effects of rejection and behavior (where possible) in terms of four broad types of long-term consequences: *academic outcomes, general psychopathology, externalizing problems* (e.g., delinquency, acting out behavior), and *internalizing problems* (e.g., depression, loneliness, low self-esteem).

Long-Term Outcomes of Peer Rejection

Academic Outcomes

Correlational studies have demonstrated statistically significant but modest relations (correlations ranging from .2 to .3) between social status (acceptance/rejection) and concurrent academic performance, with low achievement and poor school adjustment associated with peer rejection (Austin & Draper, 1984; Green, Forehand, Beck, & Vosk, 1980; Ladd, 1990; Vandell & Hembree, 1994; Wentzel, 1991; Wentzel & Asher, 1995). Is academic performance a cause or a consequence of peer rejection? If cognitive skills "cause" peer acceptance/rejection, one interpretation is that brighter children tend to be more socially savvy or mature and therefore more accepted by their peers. Evidence indicates that rejected children exhibit more limited perspective-taking and communication skills and more biased social problem solving (see Rubin et al., 1998; Crick & Dodge, 1994; Dodge & Feldman, 1990; Ladd, 1981), but it is not clear that these "social cognitive" deficits are attributable to limited cognitive or academic skills. An alternative hypothesis is suggested by Coie and Krehbiel (1984), who showed that remediation of academic deficits in a sample of low achieving rejected children resulted in improved peer acceptance. In some cases, then, peer rejection in part results from disruptive, off-task behaviors that "cover" academic failure and frustration.

More important to this review is research suggesting that early rejection affects later academic performance. During the early years, children who are rejected or less accepted in kindergarten are more likely to demonstrate poor academic performance later in the school year (Ladd, 1990) or in subsequent grades (O'Neil, Welsh, Parke, Wang, & Strand, 1997). With older children, longitudinal studies show early peer rejection to predict later grade retention (Coie, Lochman, Terry, & Hyman, 1992; Kupersmidt & Coie, 1990; Ollendick, Weist, Borden, & Green, 1992), less positive adjustment in the transition to middle school (Coie et al., 1992), increased absenteeism and truancy (DeRosier, Kupersmidt, & Patterson, 1994; Kupersmidt & Coie, 1990), and less success in academic pursuits in young adulthood (Bagwell, Newcomb, & Bukowski, 1998). Direct links between peer rejection and later academic achievement have not been clearly established (e.g., DeRosier, Kupersmidt, & Patterson, 1994). For example, Ialongo, Vaden-Kiernan, and Kellam (1998) found that early (grade 1) peer rejection was significantly related to later (grade 6) academic achievement for girls, but not boys. Similarly, Wentzel and Caldwell (1997) found that rejection in grade 6 predicted girls' (but not boys') GPA in grade 7 (study 1), but in grade 8 the prediction did not hold up when other concurrent social-emotional characteristics (antisocial and prosocial behavior, distress) were controlled (study 2).

The links between peer rejection and academic outcomes may also vary across cultures and subcultures. Those studies demonstrating concurrent correlations between rejection and poor achievement have been conducted with predominantly White, North American samples. Ethnographic research by Fordham and Ogbu (1986) revealed that some high-achieving African-American adolescents were rejected by their peers, because such behavior was perceived to be "acting white." Similarly, Suskind (1998) describes the true story of Cedric Jennings, a Black student who, like other academically successful students in his ghetto high school, was openly rejected by peers for aspiring to achieve scholastically. For these youths, rejection appeared to be a consequence of high achievement motivation; this, in turn, afforded them greater opportunity to pursue academic interests. Thus, peer rejection may sometimes unexpectedly contribute to positive academic outcomes.

Perhaps the most well-researched academic outcome associated with early peer rejection is dropping out of school (see Hymel, Comfort, Schonert-Reichl, & McDougall, 1996). Parker and Asher found support for the notion that rejected children are at much higher risk to drop out of school, even when controlling for prior achievement. These links have been replicated in more recent studies (e.g., Ollindick et al., 1992), with a small-scale meta-analysis (seven studies) by Comfort and Kishor (1994), indicating modest but significant effect sizes.

Not all studies show predictive links between early social status and later dropout, however. For example, Cairns, Cairns, and Neckerman (1989) found that dropout was best predicted by the cumulative effects of social aggression and academic difficulties, not rejection, although rejection was assessed by teachers rather than peers. Kupersmidt and Coie (1990) also failed to find that peer rejection was a significant predictor of early school dropout. However, like others, they found that a greater percentage of students who were rejected in grade five (30%) later dropped out, as compared with average (20%), popular (7%), and neglected (0%) students. Further, Kupersmidt and Coie noted that social preference (acceptance minus rejection) was a significant predictor of later dropout in analyses conducted with a White subsample.[4]

In attempting to identify the processes through which early peer rejection leads to subsequent dropout, Hymel et al.'s (1996) review of the literature indicates that students who leave school early are more likely to affiliate with peers who have lower educational values and aspirations and who themselves dropped out or are at risk for it. They also pointed out that, although early peer rejection predicts later dropout, there is no evidence that students are rejected at the time they leave school. They speculated that early peer rejection begins a cycle in which "students who are not well integrated within the mainstream classroom begin to associate with similar others—those who do not support the 'school game'—and together these students gradually disengage from school" (p. 330).

Because both aggression and rejection predict academic difficulties, both concurrently (Wentzel & Asher, 1995) and over time (Coie et al., 1992), subsequent research has attempted to tease apart the relative contributions of each in predicting later school dropout. Both Kupersmidt and Coie (1990) and Cairns et al. (1989) provided evidence that the strongest prediction of school dropout derived from indices of aggression and academic performance rather than rejection per se. More recently, French, Conrad, and Turner (1995), however, found that the combination of peer rejection and antisocial behavior (e.g., disruption, lying, cheating) best predicted subsequent school adjustment difficulties (discipline problems, lower achievement, poor attendance). Rejection may therefore contribute to subsequent school dropout only if it is concomitant with aggression (Cairns et al., 1989; Kupersmidt & Coie, 1990) or marks the beginning of a cycle of gradual school disengagement (Hymel et al., 1996).

General Psychopathology Outcomes

Parker and Asher (1987) focused on adult psychopathology as a consequence of early social difficulties. One of the early and oft-cited studies within this literature was by Cowen, Pederson, Babigian, Izzo, and Trost (1973), who found that teacher and peer assessments of acceptance/rejection in grade 3 predicted mental health problems 11–13 years later better than any other piece of information in the child's cumulative school record. The Cowen et al. study, however, did not specify the nature of the psychopathology. Parker and Asher found that the results of 10 follow-back studies consistently demonstrated that adults with psychological disorders had histories of poor peer acceptance. However, results of five follow-up studies, which more readily lend themselves to predictive conclusions, were mixed. Thus, at the time of the 1987 review, there was some inconclusive evidence that early peer difficulties are associated with a variety of psychiatric problems, including neurosis, psychosis, alcoholism, conduct disorder, and schizophrenia.

In a subsequent review, Kupersmidt et al. (1990) concluded that the role of peer rejection in the development of schizophrenia was not altogether clear and varied across boys and girls. Specifically, links between early rejection and later schizophrenia were inferred primarily from indices of early social behavior. Socially withdrawn behavior predicted later schizophrenia in girls, and both antisocial behavior and subsequent withdrawal predicted schizophrenia in boys. There was some evidence of links between later schizophrenia and teacher reports of rejection, but no studies had evaluated peer-assessed rejection as a predictor of later schizophrenia.

Three more recent longitudinal studies have demonstrated significant links between early social acceptance/rejection and psychopathology (Coie,

Christopoulous, Terry, Dodge, & Lochman, 1989; Hymel et al., 1990; Morison & Masten, 1991). Each of these studies, however, also demonstrated that early social behavior predicted later maladjustment, with aggression associated more strongly with later externalizing difficulties and withdrawal more predictive of later internalizing difficulties. Such findings foreshadowed the next wave of research that examined the independent and interactive contributions of rejection and social behavior in predicting subsequent internalizing and externalizing outcomes.

Externalizing Problems

Parker and Asher (1987) considered only one type of externalizing outcome: delinquency/criminality. Two available follow-back studies suggested that a history of peer rejection characterized the lives of adolescent or young adult offenders, and 6 out of 10 follow-up studies provided evidence that low peer acceptance predicts later criminality. These relations have been replicated in more recent studies (e.g., Kupersmidt, Burchinal, & Patterson, 1995; Ollendick et al., 1992).

Parker and Asher (1987) also found strong support from both follow-back and follow-up studies for the notion that an aggressive behavioral style is linked with later criminality. More recently, Rubin, Chen, McDougall, Bowker, and McKinnon (1995) reported that early (grade 2) aggression predicted later self-reports of delinquent activity. Given established links between aggression and rejection, researchers questioned whether peer rejection adds significantly to the prediction of later criminality, over and above aggressive behavior. Several longitudinal studies have demonstrated that, despite predictive links between early rejection and later criminality, only aggression (not rejection) predicts later delinquent behavior when both are considered as predictors (Kupersmidt & Coie, 1990; Lochman & Wayland, 1994; Rubin et al., 1995; Tremblay, Mâsse, Vitaro, & Dobkin, 1995).

Nonetheless, conclusions about the role of peer rejection in the emergence of delinquent and criminal behavior may be premature. Patterson, Capaldi, and Bank (1991) also found that the primary predictor of later delinquency was early antisocial behavior rather than peer rejection per se, but they suggested that the effects of peer rejection on later criminality may be indirect, mediated by antisocial affiliations. Specifically, they proposed that aggressive children who are generally rejected by their peers in the early grades may have restricted access to the wide range of possible peers with whom they can associate (see also Brendgen, Vitaro, & Bukowski, 1998; Dishion, Capaldi, Spracklen, & Li, 1995; Parker et al., 1995). Given the fundamental need to belong (Baumeister & Leary, 1995), these children seek peer affiliation, but they are more likely to gravitate toward similar and available others, in this case, other aggressive or antisocial peers (see Dishion, Patterson, & Griesler, 1994). As Cairns and Cairns (1991; Cairns, Cairns, Neckerman,

Gest, & Gariépy, 1988) pointed out, aggressive as well as nonaggressive children are far more likely to affiliate with their "own kind." Participation in a deviant (aggressive) peer group, in turn, increases the likelihood of antisocial and delinquent behavior.

Although research by Tremblay et al. (1995) failed to demonstrate that the deviant behavior of *best friend* contributes significantly to later delinquency, results of a growing number of studies lend support to aspects of the Patterson et al. (1991) proposal (e.g., Boivin & Vitaro, 1995; Brendgen et al., 1998; French et al., 1995; Vitaro & Tremblay, in press). For example, French et al. found that adolescents who were both rejected and antisocial in grade 8 were at greater risk for substance use and *involvement with deviant peers* in grade 10.[5] Brendgen et al. found support for a sequential model in which early adolescents who lacked close affective ties to their parents (a risk factor for delinquency) were more likely to affiliate subsequently with delinquent peers if they suffered from low self-esteem, but *only* if they were rejected by the majority of their peers, which essentially limited their access to other, nondelinquent friends. Finally, intervention research by Vitaro and Tremblay has demonstrated the effectiveness of an early delinquency prevention program with 8- to 9-year-old aggressive boys in decreasing aggressive behavior (teacher rated), reducing vandalism and stealing (self-reported), and increasing the likelihood of affiliation with nondeviant peers by age 12. Although these findings are consistent with Patterson et al.'s model, further longitudinal research is needed for a full validation of the proposed indirect effects of peer rejection on subsequent delinquency.

Interestingly, results of recent research on both delinquency (as described above) and school dropout (Hymel et al., 1996) suggest a similar causal sequence regarding the indirect effects of peer rejection. In both cases, the suggestion is that early peer rejection leads to affiliation with like-minded peers and gradual disengagement from the social mainstream. These hypotheses require further empirical research but are consistent with the growing appreciation of the critical role that children's peer groups play in development (group socialization theory; Harris, 1995).

Since the Parker and Asher (1987) review, researchers have also considered a broader range of externalizing outcomes associated with peer rejection. One obvious "externalizing outcome" is aggression or antisocial behavior. Aggression is one of the strongest correlates of peer rejection; much of the research suggests that aggression *causes* rejection (e.g., Bukowski & Newcomb, 1984; Coie et al., 1982; Coie & Kupersmidt, 1983; Dodge, 1983; Little & Garber, 1995), although others argue that rejection leads to subsequent aggression (e.g., Dodge, Bates, & Pettit, 1990; Merten, 1994). Longitudinal studies show that early peer rejection is related to later aggressive behavior (e.g., Kupersmidt et al., 1995), but that early aggression is a better predictor of later aggressive behavior than early rejection (Ialongo et al., 1998; Kupersmidt et al., 1990; Ledingham, Schwartzman, Chappell, Cristina,

& Schmidt, 1999). Thus, aggression may be a "common cause" of both rejection and subsequent aggression.

Using a composite index of externalizing outcomes, longitudinal research by Kupersmidt and Coie (1990) revealed that the likelihood of "nonspecific" externalizing outcomes in adolescence (including dropout, police contact, school suspension, grade retention, or truancy) was greater for students who were rejected in grade 5. However, subsequent analyses indicated that only grade 5 aggression, not rejection, emerged as a significant predictor of later externalizing outcomes when considered simultaneously. These findings were qualified by additional analyses of data from White students (69% of the sample) for whom the combination of aggression and rejection in grade 5 best predicted later ("nonspecific") externalizing difficulties. Indeed, the probability of some form of externalizing difficulty seven years later was 92.73% for White students who were both aggressive and rejected in grade 5.

Coie and his colleagues followed a third-grade sample of predominantly Black children and examined the early predictors of later externalizing problems (parent- and self-report of DSM criteria) in grades 6 (Coie et al., 1992) and grade 10 (Coie, Terry, Lenox, Lochman, & Hyman, 1995). Although the results of this research suggested a complex interplay of early characteristics and later outcomes for boys versus girls, the combination of early aggression and rejection seemed to provide the best prediction of later externalizing difficulties, at least for boys. Similarly, DeRosier et al. (1994) observed that the link between high levels of externalizing problems in grades 2–7 and externalizing problems four years later was exacerbated for individuals who were also rejected by peers, although this pattern was stronger for boys than girls. Using a slightly different approach, Bierman and colleagues compared aggressive-rejected, aggressive-nonrejected, and nonaggressive-rejected boys, ages 6–12. Concurrently, aggressive-rejected boys exhibited more conduct problems than comparison boys according to teacher, peer, and observer reports (Bierman, Smoot, & Aumiller, 1993). When Bierman and Wargo (1995) assessed these same boys two years later, the aggressive-rejected boys exhibited the greatest number of conduct problems relative to boys in the comparison groups.

Across studies, then, apparently the combination of aggression and rejection provides, for boys, the best prediction of later externalizing difficulties. The prediction of externalizing difficulties in girls remains unclear. One possible issue in the study of the links between aggression, rejection, and externalizing outcomes in girls is that we are only beginning to understand the unique forms that aggression takes in girls. Crick and colleagues (e.g., Crick, 1995, 1996; Crick & Grotpeter, 1995) have demonstrated that girls are more likely to engage in *relational aggression,* which involves harming others by intentionally manipulating and damaging their peer relationships (e.g., teasing, rumor spreading, exclusion). With evidence that both relational and overt aggression contribute independently to peer rejection (Crick & Grotpeter,1995), and that the degree to which children engage in *nonnormative* types of aggression predicts concurrent maladjustment (Crick, 1997), future research demands greater attention to gender as a possible moderator of the links among early rejection and aggression and later externalizing outcomes.

Internalizing Outcomes

Studies of internalizing problems associated with peer rejection have focused primarily on three major types of outcomes: self-concept, depression, and loneliness. For example, numerous studies have demonstrated significant concurrent correlations between peer rejection and loneliness from early (Cassidy & Asher, 1992) and middle childhood (e.g., Crick & Ladd, 1993) through adolescence (Parkhurst & Asher, 1992), with rejected children expressing significantly greater loneliness and social dissatisfaction than their more-accepted peers. However, the magnitude of these correlations is low (approximately .3), and rejected children, as a group, show the highest mean, as well as the highest variability, in loneliness scores (see Asher, Parkhurst, Hymel, & Williams, 1990). Thus, not all rejected children feel lonely. Modest levels of association have also been demonstrated between peer status and other internalizing problems, including low self-esteem (Harter, 1982; Hymel & Franke, 1985) and depression (Cole, 1990; Cole & Carpentieri, 1990; Ialongo et al., 1998; Patterson & Stoolmiller, 1991; Vosk, Forehand, Parker, & Rickard, 1982). Because of the modest associations between rejection and self-perceptions as well as the wide variability in self-perceptions among rejected children, researchers have attempted to specify additional factors that contribute to the likelihood of internalizing difficulties among rejected children.

A major contribution to our understanding of the etiology of internalizing outcomes comes from research on social behavior and rejected subgroups. By the end of the 1980s, Rubin and Hymel and colleagues demonstrated that negative self-perceptions and affective outcomes such as depression and loneliness were associated with withdrawn rather than aggressive social behavior, both concurrently (e.g., Hymel, Rubin, Rowden, & LeMare, 1990; Rubin et al., 1993; Rubin & Mills, 1988) and predictively (e.g., Rubin, Hymel, & Mills, 1989; Rubin & Mills, 1988).[6] Such findings paved the way for studies of rejected subgroups that demonstrated that withdrawn or submissive-rejected children report more concurrent internalizing outcomes, including negative self-perceptions, loneliness, and depression (e.g., Boivin & Begin, 1989; Boivin, Poulin, & Vitaro, 1994; Boivin, Thomassin, & Alain, 1989; Crick & Ladd, 1993; Hymel et al., 1993; Parkhurst & Asher, 1992; Patterson, Kupersmidt, & Greisler, 1990; Williams & Asher, 1987).

In teasing apart the relative contributions of withdrawn social behavior and peer rejection to feelings of loneliness, Renshaw and Brown (1993) found that withdrawal and peer acceptance/rejection contributed independently to later self-reported loneliness, but aggressive behavior did not. However, in a longer follow-up of 60 grade 2 students into their grade 9 year, Rubin et al. (1995) observed that higher reports of loneliness, depression, and poor perceptions of social competence in adolescence were predicted by social withdrawal in grade 2, but that a composite index of social competence in grade 2 (including a measure of peer acceptance /rejection) did not add significantly to this prediction. Unfortunately, this study did not evaluate peer rejection as a separate predictor of internalizing outcomes.

Boivin and colleagues (Boivin & Hymel, 1997; Boivin et al., 1995) suggested a more complicated pattern of relationships between peer rejection and social withdrawal as predictors of internalizing difficulties. Boivin and Hymel provided evidence to support a sequential mediational model in which the association between social withdrawal and negative self-perceptions (i.e., feelings of loneliness and social incompetence) was partially mediated by the quality of one's peer experiences, namely, peer rejection and, in turn, peer victimization. In other words, although socially withdrawn children are inclined to view themselves as lonelier and more socially incompetent (direct effects), these inclinations are enhanced when the withdrawn children are rejected and, in turn, victimized by peers (indirect effects). In an extension of this model, Boivin et al. replicated the initial sequence longitudinally. Specifically, increases in loneliness from one school year to the next were predicted by increases in withdrawal, which was mediated by increases in peer rejection, which was partially mediated by increases in victimization among peers. Additional analyses demonstrated that feelings of loneliness, in turn, contributed to reported depression. In other words, withdrawn children were at risk for later depression if they were rejected by peers, but even more at risk when peer rejection lead to actual poor treatment by peers (victimization) and only when these negative peer experiences lead children to feel badly about their current social situation (loneliness). Valås and Sletta (1996) provided evidence for a similar sequence of links between social withdrawal, status, loneliness, and internalizing outcomes in a Norwegian sample. Again, whether or not the individual felt badly about his or her social situation (loneliness) mediated the link between status and subsequent internalizing outcomes (low self-esteem and depression). Panak and Garber (1992) also found that the child's own perceptions of his or her rejection by peers mediated the link between rejection and subsequent depression.

Although research has generally demonstrated stronger links between social withdrawal (in combination with rejection) and internalizing outcomes, some evidence suggests that aggression is also concurrently associated with internalizing outcomes, especially depression (e.g., Cole & Carpentieri, 1990; Garber, Quiggly, Panak, & Dodge, 1991; Kovacs, Paulauskas, Gatsonis, & Richards, 1988). However, these findings are readily interpreted within Coyne's interpersonal theory of depression (Coyne, 1976; Coyne, Burchill, & Stiles, 1990), which posits that depression causes rejection rather than the reverse. Coyne proposed that depressive individuals' need for validation leads them to constantly seek reassurance and approval from others, a tendency that, over time, becomes more intense and frequent, gradually leading to peer rejection. Studies by Little and Garber (1995) and by Joiner and Barnett (1994) are consistent with this causal hypothesis.

Nevertheless, a few studies have examined the relative and combined effects of rejection and aggression on later internalizing outcomes, but results have been weak and inconsistent. In some cases, predictive links between aggressive behavior and internalizing outcomes have not been demonstrated for either depression (e.g., Hymel et al., 1990; Ialongo et al., 1998; Panak & Garber, 1992) or loneliness (Renshaw & Brown, 1993). Other studies, however, show that increases in both rejection and aggression predict depression one year later (Panak & Garber, 1992) and that the combination of rejection and antisocial behavior placed students at greater risk for later depression (French et al., 1995). Similarly, Lochman and Wayland (1994) found both aggression and peer status to predict later internalizing difficulties in boys.

Research by Coie and his colleagues suggests that the relationship here may be even more complex. When parental reports of internalizing difficulties were considered, Coie et al. (1992) found weak links between early (grade 3) aggression and later (grade 6) internalizing problems, and these were essentially accounted for by indices of rejection. However, when self-reported internalizing difficulties were considered, a significant interaction between aggression and rejection emerged, with peer rejection (social preference) predicting later internalizing difficulties for low-aggressive but not high-aggressive children. In a subsequent report, Coie et al. (1995) followed these same students into grade 10 and found that the pattern of predictive relations differed for boys and girls and for parent reports and self-reports.[7] When parent reports were considered, rejected-aggressive boys showed significant increases in internalizing difficulties, but no significant predictors emerged for girls. When self-reports of internalizing outcomes were considered, however, rejection (not aggression) predicted later internalizing difficulties for both genders. The mixed results across studies do not lend much confidence to the prediction of internalizing outcomes from indices of aggression but do support links between depression and rejection.

To summarize, links between rejection and internalizing outcomes seem clearer for boys than girls. For both boys and girls, however, the combination of social withdrawal (not aggression) *and* peer rejection increases children's risk for later internalizing difficulties. These relationships, however, are complex rather than straightforward. Although withdrawn children appear to be prone to internalizing problems, such outcomes are mediated in part by negative peer experiences, including peer rejection and victimization (Boivin & Hymel 1997; Boivin et al., 1995). One particularly critical consideration, however, is how the individual perceives the situation. Children who view themselves as rejected (Panak & Garber, 1992) and who feel lonely and socially dissatisfied (Boivin et al., 1995; Valås & Sletta, 1996) are at greater risk for internalizing problems.

Models and Processes

Research on the consequences of peer rejection began with the question of whether peer rejection was associated with particular long-term consequences. Subsequently, research shifted from identifying *what* the long-term consequences of rejection might be to determining *how* peer rejection is involved in the etiology of negative outcomes. According to Parker and Asher (1987), two implicit models that prescribe different roles for rejection have long guided this research: an incidental model and a causal model linking rejection to later maladjustment. In the incidental model, rejection is viewed as a marker rather than a true cause of later maladjustment. Underlying disturbances (e.g., family stress or personality factors, genetic predisposition) bring about deviant behaviors (e.g., aggression, withdrawal) that ultimately lead to negative consequences. That is, peer rejection is not a *cause* but rather an *indicator* of problematic social behavior and is itself a consequence of the preceding condition (Burks, Dodge, & Price, 1995). The incidental or "common cause" (Dunn & McGuire, 1992) model highlights the proposition that both peer rejection and later difficulties stem from the same underlying disturbance. With the incidental model, knowing about peer rejection might prove helpful in detecting children who may be at later risk, but variability in rejected status makes no independent contribution to the prediction of negative outcomes once the effects of negative behavior are accounted for (Parker & Asher, 1987).

Research demonstrating correlational links between rejection and various outcomes has been a useful starting point in identifying possible consequences of peer rejection, but given the concurrent nature of these data, one cannot rule out the possibility that rejection is merely incidental. For at least one of the externalizing outcomes examined in this review—aggression—the extant research suggests that rejection might best be viewed as an incidental marker of problems. Although rejection predicts later aggression (Ialongo et al., 1998; Kupersmidt et al., 1995), and some have suggested that rejection causes subsequent aggression (e.g., Merten, 1994), longitudinal research shows that early aggression is a better predictor of later aggression than rejection is (Ialongo et al., 1998; Kupersmidt et al., 1990; Ledingham et al., 1999). For other outcomes, the incidental model is not well supported by available evidence.

Most of the research conducted since 1990 has been aimed at demonstrating that rejection does *not* play an incidental role but rather is fundamental in explaining later negative adjustment. What evidence supports causal models of peer rejection? Parker and Asher's (1987) description of a causal model includes deviant or negative social behavior bringing about difficult peer experiences (e.g., rejection), which, in turn, are precursors to "deviant socialization experiences and opportunities" (p. 379) that ultimately result in poor adjustment. Poor peer relationships are a source of stress and deprive children of important socialization experiences required to develop positive social skills (Burks et al., 1995; Dunn & McGuire, 1992; Parker et al., 1995), making positive peer experience, according to Parker and Asher, "necessity not luxury." Efforts to validate causal models may be categorized into one of four research approaches: (1) demonstrating predictive links between rejection and negative outcomes over time in longitudinal designs, (2) evaluating the relative contribution of both negative social behavior and rejection in the prediction of poor outcomes, (3) considering the interactive or combined effects of behavior and rejection in predicting negative consequences, and (4) exploring the role that deviant peer experiences play in explaining the links between rejection and later maladjustment.

For the first research approach, there is no shortage of evidence (reviewed previously) in both short- and long-term longitudinal designs showing that peer rejection predicts later maladjustment outcomes in academic, externalizing, and internalizing realms. Despite these longitudinal links, one of the most compelling criticisms of the causal model has been the observation that some rejected children do not experience subsequent adjustment problems (e.g., Dunn & McGuire, 1992; Parker & Asher, 1987). In response to this criticism, the causal model has been extended beyond the straightforward link between the occurrence/nonoccurrence of rejected status and subsequent negative consequences, to examine the *transient versus chronic* and *distal versus proximal* nature of rejected experience. For example, DeRosier et al. (1994) observed that chronic (occurring over several years) and proximal (occurring in the recent past) rejection predicted both internalizing and externalizing behavior even after controlling for early adjustment. Similarly, Burks et al. (1995) observed that boys who were consistently rejected across two years were at greater risk for internalizing problems than boys who were either transiently or never rejected. Burks et al. contended that their data support a "threshold" version of the causal model in which negative consequences occur only after sufficient exposure to peer rejection moves boys beyond a threshold. Future research must define and describe the exact nature of this threshold and consider why such a model might hold for boys but not girls.

In addition to issues of chronicity and proximity, another key component in causal models linking rejection to various negative outcomes is maladaptive social behavior. Given that negative social behavior is a precursor to troubled peer relationships and is often itself a predictor of later adjustment difficulties, researchers have attempted to validate the causal model in a second way, by considering the relative and independent contributions of negative social behavior and peer rejection to the prediction of adjustment outcomes. Our review revealed that support for a "unique" causal role for peer rejection has been clearest in the realm of internalizing outcomes, with studies demonstrating that early peer rejection significantly adds to the prediction of internalizing problems (e.g., loneliness, depression), even after controlling for withdrawal or aggression (e.g., Coie et al., 1995; Lochman & Wayland, 1994; Panak & Garber, 1992; Renshaw & Brown, 1993).

The evidence for peer rejection as a unique contributor to academic and externalizing outcomes is less convincing. Although at least one study revealed that rejection was a significant predictor of academic difficulties even when aggression was controlled (Coie et al., 1992), other studies have demonstrated that aggression and not rejection predicts later academic problems (Cairns et al., 1989; Kupersmidt & Coie, 1990). Similarly, despite limited evidence that peer rejection accounts for later externalizing problems after controlling for the effects of early behavioral problems (i.e., aggression, acting out; DeRosier et al., 1994), aggression has repeatedly emerged as the more stable predictor of externalizing difficulties (Kupersmidt & Coie, 1990; Tremblay et al., 1995). In sum, rejection seems to play a stronger role in accounting for internalizing difficulties than in explaining academic or externalizing problems.

Moving beyond an examination of the independent contributions of rejection and social behavior, researchers have explored the possibility that the risk of negative consequences increases when the experience of peer rejection is coupled with negative social behavior. This third wave of research has moved the discussion of the causal model one step forward by examining a combination of child characteristics (aggression, withdrawal) and social or environmental influences (peer rejection) in a more complex and potentially realistic "interactional" model (Parker et al., 1995). Evidence for an interactional causal model varies across the domains we reviewed, with the strongest evidence for comorbidity effects observed for children who are both aggressive and rejected by their peers. Indeed, an interactional model appropriately captures the observation that rejected-aggressive children appear to be at greatest risk for academic (French et al., 1995) and externalizing problems (French et al., 1995), at least for boys (Bierman et al., 1993; Bierman & Wargo, 1995; Coie et al., 1992, 1995) and samples of Caucasian students (e.g., Kupersmidt & Coie, 1990). The interactional model is less convincing, however, in explaining the role of rejection in internalizing outcomes. Although concurrent evidence exists linking the combined experience of social withdrawal and rejection to internalizing problems (Boivin & Begin, 1989; Boivin et al., 1989, 1994; Crick & Ladd, 1993; Hymel, Bowker & Woody, 1993; Parkhurst & Asher, 1992; Patterson et al., 1990; Williams & Asher, 1987), the long-term sequence appears to be more complicated, as we will discuss shortly.

The interactional model has also afforded the opportunity to explore whether peer rejection plays a *moderating role,* altering the relationship between harmful early conditions (e.g., socialization difficulties that bring about maladaptive behaviors) and vulnerability to negative outcomes (e.g.,

Bagwell, Newcomb, & Bukowski, 1998; Dunn & McGuire, 1982). On one hand, low levels or the absence of rejection might moderate the link between deviant behavior (e.g., aggression) and problematic consequences by buffering children against maladaptive outcomes. On the other hand, the negative experience of peer rejection may exacerbate an already problematic situation and result in more damaging outcomes (e.g., Kupersmidt et al., 1990). With an interactional model, the question of whether rejection serves as a moderator can also be explored by examining the combined effects of social behavior and rejected status. Our review indicates few attempts to examine whether rejection plays a moderating role. One exception is DeRosier et al. (1994), who found that the link between early and later maladjustment (i.e., the stability of absenteeism, aggression, acting out over a three-year period) was stronger (more stable) when combined with the experience of rejection (versus no rejection). For these outcomes, then, rejection exacerbates existing problems, placing children at greater risk for adjustment difficulties. DeRosier et al. found that peer rejection played a different moderating role for internalizing outcomes. Here rejection was associated with a *decrease* in the likelihood that internalizing problems (shy/anxious, withdrawn behavior) would remain stable over time. Due to limited evidence, it is too early to draw firm conclusions about the moderating role of early peer rejection. Nevertheless, research on the consequences of peer rejection is incomplete and inadequate when we fail to consider how rejection and maladaptive social behavior operate independently and in concert.

Even more complex causal sequences also need to be considered. The fourth approach to evaluating links between rejection and adjustment involves the possibility that the effects of rejection are mediated by negative peer experiences. In this sequence, rejection leads to deviant socialization experiences (e.g., victimization by peers, negative peer affiliations) that in turn promote negative outcomes. Our review yielded three examples of this type of model. With regard to academic outcomes, Hymel et al. (1996) suggested that the path to dropping out of high school may begin with early rejection but is strengthened by affiliations with the "wrong" peer group (e.g., peers with low value for school, who are dropouts themselves). Similarly, with regard to externalizing problems such as delinquency, Patterson et al. (1991) suggested that rejected individuals who affiliate with a deviant peer group are at greater risk for delinquency. To our knowledge, the only study to actually test the mediating role of peer experiences directly was conducted by Boivin et al. (1995) for internalizing problems. They observed that the link between rejected status and subsequent internalizing difficulties (e.g., loneliness, self-concept) was at least partially mediated by whether students were victimized by their peers. Across outcome domains, then, there is some suggestion that deviant peer experiences (e.g., victimization, affiliation with delinquent/antisocial or nonacademically motivated peers) may serve as a mediator of peer rejection. These troublesome peer socialization experiences, brought about (at least in part) by peer rejection, support the more complex causal model proposed by Parker and Asher (1987), as well as recent group socialization theories of development (Harris, 1995).

Parker et al. (1995) argued that the future generation of causal models for peer rejection must also include adequate consideration of the interplay of child (i.e., maladaptive behavior, negative social cognitions) and environmental variables (i.e., poor peer relationships) that mutually influence each other over time. Parker et al. proposed a *transactional* model characterized by a cycle that begins with "disposing factors" and moves on to consider the contributions of each of three broad components of the system in the development of both cognitive/affective and behavioral consequences: negative social behaviors, negative beliefs about the self and others, and problematic peer relationships (see Parker et al., 1995, for a full description). To our knowledge, only one study to date has approximated such a transactional model. Specifically, Boivin et al. (1995) developed a "sequential mediational model" involving social behavior (withdrawal), peer rejection, negative socialization experiences (victimization), negative self-perceptions (e.g., low self-esteem, loneliness, and social dissatisfaction) and negative internalizing outcomes (depression). Children in their study who became increasingly withdrawn over time and who were subjected to growing peer rejection and victimization reported intensifying negative perceptions of their social situation, which, in turn, were linked to greater depression. Transactional models may well represent the future of research on the consequences of peer rejection, with the advantage of recognizing that "the child and the peer group form a dynamic interacting system that changes over time" (Parker et al., 1995, p. 131). To fully develop such models, however, we need to understand the processes through which self-perceptions might affect social behavior and vice versa.

Self-Perception Processes

Rejection, determined by peer sociometric evaluations, tells us nothing about the *subjective* experience of rejection. Does a child who is rejected by peers *feel* rejected? Although middle elementary school students and adolescents are generally able to accurately evaluate their status among peers (e.g., Ausebel, Schiff, & Gasser, 1952; Krantz & Burton, 1986), evidence suggests that highly rejected children express less accurate perceptions of their social status and social competence (see Cillessen & Bellmore, 1999). Further, research on rejected subgroups has demonstrated systematic variations in social self-perceptions, with withdrawn-rejected children expressing more negative self-evaluations than aggressive-rejected children (e.g., Hymel et al., 1993; Patterson et al., 1990). Particularly relevant to this review is evidence that inaccurate perceptions of one's social status predict loneliness and peer-rated internalizing problems, even after controlling for actual acceptance/rejection (Cillessen & Bellmore, 1999).

However, as Cairns and Cairns (1991) pointed out, "self-cognitions do not always have to be veridical to be functional" (p. 259). The child's own perspective on his or her social situation may be equally important, if not more important, than actual status in determining long-term effects. Consistent with these arguments, Panak and Garber (1992) found that the relation between peer rejection and depression was mediated by children's awareness of their own rejection. Rejected children who acknowledged their rejection were more depressed than rejected children who were not aware of (or did not admit) their poor status within the group.

Classroom sociometric assessments of peer rejection provide a convenient but narrow window on children's social experiences. We often fail to recognize that not all individuals who are rejected within their peer group lack peer affiliations (Cairns et al., 1988; Parker & Asher, 1993; Vandell & Hembree, 1994) and that children and adolescents do form social networks outside of the classroom setting (e.g., Internet contacts, neighborhoods, siblings, extracurricular groups), which may also include nonpeer relationships with adults (East, Hess, & Lerner, 1987; Ladd, 1983; Parker & Asher, 1987). Often researchers fail to explore these other contexts and portray the rejected individual as devoid of positive social interactions. Self-perceptions of rejection, then, may actually be based on a broader and more "accurate" view of the child's larger social world.

Finally, it is important to consider the possibility of individual differences in the value or primacy of peer affiliations, a facet hitherto largely ignored in the peer rejection literature. Baumeister and Leary (1995) argued persuasively that the need to belong is a fundamental human motivation. But clearly, individuals need and seek different types and numbers of peer relationships.

One particularly promising approach to understanding the complex ways in which individual self-perceptions might influence the long-term consequences of peer rejection comes from Kupersmidt, Buchele, Voegler, and Sedikides (1996). Consistent with adult models of both depression and loneliness, Kupersmidt et al. focused on the discrepancy between an individual's social "needs" and his or her actual and perceived social relationships. They combined the self-discrepancy model developed by Higgins and colleagues (e.g., Higgins, Klein, & Strauman, 1985) and the concept of undesired self (Ogilvie, 1987) to explain the influence of self-perceptions within the social realm. From Higgin's self-discrepancy model, Kupersmidt et al. derived three critical aspects of one's social self: Actual, Ideal, and Ought Self. Actual Social Self refers to the relations the child *actually* has established; Ideal Social Self refers to the type, quality, and quantity of peer relations the child would ideally *like* to have; and Ought Social Self refers to the types of social relations that the child (or parents or teachers) feels he or she *should* possess. Kupersmidt et al. also incorporated the notion of Undesired Social Self, which includes the bad memories of "dreaded experiences, embarrassing situations, fearsome events and unwanted emotions" (Ogilvie, 1987, p. 87).

Following Higgins's self-discrepancy theory, Kupersmidt et al. argued that the discrepancy between these various aspects of the Social Self leads to particular affective reactions, which, in turn, influence social behavior and cognition and thus contribute to particular long-term outcomes.

Although Kupersmidt et al. (1996) did not use the terms internalizing and externalizing, they posited that two of the specified self-discrepancies (Actual Self-Ideal Self and Actual Self-Ought Self) would result in outcomes that could be classified as internalizing, whereas a third type of discrepancy (Ideal Self-Undesired Self) would lead to outcomes that could be classified as externalizing. Specifically, discrepancies between Actual Self and Ideal Self (e.g., a rejected child who strongly desires to be popular and accepted) would result in "dejection-related emotions" such as feelings of disappointment or discouragement, which place the child at greater risk for loneliness or depression. Some support for this link has already been provided by Kupersmidt, Sigda, Sedikides, and Voegler (1999) for loneliness in adolescence. Alternatively, discrepancies between Actual Self and Ought Self would result in "agitation-related emotions" such as anxiety and nervousness. These affective states, in turn, may lead to such behaviors as timidity at school, refusal to speak in public, test and performance anxiety, and school phobia (again, internalizing outcomes).

However, discrepancies between Ideal Self and Undesired Self likely lead to strong negative affect that may motivate changes in social behavior and affiliations. To illustrate, Kupersmidt et al. (1996) described how a student who desires to be accepted (Ideal Self) but is consistently ignored and rejected (which, for this child, reflects his or her Undesired Self) might have a strong affective reaction (fear of being alone) and decide to affiliate with anyone who would be friendly (e.g., an antisocial peer group) rather than be without friends, resulting in problematic behaviors (externalizing outcomes). These proposals are reminiscent of earlier suggestions regarding the role of negative peer affiliations in increasing risk for delinquency (Patterson et al., 1991) and dropout (Hymel et al., 1996). The proposed Social Self Discrepancy model enhances our understanding of how individuals—each with unique conceptions of Ideal, Actual, Ought, and perhaps Undesired social selves—might seek particular types and numbers of peer relationships, follow certain paths in seeking to attain these relationships, and, when thwarted, change their cognition or behaviors in ways that contribute to externalizing and internalizing outcomes. Empirical support for the proposed model remains a task for future research.

Future Directions

Since 1987, researchers have risen to the challenges set out by Parker and Asher and have clearly established that early rejection by peers is causally linked to a variety of later maladaptive outcomes. Research on the consequences of peer rejection has demonstrated not only that peer rejection matters but also how and in what ways it matters for later development. Progress within this literature is attributable in part to the development and more widespread use of statistical procedures that allow for the testing of rather complex causal models (for examples, see the collection of articles in the special issue of *Development and Psychopathology* edited by Cicchetti and Bukowski in 1995). Rubin et al. (1998) warn us that this trend is likely to continue in future research. At the same time, Panak (1999) points to the need for some caution in our interpretation of the findings obtained from these procedures, given sample requirements and necessary assumptions for the appropriate use of these statistical tools. Despite the complexity and elegance of our causal models, however, we must keep in mind that our effect sizes are modest at best and substantial portions of the variance in long-term consequences remain unexplained. Accordingly, several areas should be addressed more fully in future research and particular questions remain unanswered.

First, we propose greater attention to variations across gender, race, and ethnicity in future research on the consequences of peer rejection. As noted throughout this review, some patterns of predictive relations are applicable only to boys or to White samples. With our increasing recognition of peer influences on child development (Harris, 1995), it becomes important to identify characteristics of the peer group that play key roles in this peer socialization process. Variations as a function of gender, race, or ethnicity may provide a useful starting point for understanding how factors unique to particular peer groups and subcultures may directly influence the outcomes associated with peer rejection.

Second, to fully appreciate the consequences of early rejection, we may need to take a second look at research that *fails* to demonstrate systematic associations involving peer rejection, despite theoretical arguments that such differences *ought* to exist. For example, one might speculate that the negative social experiences of rejected children would lead to a more negative and less trusting view of the world, less sophisticated moral reasoning, and nonnormative conceptions of friendship, yet researchers have failed to demonstrate significant differences between rejected and more accepted children in terms of either perceptions of trust (Hymel, Vaillancourt, McDougall, & Rotenberg, 1999), moral reasoning (Schonert-Reichl, 1999) or friendship conceptions (Bichard, Alden, Walker, & McMahon, 1988; Bowker & Hymel, 1987). Despite theoretical speculations, then, these social cognitive factors are not concurrent correlates or likely consequences of peer rejection. Why not?

Third, it may be useful to consider peer rejection from a resiliency framework, asking how (and why) some children seem to rise above the long-term risks associated with early peer rejection and other social difficulties. Recent articles by Miller, Brehm, and Whitehouse (1998) and by Morrison, Robertson, and Harding (1998) offer some initial discussions along these lines. We must focus on rejected students who are able to elevate their poor status within the peer group. As an initial consideration of this possibility, Sandstrom (1999) has documented some of the features associated with children who were initially rejected (grade 4) but subsequently lifted their social status (grade 5). Findings from retrospective interviews with a small group of children suggested that "improvers" (in contrast to children who were consistently rejected) took ownership of their role in peer problems, participated in extracurricular activities, and had mothers who knew their children's friends. At the same time, within their larger sample, Sandstrom and Coie also observed that rejected grade 4 boys who viewed themselves as well liked and who were viewed by peers as highly aggressive were also more likely to improve their social status in grade 5. Thus, a number of different factors may contribute to changes in social status, including characteristics of the child (behaviors, beliefs, activities, etc.), the family, and the larger social world (e.g., peer values for aggressive behavior).

Finally, we have been struck by the fact that our search for the consequences of peer rejection has focused exclusively on negative, maladaptive outcomes, with no effort to consider the possibility that, in some cases, there might be a "silver lining" to this cloud. Our emphasis on negative outcomes is certainly understandable for aggression and externalizing problems, which carry broader social implications, but may be less reasonable for peer rejection and social withdrawal. Within the literature on internalizing outcomes, the need for a more balanced perspective is suggested by studies and descriptions of withdrawn adolescents and adults that caused us to pause and to question the widely held belief that social withdrawal and rejection lead *only* to long-term social maladjustment and undesired internalizing outcomes such as loneliness, depression, and anxiety. Can the increased solitude that leads results from withdrawal and isolation contribute to more positive outcomes? There is some suggestion in the literature that this may be true.

As one example, research by Larson (see Larson, 1999, for a review) suggests a "constructive side of adolescent solitude" (p. 254). Larson has shown that adolescents (but not preadolescents) report reduced self-consciousness, increased ability to concentrate, and more positive emotional states following periods of time alone. Moreover, across several samples, Larson found that adolescents who spent moderate amounts of time alone (i.e., 20%–35% of their waking hours) were better adjusted than those who were rarely alone or alone more often. Larson suggested that intermediate amounts of time alone might well serve constructive goals, especially in terms of identity development. His suggestion is supported by research on loneliness and identity development by Goossens and Marcoen (1999). They demonstrated that adolescents who reported more positive attitudes toward being alone showed more introspection and greater exploration of alternative identities. Thus, in terms of adolescent identity development, time alone is not necessarily a bad thing. The potential benefits of solitude in childhood remain unknown.

Findings such as those just described do not negate evidence for maladaptive outcomes associated with loneliness and more extensive time alone, as Larson (1997) distinguishes between *healthy* and *unhealthy* solitude. Critical here is whether the individual *chooses* to be alone (see previous section on self-perception processes), whether the individual *uses time alone constructively*, and whether time alone is *balanced* by more social and affiliative experiences. Some suggest that a balance between socially engaged time and periods of time alone is essential for biological and psychological well-being for both children and adults (Batchelder & Winnykamen, 1995; Buchholz, 1997; Larson, 1990). However, this balance may vary considerably across individuals, with differing implications for one's later life. For example, Storr (1997) described the lives of exceptional creative adults, artists such as Goya, writers such as Kipling and P. G. Wodehouse, musicians such as Beethoven, philosophers such as Wittgenstein and Kant, and scientists such as Einstein, who within our current research paradigms and methodologies might well be described as socially withdrawn, isolated, or rejected. Storr pointed out that these individuals differed markedly from what is widely regarded as the norm in their need and predilection for solitude, spending extensive time alone engaged in constructive pursuits. Storr noted that a balance of solitude and social engagement is probably necessary in all our lives, but for the highly creative individual, greater time alone is an absolute necessity. In terms of this review, peer rejection may contribute to positive or negative long-term outcomes depending on whether the resulting increase in solitary time is consistent with personal goals and desires and used constructively to engage in other creative pursuits. Storr reminds us, however, that "the happiest lives are probably those in which neither interpersonal relationships nor impersonal interests are idealized as the only way to salvation. The desire and pursuit of the whole must comprehend both aspects of human nature" (p. 202). It appears plausible to us that when children and adolescents choose to be alone or show a preference for solitude in accomplishing certain tasks, negative consequences may not be inevitable and positive outcomes may also be possible. In contrast, if time alone stems from active rejection by other people, problems will likely result.

In conclusion, we argue that the task at hand is to consider peer rejection as part of an extremely complex developmental system. As our review demonstrates, a single pathway leading to particular negative outcomes does not characterize the experience of rejection. For many individuals, like Graham (described at the outset), the immediate consequences of being rejected by the peer group are both painful and alarming and merit ongoing and close attention. To assist rejected children, we must examine what seems to protect some rejected children who appear resilient in the face of negative peer experiences or who seem capable of improving their status. The long-term consequences of early peer rejection may vary depending on several factors. Our challenge in future research, then, is to take a broader, longer, and more balanced view of the outcomes of early peer rejection and to begin to identify those factors, both internal and external, personal, familial, and societal, which enhance the likelihood of positive outcomes and decrease the likelihood of negative consequences. Accordingly, our suggestions for future research highlight the need to explore mitigating factors (e.g., gender, race, protective factors, thresholds of experience, self-perceptions, etc.) and to acknowledge the possibility that under the right circumstances personal growth can emerge out of solitude.

At the same time, we cannot ignore the growing number of extreme and highly publicized cases in which peer rejection and victimization have been cited as major contributing factors in the worst possible consequence— death. In media reports, it appears that peer rejection can ultimately lead to suicide, death at the hands of peers, and episodes of violent retaliation toward peers. A few examples will illustrate our point. In 1982, three 10- to 14-year-olds in Norway committed suicide, leaving behind a note that pointed to peer rejection and victimization as the cause of their self-destruction (Olweus, 1993). In 1997, 16-year-old Luke Woodham murdered his mother, a former girlfriend, and another student at his high school in the southern United States, claiming that he felt unloved by his mother and despised by his peers at school (Rogers, Stewart, Klise, & Haederle, 1999). Also in 1997, 14-year-old Reena Virk of western Canada was tortured and murdered at the hands of peers, presumably in response to accusations that the victim had spread rumors about another girl ("Teen Violence," 1997). In 1999, in the United States, Eric Harris and Dylan Klebold, described as "misfits" who were rejected by their mainstream peers and increasingly involved in deviant peer subculture, murdered a teacher and 12 classmates, wounded 20 others, and then took their own lives in a planned, three-hour rampage (Cohen, 1999; Gibbs, 1999; Mitchell, 1999; Rogers et al., 1999). As the century comes to a close, we have witnessed an increasing number of incidents in which children and adolescents who were rejected, teased, and bullied by their peers have resorted to violent and destructive acts of revenge, retaliation, and self-destruction, including the murder of classmates and themselves. Although cited as a common factor across the cases cited here, the causal role of peer rejection in these horrific events can be evaluated only retrospectively. Nevertheless, the growing number of incidents recounted in the news has brought popular attention to the critical role of peer rejection and interpersonal relations in children's lives.

As researchers, educators, and parents begin to more fully appreciate the role of peer relations in children's lives (e.g., Harris, 1995), these events may serve as a crucial "wake up call" for society. In understanding the role of peer rejection in these developmental trajectories, we face a new challenge to turn the tide. The suicide death of the three youths in Norway lead ultimately to an effective national campaign against bullying in the Norway schools (see Olweus, 1993). One can only hope that the more recent series of events in North America near the end of the century will lead similarly to large-scale efforts to further our understanding of how to avoid the negative and destructive consequences of peer rejection.

Notes

1. The "buffering" effect of dyadic relationships varies as a function of the outcome considered and in some cases, friendship may contribute to negative outcomes (e.g., Kupersmidt, Burchinal, & Patterson, 1995; Hoza, Molina, Bukowski, & Sippola, 1995).

2. There is a third alternative, the probability method, but this technique is seldom used in the current literature (see Newcomb & Bukowski, 1983). Using a binomial probability model, researchers classify the frequency of liking and disliking nominations as being common (i.e., within a range one would expect on the basis of chance) or rare (i.e., outside what would be expected by chance). In this procedure, popular individuals are those who have rare liking scores and disliking scores that fall below the mean, whereas rejected individuals receive rare disliking sores and liking scores below the mean.

3. In this chapter, we consider studies in which peer rejection has been operationalized in terms of negative peer ratings, negative peer nominations, low "social preference" scores, or by classification into a rejected subgroup. In some cases, we also consider studies that have considered low peer acceptance as an index of peer rejection, although we recognize that interpretations of such studies must be made with caution.

4. See Lochman and Wayland (1994) for descriptions of other racial differences in the pattern of predictive relations observed for internalizing outcomes.

5. Research by Keenan, Loeber, Zhang, Stouthamer-Loeber, and VanKammen (1995) also provides support for the influence of affiliations with deviant peers on delinquent behavior, although this research does not deal directly with issues of peer rejection.

6. The link between withdrawal and rejection emerges developmentally (see Rubin et al., 1998). Although withdrawn behavior in preschool and kindergarten is not associated with peer dislike (Rubin, 1982), withdrawal is associated with peer rejection by middle childhood (e.g., Rubin et al., 1989) when such behavior becomes more nonnormative (Younger, Gentile, & Burgess, 1993).

7. Variations across parent and self-reports are not surprising, considering that parents tend not be good informants of their children's internalizing problems (e.g., Reynolds, Anderson & Bartell, 1985).

References

Asher, S. R., & Coie, J. D. (1990). *Peer rejection in childhood.* New York: Cambridge University Press.

Asher, S. R., & Dodge, K. H. (1986). Identification of socially rejected children. *Developmental Psychology, 22,* 444–449.

Asher, S. R., & Hymel, S. (1981). Children's social competence in peer relations: Sociometric and behavioral assessments. In J. D. Wine & M. D. Smye (Eds.), *Social competence* (pp. 125–157). New York: Guilford Press.

Asher, S. R., Parkhurst, J. T., Hymel, S., & Williams, G. A. (1990). Peer rejection and loneliness in childhood. In S. R. Asher & J. D. Coie (Eds.), *Peer rejection in childhood* (pp. 253–273). New York: Cambridge University Press.

Austin, A. M. B., & Draper, D. C. (1984). The relationship among peer acceptance, social impact and academic achievement in middle childhood. *American Educational Research Journal, 21,* 597–604.

Ausubel, D. P., Schiff, H. M., & Gasser, E. B. (1952). A preliminary study of developmental trends in socioempathy: Accuracy of perceptions of own and others sociometric status. *Child Development, 23,* 111–128.

Bagwell, C. L., Newcomb, A. F., & Bukowski, W. M. (1998). Preadolescent friendship and peer rejection as predictors of adult adjustment. *Child Development, 69,* 140–153.

Batchelder, M. L., & Winnykamen, F. (1995). Children in self-care: Homeless in the afternoons or socially provided for? *Journal of Social Distress and the Homeless, 4,* 1–32.

Baumeister, R. F., & Leary, M. R. (1995). The need to belong: Desire for interpersonal attachments as a fundamental human motivation. *Psychological Bulletin, 117,* 497–529.

Bichard, S. L., Alden, L., Walker, L. J., & McMahon, R. J. (1988). Friendship understanding in socially accepted, rejected and neglected children. *Merrill Palmer Quarterly, 34,* 33–46.

Bierman, K. L., Smoot, D. L., & Aumiller, K. (1993). Characteristics of aggressive-rejected, aggressive (nonrejected), and rejected (nonaggressive) boys. *Child Development, 64,* 139–151.

Bierman, K. L., & Wargo, J. B. (1995). Predicting the longitudinal course associated with aggressive-rejected, aggressive (non-rejected), and rejected (non-aggressive) status. *Development and Psychopathology, 7,* 669, 682.

Boivin, M., & Begin, G. (1989). Peer status and self-perception among early elementary school children: The case of rejected children. *Child Development, 60,* 591–596.

Boivin, M., & Hymel, S. (1997). Peer experiences and social self-perceptions: A sequential model. *Developmental Psychology, 33,* 135–145.

Boivin, M., Hymel, S., & Bukowski, W. M. (1995). The roles of social withdrawal, peer rejection and victimization by peers in predicting loneliness and depressed mood in childhood. *Development and Psychopathology, 7,* 765–785.

Boivin, M., Poulin, F., & Vitaro, F. (1994). Depressed mood and peer rejection in childhood. *Development and Psychopathology, 6,* 483–498.

Boivin, M., Thomassin, L., & Alain, M. (1989). Peer rejection and self-perceptions among early elementary school children: Aggressive rejectees versus withdrawn rejectees. In B. H. Schneider, G. Attili, J. Nadel, & R. P. Weissberg (Eds.), *Social competence in developmental perspective* (pp. 392–393). Boston: Kluwer Academic.

Boivin, M., & Vitaro, F. (1994). The impact of peer relationships on aggression in childhood: Inhibition through coercion or promotion through peer support. In J. McCord (Ed.), *Coercion and punishment in long-term perspectives* (pp. 183–197). New York: Cambridge University Press.

Bowker, A., & Hymel, S. (1987). *Individual differences in children's friendship conceptions: Variations as a function of age, sex, and status.* Paper presented at the annual meeting of the Canadian Psychological Association, Vancouver, BC.

Brendgen, M., Vitaro, F., & Bukowski, W. M. (1998). Affiliation with delinquent friends: Contributions of parents, self-esteem, delinquent behavior, and rejection by peers. *Journal of Early Adolescence, 18,* 244–265.

Brown, B. B. (1990). Peer groups and peer cultures. In S. S. Feldman & G. R. Elliott (Eds.), *At the threshold: The developing adolescent* (pp. 171–196). Cambridge, MA: Harvard University Press.

Buchholz, E. S. (1997). *The call of solitude: Alonetime in a world of attachment.* New York: Simon & Schuster.

Bukowski, W. M., & Newcomb, A. F. (1984). Stability and determinants of sociometric status and friendship choice: A longitudinal perspective. *Developmental Psychology, 20,* 941–952.

Burks, V., Dodge, K. A., & Price, J. M. (1995). Models of internalizing outcomes of early rejection. *Development and Psychopathology, 7,* 683–695.

Cairns, R. B., & Cairns, B. D. (1991). Social cognition and social networks: A developmental perspective. In D. J. Pepler & K. H. Rubin (Eds.), *The development and treatment of childhood aggression* (pp. 249–276). Hillsdale, NJ: Erlbaum.

Cairns, R. B., Cairns, B. D., & Neckerman, H. J. (1989). Early school dropout: Configurations and determinants. *Child Development, 60,* 1437–1452.

Cairns, R. B., Cairns, B. D., Neckerman, H. J., Gest, S. D., Gariépy, J. (1988). Social networks and aggressive behavior: Peer support or peer rejection? *Developmental Psychology, 24*(6), 815–823.

Cassidy, J., & Asher, S. R. (1992). Loneliness and peer relations in young children. *Child Development, 63,* 350–365.

Cicchetti, D., & Bukowski, W. M. (1995). Developmental processes in peer relations and psychopathology. *Development and Psychopathology, 7,* 587–589.

Cillessen, A. H. N. , & Bellmore, A. D. (1999). Accuracy of social self-perceptions and peer competence in middle childhood. *Merrill Palmer Quarterly, 45,* 650–676.

Coie, J. D., Christopoulos, C., Terry, R., Dodge, K. A., & Lochman, J. E. (1989). Types of aggressive relationships, peer rejection and developmental consequences. In B. H. Schneider, G. Attili, J. Nadel, & R. P. Weissberg (Eds.), *Social competence in developmental perspective.* Dordrecht: Kluwer Press.

Coie, J. D., & Dodge, K. A. (1983). Continuities and changes in children's social status: A five-year longitudinal study. *Merrill Palmer Quarterly, 29,* 261–282.

Coie, J. D., Dodge, K. A., & Coppotelli, H. (1982). Dimensions and types of social status: A cross-age perspective. *Developmental Psychology, 18,* 557–570.

Coie, J. D., & Krehbiel, G. (1984). Effects of academic training on the social status of low-achieving, socially rejected children. *Child Development, 55,* 1465–1478.

Coie, J. D., & Kupersmidt, J. B. (1983). A behavioral analysis of emerging social status in boys' groups. *Child Development, 54,* 1400, 1416.

Coie, J. D., Lochman, J. E., Terry, R., & Hyman, C. (1992). Predicting early adolescent disorder from childhood aggression and peer rejection. *Journal of Consulting and Clinical Psychology, 60,* 783–792.

Coie, J., Terry, R., Lenox, K., Lochman, J., & Hyman, C. (1995). Childhood peer rejection and aggression as predictors of stable patterns of adolescent disorder. *Development and Psychopathology, 7,* 697–713.

Cole, D. A. (1990). Relation of social and academic competence to depressive symptoms in childhood. *Journal of Abnormal Psychology, 99,* 422–429.

Cole, D. A., & Carpentieri, S. (1990). Social status and the comorbidity of child depression and conduct disorder. *Journal of Consulting and Clinical Psychology, 58,* 748–757.

Comfort, C., & Kishor, N. (1994). *Relations of self-esteem, alienation and popularity to school dropout: A meta-analysis.* Paper presented at the annual meeting of the Canadian Society for the Study of Education, Calgary, Alberta.

Cowen, E. L., Pederson, A., Babigian, H., Izzo, L. D., & Trost, M. A. (1973). Long term follow-up of early detected vulnerable children. *Journal of Consulting and Clinical Psychology, 41,* 438–446.

Coyne, J. C. (1976). Toward an interactional description of depression. *Psychiatry, 39,* 28–40.

Coyne, J. C., Burchill, S. A. L., & Stiles, W. (1990). An interactional perspective on depression. In C. R. Snyder & D. O. Forsyth (Eds.), *Handbook of social and clinical psychology: The health perspective* (pp. 327–349). New York: Pergamon.

Crick, N. R. (1995). Relational aggression: The role of intent attributions, feelings of distress, and provocation type. *Development and Psychopathology, 7,* 313–322.

Crick, N. R. (1996). The role of overt aggression, relational aggression, and prosocial behavior in the prediction of children's future social adjustment. *Child Development, 67,* 2317–2327.

Crick, N. R. (1997). Engagement in gender normative versus nonnormative forms of aggression: Links to social-psychological adjustment. *Developmental Psychology, 33,* 610–617.

Crick, N. R., & Dodge, K. A. (1994). A review and reformulation of social-information-processing mechanisms in children's social adjustment. *Psychological Bulletin, 115,* 74–101.

Crick, N. R., & Grotpeter, J. K. (1995). Relational aggression, gender, and social-psychological adjustment. *Child Development, 66,* 710–722.

Crick, N. R., & Ladd, G. W. (1993). Children's perceptions of their peer experiences: Attributions, loneliness, social anxiety, and social avoidance. *Developmental Psychology, 29,* 244–254.

DeRosier, M., Kupersmidt, J., & Patterson, C. (1994). Children's academic and behavioral adjustment as a function of the chronicity and proximity of peer rejection. *Child Development, 65,* 1799–1813.

Dishion, T. J., Capaldi, D., Spracklen, K. M., & Li, F. (1995). Peer ecology of male drug use. *Development and Psychopathology, 7,* 803–824.

Dishion, T. J., Patterson, G. R., & Griesler, P. C. (1994). Peer adaptation in the development of antisocial behavior: A confluence model. In L. R. Huesmann (Ed.), *Aggressive behavior: Current perspectives* (pp. 61–95). New York: Plenum Press.

Dodge, K. A. (1983). Behavioral antecedents of peer social status. *Child Development, 54,* 1386–1989.

Dodge, K. A., Bates, J. E., & Pettit, G. (1990). Mechanisms in the cycle of violence. *Science, 250,* 1678–1683.

Dodge, K. A., & Feldman, E. (1990). Issues in social cognition and sociometric status. In S. R. Asher & J. D. Coie (Eds.), *Peer rejection in childhood* (pp. 119–155). New York: Cambridge University Press.

Dunn, J., & McGuire, S. (1992). Sibling and peer relationships in childhood. *Journal of Child Psychology and Psychiatry, 33,* 67–105.

East, P. L., Hess, L. E., & Lerner, R. M. (1987). Peer social support and adjustment of early adolescent peer groups. *Journal of Early Adolescence, 7,* 153–163.

East, P. L., & Rook, K. S. (1992). Compensatory patters of support among children's peer relationships: A test using school friends, nonschool friends, and siblings. *Developmental Psychology, 28,* 163–172.

Fordham, S., & Ogbu, J. U. (1986) Black students' school success: Coping with the "burden of 'acting white.'" *Urban Review, 18,* 176–206.

French, D. C., Conrad, J., & Turner, T. M. (1995). Adjustment of antisocial and nonantisocial rejected adolescents. *Development and Psychopathology, 7,* 857–874.

Furman, W., & Robbins, P. (1985). What's the point? Selection of treatment objectives. In B. Schneider, K. H. Rubin, & J. E. Ledingham (Eds.), *Children's' peer relations: Issues in assessment and intervention* (pp. 41–54). New York: Springer-Verlag.

Garber, J., Quiggly, N. L., Panak, W. F., & Dodge, K. A. (1991). Aggression and depression in children: Comorbidity, specificity and social cognitive processing. In D. Cicchetti & S. Toth (Eds.), *Rochester Symposium on Developmental Psychopathology, Vol. 2: Internalizing and externalizing expression of dysfunction* (pp. 225–264). Hillsdale, NJ: Erlbaum.

Gibbs, N. (1999, May 3). Crime: The Littleton massacre. *Time,* pp. 25–34.

Goleman, D. (1995). *Emotional intelligence.* New York: Bantam Books.

Goossens, L., & Marcoen, A. (1999). Adolescent loneliness, self-reflection and identity: From individual differences to developmental processes. K. J. Rotenberg & S. Hymel (Eds.), *Loneliness in childhood and adolescence* (225–243). New York: Cambridge University Press.

Green, K. D., Forehand, R., Beck, S. J., & Vosk, B. (1980). An assessment of the relationship among measures of children's social competence and children's academic achievement. *Child Development, 51,* 1149–1156.

Harris, J. R. (1995). Where is the child's environment? A group socialization theory of development. *Psychological Review, 102,* 458–489.

Harris, J. R. (1998). *The nurture assumption.* New York: Free Press.

Harter, S. (1982). The perceived competence scale for children. *Child Development, 53,* 89–97.

Higgins, E. T., Klein, R., & Strauman, T. (1985). Self-concept discrepancy theory: A psychological model for distinguishing among different aspects of depression and anxiety. *Social Cognition, 3,* 51–76.

Hodges, E. V. E., Boivin, M., Vitaro, F., & Bukowski, W. M. (1999). The power of friendship: Protection against an escalating cycle of peer victimization. *Developmental Psychology, 35,* 94–101.

Hoza, B., Molina, B., Bukowski, W. M., & Sippola, L. K. (1995). Aggression, withdrawal and measures of friendship and popularity as predictors of internalizing and externalizing problems during adolescence. *Development and Psychopathology, 7,* 787–802.

Hymel, S., Bowker, A., & Woody, E. (1993). Aggressive versus withdrawn unpopular children: Variations in peer, teacher and self-perceptions in multiple domains. *Child Development, 64,* 879–896.

Hymel, S., Comfort, C., Schonert-Reichl, K., & McDougall, P. (1996). Academic failure and school drop-out: The influence of peers. In K. Wentzel & J. Juvonen (Eds.). *Social motivation: Understanding children's school adjustment* (pp. 313–345). New York: Cambridge University Press.

Hymel, S., & Franke, S. (1985). Children's peer relations: Assessing self-perceptions. In B. H. Schneider, K. H. Rubin, & J. E. Ledingham (Eds.), *Children's peer relationships: Issues in assessment and intervention* (pp. 75–92). New York: Springer-Verlag.

Hymel, S., & Rubin, K. H. (1985). Children with peer relationship and social skills problems: Conceptual, methodological and developmental issues. In G. J. Whitehurst (Ed.), *Annals of child development* (vol. 2, pp. 251–297). Greenwich, CT: JAI Press.

Hymel, S., Rubin, K. H., Rowden, L., & LeMare, L. (1990). Children's peer relationships: Longitudinal predications of internalizing and externalizing problems from middle to late childhood. *Child Development, 61,* 2004–2021.

Hymel, S., Vaillancourt, T., McDougall, P., & Rotenberg, K. R. (1999). *Children's peer relations: Maintaining trust while functioning in a social world.* Paper presented at the biennial meeting of the Society for Research in Child Development, Albuquerque, NM.

Ialongo, N. S., Vaden-Kiernan, N., & Kellam, S. (1998). Early peer rejection and aggression: Longitudinal relations with adolescent behavior. *Journal of Developmental and Physical Disabilities, 10,* 199–213.

Inderbizen, H. M. (1994). Adolescent peer social competence: A critical review of assessment methodologies and instruments. In T. H. Ollendick & R. J. Prunes (Eds.), *Advances in clinical child psychology* (vol. 16, pp. 227–259). New York: Plenum.

Joiner, T. E., & Barnett, J. (1994). A test of interpersonal theory of depression in childhood and adolescence using a projective technique. *Journal of Abnormal Child Psychology, 22,* 595–609.

Keenan, K., Loeber, R., Zhang, Q., Stouthamer-Loeber, M., & VanKammen, W. B. (1995). The influence of deviant peers on the development of boys' disruptive and delinquent behavior: A temporal analysis. *Development and Psychopathology, 7,* 715–726.

Kinney, D. (1993). From nerds to normals: The recovery of identity among adolescents from middle school to high school. *Sociology of Education, 66,* 21–40.

Kovacs, M., Paulauskas, S., Gatsonis, C., & Richards, C. (1988). Depressive disorders in children: III. A longitudinal study of comorbidity with and risk for conduct disorder. *Journal of Affective Disorder, 15,* 205–217.

Krantz, M., & Burton, C. (1986). The development of social cognition of social status. *Journal of Genetic Psychology, 147,* 89–95.

Kupersmidt, J. B., Buchele, K. S., Voegler, M. E., & Sedikides, C. (1996). Social self-discrepancy: A theory relating peer relations problems and school maladjustment. In J. Juvonen & K. R. Wentzel (Eds.), *Social motivation: Understanding children's school maladjustment* (pp. 66–97). New York: Cambridge University Press.

Kupersmidt, J., Burchinal, M., & Patterson, C. J. (1995). Developmental patterns of childhood peer relation as predictors of externalizing behavior problems. *Development and Psychopathology, 7,* 825–843.

Kupersmidt, J. B., & Coie, J. D. (1990). Preadolescent peer status, aggression and school adjustment as predictors of externalizing problems in adolescence. *Child Development, 61,* 1350–1362.

Kupersmidt, J. B., Coie, J. D., & Dodge, K. A. (1990). The role of poor peer relationships in the development of disorder. In S. R. Asher & J. D. Coie (Eds.), *Peer rejection in childhood* (pp. 274–305). Cambridge: Cambridge University Press.

Kupersmidt, J. B., Sigda, K. B., Sedikides, C., & Voegler, M. E. (1999). Social self-discrepancy theory and loneliness during childhood and adolescence. In K. R. Rotenberg & S. Hymel (Eds.), *Loneliness in childhood and adolescence* (pp. 263–279). New York: Cambridge University Press.

Ladd, G. W. (1981). Effectiveness of a social learning method for enhancing children's social interaction and peer acceptance. *Child Development, 52,* 171–178.

Ladd, G. W. (1983). Social networks of popular, average, and rejected children in school settings. *Merrill-Palmer Quarterly, 29,* 283–307.

Ladd, G. W. (1990). Having friends, keeping friends, making friends, and being liked by peers in the classroom: Predictors of children's early school adjustment? *Child Development, 61,* 1081–1100.

Landau, S., & Milich, R. (1990). Assessment of children's status and peer relations. In A. M. LaGreca (Ed.), *Through the eyes of the child: Obtaining self-reports form children and adolescents.* Boston: Allyn & Bacon.

Larson, R. W. (1990). The solitary side of life: An examination of the time people spend alone from childhood to old age. *Developmental Review, 10* (2), 155–183.

Larson, R. W. (1997). The emergence of solitude as a constructive domain of experience in early adolescence. *Child Development, 68* (1), 80–93.

Larson, R. W. (1999). On the uses of loneliness in adolescence. In K. J. Rotenberg & S. Hymel (Eds.), *Loneliness in childhood and adolescence* (pp. 244–262). New York: Cambridge Press.

Ledingham, J. E., Schwartzman, A., Chappell, D., Cristina, S., & Schmidt, D. (1999, April). *Relationships among aggression, withdrawal, and peer acceptance over a three year period.* Paper presented at the biennial meeting of the Society for Research in Child Development, Albuquerque, NM.

Little, S. A., & Garber, J. (1995). Aggression, depression, and stressful life events predicting peer rejection in children. *Development and Psychopathology, 7,* 845–856.

Lochman, J. E., & Wayland, K. K. (1994). Aggression, social acceptance and race as predictors of negative adolescent outcomes. *Journal of the American Academy of Child and Adolescent Psychiatry, 33,* 1026–1035.

Maassen, G. H. , van der Linden, J. L., & Akkermans, W. (1997). Nominations, ratings and dimensions of sociometric status. *International Journal of Behavioral Development, 21,* 179–199.

Merten, D. E. (1994). The cultural context of aggression: The transition to junior high school. *Anthropology & Education Quarterly, 25,* 29–43.

Miller, G. E., Brehm, K., & Whitehouse, S. (1998). Reconceptualizing school-based prevention for antisocial behavior within a resiliency framework. *School Psychology Review, 27,* 364–379.

Mitchell, A. (1999, 22 April). The "Terrible Tuesday" killers. *Toronto Globe and Mail,* pp. A1, A16.

Morison, P., & Masten, A. S. (1991). Peer reputation in middle childhood as a predictor of adaptation in adolescence: A seven-year follow-up. *Child Development, 62,* 991–1007.

Morrison, G. M., Robertson, L., & Harding, M. (1998). Resilience factors that support the classroom functioning of acting out and aggressive students. *Psychology in the Schools, 35,* 217–227.

Newcomb, A. F., & Bukowski, W. M. (1983). Social impact and social preference as determinants of children's peer group status. *Developmental Psychology, 19,* 856–867.

Newcomb, A. F., Bukowski, W. M., Pattee, L. (1993). Children's peer relations: A meta-analytic review of popular, rejected, neglected, controversial, and average sociometric status. *Psychological Bulletin, 111,* 99–128.

Ogilvie, D. M. (1987). The undesired self: A neglected variable in personality research. *Journal of Personality and Social Psychology, 52,* 379–385.

Ollendick, T. H., Weist, M. D., Borden, M. C., & Greene, R. W. (1992). Sociometric status and academic, behavioral, and psychological adjustment: A five-year longitudinal study. *Journal of Consulting and Clinical Psychology, 60,* 80–87.

Olweus, D. (1993). *Bullying at school: What we know and what we can do.* Oxford, UK: Blackwell.

O'Neil, R., Welsh, M., Parke, R. D. , Wang, S., & Strand, C. (1997). A longitudinal assessment of the academic correlates of early peer acceptance and rejection. *Journal of Clinical Child Psychology, 26,* 290–303.

Panak, W. F. (1999, April). *Robust standard errors in confirmatory factor analysis: Implications for child psychopathology research.* Paper presented at the biennial meeting of the Society for Research in Child Development, Albuquerque, NM.

Panak, W. F., & Garber, J. (1992). Role of aggression, rejection, and attributions in the prediction of depression in children. *Development and Psychopathology, 7,* 145–165.

Parker, J. G., & Asher, S. R. (1987). Peer relations and later personal adjustment: Are low-accepted children at risk? *Psychological Bulletin, 102,* 57–389.

Parker, J. G., & Asher, S. R. (1993). Friendship and friendship quality in middle childhood: Links with peer group acceptance and feelings of loneliness and social dissatisfaction. *Developmental Psychology, 29,* 357–389.

Parker, J. G., Rubin, K. H., Price, J., & DeRosier, M. E. (1995). Peer relationships, child development and adjustment: A developmental psychopathology perspective. In D. Cicchetti & D. Cohen (Eds.), *Developmental psychopathology,* Vol. 2: *Risk, disorder and adaptation* (pp. 96–161). New York: Wiley.

Parker, J. G., Saxon, J. L., Asher, S. R., & Kovacs, D. M. (1999). Dimensions of children's friendship adjustment: Implications for understanding loneliness. In K. R. Rotenberg & S. Hymel (Eds.), *Loneliness in childhood and adolescence*. (pp. 201–221). New York: Cambridge University Press.

Parkhurst, J. T., & Asher, S. R. (1992). Peer rejection in middle school: Subgroup differences in behavior, loneliness, and interpersonal concerns. *Developmental Psychology, 28,* 231–241.

Patterson, G. R., Capaldi, D., & Bank, L. (1991). An early starter model for predicting delinquency. In D. J. Pepler & K. H. Rubin (Eds.), *The development and treatment of childhood aggression* (pp. 139–168). Hillsdale, NJ: Erlbaum.

Patterson, G. J., Kupersmidt, J. B., & Greisler, P. C. (1990). Children's perceptions of self and of relationships with others as a function of sociometric status. *Child Development, 61,* 1335–1349.

Patterson, G. R., & Stoolmiller, M. (1991). Replications of a dual failure model for boys depressed mood. *Journal of Consulting and Clinical Psychology, 59,* 491–498.

Renshaw, P. D., & Brown, P. J. (1993). Loneliness in middle childhood: Concurrent and longitudinal predictors. *Child Development, 64,* 1271–1284.

Reynolds, W. M., Anderson, G., & Bartell, W. (1985). Measuring depression in children: A multimethod assessment investigation. *Journal of Abnormal Child Psychology, 13,* 513–526.

Rogers, P., Stewart, B., Klise, K., & Haederle, M. (1999, May 3). Lessons from the past. *People,* 51 (16), 99.

Roff, M., Sells, S. B., & Golden, M. M. (1972). *Social adjustment and personality development in children.* Minneapolis: University of Minnesota Press.

Rubin, K. H. (1982). Social and social-cognitive developmental characteristics of young isolate, normal and sociable children. In K. H. Rubin & H. S. Ross (Eds.), *Peer relationships and social skills in childhood* (pp. 353–374). New York: Springer-Verlag.

Rubin, K. H., Bukowski, W., & Parker, J. G. (1998). Peer interactions, relationships and groups. In W. Daemon (Series Ed.) and N. Eisenberg (Vol. Ed.), *Handbook of child psychology:* Vol. 3, *Social emotional and personality development* (5th ed., pp. 619–700). New York: Wiley.

Rubin, K. H., Chen, X., & Hymel, S. (1993). Socioemotional characteristics of withdrawn and aggressive children. *Merrill-Palmer Quarterly, 39,* 518–534.

Rubin, K. H., Chen, X., McDougall, P., Bowker, A., & McKinnon, J. (1995). The Waterloo longitudinal project: Predicting internalizing and externalizing problems in adolescence. *Development and Psychopathology, 7,* 751–764.

Rubin, K. H., Hymel, S., LeMare, L., & Rowden, L. (1989). Children experiencing social difficulties: Sociometric neglect reconsidered. *Canadian Journal of Behavioral Science, 21,* 94–111.

Rubin, K. H., Hymel, S., & Mills, R. (1989). Sociability and social withdrawal in childhood: Stability and outcomes. *Journal of Personality, 57,* 238–255.

Rubin, K. H., LeMare, L., & Lollis, S. (1990). Social withdrawal in childhood: Developmental pathways to peer rejection. In S. R. Asher & J. D. Coie

(Eds.), *Peer rejection in childhood* (pp. 217–249). New York: Cambridge University Press.

Rubin, K. H., & Mills, R. S. L. (1988). The many faces of social isolation in childhood. *Journal of Consulting and Clinical Psychology, 65* (6), 916–924.

Sandstrom, M. J. (1999). A developmental perspective on peer rejection: Mechanisms of stability and change. *Child Development, 70,* 955–966.

Schonert-Reichl, K. (1999). Relation of peer acceptance, friendship adjustment and social behavior to moral reasoning during adolescence. *Journal of Early Adolescence, 19,* 249–279.

Storr, A. (1997). *Solitude.* London: Harper Collins.

Suskind, R. (1998). *A hope in the unseen.* New York: Broadway Books.

Teen violence: Brutality of attack horrifies community. (1997, November 27). *Toronto Globe and Mail,* pp. A1, A12.

Terry, R., & Coie, J. D. (1991). A comparison of methods for defining sociometric status among children. *Developmental Psychology, 27,* 867–880.

Tremblay, R. E., Mâsse, L. C., Vitaro, F., & Dobkin, P. L. (1995). The impact of friends' deviant behavior on early onset of delinquency: Longitudinal data from 6–13 years. *Development and Psychopathology, 7,* 649–667.

Valås, H., & Sletta, O. (1996). *Social behavior, peer relations, loneliness and self-perceptions in middle school children: A mediational model.* Paper presented at the XIVth biennial meeting of the International Society for the Study of Behavioral Development, Quebec City, CA.

Vandell, D. L., & Hembree, S. E. (1994). Peer social status and friendship: Independent contributors to children's social and academic adjustment. *Merrill-Palmer Quarterly, 40,* 461–477.

Vitaro, F., & Tremblay, R. E. (in press). Impact of a prevention program on aggressive boys' friendships and social adjustment. *Journal of Abnormal Child Psychology.*

Vosk, B., Forehand, R., Parker, J. B., & Rickard, K. (1982). A multidimensional comparison of popular and unpopular children. *Developmental Psychology, 18,* 571–575.

Wentzel, K. R. (1991). Relations between social competence and academic achievement in early adolescence. *Child Development, 62,* 1066–1078.

Wentzel, K. R., & Asher, S. R. (1995). The academic lives of neglected, rejected, popular and controversial children. *Child Development, 66,* 754–763.

Wentzel, K. R., & Caldwell, K. (1997). Friendships, peer acceptance, and group membership: Relations to academic achievement in middle school. *Child Development, 68,* 1198–1209.

Williams, G. A., & Asher, S. R. (1987). *Peer and self perceptions of peer rejected children: Issues in classification and subgrouping.* Paper presented at the biennial meeting of the Society for Research in Child Development, Baltimore, MD.

Williams, B. T. R., & Gilmour, J. D. (1994). Annotation: Sociometry and peer relationships. *Journal of Child Psychology and Psychiatry, 35,* 997–1013.

Younger, A. J., Gentile, C., & Burgess, K. (1993). Children's perceptions of social withdrawal: Changes across age. In K. Rubin and J. B. Asendorpf (Eds.), *Social withdrawal, inhibition and shyness in childhood* (pp. 215–235). Hillsdale, NJ: Erlbaum.

PART 3

INDIVIDUAL DIFFERENCES

10

The Role of Rejection Sensitivity in People's Relationships with Significant Others and Valued Social Groups

SHERI R. LEVY, OZLEM AYDUK, AND GERALDINE DOWNEY

An event that caught the attention of America in 1998 was the shocking behavior of 13-year-old Mitchell Johnson and 11-year-old Andrew Golden, who opened fire in their schoolyard, killing four classmates and a teacher in Jonesboro, Arkansas. Friends' accounts of the events leading to the shootings revealed that Johnson was troubled by the recent divorce of his parents and by the ending of his relationship with a girl. Earlier that week, Johnson had apparently told a friend that he intended to shoot all the people at school who rejected him (Labi, 1998). Yet another tragic story in 1998 involving unrequited love is that of Julie Scully, who was murdered and dismembered by her boyfriend Giorgos Skiadopoulos in a jealous rage, supposedly triggered by her comment that she missed her young son who was living far away. In 1999, another school shooting shocked the nation; this time two high school seniors in Denver, Colorado, killed 13 classmates and a teacher before taking their own lives. Eric Harris and Dylan Klebold's rampage appears to have been, in part, a reaction to a group of peers who teased and marginalized them.

These anecdotes suggest that the fear of abandonment and feelings of rejection can be associated with crimes of passion and revenge. Research also has shown that people who lack or have insecure social bonds are susceptible to a variety of psychological difficulties, including depressive symptomalogy (e.g., Davila, Burge, & Hammen, 1997; Hammen, Burge, Daley, & Davila, 1995), mental illness (e.g., Bowlby, 1969, 1973; Leary, 1990), physical illness (see Lynch, 1979; also see Goodwin, Hunt, Key, & Samet, 1987), and even suicide (e.g., Rothberg & Jones, 1987; Trout, 1980).

Although belonging and acceptance are basic, universal needs (e.g., Bowlby, 1969, 1973; Freud, 1936; Horney, 1937; Maslow, 1962; Sullivan, 1953; for a review, see Baumeister & Leary, 1995), not everyone whose needs are being neglected responds in such maladaptive ways. It is necessary, therefore, to account for these differences. Drawing on the attachment (e.g., Bartholomew & Horowitz, 1991; Hazan & Shaver, 1987) and attributional perspectives (e.g., Dodge, 1980; Dodge & Somberg, 1987), Downey and her colleagues have proposed a cognitive-affective processing disposition, rejection sensitivity, that helps explain why individuals respond differently to perceived rejection (Downey & Feldman, 1996; Feldman & Downey, 1994).

In the following sections, we describe the rejection sensitivity (RS) model and evidence bearing on it. We review long-standing work in our laboratory on the role of RS in relationships with significant others (parental, peer, and romantic relationships) and then turn to more recent research regarding how RS can influence individuals' relationships with valued social groups and institutions. In the final section, we propose how to interrupt and break the vicious cycle of rejection sensitivity.

The Rejection Sensitivity Model

Defensive (i.e., anxious or angry) expectations of rejection by valued others represent the core of RS (see fig. 10.1). RS develops when people's needs are met repeatedly with rejection so that they come to expect significant others to reject them (link 1 of fig. 10.1). Yet, unlike an attachment perspective that views attachment style in global terms (e.g., global behavioral tendencies), RS is not a global disposition. Rather, defensive expectations of rejection are triggered only in situations that afford the possibility of rejection by valued others. Anxious expectations of rejection foster a hypervigilance for rejection cues, such that features of even innocuous social interactions are readily perceived as signs of intentional rejection (link 2 of fig. 10.1). After the behaviors of others are encoded as "rejecting" behavior, hurt and anger follow (link 3 of fig. 10.1) as well as the enactment of maladaptive behaviors (link 4 of fig.

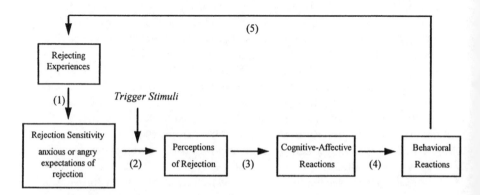

Figure 10.1   Rejection Sensitivity Model

10.1). To the extent that individuals' perceptions of rejection may be inaccurate, their negative responses to others' ambiguous behaviors can produce a self-fulfilling prophecy (e.g., Merton, 1948) in which actual rejection is elicited (link 5 of fig. 10.1).

Before we turn to a more detailed description of each link of the model, it is important to note variability in the RS cycle. First, rejection expectations lie on a continuum: low RS (LRS) individuals more calmly expect acceptance whereas high RS (HRS) individuals defensively expect rejection in ambiguous situations. Second, although HRS individuals may have all experienced prolonged or severe social rejection, their specific experiences may produce differences in, for example, their expectations (anxious vs. angry) and behavioral reactions (avoidance vs. intimacy seeking) in social situations.

The Development of Rejection Sensitivity (Link 1)

Consistent with an attachment perspective, RS is thought to develop from prior rejection experiences. Although early childhood problems between primary caregivers and children seem to have profound and long-lasting consequences for individuals' socioemotional adjustment (e.g., Bowlby, 1969, 1973, 1980; Sroufe, 1990), rejection by people other than primary caregivers also may lead to the formation of rejection expectations any time in the developmental course. In an ecological framework (Bronfenbrenner, 1979), the need to be accepted can be fulfilled or denied in many types of relationships, including proximal (parents, peers, romantic) and distal relationships (group, community, society). People can simultaneously experience social acceptance or rejection in one or more kinds of relationships.

Imagine, for example, a child who is adored and supported by her parents but who is constantly teased and rejected by her peers. Although she may be securely attached to her parents, peer rejection may lead her to expect rejection from other people such as romantic partners and colleagues. Indeed, early peer rejection has been linked to later maladjustment extending into adolescence and adulthood both in the form of externalizing problems (aggression) and internalizing problems (depression) (e.g., Bagwell, Newcomb, & Bukowski, 1998; Coie, Terry, Lenox, Lochman, & Hyman, 1998; Hecht, Inderbitzen, & Bukowski, 1998; Rudolph, Hammen, & Burge, 1997; Schwartz, McFadyen-Ketchum, Dodge, Pettit, & Bates, 1998).

However, if one experiences rejection later in life, its effects on the strength and the scope of the rejection expectations may be restricted. In this case, imagine a college senior dumped by his fiancee and emotionally traumatized. Although he may approach other potential partners with wariness and at times with expectations of rejection, we would not expect him to approach his childhood friends or his parents with defensive expectations of rejection.

In short, we propose that rejection experiences in any type of social relationship may produce defensive expectations of rejection in one or more types of relationships. That is, rejection experienced in one type of relationship (e.g., with peers) may produce expectations of rejection in current and future relationships of the same type (e.g., with other peers) and may transfer to other types of relationships (e.g., with romantic partners, within valued social groups).

Rejection Expectations and Perceptions of Rejection (Link 2)

A key assumption of the RS model is that HRS individuals' expectations of rejection are activated in situations that afford the possibility of rejection (e.g., disapproval of or a conflict with a friend or romantic partner; see Mischel & Shoda, 1995, for other situation-specific models). These expectations of rejection may take the form of anxious or angry expectations of rejection—two high arousal, negatively valenced reactions to perceived threat (Lang, 1995). As we discuss later, the type of expectation that people have may be influenced by their age and cultural or environmental factors.

For HRS individuals who have experienced rejection in past social relationships, potentially rejecting interactions are threatening not only because they think rejection is likely but also because they are uncertain when rejection will actually occur. Under these conditions, a person becomes vigilant, meticulously scanning the environment for any possible rejection cues (e.g., Compas, 1987; Krohne & Fuchs, 1991) and preparing to act defensively once cues of rejection are detected. Although vigilance may be an attempt to predict rejection and, thus, be intended as a coping strategy, it makes the individual susceptible to false alarms as the threshold for perception of rejection is lowered. Therefore, activation of anxious expectations of rejection may result in the HRS individual more readily perceiving rejection even in the innocuous behaviors of others.

Perceptions of Rejection and Reactions (Links 3 and 4)

The RS model posits that perceptions of rejection first elicit cognitive-affective reactions such as hurt, anger, and blaming self or others (link 3), which may spill over into dejection, aggression, or withdrawal (link 4). People who have a tendency to blame others when things go wrong (other-blame) may be more prone to aggressive reactions, whereas those who have a tendency to blame themselves (self-blame) may be at higher risk for depressive symptoms and withdrawal.

What is the psychological mechanism that leads HRS individuals to maladaptively react to perceived rejection? Why do HRS individuals react to ambiguously intentioned negative behavior with hostility? Given that HRS individuals are vigilant for signs of rejection, they may readily attribute harmful intent to *potential* sources of rejection and disregard contextual cues that may provide alternative explanations for others' behavior. This readiness to attribute intentional rejection to others' behaviors, in turn, may facilitate feelings of hurt and anger and even justify defensive behavioral reactions (see Dodge, 1980; Dodge, Murphy, & Buchsbaum, 1984; Dodge, Pettit, McClaskey, & Brown, 1986; Holtzworth-Munroe & Anglin, 1991; Holtzworth-Munroe & Hutchinson, 1993). For example, aggressive children who chronically expect rejection tend to attribute hostile intent to their peers' negative behaviors even when the underlying intent of their peers' behavior is ambiguous. Such attributional biases subsequently result in reactive aggression (Dodge, 1980; Dodge, Murphy, & Buchsbaum, 1984; Dodge, Pettit, McClaskey, & Brown, 1986). Likewise, wife assaulters have been found to attribute more hostile intent to their wives' behavior than nonassaulters (Holtzworth-Munroe & Hutchinson, 1993). Thus, the perceived rejection-to-defensive reactions link may be mediated by HRS individuals' readiness to attribute harmful intent to others' actions.

Coping with Sensitivity to Rejection

How do HRS individuals regulate their interactions with others? Drawing on clinical theories of coping with rejection (Ainsworth, Blehar, Waters, & Wall, 1978; Bowlby, 1969, 1973, 1980; Horney, 1937), the RS model includes two broad strategies people may use to cope with their heightened sensitivity to rejection. These strategies are associated with different behavioral reactions to perceived rejection; unfortunately, both strategies likely perpetuate the RS cycle.

For instance, some HRS individuals may try to avoid rejection by securing intimacy and unconditional love in the belief that "If you love me, you will not hurt me" (Horney, 1937, p. 96). High investment in a relationship, coupled with anxious expectations of rejection, is likely to heighten HRS individuals' propensity to perceive and overreact to minor or ambiguous cues of rejection in their significant others' behavior. This strategy may put intimacy-seeking HRS individuals at heightened risk for inappropriate attempts to avoid rejection. Specifically, they may be vulnerable to blind actions, even those they are uncomfortable doing, to please their partner and maintain the relationship (e.g., Purdie & Downey, in press).

Alternatively, some HRS individuals may try to avoid rejection by shunning intimate relationships in the belief that "If I withdraw, nothing can hurt me" (Horney, 1937, p. 96). Intimacy-avoidant HRS individuals then may attempt to shield themselves from rejection through reduced involvement in intimate relationships, such as close friendships and serious romantic relationships. Whereas this strategy may help HRS individuals avoid stormy interpersonal relationships, they may also lose opportunities for attaining the sense of acceptance missing from their lives. Therefore, this strategy may put people at risk for constant loneliness and depression.

Why do HRS individuals adopt one course of action rather than another? Relationship seeking versus avoidance strategies may be specific to a particular relationship or type of relationship. Temperamental factors such as dispositionally high inhibition also can influence the strategy used to cope with rejection sensitivity. The strategy an individual typically uses may also reflect one's early rejection experiences. Ainsworth et al. (1978), for example, suggested that consistent parental rejection may prompt avoidance of relationships, whereas intermittent rejection may prompt an ambivalent preoccupation with relationships with mixed support. These two forms of behavioral reactions also may have precursors in the kind of expectation—anxious versus angry expectations—HRS individuals possess. That is, anxious expectations of rejection may be more closely linked to ingratiating behavior, and angry expectations may be more closely linked to hostility. Although it is not completely clear what prompts HRS individuals to behave in one way or another, both relationship seeking and avoidance strategies could perpetuate rejection. As we will describe, such behavioral patterns are likely to undermine the relationships of rejection-sensitive people and result in actual rejection to become self-fulfilling prophecies (e.g., Jussim, 1986; Merton, 1968).

Operationalization of RS

The context-sensitive conceptualization of rejection sensitivity is captured in the measurement tool. The RS measure used in most of the studies described in this chapter taps expectations of rejection from important others. Respondents are asked for their expectations of rejection in hypothetical situations in which an important acquaintance or a significant other may potentially refuse their request for help, advice, or companionship. The two forms of the measure, a child/early adolescent version and late adolescent/young adult version, are similar in format. The adult rejection-sensitive measure (RSQ; Downey & Feldman, 1996) contains 18 interpersonal situations, including situations involving peers (e.g., "You ask a friend to do you a big favor"), parents (e.g., "You ask your parents to come to an occasion important to you"), and romantic partners (e.g., "You call your boyfriend/girlfriend after a bitter argument and tell him/her you want to see him/her"). The child version of the rejection sensitivity questionnaire (CRSQ; Downey, Lebolt, Rincon, & Freitas, 1998), by contrast, contains 12 situations, including items pertaining to peers (e.g., "You had a really bad fight with a friend the other day. You wonder if your friend will want to talk to you today") and teachers (e.g., "You decide to ask the teacher if you can take a video game for the weekend. You wonder if she will let you have it").

In each version of the measure, respondents are asked to rate their expectations of rejection (e.g., "I would expect that s/he would be willing to help me out") as well as their concern about the outcome (e.g., "How anxious/or angry would you be whether your friend would want to help you out"). Level of RS in each situation is calculated by multiplying the degree of concern by the degree of expectation of rejection. The adoption of an expectancy-value model (e.g., Bandura, 1986) captures the notion that HRS individuals do not merely expect rejection (as, for example, telephone solicitors do) but also are anxious or concerned about the possibility of rejection (which telephone solicitors are not).

The adult version of RSQ operationalizes the concern component for each scenario in terms of anxiety, and the CRSQ asks respondents about both how anxious and how angry they would be about the prospect of rejection in each scenario described. In the studies summarized in this chapter, the CRSQ was used with the angry component of rejection expectations rather than the anxious component of expectations. The decision to examine the consequences of angry expectations of rejection in children was based on pilot work indicating that both anxiety and anger were salient emotions for them in situations in which rejection was possible.

Because both the child and adult forms of the measure show a stable one-factor structure, a rejection sensitivity score is calculated as the average of the total (cross-situational) responses. The one-factor structure also suggests that rejection sensitivity is likely to impact different types of interpersonal relationships (e.g., peer, romantic, parent). In most of our studies, HRS individuals are defined as those with scores above the median, and the reverse is true for LRS individuals. The RS measures show good internal and test-retest reliability and discriminant validity in both the late adolescent/adult (see Downey & Feldman, 1996) and child/early adolescent samples (Downey, Lebolt, et al., 1998). Validation studies showed that RS is not redundant, in its predictive validity, with measures of introversion (Eysenck & Eysenck, 1964), self-esteem (Rosenberg, 1979), general attachment style (Hazan & Shaver, 1987; Levy & Davis, 1988), or social anxiety (Watson & Friend, 1969).

In the following sections, we show the impact of rejection sensitivity on social functioning in different relationships. We begin by describing our research on dyadic relationships (peer, parent, romantic) and then turn to our recent research on relationships with valued social groups and institutions.

Significant Dyadic Relationships

In examining each link hypothesized by the RS model in the context of significant dyadic relationships, we will lean heavily on data from college student samples, although we also will note relevant findings from younger samples.

Early Rejection and the Development of Rejection Expectations

In a study of college students, Feldman and Downey (1994) explored whether the roots of anxious expectations of rejection lie in experiences of rejection from parents. Participants completed the RSQ and then answered questions about the quality and nature of their relationships with family members during childhood. They also completed the Conflict Tactics Scale (CTS; Straus, 1979), which assessed their exposure to their parents' use of physical conflict tactics toward each other and toward them. As predicted, if college students had been exposed to frequent and severe family violence during childhood, they anxiously expected rejection in current relationships. In addition, Downey, Khouri, and Feldman (1997) found that emotional neglect and conditional love by parents were associated with heightened levels of rejection sensitivity.

Although this study suggested continuity between early experiences and later rejection expectations, its retrospective design did not allow strong causal inferences. Therefore, Downey, Bonica, and Rincon (1999) explored the relation between rejection experiences and rejection expectations in early adolescents in a longitudinal study. Specifically, fifth, sixth, and seventh graders completed the CRSQ, and their primary caregiver completed a questionnaire assessing their use of hostile and rejecting behavior toward their child. The following year when the children were in sixth to eighth grade, they completed the CRSQ a second time. Primary caregivers' reports of harsh parenting practices predicted an increase in their children's defensive expectations of rejection. These data provide support for a continuity between exposure to parenting that communicates rejection and the development of rejection expectations that guide people's feelings, thoughts, and behaviors in their future relationships. As previously discussed, our model suggests that rejection experiences involving significant others aside from parents also may lead to the development of rejection experiences. Clearly, future research should address this possibility directly. In the next section, we address the process through which defensive (anxious or angry) rejection expectations lead to both personal distress and interpersonal difficulties, and we present empirical evidence for each link hypothesized in the RS model.

Rejection Expectations and Distress and Perceptions of Rejection

We found empirical support for the hypothesized link between the activation of anxious rejection expectations, on the one hand, and increased distress and a readiness to perceive intentional rejection, on the other hand, in two studies with college students (Downey & Feldman, 1996). The first study was a laboratory experiment. After completing an initial mood scale and the RSQ, participants were introduced to a stranger of the other gender, a confederate, with whom they expected to converse during two short sessions. Following the first session, however, the experimenter informed participants in the experimental condition that their study partner (i.e., the confederate) did not want to continue with the experiment. No explanation for the confederate's behavior was given. In the control condition, the experimenter told the participants that there was not enough time to complete the second session. Subsequently, participants in both conditions completed a mood scale used to assess their post-manipulation anxious, angry, depressed, and rejected moods. In addition, the experimenter rated the participants' reaction to the manipulation. Results indicated that only HRS individuals in the experimental condition reported a significant increase in rejected mood. Such an increase was not observed for any other mood ratings and was thus restricted to feelings of rejection. Experimenter ratings of participants' negative affect also corroborated these findings: HRS individuals were perceived as being more upset and confused in reaction to the experimental manipulation. These findings were replicated with adolescents in a study using a similar paradigm (Downey, Lebolt, et al., 1998; study 2).

To establish whether anxious expectations of rejection predicted the perception of intentional rejection in a romantic partners' behavior, Downey and Feldman (1996; study 3) undertook a prospective study of college students. The study tested whether a person's rejection expectations assessed before he or she began a new romantic relationship would predict attributions of hurtful intent to a new partner's insensitive behavior (e.g., being inattentive and distant). To assess the predictive utility of the RSQ above and beyond constructs that are conceptually and empirically related to anxious expectations of rejection, participants also completed measures that assessed social anxiety (Watson & Friend, 1969), social avoidance (Watson & Friend, 1969), adult attachment styles (Hazan & Shaver, 1987; Levy & Davis, 1988), self-esteem (Rosenberg, 1979), neuroticism (Eysenck & Eysenck, 1964), and introversion (Eysenck & Eysenck, 1964). Anxious rejection expectations assessed before a romantic relationship began predicted the extent to which people would attribute hurtful intent to their new romantic partner's insensitive behavior. The prospective relationship between RS and attributions did not change when other personality dispositions were used as statistical controls, and none of these other measures was significantly related to individuals' attributions for their new partner's behavior.

Taken together, this set of findings supported three basic premises of the RS model: (1) HRS individuals experience distress and negative moods in situations that activate their expectations of rejection; (2) HRS individuals more readily feel rejected in response to ambiguous interpersonal cues than LRS individuals; and (3) activation of defensive rejection expectations occurs in situations when rejection is a possibility.

Impact of RS on Reactions to Rejection, Quality of Relationships, and Psychosocial Adjustment

Given HRS individuals' tendency to perceive intentional rejection in the ambiguous behaviors of their partners, we hypothesized that they would feel more insecure and unhappy about their relationships and respond to rejection cues by their partners with hostility, diminished support, or jealous, controlling behavior. When unjustified, these behaviors are likely to erode even the most committed partner's satisfaction with the relationship. These hypotheses were investigated in a series of studies with college undergraduates.

In one study (Downey & Feldman, 1996; study 4), college-student couples in committed nonmarital relationships completed the RSQ and provided information about themselves and their partner. As hypothesized, HRS individuals showed higher levels of concern about being rejected by their partners, irrespective of their partners' actual (self-reported) commitment to the relationship. Their concern was obvious to their partners, who perceived them to be insecure in the relationship. Partners of HRS individuals also were less satisfied with their relationship than were partners of LRS individuals. Nevertheless, HRS individuals held more exaggerated views of their partners' level of dissatisfaction than LRS individuals. An investigation of the role of HRS individuals' behaviors on their partners' dissatisfaction revealed that jealous and controlling behavior accounted for almost a third of the effect of men's RS on their female partner's relationship dissatisfaction. Hostility and lack of support accounted for over a third of the effect of women's RS on their male partner's relationship dissatisfaction.

Hypersensitivity to rejection, jealousy, and controlling behavior has been identified as characteristic of abusive men in numerous studies (e.g., Dutton, 1988; Walker, 1979, 1984). The findings of heightened levels of jealous, controlling behavior in HRS men led Downey and her colleagues to also investigate whether HRS men are more violent toward their partners than LRS men (Downey, Feldman, & Ayduk, 2000). Specifically, they hypothesized that anxious rejection expectations would predict intimate violence in men who were highly invested in romantic relationships. Downey et al. (2000) reasoned that, among men who are not invested in relationships, anxious expectations of rejection should be associated with social isolation and avoidance and thus might be related to lower intimate violence.

Cross-sectional data from male college students were used to test these hypotheses. Participants completed the RSQ, a measure of relationship investment, the CTS (Straus, 1979), the Social Avoidance and Distress Scale (SADS; Watson & Friend, 1969), and a measure of social involvement in close relationships. Dating violence was assessed by the CTS, which assesses participants' physically aggressive behavior toward a dating partner. Social isolation was indexed by the SADS, which measures people's anxiety or distress about public social situations and their tendency to avoid such situations. Relationship investment was assessed by items (e.g., "Some students feel that being able to establish romantic relationships is important") taken from Neeman and Harter's (1984) measure of the importance of a variety of interpersonal and noninterpersonal domains (e.g., relations with parents, academic achievement). Participants also reported the number of close friends they had seen or talked to on the phone in the past 2 weeks and the number of serious or committed relationships in which they had been involved.

Downey et al.'s (2000) hypotheses were confirmed. Among college men who reported relatively high investment in romantic relationships, anxious expectations of rejection predicted dating violence. Among men who reported relatively low investment in romantic relationships, anxious expectations of rejection predicted reduced involvement in close relationships with friends and romantic partners and, more generally, increased distress in and avoidance of social situations.

The relationship between RS and interpersonal difficulties also was investigated in a 1-year longitudinal study with early adolescents. Specifically, Downey, Lebolt, et al. (1998; study 3) explored whether children who expected rejection from peers and teachers experienced increased interpersonal difficulties over time. The RS model predicts that rejection expectations will lead to cognitive-affective-behavioral reactions to perceived rejection which, in turn, may elicit further rejection (e.g., victimization) and social maladjustment (e.g., getting into fights). Thus, Downey, Lebolt, et al. (1998) predicted that negative influences would be increasingly clear over the course of a year—that children who expected rejection would act in ways that elicited rejection. The children were first tested when they were in fifth, sixth, or seventh grade and then were tested with the same set of measures a year later. Children completed the CRSQ and reported acts of aggression and of being victimized. Teachers evaluated each child's aggression, social competence, and rejection sensitivity, and the dean of students provided reports of serious transgressions including fights with peers and conflicts with school personnel. The children's self-reports revealed that RS predicted differences in aggressive, antisocial behavior and being victimized. Over time, HRS children became more aggressive toward peers, showed a decline in competent classroom behavior, and became more sensitive and reactive to negative interpersonal events. Moreover, official reports revealed that, compared with LRS children, HRS children were more frequently referred for official punishment from conflicts with peers and for being defiant with adults and were more frequently suspended from school as punishment for such behavior.

In summary, the findings described here support predictions from the RS model that rejection expectations are related to negative behavioral and interpersonal outcomes, such as jealousy, controlling behavior, physical violence (among men), as well as hostility and withdrawal of support (among women). Rejection expectations also are related to troubled, volatile, and aggressive relationships with both peers and teachers and suspension from school for early adolescents.

In the next section, we describe a series of studies that test whether the link between defensive expectations of rejection and behavioral overreactions is indeed mediated through HRS individuals' readiness to perceive intentional rejection in others' negative behaviors, even when the underlying intent is ambiguous.

Perceived Rejection and Overreactions

Rejection and hostility.   The hypothesis that HRS women would display hostility to a greater extent than LRS women only in situations in which they felt rejected was investigated in a series of studies (Ayduk, Downey, Testa, Yen, & Shoda, 1999). The first study used a sequential priming-pronunciation paradigm to assess whether priming thoughts of rejection would automatically facilitate hostile thoughts. Ayduk et al. hypothesized that priming thoughts of rejection would facilitate thoughts of hostility to a greater extent in HRS than LRS women. However, they did not expect that thoughts of hostility would be more chronically accessible to HRS than LRS women, as should occur if HRS women were dispositionally more hostile than LRS women across situations.

In this paradigm, participants pronounce, as quickly as possible, a target word presented on a computer screen that is preceded by the presentation of a prime word. Time to the onset of pronunciation has been established as a reliable measure of the strength of mental associations in previous research (e.g., Bargh, Chaiken, Raymond, & Hymes, 1996; Bargh, Raymond, Pryor, & Strack, 1995). The assumption underlying this paradigm is that, to the extent that responses to target words representing a particular concept are facilitated by prime words representing another concept (as compared to a control or neutral prime), an automatic mental association exists between the concept represented by the prime and the concept represented by the target.

The results supported Ayduk et al.'s hypotheses. The HRS women began pronouncing hostility words (e.g., "hit") faster than LRS women when the words were preceded by rejection words (e.g., "abandon"). When other negative words (e.g., "vomit") served as a prime, HRS and LRS women did not differ in the onset of their pronunciation of hostile words, indicating that negative words in general do not elicit hostility from HRS women. Moreover, HRS and LRS women did not differ in the condition in which hostile words were preceded by neutral words (e.g., "board"), suggesting that HRS women are not dispositionally more hostile than LRS women.

In another laboratory experiment, Ayduk et al. (1999, study 2) also examined whether hostile thoughts activated by rejection thoughts translate into hostile behaviors. Participants were told that the goal of the study was to understand how people established on-line relationships such as through virtual dating services. First, female participants exchanged biographical sketches with a potential (fictitious) dating partner with whom they expected to interact over the Internet. Following the exchange, participants were told that the interaction would not occur. Participants in the experimental condition were told that the male participant did not want to continue with the on-line interaction part of the study and had departed. Participants in the control condition were given a situational explanation, equipment failure, for why the interaction would not occur. In contrast to the Downey and Feldman experiment (1996; study 2) in which the experimental rejection was less personal and more ambiguous and the context of the study was potentially more innocuous (a study of impression formation), the experimental manipulation in this study was a more explicit, personal rejection and the context of the study was more disconcerting (i.e., to consider potential romantic partners). Therefore, Ayduk et al. expected, and found, that HRS and LRS women in the experimental condition showed an equivalent increase in feelings of rejection following the rejection manipulation.

Participants then were given the opportunity to evaluate their impressions of their assigned partner's biographical sketch. Hostility was operationalized as the reduced positivity of the women's evaluations of their partner. In the rejection condition, HRS women evaluated their partners less positively than LRS women, whereas in the control condition, in which there was no reason to feel rejected, HRS women and LRS women had similar evaluations of their partners. Thus, the hypothesis that hostility is a specific reaction to rejection for HRS women was supported in this controlled experimental setting.

Because the ultimate goal of this program of research is to understand the impact of RS on people's ongoing relationships, Ayduk et al. (1999, study 3) also conducted a longitudinal daily diary study with undergraduate dating couples. The daily diary design allowed Ayduk et al. to examine HRS and LRS women's hostility toward romantic partners as a function of the day-to-day variation in feelings of rejection. From previous findings, Ayduk et al. hypothesized that HRS women would react in a hostile way toward their romantic partners only when they felt rejected. They used conflicts to index hostility and expected HRS women to show a higher probability of reporting conflicts than LRS women on days after they felt rejected, but not otherwise. They did not expect the likelihood of conflicts for LRS women to be related to feelings of rejection.

The analyses used a multilevel or hierarchical linear model approach, which permits the simultaneous analysis of within- and between-person variation (Bolger & Zuckerman, 1995; Bryk & Raudenbush, 1992; Kenny, Kashy, & Bolger, 1998). In short, Ayduk et al. compared the probability of women getting into conflicts with their partners following days when they felt rejected to days when they did not feel rejected. As expected, HRS women were more likely than LRS women to get into conflicts with their partners on a diary day if they had felt rejected the previous day. On days following low perceived rejection, HRS women did not differ from LRS women in likelihood of conflict.

Does a similar link between feelings and perceptions of rejection and angry overreactions exist among HRS men? Hypothesizing that men may be more concerned about social status and respect among peers (socially prescribed masculine values) than women, Ayduk and Downey (1999) have explored whether publicly threatening HRS men's status would trigger perceptions of rejection and resulting angry reactions. To test this hypothesis, they adapted the general procedure and cover story of the rejection experiment used by Ayduk et al. (1999, study 2). Unlike in the Ayduk et al. study, however, these participants (all male) were told that a male peer whom they did not know would be watching them and forming an impression of them. They were told that a video camera in the experimental room was connected to a monitor in another room where the observer would be watching them interact with their female partner while they chat over e-mail. Following the exchange of biosketches, participants in the rejection condition were told that their partner did not want to continue with the experiment, whereas participants in the control condition were told the interaction could not occur because of a situational explanation (equipment failure). Subsequently, they were asked to evaluate their impressions of their partner based on her biosketch.

Preliminary results from this study suggest that, like HRS women in the Internet rejection condition (Ayduk et al., 1999, study 2), HRS men who believed that a peer observed the rejection evaluated their partner less positively than HRS men who were in the control condition, as well as LRS men in both conditions. In contrast, HRS men in the control condition did not respond differently than LRS men. These results support a link between rejection and retaliatory hostility in men. They also suggest that rejection cues that trigger hurt and anger for HRS men may specifically jeopardize their public self and social status.

Rejection and depression.   Hostility, of course, is not the only type of reaction that HRS individuals may display in response to perceived rejection from romantic partners. Internalizing reactions such as self-blame, low self-esteem, and depression may be expressions of pain as well. To begin to address these alternative reactions to perceived rejection, Ayduk, Downey, and Kim (in press) examined whether HRS women show a heightened vulnerability to depressive symptomatology following rejection by their romantic partners. A sample of 220 female undergraduates completed the RSQ and the Beck Depression Inventory (BDI; Beck & Steer, 1987) during their first month of college. At the end of the college year, they completed the BDI for a second time. At that time, they also recorded their dating history for the intervening period. From that record, it was possible to determine whether they had experienced the ending of a romantic relationship over the course of the year and, if so, who had initiated the breakup. Findings supported the hypothesis that HRS women would be more vulnerable to depression than LRS women when their partners initiated the dissolution of their relationship. The HRS women whose romantic partners ended the relationship showed the highest increase in depressive reactions over the course of the year. Controlling for women's academic performance did not change this pattern. Therefore, these results supported two conclusions: (1) HRS women are not dispositionally more depressed than LRS women; rather, they show depressive reactions in the face of rejection, and (2) this pattern is not attributable to low academic performance, an alternative explanation for increased depression.

RS and Actual Rejection: A Self-Fulfilling Prophecy

As described in the preceding sections, anxious expectations of rejection are positively related to partner dissatisfaction among college students, and this relationship is mediated by HRS men's jealous and controlling behavior and HRS women's hostile and support-withdrawing behavior (Downey & Feldman, 1996; study 4). These results suggest that the negative behavior of HRS individuals in relationships, especially if they frequently react to innocuous behaviors on their partners' part, may erode the satisfaction of even a highly committed partner and the foundations of the relationship. Reduced partner satisfaction may eventually bring about actual rejection by the partner through the dissolution of the relationship. In this way, the legacy of RS may be maintained, at least partly, by a self-fulfilling feedback loop.

Downey, Freitas, Michealis, and Khouri (1998) directly investigated the self-fulfilling prophecy hypothesis in a daily diary study. Participants were couples in committed dating relationships; at least one partner was an undergraduate. Participants first completed a set of background measures including the RSQ, global measures of relationship satisfaction and commitment, and demographic questions. Then for the next 4 weeks, both members of each couple completed a daily structured questionnaire that included questions about participants' relationship dissatisfaction, thoughts of ending the relationship, perceptions of accepting partner behavior, and perceptions of rejecting partner behavior. A year after the completion of the diary study, one member of each couple was contacted and asked whether the couple was still together. Of the couples contacted, 29% had broken up.

In fact, RS predicted relationship breakup for both men and women, even when controlling for partners' initial level of RS, relationship satisfaction, and commitment. Data from the diary study were used to help shed light on the processes whereby RS undermines relationships for women but not men. Specifically, naturally occurring conflicts were found to trigger a process through which women's rejection expectancies led to their partners' rejecting responses, operationalized as partner-reported relationship dissatisfaction and thoughts of ending the relationship. Both of these indices of rejection predicted breakup for men and for women.

On days preceded by conflict, HRS women's partners were more likely than LRS women's partners to experience relationship dissatisfaction and to think of ending the relationship. Moreover, HRS women's partners felt significantly more negatively about the relationship on days preceded by conflict than on days that were not. The pattern was reversed, but to a nonsignificant degree, for the partners of LRS women. These findings are not attributable to the stable effects of partner background characteristics, because these are held constant in within-couple analyses. Nor can they be accounted for by the contaminating effect of the prior day's dissatisfaction and thoughts of ending the relationship, which were also held constant in the analyses.

The differential impact of conflict on the partners of HRS and LRS women was evident to the women. On days preceded by conflict, HRS women perceived partners to be less accepting and more withdrawn. This link was partially mediated by partner satisfaction and commitment. Conflicts did not precipitate changes in relationship satisfaction or commitment for HRS and LRS men's partners. Thus, these findings add to accumulating evidence that typical conflicts may be more appropriate contexts for examining the impact of women's than of men's relationship cognitions.

Overall, these findings implicate conflicts as critical situations in which to examine the processes leading to the fulfillment of HRS women's rejection expectations. The next step was to examine what happened during the conflicts between HRS women and their partners that might account for the partners' heightened feeling of rejection of the relationship postconflict. Toward this end, Downey, Freitas, et al. (1998; study 2) used a behavioral observation paradigm developed by Gottman (1979) to test whether women's conflict behavior mediated the relation between their rejection expectancies and their partners' postconflict rejecting reactions. Participants were college-age couples in the early stages of an exclusive dating relationship. In an initial session, each member of the couple separately completed a background questionnaire that included measures of RS, relationship satisfaction and commitment, and demographic information. One to two weeks later, couples came into the laboratory to be videotaped while discussing an unresolved relationship issue.

On arrival, both members separately completed a measure of their current mood. Both members of each couple selected five topics of ongoing conflict from a list of 19 and then marked the most salient one. The experimenters then assigned the couples to discussion topics picked by both members. Common themes among these topics were "spending time together," "other friendships," "commitment," and "sex" (HRS and LRS individuals chose similar topics). To reduce distraction, couples were videotaped for 20 minutes by a camera set up behind a one-way mirror. After the interaction, participants completed a second mood questionnaire, which assessed how angry, anxious, and sad they felt when they thought of their partner and their relationship.

Videotaped interactions were coded using the Marital Interaction Coding System-IV (MICS-IV) (Weiss & Summers, 1983) by coders at the University of Oregon Marital Studies Program. In the analyses, behavior codes that included both verbal and nonverbal behaviors were combined to form a Negative Behavior composite, and the proportion of total negative behavior was calculated.

Results showed that partners of HRS women were more angry and more resentful about the relationship following the conflict discussion than were partners of LRS women. This difference reflected a nonsignificant increase in the anger of partners of HRS women and a significant decline in the anger of LRS women's partners. Controlling for partners' preconflict anger, relationship commitment and satisfaction did not change this relationship. Next, Downey et al. tested the hypothesis that the relationship between RS and partners' postconflict anger for women was mediated by women's negative behavior during the conflict. Path analyses indicated that women's negative behavior accounted for 54% of the effect of women's RS on their partners' change in anger. Consistent with the findings from the diary study, men's RS predicted neither their conflict behavior nor their partners' postconflict anger.

Together with the findings from the diary study, these results provide evidence that people's expectations influence, rather than merely reflect, the reality of their ongoing relationships. In other words, rejection expectations can lead people to behave in ways that actually elicit rejection from others, confirming people's initial expectations about the likelihood of rejection. This self-fulfilling prophecy, we believe, is one reason why it may be difficult to intervene in this RS cycle. Because HRS individuals are active participants in the construction of their social worlds, their tendency to expect, perceive, and overreact to rejection may simply increase their likelihood of being rejected.

Summary

The empirical evidence described here points to rejection sensitivity as a cognitive-affective processing disposition to anxiously expect, readily perceive, and overreact to rejection and as a risk factor for difficulties in dyadic relationships during late adolescence. To review, rejection cues activate anxious expectations of rejection and thus elicit negative affect and distress in HRS individuals. When anxious rejection expectations are activated, HRS individuals, more readily than LRS individuals, perceive rejection in the ambiguous behaviors of their romantic partners as well as new acquaintances. In turn, their perceptions and feelings of rejection automatically elicit negative affect (anger and hurt) and lead not only to maladaptive interpersonal behaviors (retaliatory hostility and negative conflict tactics) but also to intrapersonal difficulties (depression).

Given their readiness to perceive rejection, HRS individuals tend to overestimate their partners' dissatisfaction with the relationship. Over time, partners characterize HRS women as hostile and unsupportive and HRS men as jealous and controlling, and they report lower levels of relationship satisfaction than partners of LRS individuals (Downey & Feldman, 1996, study 4). It is not surprising, then, that the relationships of HRS individuals are more likely to dissolve than the relationships of LRS individuals, reflecting a self-fulfilling prophecy that may maintain and perpetuate the RS dynamic (Downey, Freitas, et al., 1998, study 1). To conclude this section, we mention implications of these findings and offer directions for future research.

Implications and Future Directions

Self-control ability as a buffer against overreactions to rejection.   A self-fulfilling prophecy may not always emanate from the romantic relationships of HRS individuals. People bring not only their vulnerabilities to social situations but also strengths that may then counteract the effects of the former. For example, in HRS individuals, self-control competencies may reduce the risk of negative outcomes.

As previously discussed, biases in attributions of intent may be one information-processing mechanism that links rejection sensitivity with overreactions (Downey & Feldman, 1996, study 3). Research indeed indicates that biases in attributions of intent characterize aggressive children and adult men (e.g., Dodge, 1980; Dodge & Somberg, 1987; Holtzworth-Munroe & Hutchinson, 1993). Activation of rejection expectations may lead HRS individuals to focus on the internal (e.g., their affective states) as well as external threat-related cues (e.g., behaviors of the perpetrator) but to disregard contextual cues that may provide alternative (and more benign) explanations for others' behaviors. Consequently, RS may facilitate feelings of anger and defensive behavioral overreactions through a readiness to attribute hostile intent to the potential source of rejection.

HRS individuals who can avoid such biases may be buffered against the relatively automatic reactions to perceived rejection in the RS cycle. How could HRS individuals avoid such biases? They can inhibit their tendencies to focus on the emotional and arousing aspects of interpersonal interactions or they can access attentional-cognitive strategies to construe trigger features of interpersonal situations in less emotional terms. Preliminary evidence supports these possibilities. In both early and late adolescent samples, strategic self-control (as measured by ability to delay gratification during early childhood) among HRS individuals was related to higher levels of self-worth, self-esteem, and peer acceptance and lower levels of aggression (Ayduk, Mendoza-Denton, Downey, Mischel, Peake, & Rodriguez, in press). Although future work needs to directly test the causal impact of self-control strategies on the link between anxious rejection expectations and maladaptive overreactions in HRS individuals, these preliminary results suggest that interventions aimed at individuals' cognitive-affective information-processing system and coping mechanisms may be effective. We will return to intervention strategies for reducing RS in the final section of the chapter.

Early adolescent romantic relationships.   So far, Downey and her colleagues' research into the implications of RS for romantic relationships has focused on college students' dating relationships. Many people, however, first become romantically involved during middle school years. These short-lived romances provide the context for sexual experimentation and socioemotional development (Erikson, 1968; Sullivan, 1953), the lessons likely to set the scripts for future relationships.

Accordingly, we have started investigating the romantic relationships of middle school children. We are particularly interested in understanding how often HRS girls engage in socially motivated delinquent behavior to prevent rejection or gain acceptance from their boyfriends. We hypothesize that the desire to prevent rejection and gain acceptance may motivate HRS girls toward compliance and self-silencing (Jack, 1991) in situations of disagreement with delinquency-prone boyfriends, which would put them at higher risk for cutting classes, joining gangs, or having unprotected sex. Compliance also can reinforce a perpetrator's abusive behavior, increasing the risk of future victimization. In support of these hypotheses, our preliminary findings indicate that, compared to LRS girls, HRS girls were more willing to do things they know are wrong to keep their boyfriends (Purdie & Downey, in press).

At the same time we are exploring whether RS is a risk factor for boys in the development of coercive conflict resolution strategies with dating partners. We are also investigating the possibility that RS may be related to social delinquency among boys. In their search for approval and acceptance, for example, HRS boys may be more likely to join gangs than LRS boys. In subsequent sections, we elaborate on how RS may play itself out in intragroup relationships.

Relationships with Valued Social Groups and Institutions

The findings reviewed thus far indicate that rejection expectations in one type of dyadic relationship (e.g., with peers) influence similar current and future dyadic relationships as well as extend to other types of relationships (e.g., with romantic partners). We wondered whether rejection sensitivity developing out of rejecting experiences with significant individuals also influences people's experiences within valued social *groups*. Are intragroup interactions threatening to HRS individuals, or are the effects of rejection sensitivity specific to dyadic relationships? Do the rejection sensitivity processes governing perception of individual others also apply to groups of others? Are the same cognitive, affective, and behavioral reactions elicited in response to perceptions of rejection by groups of others as by individual others?

Such questions are part of the broader debate of whether impression formation of individuals is similar to that of groups. Based on an extensive review, Hamilton and Sherman (1996) concluded that the same fundamental information-processing system underlies impression formation of individuals and groups, but that specific processes and their results can differ for individual and group targets. For instance, some research suggests that perceivers tend to expect more stability in an individual than in a group (e.g., McConnell, Sherman, & Hamilton, 1997), and research indeed indicates that impressions formed of individuals tend to be more stable (i.e., resistant to counter-expectant information) than impressions of groups (e.g., Weisz & Jones, 1993). Whereas a growing body of work indicates that, in general, perceivers process information differently for individual and group targets, some research on individual differences has shown that differences lie in the targets as well as in the perceivers. Research by Dweck and her colleagues, for instance, shows that perceivers' dynamic versus static views of human attributes predict the same pattern of attributions and judgments regardless of the target—self, individual other, or group (see Levy & Dweck, 1998).

In the studies reviewed next, we pursued the possibility that rejection sensitivity operates consistently across individual and group targets. Reasoning that relationships with a single individual and a group of individuals are similar in that both can provide or deny acceptance, we hypothesized that rejection expectations would have similar cognitive, affective, and behavioral influences on people's relationships with groups as on people's relationships with individuals.

Perceptions of Rejection Within Groups and Cognitive-Affective Reactions

One group context likely to trigger concerns about rejection is a transition to an unfamiliar yet important group setting (e.g., entering college and beginning a job in a new corporation). The meaning and intentions behind others' behaviors are not clear in such contexts. Transitions tend to be difficult times because (1) social networks are disrupted and changed (e.g., Lewin, 1947), and (2) new schemas are developing and information is being integrated into existing ones (e.g., Ruble, 1994). Accordingly, transitions such as to parenthood (e.g., Ruble, Fleming, Hackel, & Stangor, 1988) and to new school settings (e.g., Eccles & Midgley, 1990; Simmons, Rosenberg, & Rosenberg, 1973) make people vulnerable to depression and to self-doubt. Although new life phases may be inherently stressful for most people (e.g., Hormuth, 1990), HRS individuals may experience heightened stress during these times because of their rejection expectations. Ruble's phase model of transitions (1994) proposes that an individual's expectations when entering a transitional state can influence the outcome of that transition. As an example, maternal expectations formed during pregnancy affect postpartum mothering self-definitions (e.g., Deutsch, Ruble, Fleming, Brooks-Gunn, & Stangor, 1988).

On the basis on this reasoning, Levy, Eccleston, Mendoza-Denton, and Downey (1999; study 1) selected a transitional context—entrance to college—for an initial examination of the influence of rejection sensitivity on relationships within important institutions. With the upheaval of leaving home (perhaps for the first time) and becoming independent, the transition surely can be threatening and uncertain. Past work has indeed shown that this transition can trigger negative affective states (depression and anxiety) and disengagement from university activities (e.g., Hoyle & Crawford, 1994;

also see Ethier & Deaux, 1994). Such reactions seem likely to be accentuated for those entering college with expectations of social rejection and with a tendency to perceive intentional rejection in innocuous or ambiguous social interactions. In some cases, representatives of the university may unintentionally communicate rejection to incoming students. For example, residence advisors, professors, counselors, and financial aid advisors, to name a few university representatives, may be unavailable or unhelpful in meeting new students' needs. And HRS individuals are likely to perceive rejection in such encounters rather than take into account the inherent stress of transitional periods for all involved. In short, Levy et al. hypothesized that the college transition would trigger rejection concerns in HRS individuals, and the same basic set of cognitive-affective-behavioral reactions HRS individuals display in dyadic interactions would emerge during this transition into a new social institution.

Entering college students initially were contacted during orientation and were asked to complete the RSQ measure and then to complete a short, structured diary at the end of each day during their first 3 weeks of college. The main dependent measure from the daily diary was the extent to which participants felt as though they fit into the university community. We predicted that perceptions of rejection among HRS students would appear as soon as the students entered college and would lead to low reported levels of belonging at the college.

Hierarchical linear modeling analyses indicated that HRS students felt less of a sense of belonging than LRS students when they first arrived, and this initial gap widened over time. That is, LRS students had an increasing sense of belonging over the first 3 weeks, indicating that they were adapting and easing through the stressful transition. In contrast, HRS students' sense of belonging did not increase during the 3-week transition. Moreover, when students were contacted at the end of the academic year, Levy et al. found that the difference in sense of belonging between HRS and LRS students persisted. Why did HRS individuals feel more alienated even after the initial transition period? One possibility is that over time an increasing number of possibilities for rejection may make it difficult for HRS individuals to overcome initial feelings of alienation or rejection.

Like HRS individuals in past studies experiencing negative affective reactions in romantic relationships (e.g., Downey & Feldman, 1996; Downey, Freitas, et al., 1998), these HRS individuals also reported more negative feelings about the university than did LRS individuals. For example, HRS individuals felt significantly less satisfaction with the university, less respect for the university, and less trust in the university to make decisions good for everyone. Additionally, unlike LRS students, HRS students reported less willingness to recommend the university to a friend who was accepted for admission, suggesting that they might be likely to act on their more negative evaluations of the university.

Could the differences between HRS and LRS students' beliefs and feelings about the university reflect differences in their academic performance expectations or differences in their actual performance during the first semester of college? Such alternative explanations for these findings seem unlikely because rejection sensitivity levels did not relate to reported high school grade point average or to reported fall semester grade point average. Rather, these results suggest that students' preexisting expectations of rejection colored their initial and lasting impressions of a new social institution.

Coping Strategies

How do HRS individuals cope with perceived rejection in group settings? According to the rejection sensitivity model, higher levels of RS can lead to both relationship avoidance and relationship preoccupation. Our preliminary findings suggest that these coping strategies apply when HRS individuals regulate their social relations within valued social organizations.

Avoidance strategies. In the longitudinal diary study just described, Levy et al. also explored differences in behavioral responses as a function of rejection sensitivity. Much research has shown that people tend to react to threatening, uncertain experiences (like the transition to college) by withdrawing into a close-knit group—usually bonding with several others in the same setting. For instance, highly cohesive small groups can grow naturally out of life-threatening experiences (e.g., Elder & Clipp, 1988) and severe initiation into an organization (e.g., Hautaluoma, Enge, Mitchell, & Rittwager, 1991). Given the greater likelihood that HRS individuals will identify threat (i.e., perceive rejection) in an uncertain context, we expected that they might be more likely to react to the college transition by limiting their social circles.

The college environment provides incoming students with a variety of people with whom to affiliate. Who would HRS individuals tend to seek out? People generally tend to seek friends and partners similar in interests, age, and race (e.g., Cash, Janda, Byrne, Murstein, Merighi, & Malloy, 1994; Hallinan & Williams, 1987; Moreland & Zajonc, 1982), and the same is true in group memberships (e.g., Diehl, 1988; Osbeck, Moghaddam, & Perreault, 1997). Pursuing others similar to oneself increases the likelihood of acceptance, increases social-verification (e.g., Hardin & Higgins, 1996; Shah, Kruglanski, & Thompson, 1998), and reduces uncertainty (e.g., Hogg & Abrams, 1993). Are HRS individuals especially likely to restrict their relationships to similar others in response to uncertain group experiences such as entering college (cf. Ethier & Deaux, 1994)?

To examine this question among participants in the diary study, Levy et al. obtained measures of friendship at the end of the academic year. Participants were asked to list all of the close friends they had made and to list their characteristics such as age, sex, and race. In addition, to explore whether respondents sought out clearly defined groups of similar others, we asked them to report their affiliations with campus clubs and organizations.

The analysis of respondents' lists of close friends revealed two key findings. First, HRS individuals listed fewer friends than did LRS individuals, indicating that some HRS individuals either could not make friends, were unable to maintain new friendships, or avoided social interaction. Second, HRS students who made new friends reported, as predicted, fewer friends with differing characteristics (i.e., other-race friends) than LRS students, suggesting that they were more likely to limit their social relations to friends with similar characteristics. To test the hypothesis that HRS individuals might try to affiliate with similar others by joining relatively homogeneous clubs on campus, we restricted our analysis to the largest such club on campus, race-minority organizations. Results indeed indicated that those racial minority students who were high in rejection sensitivity were more likely than those who were low in rejection sensitivity to join an ethnic organization on campus.

In summary, the greater students' level of rejection sensitivity, the more the students seemed to react to a threatening social transition by limiting social relations over the course of the first year.

Social preoccupation strategies. In group settings, do HRS individuals also display the other coping strategy—social preoccupation—characteristic of some HRS individuals in dyadic settings? In another study with college students, Levy et al. (1999; study 2) explored whether HRS individuals exhibit social preoccupation strategies for gaining acceptance in groups with which they identify. Levy et al. hypothesized that HRS individuals who perceive rejection from a valued group of which they are a member may try to win group approval with ingratiating behavior. In this study, college students were asked to select the group with which they identify the most and to answer a series of questions about their standing and role in the group. As a measure of perceived rejection in the group, participants were asked to evaluate how isolated they felt and how well they fit in the group. Students were also asked for their willingness to comply with group rules and standards.

As predicted, the more rejection sensitive individuals were, the more isolated they reported feeling in the group they identified as most important to them. Thus, in the same way HRS individuals have trouble meeting their social needs within relationships with significant others (i.e., romantic partners), they also have trouble meeting their needs within valued social groups. Levy et al. additionally explored whether HRS individuals adopt strategies for dealing with feelings of isolation within valued groups different from those LRS individuals use. To examine this, we regressed participants' willingness to comply with group rules on RS, feelings of isolation, and the interaction between RS and feelings of isolation. Only the interaction was significant, indicating that HRS and LRS individuals reported nearly opposite patterns of compliance. That is, LRS students who felt the most isolated in the group reported the least willingness to adhere to the group's rules, whereas HRS students who felt the most isolated in the valued group reported the greatest willingness to adhere to the group's rules. The HRS students' greater obedience to the group's rules is somewhat paradoxical. One would think that an individual who feels isolated in a group would feel less allegiance and commitment to a group and, thus, be less willing to adhere to its rules. The HRS individuals' greater willingness to adopt group rules, even when they feel isolated, may reflect more than just a strategy for gaining acceptance. Adopting group norms may also provide a "social reality." As Hardin and Higgins (1996) noted, social groups can serve the function of creating a social reality by being a source of social verification and comparison (also see Festinger, 1954; Shah et al., 1998). Future work will investigate whether HRS individuals' behavior within groups reflects their pursuit of needs such as social acceptance and verification.

Summary

Rejection expectations can negatively influence individuals' perceptions of and relations within familiar and valued groups as well as negatively color their impressions of an unfamiliar group whose behavioral intentions may appear ambiguous. Rejection sensitivity prompted negative affect, dissatisfaction, and both social preoccupation and avoidance coping strategies. Hence, the RS model developed to account for dynamics in dyadic relationships seems also to apply to how people think, feel, and respond to social groups and institutions. These findings suggest that rejection sensitivity affects social perception and behavior consistently across individual and group targets.

Implications and Future Directions

The influence of RS on transitional periods other than college.   To follow up on our initial findings showing that HRS students struggle more with the college transition than do LRS students, we will be exploring the consequences of RS through the transition in greater detail throughout the 4 years of college. Since entering college is only one of the many transitions people face, an important future direction is to trace the consequences of RS through other important life phases. A particularly important and stressful transition is the one to junior high or middle school (e.g., Eccles & Midgley, 1990; Simmons et al., 1973). During this period, adolescents face many challenges—puberty, dating, more challenging school work, and shifting peer groups. How HRS individuals fare during such a transition may be particularly illuminating. This transition allows for tests of how RS influences emerging romantic relationships and shifts in reference groups. The transition to junior high or middle school presents an opportunity to investigate the implications of RS for individuals' dyadic relationships and relationships with groups. As a side note, other transition periods also open up possibilities for simultaneously examining the role of RS in different relationships. That is, a well-studied and also extremely stressful period is the transition to parenthood (e.g., Ruble et al., 1988) when consequences of RS could be tracked in marital relationships as well as in newly developing relationships with children.

In-group favoritism and out-group devaluation.   Our findings suggest that HRS individuals may exhibit more in-group favoritism than LRS individuals. In the diary study of the transition to college, HRS students were more likely to affiliate with groups of similar others, and in the study of group identity, HRS students were more willing to comply with their in-groups' rules. Given that strongly identifying with in-groups and in-group favoritism often promotes out-group devaluation (see Brewer & Brown, 1998), we anticipate that even HRS individuals who have found a secure base (however temporary) within a group would hold stronger negative views of out-groups than LRS individuals. Furthermore, devaluing out-groups may also be a strategy for gaining in-group acceptance.

Could RS then be a motivating factor in prejudice? Social rejection as an explanation for developing prejudice has a precedent in the classic personality explanation of prejudice—the authoritarian personality (Adorno, Frenkel-Brunswick, Levinson, & Sanford, 1950). Working within a psychodynamic framework, Adorno et al. portrayed this personality syndrome as arising from early childhood experiences, particularly from parents' threatening, forbidding, and punitive responses to their child's "unconventional" behavior. These difficult childhood experiences were thought to contribute to the development of an inadequate ego, which relied on defense mechanisms (such as projection of anger toward out-groups rather than toward parents) to release the aggressive and sexual impulses of their poorly controlled "ids." Although this work was criticized on theoretical (the untestable nature of psychoanalytic theory), conceptual (vague operationalization), and methodological grounds (psychometric properties of the F-scale), higher prejudice levels were found among authoritarians. These shortcomings have been subsequently addressed, and researchers have continued to find that authoritarians tend to be prejudiced toward a wide variety of groups (see Altemeyer, 1998). We are currently exploring how our construct relates to authoritarianism and fits with other motivational explanations of prejudice (e.g., self-esteem maintenance: Fein & Spencer, 1997).

Marginalization and joining "fringe" groups.   People who are socially rejected often become marginalized members of society. The findings from the diary study in which HRS first-year college students seemed to seek out subgroups of similar others (i.e., student clubs) in their college may reflect a more general process through which rejected people opt out of broader, more mainstream groups and into more marginalized, fringe groups. As HRS individuals have been shown to feel more isolated within mainstream institutions, some HRS individuals may find solace in marginalized peer groups.

What kind of marginalized groups might draw HRS individuals? In the *Nature of Prejudice*, Gordon Allport (1954) suggested that "it may well turn out that followers [of demagogues] are nearly all individuals who have felt themselves to be somehow rejected" (p. 392). Could our work then have implications for understanding membership and activities within extreme groups such as cults, marginalized political groups, and even "hate" groups (i.e., groups organized around the hatred of political, religious, ethnic, or racial groups)? Although there is little empirical work on the psychological characteristics of such group members, the theme of social rejection runs through the literature on these types of groups. As one example, hate group members tend to come from troubled homes in which divorce, separation, and abuse (physical abuse; drug abuse) are prevalent (Hamm, 1993) and in which there are no positive role models (e.g., Wang, 1994). Although social factors may lead people to join such groups, the ideology of these groups may not be the primary motive. Rather, finding a place to belong may be an underlying motivation.

Besides fitting the characteristics of individuals prone to join extreme or marginalized groups, our model also may explain in part what motivates people to carry out violent acts once they enter such groups. Results from the group identity study, in which HRS individuals who felt isolated in a group reported greater willingness to adopt group rules and standards, suggest that some HRS individuals may blindly follow group rules to gain acceptance. Thus, people who blindly follow a group norm and act in violent, socially deviant ways may actually be seeking the positive, socially valued goal of obtaining acceptance. We are not suggesting that all fringe or subversive group members are HRS or that all HRS individuals would join fringe or subversive groups if they were available; however, interesting, important links may connect our work and work on such groups.

Strategies for Breaking the RS Cycle

In the previous sections, we delineated processes that promote and maintain the RS cycle within a variety of social relationships. We also have begun to investigate how these detrimental processes can be interrupted and how the cycle can be broken. In this section, we propose diverse approaches for undermining links in the RS cycle. We focus on interventions that specifically challenge the damaging perceptions, cognitions, and behavioral patterns characteristic of HRS individuals, and, consistent with an ecological framework, we also discuss interventions targeting HRS individuals' social environments. While tracing each intervention possibility, we also note potential obstacles to change, and, unfortunately, these are numerous.

Targeting the HRS Individual

Breaking specific links in the RS cycle.   Attacking perceptions of rejection may be a good place to start undermining the RS cycle (link 2 of Figure 10.1). As previously noted, HRS individuals attribute hurtful intent to the ambiguous behaviors of others (also see Dodge, 1980; Dodge et al., 1986). An intervention strategy, then, would be to replace attributional biases of harmful intent with alternative explanations such as situational attributions. Several attributional retraining programs seem particularly apt for HRS individuals (for reviews of attributional theory and therapy, see Graham & Folkes, 1990).

For example, Hudley and Graham (1993) designed a social cognitive intervention to lessen 10–12-year-old boys' hostile attributional biases in negative social encounters of ambiguous causal origins. During 12 sessions across a 4-month period, the boys in the experimental condition role-played less violent (more adaptive) responses to hypothetical and laboratory simulations of peer provocation. The intervention included training in accurately interpreting the verbal and behavioral cues of others and in making attributions to nonhostile intent. In addition, children were taught how to respond to negative outcomes without hostility, a component of the intervention that could beneficially undermine affective reactions characteristic of some HRS individuals (link 3 of fig. 10.1). Hudley and Graham found that boys' tendency to attribute malicious intent to ambiguous peer provocations could be retrained (at least temporarily). Such an intervention also could also be adopted for older age groups and seems particularly appropriate for HRS individuals who tend to react to perceived rejection with hostility and violence.

A more indirect attributional retraining procedure that Mark Schaller and colleagues developed with college students (e.g., Schaller, Asp, Rosell, & Heim, 1996) also may prove helpful in undermining HRS individuals' negative attributions of others' intentions. To teach participants to be attentive to alternative explanations for others' behaviors and outcomes (nondispositional explanations), Schaller and colleagues gave participants 40 minutes of statistical training in the *logic* of analysis of covariance (ANCOVA). They reasoned that the ANCOVA training would show that obvious inferences sometimes can be wrong. Specifically, participants were provided with scenarios (e.g., win-loss records of two fictitious tennis players from two leagues) and then led through the logic of ANCOVA to uncover a confounding variable in drawing an impression of the targets (e.g., in determining who was the better player, one needed to consider the competitiveness of each league and the number of games of each player). Schaller et al. found that participants who received the training were less likely than those who did not receive training to form erroneous judgments of others. Although this intervention training should be adapted to social situations more applicable to HRS individuals, training HRS individuals to attend to the details of social situations could help them recognize nonhurtful intentions in others and in turn arrive at less erroneous and malicious dispositional conclusions about others' behaviors.

Beyond attributional retraining interventions, other preexisting interventions could be adapted to attack different links in the RS cycle. For example, interventions that target people's emotional competence could address the cognitive-affective component of RS (link 3 of fig. 10.1) by helping HRS individuals better identify others' feelings toward them and better regulate their own reactive feelings toward others. The PATHS program (Promoting Alternative Thinking Strategies; Greenberg, Kusche, Cook, & Quamma, 1995), an emotion-focused school-based unit for elementary school–age children, seems particularly well-suited for their purpose. For three days a week during one school year, classroom teachers and PATH staff taught second- and third-grade children to attend to their own and others' feelings, to correctly label them, to discuss them, and to decide under what circumstances to keep their feelings private or make them public. Children were also taught how to control their emotions using a simple metaphor—a traffic light (also see Weissberg, Caplan, & Bennetto, 1988). A poster of a traffic light was placed in each class with a red light referring to "Stop—Calm Down," a yellow light referring to "Go Slow—Think," and a green light signaling "Go—Try My Plan." Greenberg et al. found that children in regular and special needs classrooms (e.g., children with severe behavioral problems) who participated in the intervention had a better understanding of cues for recognizing emotions in others, identifying their own emotions, managing their own emotions, and appreciating the malleability of feelings than did children in the control condition. These data may suggest that HRS individuals need not be singled out (and potentially stigmatized) while they learn to monitor and control their emotions in stressful social situations.

Finally, to undermine hostile behavioral patterns characteristic of some HRS individuals (link 4 of fig. 10.1), antisocial behavioral and aggression reduction intervention programs could be utilized (e.g., Aber, Jones, Brown, Chaudry, & Samples, 1998; Huesmann et al., 1996). Besides focusing specifically on how individuals overcome hostile behavior, some of these interventions also focus on the role of individuals' social networks (parents, teachers, and peers) in different contexts (classroom, playground, home) in the expression and perpetuation of hostile reactions. The multifaceted nature and ecological approach of these interventions complement our conception of diverse factors influencing RS, and, thus, these interventions may be particularly worthwhile for HRS individuals who have experienced prolonged or severe rejection in different relationships and settings. For example, Resolving Conflict Creatively Program (RCCP; Aber et al., 1998) is a social skills improvement program in which elementary school children are taught negotiation and problem-solving skills for dealing with social conflict. Classroom teachers are trained to use a variety of techniques such as role-playing and small group discussions to guide children in resolving conflicts nonaggressively. Additionally, as part of the program, a subset of children is nominated and trained to serve as conflict resolution mediators in and out of the classroom. From the fall to spring semester, Aber et al. (1998) found that children who were exposed to many RCCP lessons ($M = 23$ lessons) had less aggressive interpersonal negotiation strategies in reactive situations than did children who received only a few lessons ($M = 2$ lessons) or no RCCP lessons. These promising preliminary findings suggest that programs such as RCCP may prove successful in reducing aggressive behavioral reactions among HRS individuals.

Believing in the potential for change.   To begin the process of undermining their heightened rejection concerns, HRS individuals need not only sufficient motivation but probably also the belief that "change" is possible. When one believes that people can change, then the dynamics of specific person-situation interactions can change. Those who are encouraged to believe that people are dynamic actors in specific situations can perhaps break the domino effect of the RS chain. Believing that change is possible both for oneself (e.g., "I can change my expectations and behavior") and for valued others (e.g., "he [or she or they] can become less rejecting") would be beneficial. Some research has provided encouraging support for persuading individuals to (at least temporarily) adopt the view that people can change (Chiu, Hong, & Dweck, 1997; Levy, Stroessner, & Dweck, 1998). Moreover, this line of work by Dweck and her colleagues also suggests that people who view human nature as malleable are less prone to engage in detrimental attributions and judgments. That is, they make weaker trait judgments (Chiu et al., 1997, Levy & Dweck, 1999; Levy et al., 1998), expect less cross-situational behavioral consistency in others (Chiu et al., 1997), and make more situational attributions for others' behavior (Levy & Dweck, 1999; Levy et al., 1998). However, believing that others, such as one's partner, can change may not be without costs; people with a malleable view of human nature may, for example, stay too long in destructive relationships, not knowing when to give up (e.g., see Janoff-Bulman & Brickman, 1982).

Reducing RS Through Supportive Social Relationships

Supportive relationships may be key in breaking the rejection-sensitivity cycle. First, an accepting relationship may reduce HRS individuals' future expectations of rejection. Second, supportive others who are not rejection sensitive can serve as models because they generate fewer malevolent explanations for others' behavior and use adaptive conflict resolution strategies. As previously mentioned, violence intervention programs show that training parents, teachers, and peers to support children to overcome their antisocial behavior can be successful. Moreover, research indicates that a supportive partner can help women break intergenerational cycles of child abuse (e.g., Egeland, Jacobvitz, & Sroufe, 1988; Quinton, Rutter, & Liddle,

1984), and parental support can buffer peer-rejected children from negative outcomes (e.g., Patterson, Cohn, & Kao, 1989).

A possible barrier to the use of supportive relationships as a tool for breaking the RS cycle is getting HRS individuals involved in "healthy," supportive relationships—getting them to seek out and identify supportive relationships. This may be especially difficult for HRS individuals who are socially withdrawn. One social avenue particularly well-suited to these individuals is the Internet, which has opened up possibilities (e.g., chat-rooms, newsgroups, on-line dating services) for people to interact with others in a relatively anonymous way, thereby providing a possible safe context for seeking acceptance. Parks and Roberts (1998), for instance, found that virtual environments known as MOOs (Multi-User Dimensions, Object-Oriented) stimulated the formation of personal relationships including close friendships and relationships that transferred to off-line, face-to-face intimate relationships (also see Parks & Floyd, 1996). Perhaps most applicable to our research on rejection sensitivity is the finding that the Internet has been successfully used by individuals who otherwise have difficulty reaching out for social support (e.g., people with marginalized or stigmatized social identities). McKenna and Bargh (1998) have recently shown that people with marginalized identities who participate in Internet newsgroups can develop greater self-acceptance. Broader-based evaluations of self-help resources and on-line therapy are also under way and appear promising (King & Morreggi, 1998).

Furthermore, HRS individuals may need help in identifying truly supportive relationships. Although future work needs to address this issue directly, some HRS individuals may have difficulty identifying supportive social networks. For example, they may not be sufficiently selective and thus enter into relationships with anyone who shows interest or support. They also may place so much value on one dimension of their partner or group members—acceptance—that they are blind to other potentially harmful characteristics. They may enter or stay in abusive relationships with partners or join groups that engage in violent acts toward others or that make other potentially harmful demands as a condition of membership. Individual, family, and couples therapy can also help people identify healthy relationships and learn to trust others (e.g., Ginsberg, 1997). Additionally, school-based interventions that specifically assist students in recognizing and building healthy relationships may be helpful. Two examples are the Youth Relationships Project, which raises middle adolescents' awareness of how to identify and avoid patterns of violence unfolding in relationships (e.g., Wolfe, Wekerle, & Scott, 1997) and cooperative learning classrooms, which foster healthy relationships among school-age children (e.g., McCallum & Bracken, 1993).

Supportive relationships may be crucial to breaking the RS cycle, yet it is unclear whether finding acceptance in one relationship (e.g., with a romantic partner) can help a person overcome RS. Special consideration will need to be given the possibility that acceptance in one type of relationship (e.g., finding a supportive intimate partner) can lead to rejection in another type of relationship (e.g., parents may not approve of one's significant other).

Timing of Interventions

Early interventions often have been heralded as the best strategy for improving social, cognitive, and academic outcomes of at-risk youths (such as those targeted by Project Headstart). After an extensive review, Ramey and Ramey (1998) concluded that early academic and cognitive interventions are indeed effective. Moreover, Coie (1996) reiterated the need for early social interventions, noting the early detection of violence and antisocial behavior among adolescents (i.e., as young as age 6 or 7) and the accumulating deficits, levels of subsequent violence, and academic failure with age. Therefore, identifying and interrupting rejection sensitivity as early as possible is clearly ideal.

When intervening early is not possible, another promising opportunity to instigate change may be times of environmental or experiential change. Although our findings suggest that HRS individuals' expectations can be confirmed or self-fulfilled during transitions, Ruble's phase model of transitions (1994) additionally suggests that preexisting beliefs and expectations may be challenged during passage through new life phases. For example, expectations about the characteristics that distinguish men from women were shown to become flexible and susceptible to change during adolescents' transition to junior high school (Alfieri, Ruble, & Higgins, 1996). If such well-defined expectations of others (such as gender) can be challenged during transitions, perhaps rejection expectations also can be challenged during such periods. Why are preexisting beliefs susceptible to change during these periods? Ruble proposed three core phases of transitions: construction, consolidation, and integration. Transitions are thought to prompt a construction phase in which people actively seek information to understand changes. Information seeking continues in the consolidation phase as new conclusions about the self and others are incorporated in knowledge structures. In the final phase (integration), new conclusions are elaborated and integrated into one's identity (perhaps rigidly, if no counterinformation is subsequently received). Therefore, HRS individuals may be receptive to interventions (e.g., some of the strategies we suggested) during periods of transition, when people may be willing to redefine themselves and shed old expectations.

Summary

In sum, we have identified a number of strategies for interrupting the RS cycle. Incorporating these strategies into a broad intervention may ultimately prove fruitful. Several components of such an intervention would draw on preexisting interventions (i.e., attributional retraining, emotional competence, and antisocial behavior interventions) to target specific links in the RS cycle. Another component would be training individuals in identifying and maintaining supportive social networks. Beyond directly addressing HRS individuals' cognitions, affects, and behaviors, the intervention could consist of an outreach program targeting the individuals' social networks in the home (e.g., parents and other family members) and outside the home (e.g., peers, teachers) for education about HRS individuals' special needs. Moreover, because social norms can be such a powerful force in the acceptability of antisocial behavior (e.g., Anderson, 1994; Cohen, 1998), the intervention could include a component addressing how particular environments make individuals vulnerable to RS. Finally, and ideally, the intervention would begin in early childhood and continue through late childhood. Clearly, taking steps toward testing one or more specific components of such a broad-based intervention is an important direction for our research.

Conclusion

In this chapter, we have described how RS can be maladaptive, negatively influencing how people think, feel, and behave in different relationships. We have shown how RS can be self-fulfilling and can be carried from one type of relationship to another (e.g., from relationships with parents to relationships with romantic partners).

It is important to highlight here that all rejection-sensitive individuals are *not* the same; HRS individuals may have different kinds of expectations (anxious vs. angry) and behavioral reactions (avoidance vs. intimacy seeking), and these differences may depend on their environments (e.g., the acceptability of different expressions of frustration, their specific experiences). Moreover, the differences between LRS individuals and HRS individuals lie on a continuum.

In closing, this chapter has highlighted how some people develop heightened needs for acceptance in response to severe and prolonged forms of social rejection and how these urgent attempts to gain acceptance can undermine their success. The cycle of rejection also can have negative repercussions for those in contact with rejected individuals, as dramatically demonstrated all too often in tragic news stories, such as the school shootings in Jonesboro and Denver. Further investigations of RS may broaden our understanding of the processes underlying these consequences and may in turn contribute to our understanding of how to divert them.

References

Aber, J. L., Jones, S. M., Brown, J. L., Chaudry, N., & Samples, F. (1998). Resolving conflict creatively: Evaluating the developmental effects of a school-based violence prevention program in neighborhood and classroom context. *Development and Psychopathology, 10,* 187–213.

Adorno, T. W., Frenkel-Brunswick, E., Levinson, D. J., & Sanford, R. N. (1950). *The authoritarian personality*. New York: Harper.

Ainsworth, M., Blehar, M., Waters, E., & Wall, S. (1978). *Patterns of attachment: A psychological study of the strange situation*. Hillsdale, NJ: Erlbaum.

Alfieri, T., Ruble, D. N., & Higgins, E. T. (1996). Gender stereotypes during adolescence: Developmental changes and the transition to junior high school. *Developmental Psychology, 32,* 1129–1137.

Allport, G. W. (1954). *The nature of prejudice*. Reading, MA: Addison-Wesley.

Altemeyer, B. (1998). The other "authoritarian personality." *Advances in Experimental Social Psychology, 30,* 47–92.

Anderson, E. (1994). The code of the streets. *Atlantic Monthly,* 81–94.

Ayduk, O., & Downey, G. (1999). *Rejection sensitivity and anger in men*. Unpublished data, Columbia University.

Ayduk, O., Downey, G., & Kim, M. (in press). Rejection sensitivity and depression in women. *Personality and Social Psychology Bulletin.*

Ayduk, O., Downey, G., Testa, A., Yen, Y., & Shoda, Y. (1999). Does rejection elicit hostility in high rejection sensitive women. *Social Cognition, 17,* 245–271.

Ayduk, O., Mendoza-Denton, R., Downey, G., Mischel, W., Peake, P., & Rodriguez, M. (in press). Regulating the interpersonal self: Strategic self-regulation for coping with rejection sensitivity. *Journal of Personality and Social Psychology.*

Bagwell, C. L, Newcomb, A. F., & Bukowski, W. M. (1998). Preadolescent friendship and peer rejection as predictors of adult adjustment. *Child Development, 69,* 140–153.

Bandura, A. (1986). *Social foundations of thought and action: A social cognitive theory*. Englewood Cliffs, NJ: Prentice-Hall.

Bargh, J. A., Chaiken, S., Raymond, P., & Hymes, C. (1996). The automatic evaluation effect: Unconditional automatic attitude activation with a pronunciation task. *Journal of Experimental Social Psychology, 32,* 104–128.

Bargh, J. A., Raymond, P., Pryor, J. B., & Strack, F. (1995). Attractiveness of the underling: An automatic power → sex association and its consequences for sexual harassment and aggression. *Journal of Personality and Social Psychology, 68,* 768–781.

Bartholomew, K., & Horowitz, L. M. (1991). Attachment styles among young adults: A test of a four category model. *Journal of Social and Personality Psychology, 61,* 147–178.

Baumeister, R. F., & Leary, M. R. (1995). The need to belong: Desire for interpersonal attachments as a fundamental human motivation. *Psychological Bulletin, 117,* 497–529.

Beck, A. T., & Steer, R. A. (1987). *Manual for the Revised Beck Depression Inventory*. San Antonio, TX: Psychological Corporation.

Bolger, N., & Zuckerman, A. (1995). A framework for studying personality in the stress process. *Journal of Personality and Social Psychology, 69,* 890–902.

Bowlby, J. (1969). *Attachment and loss, Vol. 1: Attachment*. New York: Basic Books.

Bowlby, J. (1973). *Attachment and loss, Vol. 2: Separation.* New York: Basic Books.

Bowlby, J. (1980). *Attachment and loss, Vol. 3: Loss, sadness, and depression.* New York: Basic Books.

Brewer, M. B., & Brown, R. J. (1998). Intergroup relations. In D. T. Gilbert, S. T. Fiske, & G. Lindzey (Eds.), *Handbook of social psychology* (4th ed., vol. 2, pp. 554–594). New York: McGraw Hill.

Bronfenbrenner, U. (1979). *The ecology of human development: Experiments by nature and design.* Cambridge, MA: Harvard University Press.

Bryk, A. S., & Raudenbush, S. W. (1992). Toward a more appropriate conceptualization of research on school effects: A three-level hierarchical linear model. *American Journal of Education, 97,* 65–108.

Cash, T. F., Janda, L. H., Byrne, D., Murstein, B. I., Merighi, J. R, & Malloy, T. E. (1994). Interpersonal attraction. In W. A. Lesko et al. (Eds.), *Readings in social psychology: General, classic, and contemporary selection* (2nd ed., pp. 171–187). Boston: Allyn & Bacon.

Chiu, C., Hong, Y., & Dweck, C. S. (1997). Lay dispositionism, culture and implicit theories of personality. *Journal of Personality and Social Psychology, 73,* 19–30.

Cohen, D. (1998). Culture, social organization, and patterns of violence. *Journal of Personality and Social Psychology, 75,* 408–419.

Coie, J. D. (1996). Prevention of violence and antisocial behavior. In R. D. Peters, R. J. McMahon, et al. (1996). *Preventing childhood disorders, substance abuse, and delinquency. Banff international behavioral science series, Vol. 3* (pp. 1–18). Thousand Oaks, CA: Sage.

Coie, J., Terry, R., Lenox, K., Lochman, J., & Hyman, C. (1998). Childhood peer rejection and aggression as predictors of stable patterns of adolescent disorder. *Development & Psychopathology, 10,* 587–588.

Compas, B. E. (1987). Coping with stress during childhood and adolescence. *Psychological Bulletin, 101,* 393–403.

Davila, J., Burge, D., & Hammen, C. (1997). Why does attachment style change? *Journal of Personality and Social Psychology, 73,* 826–838.

Deutsch, F. M., Ruble, D. N., Fleming, A., Brooks-Gunn, J., & Stangor, C. S. (1988). Information seeking and maternal self-definition during the transition to motherhood. *Journal of Personality and Social Psychology, 55,* 420–431.

Diehl, M. (1988). Social identity and minimal groups: The effects of interpersonal and intergroup attitudinal similarity on intergroup discrimination. *British Journal of Social Psychology, 27,* 289–300.

Dodge, K. (1980). Social cognition and children's aggressive behavior. *Child Development, 51,* 162–170.

Dodge, K., Murphy, R. R., & Buchsbaum, K. (1984). The assessment of intention-cue detection skills in children: Implications for developmental psychopathology. *Child Development, 55,* 163–173.

Dodge, K., Pettit, G., McClaskey, C., & Brown, M. (1986). Social competence in children. *Monographs of the Society for Research in Child Development, 51,* 1–85.

Dodge, K., & Somberg, D. (1987). Hostile attributional biases among aggressive boys are exacerbated under conditions of threat to self. *Child Development, 58,* 213–224.

Downey, G., Bonica, C., & Rincon, C. (1999). *Harsh parenting and rejection sensitivity: A longitudinal study.* Unpublished data, Columbia University.

Downey, G., & Feldman, S. (1996). Implications of rejection sensitivity for intimate relationships. *Journal of Personality and Social Psychology, 70,* 1327–43.

Downey, G., Feldman, S., & Ayduk, O. (2000). Rejection sensitivity and male violence in romantic relationships. *Personal Relationships, 7,* 45–61.

Downey, G., Freitas, A. L., Michealis, B., & Khouri, H. (1998). The self-fulfilling prophecy in close relationships: Do rejection sensitive women get rejected by romantic partners? *Journal of Personality and Social Psychology, 75,* 545–560.

Downey, G., Khouri, H., & Feldman, S. (1997). Early interpersonal trauma and later adjustment: The mediational role of rejection sensitivity. In D. Cicchetti, S. L. Toth, et al. (Eds.), *Developmental perspectives on trauma: Theory, research, and intervention. Rochester symposium on developmental psychology, Vol. 8* (pp. 85–114). Rochester, NY: University of Rochester Press.

Downey, G., Lebolt, A., Rincon, C., & Freitas, A. L. (1998). Rejection sensitivity and children's interpersonal difficulties. *Child Development, 69,* 1072–1089.

Dutton, D. G. (1988). *The domestic assault of women: Psychological and criminal justice perspectives.* Boston: Allyn & Bacon.

Eccles, J. S., & Midgely, C. (1990). Changes in academic motivation and self-perception during adolescence. In R. Montemayor, G. Adams, & T. Gullotta (Eds.), *From childhood to adolescence: A transitional period?* (pp. 134–155). Newbury Park, CA: Sage.

Egeland, B., Jacobvitz, D., & Sroufe, L. A. (1988). Breaking the cycle of abuse. *Child Development, 59,* 1080–1088.

Elder, G. H., & Clipp, E. C. (1988). Wartime losses and social bonding: Influences across 40 years in men's lives. *Psychiatry, 51,* 177–198.

Erikson, E. H. (1968). *Identity: Youth and crisis.* New York: Norton.

Ethier, K. A., & Deaux, K. (1994). Negotiating social identity when contexts change: Maintaining identification and responding to threat. *Journal of Personality and Social Psychology, 67,* 243–251.

Eysenck, H. J., & Eysenck, S. B. G. (1964). *Manual of the Eysenck Personality Inventory.* San Diego: Educational and Industrial Testing Service.

Fein, S., & Spencer, S. J. (1997). Prejudice as self-image maintenance: Affirming the self through derogating others. *Journal of Personality and Social Psychology, 73,* 31–44.

Feldman, S., & Downey, G. (1994). Rejection sensitivity as a mediator of the impact of childhood exposure to family violence on adult attachment behavior. *Development and Psychopathology, 6,* 231–247.

Festinger, L. (1954). A theory of social comparison processes. *Human Relations, 7,* 117–140.

Freud, S. (1936). *The ego and the mechanisms of defense* (C. Baines, Trans.). New York: International Universities Press.

Ginsberg, B. G. (1997). *Relationship enhancement family therapy.* New York: Wiley.

Goodwin, J. S., Hunt, W. C., Key, C. R., & Samet, J. M. (1987). The effect of marital status on stage, treatment, and survival of cancer patients. *Journal of American Medical Association, 258,* 3125–3130.

Gottman, J. M. (1979). Detecting cyclicity in social interaction. *Psychological Bulletin, 86,* 338–348.

Graham, S., & Folkes, V. S. (Eds.). (1990). *Attribution theory: Applications to achievement, mental health, and interpersonal conflict.* Hillsdale, NJ: Lawrence Erlbaum.

Greenberg, M. T., Kusche, C. A., Cook, E. T., & Quamma, J. P. (1995). Promoting emotional competence in school-aged children: The effects of the PATHS curriculum. *Development and Psychopathology, 7,* 117–136.

Hallinan, M. T., & Williams, R. A. (1987). The stability of students' interracial friendships. *American Sociological Review, 52,* 653–664.

Hamilton, D. L., & Sherman, S. J. (1996). Perceiving persons and groups. *Psychological Review, 103,* 336–355.

Hamm, M. S. (1993). *American skinheads: The criminology and control of hate crime.* Westport, CT: Praeger.

Hammen, C. L., Burge, D., Daley, S. E., & Davila, J. (1995). Interpersonal attachment cognitions and prediction of symptomatic responses to interpersonal stress. *Journal of Abnormal Psychology, 104,* 436–443.

Hardin, C. D., & Higgins, E. T. (1996). Shared reality: How social verification makes the subjective objective. In R. M. Sorrentino, E. T. Higgins, et al. (Eds.), *The interpersonal context. Handbook of motivation and cognition* (pp. 28–84). New York: Guilford Press.

Hautaluoma, J. E., Enge, R. S., Mitchell, T. M., & Rittwager, F. J. (1991). Early socialization into a work group: Severity of initiations revisited. *Journal of Social Behavior and Personality, 6,* 725–748.

Hazan, C., & Shaver, P. (1987). Romantic love conceptualized as an attachment process. *Journal of Personality and Social Psychology, 52,* 511–524.

Hecht, D. B., Inderbitzen, H. M., & Bukowski, A. L. (1998). The relationship between peer status and depressive symptoms in children and adolescents. *Journal of Abnormal Child Psychology, 26,* 153–160.

Hogg, M., & Abrams, D. (1993). Towards a single process uncertainty-reduction model of social motivation in groups. In M. A. Hogg & D. Abrams (Eds.), *Group motivation* (pp. 173–190). New York: Harvester Wheatsheaf.

Holtzworth-Munroe, A., & Anglin, K. (1991). The competency of responses given by maritally violent versus nonviolent men to problematic marital situations. *Violence and Victims, 6,* 257–269.

Holtzworth-Munroe, A., & Hutchinson, G. (1993). Attributing negative intent to wife behavior: The attributions of maritally violent versus nonviolent men. *Journal of Abnormal Psychology, 102,* 206–211.

Hormuth, S. E. (1990). *The ecology of the self: Relocation and self-concept change.* Cambridge: Cambridge University Press.

Horney, K. (1937). *The neurotic personality of our time.* New York: Norton.

Hoyle, R. K., & Crawford, A. M. (1994). Use of individual-level data to investigate group phenomena: Issues and strategies. *Small Group Research,* *25,* 464–485.

Hudley, C., & Graham, S. (1993). An attributional intervention to reduce peer-directed aggression among African American boys. *Child Development,* *64,* 124–138.

Huesmann, L. R., Maxwell, C. D., Eron, L., Dahlberg, L. L., Guerra, N. G., Tolan, P. H., VanAcker, R., & Henry, D. (1996). Evaluating a cognitive/ecological program for the prevention of aggression among urban youth. *American Journal of Preventive Medicine, 12*(5 suppl), 120–128.

Jack, D. C. (1991). *Silencing the self: Women and depression.* Cambridge, MA: Harvard University Press.

Janoff-Bulman, R., & Brickman, P. (1982). Expectations and what people learn form failure. In N. T. Feather (Ed.), *Expectations and actions: Expectancy-value models in psychology* (pp. 207–237).). Hillsdale, NJ: Erlbaum.

Jussim, L. (1986). Self-fulfilling prophecies: A theoretical and integrative review, *Psychological Review, 93,* 425–445.

Kenny, D. A., Kashy, D., & Bolger, N. (1998). Data analysis in social psychology. In D. Gilbert, S. Fiske, & G. Lindzey (Eds.), *Handbook of social psychology* (4th ed., pp. 233–268). New York: McGraw Hill.

King, S. A., & Morreggi, D. (1998). Internet therapy and self help groups: The pros and cons. In J. Gackenbach et al. (Ed.), *Psychology and the internet: Intrapersonal, interpersonal, and transpersonal implications* (pp. 77–109). San Diego: Academic Press.

Krohne, H. W., & Fuchs, J. (1991). Influence of coping dispositions and danger-related information on emotional and coping reactions of individuals anticipating an aversive event. In C. D. Speileberger, I. G. Sarason, J. Strelau, & J. M. T. Brebner (Eds.), *Stress and anxiety, Vol. 13. The series in clinical psychology and the series in clinical and community psychology* (pp. 131–155). New York: Hemisphere.

Labi, N. (April, 1998). The hunter and the choirboy. *Time,* 151.

Lang, P. J. (1995). The emotional probe. *American Psychologist, 50,* 372–385.

Leary, M. (1990). Responses to social exclusion: Social anxiety, jealousy, loneliness, depression, and low self-esteem. *Journal of Social and Clinical Psychology, 9,* 221–229.

Levy, M. B., & Davis, K. (1988). Lovestyles and attachment styles compared: Their relations to each other and to various relationship characteristics. *Journal of Social and Personal Relationships, 5,* 439–471.

Levy, S. R., & Dweck, C. S. (1998). Trait- versus process-focused social judgment. *Social Cognition, 16,* 151–172.

Levy, S. R., & Dweck, C. S. (1999). The impact of children's static vs. dynamic conceptions of people on stereotype formation. *Child Development, 70,* 1163–1180.

Levy, S. R., Eccleston, C., Mendoza-Denton, R., & Downey, G. (1999). *Rejection sensitivity in group processes.* Unpublished manuscript.

Levy, S. R., Stroessner, S. J., & Dweck, C. S. (1998). Stereotype formation and endorsement: The role of implicit theories. *Journal of Personality and Social Psychology, 74,* 1421–1436.

Lewin, K. (1947). Group decision and social change. In T. M. Newcomb &

E. L. Hartley (Eds.), *Readings in social psychology* (pp. 330–344). New York: Holt.

Lynch, J. J. (1979). *The broken heart: The medical consequences of loneliness.* New York: Basic Books.

Maslow, A. H. (1962). *Toward a psychology of being.* New York: Van Nostrand.

McCallum, R. S., & Bracken, B. A. (1993). Interpersonal relations between school children and their peers, parents, and teachers. *Educational Psychology Review, 5,* 155–176.

McConnell, A., Sherman, J. W., & Hamilton, D. L. (1997). Target entitativity: Implications for information processing about individual and group targets. *Journal of Personality and Social Psychology, 72,* 750–762.

McKenna, K., & Bargh, J. (1998). Coming out in the age of the internet: Identity "de-marginalization" through virtual group participation. *Journal of Personality and Social Psychology, 75,* 681–694.

Merton, R. K. (1948). The self-fulfilling prophecy. *Antioch Review, 8,* 193–210.

Mischel, W., & Shoda, Y. (1995). A cognitive-affective system theory of personality: Reconceptualizing situations, dispositions, dynamics, and invariance in personality structures. *Psychological Review,* 246–268.

Moreland, R. L., & Zajonc, R. B. (1982). Exposure effects in person perception: Familiarity, similarity, and attraction. *Journal of Experimental Social Psychology, 18,* 395–415.

Neeman, K., & Harter, S. (1984). *The self-perception profile for college students.* Unpublished manuscript, University of Denver.

Osbeck, L. M., Moghaddam, F. M., & Perreault, S. (1997). Similarity and attraction among majority and minority groups in a multicultural context. *International Journal of Intercultural Relations, 21,* 113–123.

Parks, M. R., & Floyd, K. (1996). Making friends in cyberspace. *Journal of Communication, 46,* 80–97.

Parks, M. R., & Roberts, L. D. (1998). "Making MOOsic": The development of personal relationships on line and a comparison to their off line counterparts. *Journal of Social and Personal Relationships, 15,* 517–537.

Patterson, C., Cohn, D., & Kao, B. (1989). Maternal warmth as a protective factor against risks associated with peer rejection among children. *Development and Psychopathology, 1,* 21–38.

Purdie, V., & Downey, G. (in press). Rejection sensitivity: A psychological legacy of victimization that places adolescent girls at risk in romantic relationships. *Child Maltreatment.*

Quinton, D., Rutter, M., & Liddle, C. (1984). Institutional rearing, parenting difficulties, and marital support. *Psychological Medicine, 14,* 107–24.

Ramey, C. T., & Ramey S. L. (1998). Early intervention and early experience. *American Psychologist, 53,* 109–120.

Rosenberg, M. (1979). *Conceiving the self.* New York: Basic Books.

Rothberg, J. M., & Jones, F. D. (1987). Suicide in the U.S. Army: Epidemiological and periodic aspects. *Suicide and Life-Threatening Behavior, 17,* 119–132.

Ruble, D. N. (1994). A phase model of transitions: Cognitive and motivational consequences. *Advances in Experimental Social Psychology, 26,* 163–214.

Ruble, D. N., Fleming, A. S., Hackel, L., & Stangor, C. S. (1988). Changes in the marital relationship during the transition to motherhood: Effects of violated expectations concerning division of household labor. *Journal of Personality and Social Psychology, 55*, 78–87.

Rudolph, K. D., Hammen, C., & Burge, D. (1997). A cognitive-interpersonal approach to depressive symptoms in preadolescent children. *Journal of Abnormal Child Psychology, 25*, 33–45.

Schaller, M., Asp, C., Rosell, M. C., & Heim, S. J. (1996). Training in statistical reasoning inhibits the formation of erroneous group stereotypes. *Personality and Social Psychology Bulletin, 22*, 829–844.

Schwartz, D., McFadyen-Ketchum, S. A., Dodge, K. A, Pettit, G. S., & Bates, J. E. (1998). Peer group victimization as a predictor of children's behavior problems at home and in school. *Development and Psychopathology, 10*, 87–99.

Shah, J. Y., Kruglanski, A. W., & Thompson, E. P. (1998). Membership has its (epistemic) rewards: Need for closure effects on in-group bias. *Journal of Personality and Social Psychology, 75*, 383–393.

Simmons, R. G., Rosenberg, F., & Rosenberg, M. (1973). Disturbance in the self-image at adolescence. *American Sociological Review, 38*, 553–568.

Sroufe, L. A. (1990). An organizational perspective on the self. In D. Cicchetti & M. Beeghly (Eds.), *The self in transition: Infancy to childhood, The John D. and Catherine T. MacArthur Foundation series on mental health and development.* (pp. 281–307). Chicago: University of Chicago Press.

Straus, M. A. (1979). Measuring intrafamily conflict and violence: The Conflict Tactics (CT) Scale. *Journal of Marriage and the Family, 41*, 75–88.

Sullivan, H. S. (1953). *The interpersonal theory of psychiatry.* New York: Norton.

Trout, D. L. (1980). The role of social isolation in suicide. *Suicide and Life-Threatening Behavior, 10*, 10–23.

Walker, L. E. (1979). *The battered woman.* New York: Harper & Row.

Walker, L. E. (1984). *The battered woman syndrome.* New York: Springer.

Wang, A. Y. (1994). Pride and prejudice in high school gangs. *Adolescence, 29*, 281–291.

Watson, D., & Friend, R. (1969). Measurement of social-evaluative anxiety. *Journal of Consulting and Clinical Psychology, 33*, 448–457.

Weiss, R. L., & Summers, K. (1983). Marital interaction coding system III. In E. Filsinger (Ed.), *Marriage and family assessment* (pp. 35–115). Beverly Hills, CA: Sage.

Weissberg, R. B., Caplan, M. Z., & Bennetto, L. (1988). *The Yale-New Haven middle-school social problem solving (SPS) program.* New Haven, CT: Yale University.

Weisz, C., & Jones, E. E. (1993). Expectancy disconfirmation and dispositional inference: Latent strength of target-based and category-based expectations, *Personality and Social Psychology Bulletin, 19*, 563–573.

Wolfe, D. A., Wekerle, C., & Scott, K. (1997). *Alternatives to violence: Empowering young youth to develop healthy relationships.* Thousand Oaks, CA: Sage.

11

Individual Differences in Reactions to Rejection

KRISTINE M. KELLY

Close, relatively enduring personal relationships are a fundamental part of human life. People spend most of their daily lives in the presence of and interacting with important others (Larson, Csikszentmihalyi, & Graef, 1982). Even when alone, individuals spend much of their time thinking about significant others. Plentiful empirical evidence has demonstrated that the status and quality of these close personal ties predict health and personal adjustment. Indeed, physical and psychological well-being are strongly related to the perception of being part of a social network in which one feels needed and respected and from which one may receive help, comfort, information, and advice (Sarason & Sarason, 1985). Individuals who lack satisfying relationships with other people are much more susceptible to stress and stress-induced physical illness (Cobb, 1976), psychopathology (Hamachek, 1992), eating disorders (Schmidt, Tiller, & Morgan, 1995), fatal heart attacks (Lynch, 1979), posttraumatic stress disorder (Hobfall & London, 1986), and suicide (Holmes, Mateczun, Lall, & Wilcove, 1998) than those who are integrated in a rich network of receptive, attentive others. Furthermore, people are more likely to die as a result of serious illnesses or other personal misfortunes if they have relatively few social ties (Hazuda, 1994; Orth-Gomer, 1994).

These investigations suggest that people who lack a supportive network of friends and relatives are vulnerable to a host of psychological and physical problems because they lack something essential available only through interpersonal relationships. In fact, interpersonal involvement is seemingly so necessary for human well-being that some researchers have proposed that humans possess an evolved psychological mechanism that motivates them to seek and maintain a minimum quantity of lasting, positive, and meaningful personal relationships with other people and to resist the dissolution of existing relationships (Baumeister & Leary, 1995). One of the major catalysts driving much of human behavior is likely this desire to be interpersonally connected with others.

Precisely because close interpersonal relationships are so important, events that threaten their continuation are among the most traumatic in people's lives. The termination of an intimate relationship, through death, divorce, and other means, is widely regarded as the most stressful event one can experience (Holmes & Rahe, 1967; Weiss, 1974). Although distress understandably arises as a result of ending a marriage or a friendship or losing one's job, considerable anxiety follows when one's connection with *any* social group or personal relationship is severed or when one does not feel accepted by a particular person or group (Baumeister & Leary, 1995). Indeed, the breakdown of both intimate and relatively superficial relationships appears to exact significant cognitive and emotional consequences.

Although everyone is subject to powerful negative emotions following social exclusions, a substantial body of research shows that individuals react to real and perceived rejection differently. Some people seem relatively unaffected by threats to their inclusion status, whereas others are hypervigilant to criticism, have a low threshold for disapproval, and are likely to feel rejected across a variety of situations. These people, in turn, respond in varying ways to rejection, from mild irritation to raging anger and violent behaviors. The popular media have increasingly reported incidents of violence following rejection events, such as being fired from a job, denied a promotion, or spurned by a romantic partner. In 1998, two boys opened fire on their gradeschool classmates and teachers in Jonesboro, Arkansas, killing five and wounding ten. One explanation offered for their behavior was that one of the boys was upset after being rejected by a girl (Gegax, Adler, & Pedersen, 1998).

Fortunately, most people do not respond to rejection as maliciously as these individuals did. However, the brutal nature of such incidents compels an examination of the reasons for differing reactions to rejection. In the last decade, a number of writers have called for research examining the role of individual differences in reactions to real or perceived rejection (e.g., Jones, 1990). In response, psychologists and other behavioral scientists have recently begun to study people's perceptions of and reactions to interpersonal difficulties such as social rejection, ostracism, unrequited love, and the "silent treatment." One purpose of this chapter is to review such studies to identify the emotional, behavioral, and cognitive factors associated with social rejection. These studies provide evidence of what it is like to feel rejected as well as indirect evidence of predisposing factors causing rejection. A second purpose is to examine the characteristics that exacerbate or ameliorate one's reactions to rejection.

The chapter contains three sections. The first briefly discusses the nature of rejection, that is, the kinds of incidents that evoke feelings of rejection, and also examines a few of the precursors of rejection and exclusion. The second section presents research on behaviors and psychological processes that result from rejection experiences. The last section explores the underlying traits associated with negative responses to rejection as well as the duration of such responses.

Characterizing Interpersonal Rejection

Facing rejection is one of the risks of becoming intimately involved in a personal relationship. The mere possibility of rejection may make blind dates, applications for graduate school and jobs, and efforts to obtain membership in sororities, fraternities, and other organizations anxiety-provoking. The potential for rejection invariably associated with these events creates tension in the initial stages of a relationship. Of course, rejection can, and often does, occur once relationships are established.

To investigate the relational context of perceived rejection, I recently asked approximately 100 undergraduate students to briefly describe a situation that resulted in their feeling rejected. A sample of some prototypical responses follows:

> I was in love with this guy. But the week after I stayed the night with him, he totally dissed me for some ugly, mean girl.

> On Valentine's Day I bought a box of chocolates and a dozen long-stemmed roses and gave them to a woman when I asked her to go out with me. She said, "No."

> My sister's boyfriend and I got into an argument, and my sister took his side. Even though my sister and I had always been close, I haven't spoken to her in over a month.

> After I graduated from high school I wanted to go into the Navy. I took the military requirement exam and was informed that I did not pass. The worst part was that the test was not that hard.

> I tried out for the cheerleading squad and didn't make it.

> My best friend and I made plans to go on a trip and then she went with someone else instead.

As shown in these narratives, when people are asked to recall a time when they felt rejected, they typically report incidents of betrayal in romantic or other close relationships, spurning by a potential romantic partner, or being denied admittance to a desired organization or group.

Additionally, most instances of social rejection contain a common element: violations of the individual's expectations. People's expectations when entering into or continuing an existing relationship generally include being liked by others, having interpersonal power, and having attentive and supportive relational partners. After all, people would have little reason to form interpersonal ties with other individuals or groups if the relationship did not hold some potential for acceptance and at least occasional happiness and satisfaction. These expectations may not be overtly conveyed to others, and their logic depends on the situation. The experience of being excluded, ignored, or spurned is strongly felt because it typically takes one by surprise. One's expectations about the type and amount of attention that one should receive in a social interaction are not fulfilled.

Investigators have consistently found that people are affected much more strongly by negative experiences than they are by positive experiences. For example, people tend to remember more accurately messages that have negative content than positive content (Fiske, 1982) and are influenced more by negative interaction styles than by positive ones and by negative voice tones than by positive voice tones (Adams & Moore, 1996; Gottman, 1979; Levenson & Gottman, 1983). One explanation is that most people expect positive outcomes in their lives (Fischoff, Slovic, & Lichtenstein, 1977; Kahneman & Tversky, 1979; Swann, Hixon, Stein-Seroussi, & Gilbert, 1990; Swann & Read, 1981). Indeed, the daily lives of most people are not characterized by a constant bombardment of negative events. Thus, when negative events do occur, they stand out against the background of relative positivity, are attended to more directly, and thereby become more salient than the expected positive outcomes.

Researchers who have examined the specific effects of expectancy violations (e.g., Burgoon & Hale, 1988; Jussim, Fleming, Coleman, & Kohberger, 1996) have discovered that the discrepant behavior of others tends to elicit extreme judgments in the direction of the expectancy violation. As applied to rejection situations, this finding suggests that when an individual assesses a particular situation and concludes that the odds favor his or her acceptance, a negative violation of this expectation (rejection) causes feelings of distress. The greater the violation and the greater the importance of the rejection to one's self-image, the greater the uncomfortable psychological arousal (Rosen, Mickler, & Spiers, 1985).

The breaching of expectations is a two-way street. As I said, distress following a rejection experience may derive partly from violation of certain expectations. However, violation of expectations may also be a primary reason for being rejected in the first place. Investigations into such topics as sexual behavior (Morris, 1965), aggression, submissiveness, and isolation (French, 1988; Parkhurst & Asher, 1992), depression (Strack & Coyne, 1983), and relationship dissatisfaction (Downey, Freitas, Michaelis & Khouri, 1998) have demonstrated that individuals perceived as "different" are more likely than conforming individuals to be identified as deviant and punished by social exclusion, including physical ridicule, spatial separation, and interpersonal ostracism.

Clearly, failure to conform to the expectations of others can lead to social exclusion (Schachter, 1959), as demonstrated in one study in which grade-school students were asked to convey their reasons for rejecting a fellow student across five situations (e.g., not selecting the student as a representative, not playing with the student). Participants (67%–84%) reported that social deviance (e.g., abuses others, is quarrelsome, shirks work, cannot talk to others) was the strongest factor responsible for rejecting their peers (Bhojak & Mehta, 1970).

In another interesting illustration, Dexter and Jordan (1988) related that Victorian children who disobeyed their parents were "put into Coventry."

For a prescribed time everyone ignored them. In interviews after they had become adults, many of them said they would rather have endured a physical beating. Even today people labeled as deviant or nonconforming—in other words, those who violate the expectations of others—find themselves marginalized and prevented from engaging in some forms of social participation (Freilich, 1991). Individuals who violate locally defined expectations may thus be discriminated against and may have a lower chance of finding mates and reproducing (Cavalli-Sforza & Feldman, 1981). Indeed, disobeying social etiquette adversely affects romantic attractiveness, competence, trustworthiness, and quality of social interactions (Wenegrat, Castillo-Yee, & Abrams, 1996). Of course, violation of social standards is only one reason why people are shunned and rejected, but it appears to be among the most common.

Reactions to Rejection

A number of studies have found that social disapproval, exclusion, and ostracism strongly predict powerful psychological distress. The sense of being rejected has been implicated in the experience of anger, irritation, unhappiness, disappointment, jealousy, hurt feelings, low self-esteem, loneliness, jealousy, social anxiety, and depression (Asher, Parkhurst, Hymel, & Williams, 1990; Kupersmidt & Patterson, 1991; Leary, Springer, Negel, Ansell, & Evans, 1998; Maccoby & Martin, 1983; Pearson, Kelly, & Ryan, 1998; Yurak, LoSchiavo, & Kerrigan, 1999). Furthermore, these affective consequences tend to covary. For example, people feel anxious when they face the possibility of losing important relationships, depressed when existing relationships end, and lonely when they lack satisfying connections with other people (Leary, 1990; Leary & Downs, 1995; Tambor & Leary, 1993).

In this section, studies are categorized on the basis of their emphasis on self-esteem, loneliness, jealousy, social anxiety, and depression as reactions to rejection because these factors have received the most attention in the literature. Although many studies examined multiple reactions to rejection, I will discuss their results pertaining to the various responses separately to preserve the flow of the review. After examining affective responses, I will turn to cognitive and behavioral reactions to rejection.

Self-Esteem

A considerable number of studies have shown that state self-esteem is strongly related to the degree to which an individual feels included and accepted by other people. Lowered self-esteem has been associated with the experience of being ridiculed (Carlton-Ford, Miller, Nealeigh, & Sanchez, 1997), internalizing negative feedback from others (Kernis, Cornell, Sun,

Berry, & Harlow, 1993), parental rejection (Litovsky & Dusek, 1985; Morvitz & Motta, 1992), exclusion by peers (Eskilson, Wiley, Meuhlhauer, & Dodder, 1986), insecure relations with others, and estrangement from one's partner (Brennan & Bosson, 1998).

One line of research has proposed that self-esteem functions as a "sociometer," a cognitive-affective gauge that monitors the social environment for cues indicating disapproval, rejection, or exclusion (Leary & Downs, 1995; Leary, Tambor, Terdal, & Downs, 1995). The sociometer theory suggests that level of self-esteem depends on one's previous experiences of inclusion or exclusion. People who are frequently ignored, avoided, or rejected develop lower self-esteem than those who repeatedly experience social inclusion. Further, low trait self-esteem not only indicates a history of rejection but also represents one's lack of confidence that he or she will, in the future, be accepted by others.

Many studies have supported the sociometer model, and the causal link between rejection and self-esteem has been tested in a number of ways. Some researchers have focused on the effects of rejection imagery on self-ratings, whereas others have placed research participants in real rejection situations in the laboratory. Tambor and Leary (1993) asked participants to read scenarios that depicted them in hypothetical social situations where they were included or rejected by other people. Across all the scenarios, participants reported that rejection greatly lowered their self-esteem. Wilcox and Mitchell (1977) obtained similar results. In their study, subjects evaluated themselves before and after imagining being aboard a lifeboat or being ejected from the lifeboat for lack of room. Comparisons of self-esteem for accepted and rejected individuals showed negative changes only for the rejected subjects.

In one of the earliest experiments designed to examine the effects of actual rejection on self-evaluation, Pepitone and Wilpizeski (1960) had one participant and two confederates discuss their views on a controversial topic for 15 minutes. The confederates took the opposing position for half the participants (rejection condition) and agreed with the position of the remaining participants (inclusion condition). After the conversation, participants felt worse about themselves after rejection than inclusion.

In a more recent laboratory experiment, Leary et al. (1995) informed subjects that they were either included or excluded from a work group based on either the preferences of the other group members or random assignment. Those who thought the group had purposely rejected them subsequently evaluated themselves much more negatively than the participants who had been randomly excluded or included by choice.

In summary, self-esteem is a construct closely associated with feeling satisfied with the interpersonal aspects of one's life. Further, self-esteem may operate as a sociometer that monitors the environment for signs of impending rejection. High self-esteem has been directly related to relational fulfillment and closeness with family and friends. Low self-esteem is associated with relational problems, especially feeling ignored or unaccepted.

Loneliness

Social rejection also has an impact on loneliness. Studies have shown that lonely individuals tend to be dissatisfied with their social and intimate relationships, even though they spend just as much time interacting with others as nonlonely people do (Jones, Carpenter, & Quintana, 1985). Loneliness is associated with inhibited social interactions in that, compared to nonlonely people, lonely people are less sociable and less friendly with their interaction partners. Consequently, others often view them as socially deviant (Sloan & Solano, 1984) and may exclude them.

Although the nature of the causal relationship between rejection and loneliness has not been fully determined, Jones and Carpenter (1986) reported indirect evidence that repeated rejection can produce loneliness. Other studies that have asked subjects to imagine themselves in various social situations also found that feeling rejected elicited loneliness. Subjects who imagined that they were unable to find dating partners or make friends or that they were being ignored by others felt more lonely than those who imagined being included (Craighead, Kimball, & Rehak, 1979; Tambor & Leary, 1993).

In a laboratory experiment that more directly examined the link between rejection and loneliness, Geller, Goodstein, Silver, and Sternberg (1974) instructed female subjects to engage in a conversation with two confederates. The confederates ignored some women for 10 minutes, and others participated in a normal conversation. A larger percentage of women who were ignored than those who were not ignored said that they felt "alone" and "withdrawn."

Much of the available information on the development of loneliness has come from research on children and adolescents. Investigators often use peer nominations to assess students' sociometric status, that is, the popularity of each student with his or her classmates. Plentiful evidence suggests that rejected students report the highest level of loneliness, social dissatisfaction, and worry of any group of students (Asher & Wheeler, 1985; Boivin, Poulin, & Vitaro, 1994; Parkhurst & Asher, 1992). In a longitudinal study designed to predict loneliness one year after obtaining sociometric peer nominations, Boivin, Hymel, and Bukowski (1995) found that increased loneliness over the year was associated with a decrease in peer status (i.e., being less liked by peers). Furthermore, lonely children at time 2 had experienced more rejection initially and had become more rejected over the year. These results point to one of the difficulties in precisely describing reactions to rejection: rejection often results in interpersonal deficiencies, such as social withdrawal and loneliness, which are often interpreted by others as unfriendliness or arrogance. These perceptions, in turn, cause others to reject the lonely individual even more, which intensifies the loneliness, and on and on.

Social Anxiety

Social anxiety and its role in interpersonal relationships have also received regular attention in the social rejection literature. In fact, one theoretical treatment asserts that anxiety results from actual or threatened exclusion from important social groups (Baumeister & Tice, 1990) or even from general society. Social exclusion theory proposes that because humans cannot survive and reproduce outside a group environment, anxiety evolved as a reaction to real or even potential exclusion. The negative affect that characterizes anxiety activates certain cognitions that prompt a person to terminate the undesirable behavior and engage in other behaviors more likely to result in acceptance and inclusion. Further, through experiencing anxiety, individuals learn which actions are associated with rejection (such as appearing unattractive or performing incompetently at work) and avoid them. This interpersonal threat may explain why people often feel uncomfortable when others, even perfect strangers, consider them overweight; if perceived by others as an undesirable social participant, one runs the risk of potential exclusion (Leary, 1990). Berman, Berman, Heymsfield, Fauci, and Ackerman (1992) found that, in a sample of obese individuals, extreme concern with appearance and high sensitivity to rejection were reported or observed frequently during interviews.

Empirical data support exclusion theory and the direct link between rejection and anxiety. For example, Tambor and Leary (1993) constructed scenarios that depicted two situations in which an individual is socially evaluated: a party and a first date. After reading the scenarios and imagining that they had been either included or excluded by the other people in the situation, rejected subjects reported far more anxiety than included subjects.

In another study (Zeidner, 1994), college students were assessed immediately before a final exam period to predict state anxiety under evaluative conditions that presumably implied the possibility of rejection (a poor grade). Results indicated that one of the best predictors of anxiety was concern about social evaluation. However, social evaluative trait anxiety failed to predict state anxiety under nonevaluative conditions.

In Geller et al.'s (1974) study in which women were either ignored or included in a conversation with two confederates, 41% of the ignored women indicated that they had felt "anxious" during the conversation, as opposed to only 15% of the included women. Finally, in a study that examined social anxiety and cardiovascular reactivity in stressful situations, Burns (1995) found that men who had elevated anxiety exhibited the largest diastolic blood pressure increases while their reaction-time abilities were being critiqued by a confederate.

In brief, numerous studies have demonstrated that feeling rejected or excluded leads to social anxiety. Social anxiety has been produced by rejecting participants in laboratory studies as well as in studies asking them to merely imagine themselves being excluded. The results were similar whether anxiety was assessed via self-report or physiological measures.

Depression

Interpersonal rejection may not be the only reason why people feel depressed, but it is certainly one important source. Much of the research devoted to understanding the sources of depression has focused on threats to one's inclusion status, such as divorce, death of a loved one, losing one's job, moving to a new city, and so on. Several studies testify to the connection between social rejection and depression. Tambor and Leary (1993) found that depression is inversely related to the degree one feels accepted or included. Similarly, in a sample of preadolescent girls, Kupersmidt and Patterson (1991) showed that low peer acceptance was the sole predictor of depression. Finally, in observations of children who had moved to a new school, Panak and Garber (1992) found that the children's perceptions of their social acceptance predicted depressive symptoms one year later.

Jealousy

A few studies have attempted to connect social rejection and jealousy. One study (Peretti & Pudowski, 1997) showed that, for college men, jealousy in romantic dating relationships was associated with feelings of rejection and loss of affection, but this effect was different for women. For college women, jealousy was associated with feelings of low self-esteem and inadequacy (which, as has been shown, are peripherally indicative of rejection).

Mathes, Adams, and Davies (1985) presented men and women with hypothetical situations depicting termination of one's romantic relationship for various reasons. For example, in one scenario the participants imagined that their partner fell in love with someone else and ended their relationship. Participants reported feeling greater levels of jealousy under circumstances when they were rejected due to a rival than in any other relationship loss situation. Thus, jealousy appears to ensue specifically from rejection that results from the presence of a third party.

Cognitive Responses

Rejection appears to have important effects on an individual's cognitive processes. Numerous studies have identified cognitive factors that characterize reactions to rejection, such as explanations to account for the rejection, particularly if it is unexpected. These explanations usually involve attributing the cause of rejection to characteristics of the rejecting person(s), to one's own inadequacies, or to circumstances in the environment (Kelley, 1973).

A body of research has revealed that rejection leads to attributions of responsibility regarding the self and the rejecting others. For instance, rejected persons feel that others dislike them and do not value their opinions (Pepitone & Wilpizeski, 1960), attribute their rejection to the negative characteristics or personality of the other people in the situation (Cheuk & Rosen, 1994; Rosen, Mickler, & Collins, 1987), and feel as though they have little control of events causing their rejection (Toner & Munro, 1996). Other work has shown that, when compared to people who feel welcomed and included in a group, rejected individuals report liking the other people in the group less (Pepitone & Wilpizeski, 1960), specifically rating them as less friendly, attractive, considerate, intelligent, cooperative, and kind (Kelly, 1999). They also evaluate them as less competent (Rosen, Mickler, & Spiers, 1986) and express a stronger desire to avoid future contact with them (Cheuk & Rosen, 1994; Rosen, Mickler, & Collins, 1987).

A study by Snoek (1962) suggests that the type and the intensity of the rejection also differentially affect cognitive processes. Specifically, personal rejection elicited less liking for the rejecting group than nonpersonal rejection, and participants' willingness to join a different group was greater after strong rather than after mild rejection. A study by Geller et al. (1974) examined the attributions of participants who had been ignored for 10 minutes by two confederates. External attributions were made by 76% of the subjects, whereas only 24% attributed their rejection to something about themselves. Other findings suggest that individuals evaluate others the most negatively after being rejected and most positively after being included or accepted (Bennett & Dewberry, 1994; Rosen, Mickler, & Collins, 1987).

Behavioral Correlates

In one of the few extensive analyses of the behavioral consequences of rejection, Williams and Sommer (1997) identified several prototypical behaviors of individuals rejected in the laboratory. In their experiment, participants were either included or excluded by two confederates in a ball-tossing game. Rejected participants initially attempted to engage the confederates by smiling and looking at them. When such behaviors did not result in inclusion, they typically looked around, frowned, and finally withdrew from the interaction. Some participants initiated other behaviors such as studying, balancing their checkbooks, or looking in their wallets (Williams & Zadro, chapter 2, this volume).

Other laboratory studies have demonstrated that a person engages in more yielding behaviors following rejection than inclusion. Individuals who were negotiating with others over a computer network tended to decrease their requests for profit following rejection and to increase their requests following inclusion (Thye, Lovaglia, & Markovsky, 1997). In other words, conciliatory behavior was more likely after exclusion, and aggressive behavior was more likely after inclusion. Later, when they could monetarily reward a person with whom they had interacted, ignored participants gave the other person significantly less money than did the included participants (Geller et al., 1974). These results suggest that rejection experiences may be associated with passive-aggressive behavior. The rejecting interaction elicited a conservative response, followed by spiteful behavior when the rejected persons controlled the allocation of resources.

Other research has examined behavioral consequences of rejection in children, adolescents, and adults under naturalistic circumstances. Compared with their nonrejected peers, rejected individuals tend to be more aggressive and disruptive (e.g., starting fights and insulting others), less prosocial (e.g., not sharing with or helping others), more restless, explosive, bossy, unhappy, immature, socially isolated, and oversensitive (Attili, Vermigli, & Schneider, 1997; Bierman & Wargo, 1995; Cantrell & Prinz, 1985; Coie et al., 1982; Dodge et al., 1982). Teachers rated rejected students significantly higher on aggression, nervousness, overactivity, inattentiveness, unpopularity, and social withdrawal than nonrejected students (Cantrell & Prinz, 1985). Maternal rejection is also reportedly a positive predictor of hostile behaviors (Ojiha & Pramanick, 1995). In fact, in one study adult men who recalled early memories of parental rejection tended to be abusive toward their spouses (Dutton, 1995).

In sum, researchers investigating rejection have painted a mixed picture of the rejected individual. Generally, rejected persons engage in social withdrawal and capitulation as well as aggressive, disruptive, and hostile behaviors. Further research should focus on personal or situational factors that may intensify this relationship between rejection and behavior.

Personal Characteristics as Moderators of Reactions to Rejection

As we have seen, studies reveal that even seemingly inconsequential rejection can have a powerful effect on emotional, cognitive, and behavioral reactivity. Indeed, negative response to being ignored, excluded, or rejected appears to be universal. However, despite these associations between rejection and aversive consequences, research also shows that people react differently to rejection. Most of us can think of people who have endured rejection yet remain unruffled, optimistic, and confident and other people who become antagonistic or withdrawn under the same circumstances. Researchers have identified relatively stable individual differences in the extent to which people respond to real, potential, or perceived rejection.

Investigators have focused on identifying underlying traits associated with heightened responses to rejection. In particular, rejection sensitivity, self-esteem, narcissism, attachment style, social anxiety, social support, depression, and gender have been identified as moderators of responses to real, anticipated, and imagined rejection. This section reviews the limited empirical evidence on the outcomes of interpersonal rejection from an individual-differences perspective.

Rejection Sensitivity

Geraldine Downey and her colleagues (Downey, Khouri, & Feldman, 1997; Levy, Ayduk, & Downey, chapter 10, this volume) have proposed a theory that seeks to clarify the causes and consequences of rejection sensitivity. According to their model, when a child experiences rejection from emotionally abusive, physically abusive, neglectful, or critical parents, he or she learns to expect rejection and eventually begins to overreact. Empirical studies have provided support for a link between parental rejection and children's well-being (Maccoby & Martin, 1983). Although rejection-sensitive individuals affiliate with other people just as much as their low-sensitive counterparts (Ando, 1978), numerous studies have confirmed that rejection sensitivity is negatively related to an individual's relationships through adulthood. For example, people sensitive to rejection were unwilling to affiliate with persons holding attitudes different than their own (Mehrabian, 1970), rated themselves as less compatible with persons of different status, and conformed more to high-status persons (Mehrabian & Ksionzky, 1974) than people who were sensitive to rejection. In addition, sensitivity to rejection has been found to inhibit self-disclosure at the early stages of friendship (Ando, 1978).

Researchers have focused on the effects of rejection sensitivity within the context of romantic relationships. In one study rejection-sensitive people perceived the inattentive, negative, or ambiguous behavior of their romantic partner as purposely hurtful and intentionally rejecting (Downey & Feldman, 1996). Further, compared to their less sensitive counterparts, they were less satisfied with their romantic relationships and perceived that their partners were dissatisfied as well. Sensitivity to rejection has been associated with avoidance of conflict situations in which rejection was a possibility (Mehrabian, 1970), strong feelings of rejection in response to ambiguous feedback, and negative behavioral reactions to this information (Downey & Feldman, 1996).

Research has also shown that men and women who have high rejection sensitivity often react differently in rejection situations. Rejection-sensitive men displayed jealousy in response to relational threats (Downey et al., 1997) and were at risk for aggressive and physically violent behavior toward their partner, particularly those men who were highly invested in the relationship (Downey et al., 1997). In contrast, women who were highly sensitive to rejection were hostile and emotionally unsupportive with their partners and felt rejected, which often led to fights with their partners. During these fights these women's behavior was hostile and rejecting (Downey et al., 1997).

Several basic findings have emerged from studies of rejection sensitivity. First, early rejection experiences have been shown to affect the degree to which people are sensitive to real and potential rejection. Second, sensitivity to rejection has been reliably related to pessimistic cognitive patterns that are unjustified from the information presented (e.g., ambiguous behavior of another person). Third, rejection-sensitive men and women tend to behave differently under threat of rejection. Men tend toward physical aggression, whereas women tend to be hostile.

Trait Self-Esteem

One of the most fruitful lines of research on moderators of reactions to rejection has focused on trait self-esteem. High self-esteem appears to buffer a person from the negative affect resulting from rejection. One recent study showed that, although people generally tended to be upset by social rejection, low self-esteem individuals excluded from playing a game with two confederates were the most sensitive to rejection (Kelly, Lifka, & Schelling, 1998). Individuals with high self-esteem reported significantly less negative affect following rejection than their low self-esteem counterparts. In another study, high self-esteem individuals also experienced fewer negative reactions to negative feedback from their partner (Brennan & Bosson, 1998).

Other research that examined romantic partner rejection concurred with this pattern of effects. A sample of dating women completed a measure of depression and self-esteem. Six weeks later their depression was again assessed. The male partners of these women completed a scale that measured their rejection of their partner (negative evaluation of their partner's worth as a person). Rejection by male partners predicted an increase in depression only for women who had low self-esteem. In other words, rejection predicted future depressive symptoms solely among women with low self-esteem (Katz, Beach, & Joiner, 1998).

Related research suggests that self-esteem interacts with particular features of the rejection episode. For example, Haupt and Leary (1997) found that people with low trait self-esteem exhibited lower state self-esteem when they were excluded from a group for personal rather than random reasons. Other research showed that low self-esteem participants felt more accepted and welcomed when they were included rather than excluded; however, high self-esteem participants felt equally accepted whether they were included or excluded based on random assignment or their personal characteristics (Nezlek, Kowalski, Leary, Blevins, & Holgate, 1997).

Narcissism

Distress following rejection may intensify according to the level of one's narcissism. Narcissists consistently report strong negative emotional responses to unpleasant social interactions (Rhodewalt, Madrian, & Cheney, 1998) and react to failure with anger, anxiety, and low self-esteem, particularly when the failure follows initial success (Rhodewalt & Morf, 1998). Further, people who score high on narcissism tend to externalize their failure by blaming others (Rhodewalt & Morf, 1998), evaluate individuals who outperform them especially negatively (Morf & Rhodewalt, 1993), and rate anyone who offers negative feedback as less competent than those who provided positive feedback (Kernis & Sun, 1994).

Attachment Style

Children develop different types of emotional bonds to those who care for them. The attachment styles that develop in childhood appear to be relatively stable into adulthood and are reflected in emotional patterns associated with romantic relationships, reactions to rejection, and other interpersonal challenges throughout one's life (Brennan & Shaver, 1995). For example, avoidant people grieve less after the termination of love affairs than their secure and anxious-ambivalent counterparts (Simpson, 1990).

Brennan and Bosson (1998) found reliable attachment style differences in individuals' reactions to feedback from their romantic partners. Individuals with a dismissive attachment style (i.e., those who avoid depending on others) or a fearful attachment style (i.e., those who want closeness but fear abandonment) were averse to partner feedback, and those with fearful and preoccupied styles (i.e., those who feel that others are reluctant to get as close as they would like) responded to feedback from their partner with distress. Further, individuals with preoccupied or fearful-avoidant attachment styles were the most likely to be depressed in a distressing relationship (Carnelley, Pietromonaco, & Jaffe, 1994).

Another study investigating attachment in the context of rejection found that highly anxious-ambivalent individuals experienced greater distress than their less anxious counterparts in response to a relationship-threatening task (their romantic partner evaluating another potential dating partner on physical and sexual attractiveness). These individuals also reported declines in perceived closeness of their relationship and were more likely to break up within a 4-month period (Simpson, Ickes, & Grich, 1999).

Social Anxiety

Substantial empirical literature suggests that highly anxious people behave differently than less anxious people. Anxious individuals' tense and inhibited behaviors are also associated with a high motivation to avoid rejection and disapproval from others (Miller, 1995), often because they have frequently heard others disparaging them (Dion, Dion, & Keelan, 1995). Further, persons high in social fear react with more negative facial electromyographic (EMG) activity when exposed to angry facial expressions and less positive facial EMG activity when exposed to happy facial expressions than subjects low in social fear (Dimberg, 1997).

In an early study that addressed the relationship between self-conscious anxiety and responses to rejection, Fenigstein (1979) instructed female participants to wait in a room with two confederates who either included or excluded them from their conversation. Results indicated that publicly self-conscious women reacted the most negatively to being rejected, disliked the confederates, and wanted to avoid future contact with them.

To examine how individual differences in anxiety affect how individuals cope with the threat of social rejection, Zeidner (1994) assessed students' trait anxiety and coping styles before they underwent a stressful evaluative event (a final exam). Results indicated that students who scored high in trait anxiety were likely to use negative coping styles, such as focusing on emotions and making excuses, in response to the potential for rejection (receiving a bad grade). Highly anxious students apparently try to ameliorate their anxiety in stressful situations instead of focusing on how to solve the problem.

Another study examined anxious and nonanxious individuals' reactions to positive or negative feedback concerning their performance on a test (Lake & Arkin, 1985). The researchers found that, following unfavorable evaluations, highly anxious individuals rated the evaluator as more perceptive and the feedback as more accurate and displayed much less positive affect than their counterparts who were low in social anxiety. High anxiety apparently is associated with a number of indexes of resignation and ineffective coping in response to any form of negative personal assessment.

Considerable evidence suggests that anxious persons subscribe to pessimistic views of others, especially in rejection situations. For example, research has demonstrated that socially anxious individuals make stable, internal attributions for their social failures (Arkin, Appelman, & Burger, 1980). However, a more recent study assessed the moderating effects of anxiety across varying rejection conditions (Jobe, 1999). Each college student participant was placed in a group that contained five confederates. They were told that five of the six individuals would be engaging in a group task and one person would serve as the "control," who would work on math problems in a separate room. Group membership was ostensibly determined by a vote for the five individuals one most wanted to work with. The subject was subsequently informed that he or she had received the least number of votes. This rejection paradigm contained three conditions: Private-Alone, wherein the participant was rejected while in a room alone; Public-Alone, wherein the participant was rejected in front of the rest of the group (confederates); and Together, wherein the participant was rejected along with one of the confederates. After being informed of the voting, participants were asked to make attributions for the cause of their rejection. Results indicated that these attributions differed not only across rejection context but also for anxiety. Participants high in evaluative anxiety made more internal and stable attributions in the Public-Alone condition and less internal and stable attributions in the Private-Alone condition. Attributions in the Together condition were not reliably moderated by anxiety. These data suggest that anxious individuals may blame their social failures on themselves only when they are the sole outcast and in the presence of the rejecting others. Conversely, under private circumstances, they tend to blame the situation or the other people.

Social Support

Broadly, social support refers to the perception that others are available and willing to provide one with emotional or instrumental aid. Research on social support has emphasized the importance of interpersonal relationships in physical and psychological well-being. Strong social support can buffer one from the harmful effects of stress, and rejection is particularly stressful.

Recent research has indicated that a network of interpersonal relationships may ameliorate one's negative attributions for rejection. Ross, Lutz, and Lakey (1999) asked subjects to complete a measure of social support. The subjects then were presented with hypothetical situations that depicted the subject in need of social support but not getting it (i.e., ambiguous rejection). Participants subsequently noted the apparent cause of the lack of support and rated this cause for internality, globality, and stability. Results indicated that persons with low perceived social support made more negative attributions for failed support than participants high in perceived social support. In confirmation, a follow-up study found that women who rated themselves low in social support experienced greater reductions in positive affect after discussing rejection/failed support experiences than women who had high support.

Other research showed that institutionalized children (who were more socially deprived than noninstitutionalized children) exhibited a greater fear of social rejection, stronger affiliation motivation, and lower self-esteem than the noninstitutionalized children (Youngleson, 1973). Feeling well-integrated in a supportive network of friends and family may temper the association between rejection and negative affect and attributions.

Depression

A growing body of evidence suggests that depressed people are more sensitive to rejection than are nondepressed individuals. In Zeidner's (1994) study, subjects completed a depression inventory before undergoing a threatening evaluation (final exam). Facing the mere possibility of rejection (a low test score), depressed students employed emotion-oriented and avoidance coping styles, thereby refusing to address the threatening situation directly by trying to increase their likelihood of success.

Nezlek et al. (1997) found that depressed participants' feelings of rejection depended on whether they were included or excluded from the group either randomly or because of the other members' evaluations of their personal characteristics. Specifically, depressed individuals reported feeling less accepted and welcomed and evaluated themselves more negatively when they were excluded based on the others' votes than when they were randomly excluded. In contrast, nondepressed participants felt less welcomed and accepted in both rejection conditions than in the inclusion conditions.

Gender Differences

Williams and Sommer (1997) provided empirical evidence of gender differences in behavioral reactions following rejection. Their results indicated that ostracized men were more likely to exhibit social loafing on a subsequent group task, whereas women, after being ostracized, tended to compensate by working harder than normal on the group task. These findings confirm an earlier study in which men were less likely than women to want to work with the rejecting group on another task (Predmore & Williams, 1983). Men and women may cope with rejection differently. Women tended to withdraw during rejection but then worked harder for the group when given the opportunity later to improve their evaluation by the group. In contrast, men tended to occupy themselves by object manipulation (e.g., looking in their wallets) while they were being ignored, concealing any emotional reactions to the situation and attempting to convey to others that they did not care. Therefore, they did not feel the need to contribute to the group to improve their status because they wanted to appear nonchalant (i.e., they didn't want to be included in the first place).

A study that focused on the relationship between extramarital sex and jealousy responses (Buunk, 1995) illustrates that men and women respond to specific types of interpersonal rejection (their partner having an affair with someone else) quite differently. Women seemed to adapt to the adultery of their partner, especially when they had experienced a history of unfaithfulness by their partner. Women were less likely to respond with anger and disappointment but more apt to feel self-doubt. These patterns were considerably less evident for men.

Finally, in a recent study that examined perceptions of men's and women's responses to the threat of rejection, people were more likely to deem verbal aggression an appropriate response to being teased for men than for women (Lightner, Pike, & Lawrence, 1999).

Overall, then, only a few studies have examined gender differences in reactions to rejection. These studies generally indicate that men tried to mask their emotions and rebuff the rejecting others when given the chance. Men also responded to rejection with anger, a response socially acceptable for men but less so for women (to the extent that aggressive behavior is associated with anger). Women withdrew during rejection but then fervently worked with the rejecting others when given the opportunity; furthermore, they were more likely to internalize the rejection experience.

Summary

For many people, exclusion is a salient part of their social lives and a source of unhappiness. The literature has identified relationships between rejection and a variety of personality factors, behavioral tendencies, attributional processes, and social interaction patterns. The data from these studies also imply that reactions to rejection can be influenced by rejection sensitivity, self-esteem, narcissism, attachment style, anxiety, social support, depression, and gender. Together, these characteristics influence the way people perceive, evaluate, and respond to rejection.

People also tend to interpret rejection within the context of their life experiences. Individuals who have repeatedly experienced rejection tend to be unhappy and distressed. Thus, a history of rejection seemingly contributes to psychological maladjustment and a pessimistic sense of self. A survey of the literature suggests that these individuals are the most likely to display negative reactions to social rejection. In one comprehensive study, Kelly (1999) found that people who responded negatively to rejection tended to see themselves as anxious, lonely, embarrassable, socially detached, and low in self-esteem. People with less negative emotional responses to rejection, in contrast, regarded themselves as socially integrated. Furthermore, certain excluded individuals interpreted their own emotional reactions and behaviors differently from included individuals. Rejected subjects who scored high in social alienation, anxiety, compulsivity, and passive-aggression tended to attribute their rejection to external, unstable, and uncontrollable causes. In other words, they believed they were rejected because of things other than their enduring personal characteristics. The reverse was true for included individuals. Those who scored high on measures of loneliness, hostility, and dysphoria made external attributions for being *included* by the other group members.

The research reviewed in this chapter demonstrates that certain components of individuals' personality may moderate the way they cope with rejection. Of particular relevance is the finding that people who fare well even in the face of rejection seem to have a global orientation toward high self-esteem, secure attachment, low anxiety, and so forth, suggesting that an individual's sense of optimism, serenity, and positive self-worth affect reactions to rejection.

Although more research is needed that delves into the dimensions of individual difference variables related to people's reactions to rejection, the available data suggest that interactions between personal tendencies and situational components play an important role in responses to rejection. Ultimately, a more complete model of reactions may be developed that thoroughly delineates the relationship between affect, cognitions, behaviors, and physiology and specifies how characteristics of the person and the situation together produce affective, cognitive, and behavioral reactions to interpersonal rejection.

References

Adams, J. M., & Moore, D. S. (1996). *The assessment of interpersonal interaction: A methodological alternative.* Unpublished manuscript, University of Tennessee.

Ando, K. (1978). Self-disclosure in the acquaintance process: Effects of affiliative tendency and sensitivity to rejection. *Japanese Psychological Research, 20,* 194–199.

Arkin, R. M., Appelman, A. J., & Burger, J. M. (1980). Social anxiety, self-presentation, and the self-serving bias in causal attribution. *Journal of Personality and Social Psychology, 38,* 23–35.

Asher, S. R., Parkhurst, J. T., Hymel, S., & Williams, G. A. (1990). Peer rejection and loneliness in childhood. In S. R. Asher & J. D. Coie (Eds.), *Peer rejection in childhood* (pp. 253–273). New York: Cambridge University Press.

Asher, S. R., & Wheeler, V. A. (1985). Children's loneliness: A comparison of rejected and neglected peer status. *Journal of Consulting and Clinical Psychology, 53,* 500–505.

Attili, G., Vermigli, P., & Schneider, B. H. (1997). Peer acceptance and friendship patterns among Italian schoolchildren within a cross-cultural perspective. *International Journal of Behavior Development, 21,* 277–288.

Baumeister, R. F., & Leary, M. R. (1995). The need to belong: Desire for interpersonal attachments as a fundamental human motivation. *Psychological Bulletin, 117,* 497–529.

Baumeister, R. F., & Tice, D. M. (1990). Anxiety and social exclusion. *Journal of Social and Clinical Psychology, 9,* 165–195.

Bennett, M., & Dewberry, C. (1994). "I've said I'm sorry, haven't I?" A study of the identity implications and constraints that apologies create for their recipients. *Current Psychology: Developmental, Learning, Personality, Social, 13,* 10–20.

Berman, W. H., Berman, E. R., Heymsfield, S., Fauci, M., & Ackerman, S. (1992). The incidence and comorbidity of psychiatric disorders in obesity. *Journal of Personality Disorders, 6,* 168–175.

Bhojak, B. L., & Mehta, P. (1970). An investigation into the causes responsible for social rejection. *Indian Journal of Social Work, 30,* 315–324.

Bierman, K. L., & Wargo, J. B. (1995). Predicting the longitudinal course associated with aggressive-rejected, aggressive-nonrejected, and rejected-nonaggressive status. *Development and Psychopathology, 7,* 669–682.

Boivin, M., Hymel, S., & Bukowski, W. M. (1995). The roles of social withdrawal, peer rejection, and victimization by peers in predicting loneliness and depressed mood in childhood. *Development and Psychopathology, 7,* 765–785.

Boivin, M., Poulin, F., & Vitaro, F. (1994). Depressed mood and peer rejection in childhood. *Development and Psychopathology, 6,* 483–498.

Brennan, K. A., & Bosson, J. K. (1998). Attachment-style differences in attitudes toward and rejections to feedback from romantic partners: An exploration of the relational bases of self-esteem. *Personality and Social Psychology Bulletin, 24,* 699–714.

Brennan, K. A., & Shaver, P. R. (1995). Dimensions of adult attachment, affect regulation, and romantic relationship functioning. *Personality and Social Psychology Bulletin, 21,* 267–283.

Burgoon, J. K., & Hale, J. L. (1988). Nonverbal expectancy violations: Model elaboration and application to immediacy behaviors. *Communication Monographs, 55,* 58–79.

Burns, J. W. (1995). Interactive effects of traits, states, and gender on cardio-vascular reactivity during different situations. *Journal of Behavioral Medicine, 18,* 279–303.

Buunk, B. P. (1995). Sex, self-esteem, dependency, and extradyadic sexual experiences as related to jealousy responses. *Journal of Social and Personal Relationships, 12,* 147–153.

Cantrell, V. L., & Prinz, R. J. (1986). Multiple perspectives of rejected, ne-glected, and accepted children: Relation between sociometric status and behavioral characteristics. *Journal of Consulting and Clinical Psychology, 53,* 884–889.

Carlton-Ford, S., Miller, R., Nealeigh, N., & Sanchez, N. (1997). The effects of perceived stigma and psychological over-control on the behavioural prob-lems of children with epilepsy. *Seizure, 6,* 383–391.

Carnelley, K. B., Pietromonaco, P. R., & Jaffe, K. (1994). Depression, working models of others, and relationship functioning. *Journal of Personality and Social Psychology, 66,* 127–140.

Cavalli-Sforza, L. L., & Feldman, M. W. (1981). *Cultural transmission and evolution: A quantitative approach.* Princeton, NJ: Princeton University Press.

Cheuk, W. H., & Rosen, S. (1994). Validating a "spurning scale" for teachers. *Current Psychology, 13,* 241–247.

Cobb, S. (1976). Social support as a moderator of life stress. *Psychosomatic Medicine, 38,* 300–314.

Coie, J. D., Dodge, K. A., & Coppotelli, H. (1982). Dimensions and types of social status: A cross-age perspective. *Developmental Psychology, 18,* 557–570.

Craighead, W. E., Kimball, W. H., & Rehak, P. (1979). Mood changes, physio-logical responses, and self-statements during social rejection imagery. *Journal of Consulting and Clinical Psychology, 47,* 385–396.

Dexter, D. (Producer) & Jordan, P. J. (Director). (1988). *The power of listening* [Video]. Carlsbad, CA: CRM/McGraw-Hill Films.

Dimberg, U. (1997). Social fear and expressive reactions to social stimuli. *Scandinavian Journal of Psychology, 38,* 171–174.

Dion, K. L., Dion, K. K., & Keelan, J. P. (1990). Appearance anxiety as a di-mension of social-evaluative anxiety: Exploring the ugly-duckling syn-drome. *Contemporary Social Psychology, 14,* 220–224.

Dodge, K. A., Coie, J. D., & Brakke, N. P. (1982). Behavior patterns of socially rejected and neglected preadolescents: The role of social approach and ag-gression. *Journal of Abnormal Child Psychology, 10,* 389–409.

Downey, G., & Feldman, S. I. (1996). Implications of rejection sensitivity for intimate relationships. *Journal of Personality and Social Psychology, 70,* 1327–1343.

Downey, G., Freitas, A. L., Michaelis, B., & Khouri, H. (1998). The self-fulfilling prophecy in close relationships: Rejection sensitivity and rejection by romantic partners. *Journal of Personality and Social Psychology, 75,* 545–560.

Downey, G., Khouri, H., & Feldman, S. I. (1997). Early interpersonal trauma and later adjustment: The mediational role of rejection sensitivity. In D. Cicchetti & S. Toth (Eds.), *Developmental perspectives on trauma: Theory, research, and intervention* (pp. 85–114). Rochester, NY: University of Rochester Press.

Dutton, D. G. (1995). Male abusiveness in intimate relationships. *Clinical Psychology Review, 15,* 567–581.

Eskilson, A., Wiley, M. G., Meuhlhauer, G., & Dodder, L. (1986). Parental pressure, self-esteem, and adolescent reported deviance: Bending the twig too far. *Adolescence, 21,* 505–515.

Fenigstein, A. (1979). Self-consciousness, self-attention, and social interaction. *Journal of Personality and Social Psychology, 37,* 75–86.

Fischoff, B., Slovic, P., & Lichtenstein, S. (1977). Knowing with certainty: The appropriateness of extreme confidence. *Journal of Experimental Psychology: Human Perception and Performance, 3,* 552–564.

Freilich, M. (1991). Smart rules and proper rules: A journey through deviance. In M. Freilich, D. Raybeck, & J. Savishinsky (Eds.), *Deviance: Anthropological perspectives.* New York: Bergin & Garvey.

French, D. C. (1988). Heterogeneity of peer-rejected boys: Aggressive and non-aggressive subtypes. *Child Development, 59,* 976–985.

Gegax, T. T., Adler, J., & Pedersen, D. (1988, April 6). The boys behind the ambush. *Newsweek, 131,* 20–24.

Geller, D. M., Goodstein, L., Silver, M., & Sternberg, W. C. (1974). On being ignored: The effects of the violation of implicit rules of social interaction. *Sociometry, 37,* 541–556.

Gottman, J. M. (1979). *Marital interaction.* New York: Academic Press.

Hamachek, D. (1992). *Encounters with the self.* 4th ed. San Diego: Harcourt Brace Jovanovich.

Haupt, A. L., & Leary, M. R. (1997). The appeal of worthless groups: Moderating effects of trait self-esteem. *Group Dynamics, 1,* 124–132.

Hazuda, H. P. (1994). A critical evaluation of U. S. epidemiological evidence and ethnic variation. In S. A. Shumaker & S. M. Czajkowski (Eds.), *Social support and cardiovascular disease* (pp. 119–142). New York: Plenum.

Hobfall, S. E., & London, P. (1986). The relationship of self-concept and social support to emotional distress among women during the war. *Journal of Social and Clinical Psychology, 4,* 189–203.

Holmes, E. K., Mateczun, J. M., Lall, R., & Wilcove, G. L. (1998). Pilot study of suicide risk factors among personnel in the United States Marine Corps (Pacific Forces). *Psychological Reports, 83,* 3–11.

Holmes, T. H., & Rahe, R. H. (1967). The Social Readjustment Rating Scale. *Journal of Psychosomatic Research, 11,* 213–218.

Jobe, R. L. (1999). *The effects of context and disposition on reactions to social rejection.* Unpublished master's thesis, Western Illinois University.

Jones, W. H. (1990). Loneliness and social exclusion. *Journal of Social and Clinical Psychology, 9,* 214–220.

Jones, W. H., & Carpenter, B. N. (1986). Shyness, social behavior, and relationships. In W. H. Jones, J. M. Cheek, & S. R. Briggs (Eds.), *Shyness: Perspectives on research and treatment* (pp. 227–238). New York: Plenum.

Jones, W. H., Carpenter, B. N., & Quintana, D. (1985). Personality and interpersonal predictors of loneliness in two cultures. *Journal of Personality and Social Psychology, 48,* 1503–1511.

Jussim, L., Fleming, C. J., Coleman, L., & Kohberger, C. (1996). The nature of stereotypes II: A multiple process model of evaluations. *Journal of Applied Social Psychology, 26,* 283–312.

Kahneman, D., & Tversky, A. (1979). Intuitive prediction: Biases and corrective procedures. *Management Science, 12,* 313–327.

Katz, J., Beach, S. R., & Joiner, T. E. (1998). When does partner devaluation predict emotional distress? Prospective moderating effects of reassurance-seeking and self-esteem. *Personal Relationships, 5,* 409–421.

Kelley, H. (1973). Processes of causal attribution. *American Psychologist, 28,* 107–128.

Kelly, K. M. (1999). *Measurement and manifestation of the need to belong.* Unpublished doctoral dissertation, University of Tennessee.

Kelly, K. M., Lifka, A. M., & Schelling, C. M. (1998, April). *Effects of self-esteem and social exclusion on self- and other-evaluations.* Poster presented at the Western Psychological Association and Rocky Mountain Psychological Association Joint Convention, Albuquerque.

Kernis, M. H., Cornell, D. P., Sun, C. R., Berry, A., & Harlow, T. (1993). There's more to self-esteem than whether it is high or low: The importance of stability of self-esteem. *Journal of Personality and Social Psychology, 65,* 1190–1204.

Kernis, M. H., & Sun, C. R. (1994). Narcissism and reactions to interpersonal feedback. *Journal of Research in Personality, 28,* 4–13.

Kupersmidt, J. B., & Patterson, C. J. (1991). Childhood peer rejection, aggression, withdrawal, and perceived competence as predictors of self-reported behavior problems in preadolescence. *Journal of Abnormal Child Psychology, 19,* 427–449.

Lake, E. A., & Arkin, R. M. (1985). Reactions to objective and subjective interpersonal evaluation: The influence of social anxiety. *Journal of Social and Clinical Psychology, 3,* 143–160.

Larson, R., Csikszentmihalyi, M., & Graef, R. (1982). Time alone in daily experience: Loneliness or renewal? In L. A. Peplau & D. Perlman (Eds.), *Loneliness: A sourcebook of current theory, research, and therapy* (pp. 44–53). New York: Wiley-Interscience.

Leary, M. R. (1990). Responses to social exclusion: Social anxiety, jealousy, loneliness, depression, and low self-esteem. *Journal of Social and Clinical Psychology, 9,* 221–229.

Leary, M. R., & Downs, D. (1995). Interpersonal functions of the self-esteem motive. In M. H. Kernis (Ed.), *Efficacy, agency, and self-esteem* (pp. 123–144). New York: Plenum.

Leary, M. R., Springer, C., Negel, L., Ansell, E., & Evans, K. (1998). The causes, phenomenology, and consequences of hurt feelings. *Journal of Personality and Social Psychology, 74,* 1225–1237.

Leary, M. R., Tambor, E. S., Terdal, S. K., & Downs, D. L. (1995). Self-esteem as an interpersonal monitor: The sociometer hypothesis. *Journal of Personality and Social Psychology, 68,* 518–530.

Levenson, R. W., & Gottman, J. M. (1983). Marital interaction: Physiological linkage and affective exchange. *Journal of Personality and Social Psychology, 45,* 587–597.

Lightner, R., Pike, C., & Lawrence, L. (1999, April). *Current and retrospective responses to ratings of teasing.* Poster presented at the annual meeting of the Midwestern Psychological Association, Chicago.

Litovsky, V. G., & Dusek, J. B. (1985). Perceptions of child rearing and self-concept development during the early adolescent years. *Journal of Youth and Adolescence, 14,* 373–387.

Lynch, J. J. (1979). *The broken heart: The medical consequences of loneliness.* New York: Basic Books.

Maccoby, E. E., & Martin, J. A. (1983). Socialization in the context of the family: Parent-child interaction. In E. M. Hetherington (Ed.), *Handbook of child psychology* (vol. 4, pp. 1–101). New York: Wiley.

Mathes, E. W., Adams, H. E., & Davies, R. M. (1985). Jealousy: Loss of relationship rewards, self-esteem, depression, anxiety, and anger. *Journal of Personality and Social Psychology, 48,* 1552–1561.

Mehrabian, A. (1970). The development and validation of measures of affiliative tendency and sensitivity to rejection. *Educational and Psychological Measurement, 30,* 417–428.

Mehrabian, A., & Ksionzky, S. (1974). *A theory of affiliation.* Lexington, MA: Health.

Miller, R. S. (1995). On the nature of embarrassability: Shyness, social evaluation, and social skill. *Journal of Personality, 63,* 315–339.

Morf, C. C., & Rhodewalt, F. (1993). Narcissism and self-evaluation maintenance: Explorations in object relations. *Personality and Social Psychology Bulletin, 19,* 668–676.

Morris, D. R. (1965). *The washing of the spears: The rise and fall of the Zulu nation.* New York: Simon & Schuster.

Morvitz, E., & Motta, R. W. (1992). Predictors of self-esteem: The roles of parent-child perceptions, achievement, and class placement. *Journal of Learning Disabilities, 25,* 72–80.

Nezlek, J. B., Kowalski, R. M., Leary, M. R., Blevins, T., & Holgate, S. (1997). Personality moderators of reactions to interpersonal rejection: Depression and trait self-esteem. *Personality and Social Psychology Bulletin, 23,* 1235–1244.

Ojiha, H., & Pramanick, M. (1995). Parental behaviour as related to some personality traits of adolescents. *Psychologia: An International Journal of Psychology in the Orient, 38,* 31–37.

Orth-Gomer, K. (1994). The significance of interaction in behavioral medicine. *Homeostasis in Health and Disease, 35,* 6–15.

Parkhurst, J. T., & Asher, S. R. (1992). Peer rejection in middle school: Subgroup differences in behavior, loneliness, and interpersonal concerns. *Developmental Psychology, 28,* 231–241.

Panak, W. F., & Garber, J. (1992). Role of aggression, rejection, and attributions in the prediction of depression in children. *Development and Psychopathology, 4,* 145–165.

Pearson, R. L., Kelly, K. M., & Ryan, R. L. (1998, April). *The relationship between perceptions of parental practices and evaluation of self.* Poster presented at the meeting of the Midwestern Psychological Association, Chicago.

Pepitone, A., & Wilpizeski, C. (1960). Some consequences of experimental rejection. *Journal of Abnormal and Social Psychology, 60,* 359–364.

Peretti, P. O., & Pudowski, B. C. (1997). Influence of jealousy on male and female college daters. *Social Behavior and Personality, 25,* 155–160.

Predmore, S., & Williams, K. D. (1983, May). *The effects of social ostracism on affiliation.* Paper presented at the meeting of the Midwestern Psychological Association, Chicago.

Rhodewalt, F., Madrian, J. C., & Cheney, S. (1998). Narcissism, self-knowledge organization, and emotional reactivity: The effect of daily experiences on self-esteem and affect. *Personality and Social Psychology Bulletin, 24,* 75–87.

Rhodewalt, F., & Morf, C. C. (1998). On self-aggrandizement and anger: A temporal analysis of narcissism and affective reactions to success and failure. *Journal of Personality and Social Psychology, 74,* 672–685.

Rosen, S., Mickler, S. E., & Collins II, J. E. (1987). Reactions of would-be helpers whose offer of help is spurned. *Journal of Personality and Social Psychology, 53,* 288–297.

Rosen, S., Mickler, S. E., & Spiers, C. (1985). The spurned philanthropist. *Humboldt Journal of Social Relations, 13,* 145–158.

Ross, L. T., Lutz, C. J., & Lakey, B. (1999). Perceived social support and attributions for failed support. *Personality and Social Psychology Bulletin, 25,* 896–909.

Sarason, I. G., & Sarason, B. R. (Eds.). (1985). *Social support: Theory, research, and applications.* Dordrecht, Netherlands: Martinus Nijhof.

Schachter, S. (1959). *The psychology of affiliation.* Stanford, CA: Stanford University Press.

Schmidt, U., Tiller, J., & Morgan, H. G. (1995). The social consequences of eating disorders. In G. I. Szmukler & C. Dare (Eds.), *Handbook of eating disorders: Theory, treatment, and research* (pp. 259–270). Chichester, England: Wiley.

Simpson, J. A., Ickes, W., & Grich, J. (1999). When accuracy hurts: Reactions to anxious-ambivalent dating partners to a relationship-threatening situation. *Journal of Personality and Social Psychology, 76,* 754–769.

Sloan, W. W., & Solano, C. H. (1984). The conversational styles of lonely males with strangers and roommates. *Personality and Social Psychology Bulletin, 10,* 293–301.

Snoek, J. D. (1962). Some effects of rejection upon attraction to a group. *Journal of Abnormal and Social Psychology, 64,* 175–182.

Strack, S., & Coyne, J. C. (1983). Social confirmation of dysphoria: Shared and private reactions to depression. *Journal of Personality and Social Psychology, 44,* 798–806.

Swann, W. B., Jr., Hixon, J. G., Stein-Seroussi, A., & Gilbert, D. T. (1990). The fleeting gleam of praise: Cognitive processes underlying behavioral reactions to self-relevant feedback. *Journal of Personality and Social Psychology, 59,* 17–26.

Swann, W. B., & Read, S. J. (1981). Acquiring self-knowledge: The search for feedback that fits. *Journal of Personality and Social Psychology, 41,* 1119–1128.

Tambor, E. S., & Leary, M. R. (1993). *Perceived exclusion as a common factor in social anxiety, loneliness, jealousy, depression, and low self-esteem.* Unpublished manuscript, Wake Forest University.

Thye, R. S., Lovaglia, M. J., & Markovsky, B. (1997). Responses to social exchange and social exclusion in networks. *Social Forces, 75,* 1031–1047.

Toner, M. A., & Munro, D. (1996). Peer social attributions and self-efficacy of peer-rejected preadolescents. *Merrill-Palmer Quarterly, 42,* 339–357.

Wenegrat, B., Castillo-Yee, E., & Abrams, L. (1996). Social norm compliance as a signaling system. II. Studies of fitness-related attributions consequent on a group norm violation. *Ethology and Sociobiology, 17,* 417–429.

Weiss, R. S. (1974). The provisions of social relationships. In Z. Rubin (Ed.), *Doing unto others* (pp. 17–26). Englewood Cliffs, NJ: Prentice-Hall.

Wilcox, J., & Mitchell, J. (1977). Effects of group acceptance/rejection on self-esteem levels of individual group members in a task-oriented problem-solving group interaction. *Small Group Behavior, 8,* 169–178.

Williams, K. D., & Sommer, K. L. (1997). Social ostracism by coworkers: Does rejection lead to loafing or compensation? *Personality and Social Psychology Bulletin, 23,* 693–706.

Youngleson, M. L. (1973). The need to affiliate and self-esteem in institutionalized children. *Journal of Personality and Social Psychology, 26,* 280–286.

Yurak, T. J., LoSchiavo, F. M., & Kerrigan, L. G. (1999, April). *Reactions to social exclusion.* Poster presented at the annual meeting of the Midwestern Psychological Association, Chicago.

Zeidner, M. (1994). Personal and contextual determinants of coping and anxiety in an evaluative situation: A prospective study. *Personality and Individual Differences, 16,* 899–918.

Author Index

Subject Index